terra australis 53

Terra Australis reports the results of archaeological and related research within the south and east of Asia, though mainly Australia, New Guinea and Island Melanesia — lands that remained terra australis incognita to generations of prehistorians. Its subject is the settlement of the diverse environments in this isolated quarter of the globe by peoples who have maintained their discrete and traditional ways of life into the recent recorded or remembered past and at times into the observable present.

List of volumes in Terra Australis

1. *Burrill Lake and Currarong: Coastal Sites in Southern New South Wales.* R.J. Lampert (1971)
2. *Ol Tumbuna: Archaeological Excavations in the Eastern Central Highlands, Papua New Guinea.* J.P. White (1972)
3. *New Guinea Stone Age Trade: The Geography and Ecology of Traffic in the Interior.* I. Hughes (1977)
4. *Recent Prehistory in Southeast Papua.* B. Egloff (1979)
5. *The Great Kartan Mystery.* R. Lampert (1981)
6. *Early Man in North Queensland: Art and Archaeology in the Laura Area.* A. Rosenfeld, D. Horton and J. Winter (1981)
7. *The Alligator Rivers: Prehistory and Ecology in Western Arnhem Land.* C. Schrire (1982)
8. *Hunter Hill, Hunter Island: Archaeological Investigations of a Prehistoric Tasmanian Site.* S. Bowdler (1984)
9. *Coastal South-West Tasmania: The Prehistory of Louisa Bay and Maatsuyker Island.* R. Vanderwal and D. Horton (1984)
10. *The Emergence of Mailu.* G. Irwin (1985)
11. *Archaeology in Eastern Timor, 1966–67.* I. Glover (1986)
12. *Early Tongan Prehistory: The Lapita Period on Tongatapu and its Relationships.* J. Poulsen (1987)
13. *Coobool Creek.* P. Brown (1989)
14. *30,000 Years of Aboriginal Occupation: Kimberley, North-West Australia.* S. O'Connor (1999)
15. *Lapita Interaction.* G. Summerhayes (2000)
16. *The Prehistory of Buka: A Stepping Stone Island in the Northern Solomons.* S. Wickler (2001)
17. *The Archaeology of Lapita Dispersal in Oceania.* G.R. Clark, A.J. Anderson and T. Vunidilo (2001)
18. *An Archaeology of West Polynesian Prehistory.* A. Smith (2002)
19. *Phytolith and Starch Research in the Australian-Pacific-Asian Regions: The State of the Art.* D. Hart and L. Wallis (2003)
20. *The Sea People: Late-Holocene Maritime Specialisation in the Whitsunday Islands, Central Queensland.* B. Barker (2004)
21. *What's Changing: Population Size or Land-Use Patterns? The Archaeology of Upper Mangrove Creek, Sydney Basin.* V. Attenbrow (2004)
22. *The Archaeology of the Aru Islands, Eastern Indonesia.* S. O'Connor, M. Spriggs and P. Veth (eds) (2005)
23. *Pieces of the Vanuatu Puzzle: Archaeology of the North, South and Centre.* S. Bedford (2006)
24. *Coastal Themes: An Archaeology of the Southern Curtis Coast, Queensland.* S. Ulm (2006)
25. *Lithics in the Land of the Lightning Brothers: The Archaeology of Wardaman Country, Northern Territory.* C. Clarkson (2007)
26. *Oceanic Explorations: Lapita and Western Pacific Settlement.* S. Bedford, C. Sand and S. P. Connaughton (eds) (2007)
27. *Dreamtime Superhighway: Sydney Basin Rock Art and Prehistoric Information Exchange.* J. McDonald (2008)
28. *New Directions in Archaeological Science.* A. Fairbairn, S. O'Connor and B. Marwick (eds) (2008)
29. *Islands of Inquiry: Colonisation, Seafaring and the Archaeology of Maritime Landscapes.* G. Clark, F. Leach and S. O'Connor (eds) (2008)
30. *Archaeological Science Under a Microscope: Studies in Residue and Ancient DNA Analysis in Honour of Thomas H. Loy.* M. Haslam, G. Robertson, A. Crowther, S. Nugent and L. Kirkwood (eds) (2009)
31. *The Early Prehistory of Fiji.* G. Clark and A. Anderson (eds) (2009)
32. *Altered Ecologies: Fire, Climate and Human Influence on Terrestrial Landscapes.* S. Haberle, J. Stevenson and M. Prebble (eds) (2010)
33. *Man Bac: The Excavation of a Neolithic Site in Northern Vietnam: The Biology.* M. Oxenham, H. Matsumura and N. Kim Dung (eds) (2011)
34. *Peopled Landscapes: Archaeological and Biogeographic Approaches to Landscapes.* S. Haberle and B. David (eds) (2012)
35. *Pacific Island Heritage: Archaeology, Identity & Community.* J. Liston, G. Clark and D. Alexander (eds) (2011)
36. *Transcending the Culture–Nature Divide in Cultural Heritage: Views from the Asia-Pacific region.* S. Brockwell, S. O'Connor and D. Byrne (eds) (2013)
37. *Taking the High Ground: The archaeology of Rapa, a fortified island in remote East Polynesia.* A. Anderson and D.J. Kennett (eds) (2012)
38. *Life on the Margins: An Archaeological Investigation of Late Holocene Economic Variability, Blue Mud Bay, Northern Australia.* P. Faulkner (2013)
39. *Prehistoric Marine Resource Use in the Indo-Pacific Regions.* R. Ono, A. Morrison and D. Addison (eds) (2013)
40. *4000 Years of Migration and Cultural Exchange: The Archaeology of the Batanes Islands, Northern Philippines.* P. Bellwood and E. Dizon (eds) (2013)
41. *Degei's Descendants: Spirits, Place and People in Pre-Cession Fiji.* Aubrey Parke. M. Spriggs and D. Scarr (eds) (2014)
42. *Contextualising the Neolithic Occupation of Southern Vietnam: The Role of Ceramics and Potters at An Son.* C. Sarjeant (2014)
43. *Journeys into the Rainforest: Archaeology of Culture Change and Continuity on the Evelyn Tableland, North Queensland.* Å. Ferrier (2015)
44. *An Archaeology of Early Christianity in Vanuatu: Kastom and Religious Change on Tanna and Erromango, 1839–1920.* J.L. Flexner (2016)
45. *New Perspectives in Southeast Asian and Pacific Prehistory.* P.J. Piper, H. Matsumura and D. Bulbeck (eds) (2017)
46. *Ten Thousand Years of Cultivation at Kuk Swamp in the Highlands of Papua New Guinea.* J. Golson, T. Denham, P. Hughes, P. Swadling and J. Muke (eds) (2017)
47. *The Archaeology of Rock Art in Western Arnhem Land, Australia.* B. David, P. Taçon, J-J. Delannoy, J-M. Geneste (eds) (2017)
48. *The Archaeology of Sulawesi: Current Research on the Pleistocene to the Historic Period.* S. O'Connor, D. Bulbeck and J. Meyer (eds) (2018)
49. *Drawing in the Land: Rock Art in the Upper Nepean, Sydney Basin, New South Wales.* J. Dibden (2019)
50. *The Spice Islands in Prehistory: Archaeology in the Northern Moluccas, Indonesia,* P. Bellwood (ed.) (2019)
51. *Archaeologies of Island Melanesia: Current approaches to landscapes, exchange and practice,* M. Leclerc and J. Flexner (eds) (2019)
52. *Debating Lapita: Distribution, Chronology, Society and Subsistence,* S. Bedford and M. Spriggs (eds) (2019)

terra australis 53

Forts and Fortification in Wallacea

Archaeological and Ethnohistoric Investigations

Edited by Sue O'Connor, Andrew McWilliam and Sally Brockwell

PRESS

Published by ANU Press
The Australian National University
Acton ACT 2601, Australia
Email: anupress@anu.edu.au

Available to download for free at press.anu.edu.au

A catalogue record for this book is available from the National Library of Australia

ISBN (print): 9781760463885
ISBN (online): 9781760463892

WorldCat (print): 1191864602
WorldCat (online): 1191863464

DOI: 10.22459/TA53.2020

This title is published under a Creative Commons Attribution-NonCommercial-NoDerivatives 4.0 International (CC BY-NC-ND 4.0).

The full licence terms are available at creativecommons.org/licenses/by-nc-nd/4.0/legalcode

Terra Australis Editorial Board: Sue O'Connor, Sally Brockwell, Ursula Frederick, Tristen Jones, Ceri Shipton and Mathieu Leclerc
Series Editor: Sue O'Connor

Cover design and layout by ANU Press.

Cover photograph: Massive walls surrounding Mapulo, a fortified settlement at the head of the Vero Valley, eastern Timor-Leste, with Mario dos Santos Loyola. Photo by Sue O'Connor.

This edition © 2020 ANU Press

Contents

Acknowledgements — vii
List of figures — ix
List of tables — xv

1. Forts and fortifications in Wallacea — 1
   Sue O'Connor, Andrew McWilliam and Sally Brockwell

Archaeology of forts

2. The fortified settlement of Macapainara, Lautem District, Timor-Leste — 13
   Sue O'Connor, David Bulbeck, Noel Amano Jr, Philip J. Piper, Sally Brockwell, Andrew McWilliam, Jack N. Fenner, Jack O'Connor-Veth, Rose Whitau, Tim Maloney, Michelle C. Langley, Mirani Litster, James Lankton, Bernard Gratuze, William R. Dickinson, Anthony Barham and Richard C. Willan

3. The Ira Ara site: A fortified settlement and burial complex in Timor-Leste — 49
   Peter V. Lape, John Krigbaum, Jana Futch, Amy Jordan and Emily Peterson

4. Excavations at the site of Vasino, Lautem District, Timor-Leste — 67
   Sally Brockwell, Sue O'Connor, Jack N. Fenner, Andrew McWilliam, Noel Amano Jr, Philip J. Piper, David Bulbeck, Mirani Litster, Rose Whitau, Jack O'Connor-Veth, Tim Maloney, Judith Cameron, Richard C. Willan and William R. Dickinson

5. The site of Leki Wakik, Manatuto District, Timor-Leste — 101
   Jack N. Fenner, Mirani Litster, Tim Maloney, Tse Siang Lim, Stuart Hawkins, Prue Gaffey, Sally Brockwell, Andrew McWilliam, Sandra Pannell, Richard C. Willan and Sue O'Connor

Social history of forts

6. Social drivers of fortified settlements in Timor-Leste — 135
   Andrew McWilliam

7. The indigenous fortifications of South Sulawesi, Indonesia, and their sociopolitical foundations — 153
   David Bulbeck and Ian Caldwell

8. Forts on Buton Island: Centres of settlement, government and security in Southeast Sulawesi — 187
   Hasanuddin

9. Forts of the Wakatobi Islands in Southeast Sulawesi — 211
   Nani Somba

10. Historical and linguistic perspectives on fortified settlements in Southeastern Wallacea: Far eastern Timor in the context of southern Maluku — 221
    Antoinette Schapper

Conclusion and future directions

11. Surveys of fortified sites in Southern Wallacea   249
    Sue O'Connor, Shimona Kealy, Andrew McWilliam, Sally Brockwell, Lucas Wattimena, Marlon Ririmasse, Mahirta, Alifah, Sandra Pannell, Stuart Hawkins, Mohammad Husni and Daud Tanudirjo

12. Conclusion   283
    Andrew McWilliam, Sue O'Connor and Sally Brockwell

Contributors   289

Acknowledgements

In Timor-Leste, we extend our thanks and appreciation to staff of the Ministry of Education and Culture (now Ministry of Higher Education, Science and Culture, Secretary of State for Art and Culture and National Directorate of Cultural Heritage), and the National Directorate of Forestry in the Ministry of Agriculture and Fisheries who assisted us in the course of this research. Permissions for the archaeological excavations and surveys were obtained from the Ministry of Education and Culture. In Dili, we particularly thank Virgılio Simith, Cecılia Assis, Abílio da Conceição Silva and Nuno Vasco Oliveira for facilitating this process. We also acknowledge the support of the Director of Protected Areas and National Parks, National Directorate of Forestry, Manuel Mendes, who gave us permission to carry out excavations at Macapainara and survey the eastern end of the island—areas that lie within the boundaries of the Nino Konis Santana National Park. We acknowledge the respective *Xefe de Suco* and the people of Com, Ira Ara, Laleia, Moro-Parlamento and Tutuala villages whose enthusiastic support and assistance made this research possible. In Com, we particularly thank Edmundo Da Cruz and his wife Robella Mendez. In Manatuto, we thank Estefan Guterres for guiding us in the field and his and his wife Rosa's generous hospitality. We thank Carmen Dos Santos for assisting us in the field and providing translation support. Rintaro Ono is thanked for his assistance in Timor-Leste during the excavation of Macapainara, as are Luke Atkinson and Samantha Cooling for excavations at Leki Wakik. In West Sumba, we thank David Mitchell and local people for their guidance and expert knowledge. The surveys for fortified settlements in Kisar and Babar Islands were undertaken on Foreign Research Permit visas issued by the Indonesian Government agency RISTEK to O'Connor: 1456/FRP/SM/VII/2015 and 3024/FRP/E5/Dit.KI/IX/2017. We would like to thank the staff of Balai Arkeologi Maluku in Ambon for facilitating our research in the region. We would also like to thank Benyamin Th. Noach ST, Bupati of Kabupaten Maluku Barat Daya (Regent of the Maluku Barat Daya Regency) for supporting our surveys in the region and for his hospitality while staying on Kisar. We thank Emeritus Professor James Fox (The Australian National University (ANU)) for advice on texts and discussions over many years with the editors about the causes and consequences of fortification in the Wallacean Archipelago. We acknowledge the generosity and expertise of the anonymous reviewers whose comments strengthened the papers in this volume. Chapters 1 and 11 benefited from the use of the Portuguese Infrastructure of Scientific Collections (PRISC.pt). Publication was supported by the ANU Publication Subsidy Fund administered by ANU Press, the School of Culture, History and Language, ANU College of Asia and the Pacific, and the School of Social Sciences, Western Sydney University. We thank our copyeditor Beth Battrick of Teaspoon Consulting and the staff of ANU Press, in particular Emily Tinker and Lorena Kanellopoulos. Shimona Kealy's contribution to Chapter 11 was funded by the Australian Research Council (ARC) Centre of Excellence for Australian Biodiversity and Heritage (CE170100015). The research in Timor-Leste, Babar, Kisar and Sumba was supported by grants from ARC (DP0556210, LP0776789, DP0878543, FL120100156), and conducted under the auspices of ANU.

List of figures

Figure 1.1. Map of study area. 2

Figure 1.2. The stronghold of Sauo. 3

Figure 1.3. Massive limestone rubble walls, Vero Valley, with Andrew McWilliam. 4

Figure 1.4. Grave and sacrificial platform at Masui. 5

Figure 1.5. Manatuto. 6

Figure 2.1. Location of Macapainara. 14

Figure 2.2. 'Batu Makassar' flat circular stone at Ili Vali with upright stone next to it. Both are shaped from a fine-grained sedimentary rock. 14

Figure 2.3. Double grave at Macapainara. 15

Figure 2.4. Chinese Blue and White tradeware. 15

Figure 2.5. South section of Squares C and D, Macapainara, showing stratigraphic units. 17

Figure 2.6. Glass and shell beads from Macapainara (sample). 22

Figure 2.7. Decorated sherds from Macapainara. 24

Figure 2.8. Recognised Macapainara vessels with sherds from separate spits. 25

Figure 2.9. Macapainara jar rim shapes. 27

Figure 2.10. Vertical distribution of stone artefacts in each square relative to spit. 29

Figure 2.11. Margins of typical chert retouched flakes, thought to be strike-a-light tools. 30

Figure 2.12. Distribution of Macapainara vertebrate faunal remains, and associated weathering (NISP). 31

Figure 2.13. Total shell weight from Macapainara Squares A, C and D (g). 35

Figure 2.14. Worked and utilised sea shells from Macapainara. 35

Figure 2.15. Worked *Rochia*, *Tectus* and *Turbo* shells. 37

Figure 2.16. *Conomurex luhuanus* shell spindle whorls. 38

Figure 2.17. Bone artefacts. 38

Figure 3.1. Map of the Ira Ara site. 51

Figure 3.2. Ira Ara south mound edge showing disturbed section, July 2005. 51

Figure 3.3. The Ira Ara *sikua*, with spring pool and mound in background, July 2004. 52

Figure 3.4. Ira Ara northeast section of Units 2 and 3 (Burials 1 and 2). 53

Figure 3.5. Plan view of Ira Ara Burials 1 and 2. 54

Figure 3.6. Earthenware pot from Ira Ara Burial 1. 58

Figure 3.7. Ira Ara Burial 2 showing position of groundstone artefact and fragmented earthenware pot and lid. 59

Figure 3.8. Dice from Ira Ara Burial 2. 59

Figure 3.9. Selected lithic artefacts from Ira Ara. 62

Figure 3.10. Relative frequency of lithic artefact types from Ira Ara. 63

Figure 4.1. Location of Vasino and other fortified sites in Timor-Leste. 67

Figure 4.2. Vasino walls and prickly pear. 68

Figure 4.3. Vasino *batu Makassar* grave. 68

Figure 4.4. Vasino plan of fortifications and features. 69

Figure 4.5. Vasino carved wooden pole (*tei* or *ete uru ha'a*). 69

Figure 4.6. Vasino Square A section drawing. 70

Figure 4.7. Vasino Squares C and D section drawing. 71

Figure 4.8. Vasino Squares E, F and G section drawing. 72

Figure 4.9. Vasino Square H: photo of section. 73

Figure 4.10. Vasino radiocarbon dates (excludes shell-based dates). 75

Figure 4.11. Vasino Bayesian model. 76

Figure 4.12. Vasino earthenware pottery rims. 79

Figure 4.13. Vasino earthenware reconstructible contours. 80

Figure 4.14. Vasino distribution of vertebrate remains Squares A–H (NISP). 86

Figure 4.15. Vasino top 10 shell taxa by MNI and weight (g). 91

Figure 4.16. Vasino shellfish habitat by MNI (FW=Freshwater). 92

Figure 5.1. Timor-Leste map showing the location of Leki Wakik. 102

Figure 5.2. Leki Wakik site plan view. 103

Figure 5.3. Leki Wakik circular stone arrangements. 104

Figure 5.4. Typical view of Leki Wakik in August 2011. 105

Figure 5.5. Leki Wakik large black slab stone considered sacred by Laleia villagers. 106

Figure 5.6. Leki Wakik magnetometry grid locations. 110

Figure 5.7. Leki Wakik Test Pits A and C in the northern area of site. 111

Figure 5.8. Leki Wakik Test Pit A section drawing. 111

Figure 5.9. Leki Wakik southeastern excavation area. 112

Figure 5.10. Leki Wakik Test Pit B profile drawing. 112

Figure 5.11. Leki Wakik Test Pit B calibrated marine shell and charcoal radiocarbon dates. 113

Figure 5.12. Leki Wakik Test Pit C section drawing. 113

Figure 5.13. Leki Wakik Test Pit D section drawing. 114

Figure 5.14. Leki Wakik Test Pit E section drawing. 114

Figure 5.15. Leki Wakik lithics counts (A) and weights (B) by test pit. 115

Figure 5.16. Leki Wakik examples of decorated sherds. 116

Figure 5.17. Leki Wakik rim type 1.	116
Figure 5.18. Leki Wakik cumulative artefact weight per spit.	123
Figure 5.19. Leki Wakik artefact weight density per spit.	124
Figure 5.20. Leki Wakik tradeware density by test pit.	124
Figure 7.1. South Sulawesi: main topographical features and language boundaries.	154
Figure 7.2. South Sulawesi hilltop settlements with and without evidence of fortifications.	159
Figure 7.3. South Sulawesi fortifications (excluding fortified hilltop sites).	162
Figure 7.4. Time chart of South Sulawesi's dated fortifications.	168
Figure 7.A1. Cross-section and plans for Benteng Kale Goa and Anaq Goa.	176
Figure 7.A2. 'Dutch sketch of Goa c. 1776' (above) compared to relevant data from Bulbeck's (1992) survey of Kale Goa (below).	177
Figure 7.A3. Plan of Benteng Baebunta, Luwu (theodolite and staff survey).	185
Figure 7.A4. Plan of Benteng Matano, Luwu (theodolite and staff survey).	186
Figure 8.1. A steep section of the route to Fort Koncu.	193
Figure 8.2. The remaining wall structure of Fort Koncu on the eastern side.	194
Figure 8.3. Wa Kaa Kaa's grave.	195
Figure 8.4. An etched rock said to have been the place of royal agreement.	196
Figure 8.5. Limestone arrangement in the shape of a ring thought to symbolise the centre of the world.	197
Figure 8.6. The ruins of the wall structure of Fort Liwu.	198
Figure 8.7. One of the corner bastions of Fort Liwu.	198
Figure 8.8. One of the ancient cannons in Fort Liwu now placed on the coast at Wabula.	199
Figure 8.9. One of the ancient tombs inside Fort Liwu.	200
Figure 8.10. Plan of Fort Liwu in Wabula.	200
Figure 8.11. The former *mihrab* (a niche in the wall of a mosque) inside Fort Liwu, which also functioned as a tomb.	201
Figure 8.12. One of the gates into Fort Kombeli on the western side.	202
Figure 8.13. The restored tomb of one of the *Parabela*.	202
Figure 8.14. Fort Kombeli tomb made of coral rock.	202
Figure 8.15. Plan of Fort Takimpo.	203
Figure 8.16. Fort Takimpo walls.	203
Figure 8.17. Main gateway into Fort Takimpo.	204
Figure 8.18. Mosque inside Fort Takimpo.	205
Figure 8.19. The inauguration stage in Fort Takimpo.	205
Figure 9.1. Fort Kaledupa.	214
Figure 9.2. Kaledupa Mosque.	215

Figure 9.3. Fort Liya. 216

Figure 9.4. Fort Liya. 217

Figure 10.1. Area of southern Maluku and eastern Timor where fortified villages are concentrated (shaded blue). 222

Figure 10.2. Layers of stone walls leading up to the gate of a fortified village in the mountains of the Kei Island. 225

Figure 10.3. The thick, more than 2 m high *lutur*, or stone wall, that made up the base of mosque of the old Ujir village and which doubled as a fortification, located strategically at the water's edge. 228

Figure 10.4. Remains of the stone wall around Omtufu village, Yamdena, Tanimbar Islands c. 1920. 230

Figure 10.5. One of the entry gates to Omtufu village, Yamdena, Tanimbar Islands c. 1903, shown in use with palisading of sharpened stakes and two guards standing off to the gate's left. 230

Figure 10.6. The landward gate of Wakpapapi, Babar, Babar Islands, with a steep ladder leading up to the palisaded stone wall. 231

Figure 10.7. Gate over the stone wall of Lawawang village, Marsela, Babar Islands. 232

Figure 10.8. Stone wall palisaded with bamboo around Latalola village, Marsela, Babar Islands. 233

Figure 10.9. A Letinese walled village in the top right-hand corner of the frontispiece of Barchewitz (1751). 234

Figure 10.10. Hilltop fortified village on Luang Island. 236

Figure 10.11. Wulur village on Damar island enclosed by a stone wall visible behind villagers. 237

Figure 10.12. Distribution of #lutuR in Southeastern Wallacea. 239

Figure 11.1. Map showing survey locations. 249

Figure 11.2. Map showing the location of identified fort sites in Sumba Barat (West Sumba). 251

Figure 11.3. Paletirua fortified village. 252

Figure 11.4. Map of fortified sites located in Timor-Leste. 253

Figure 11.5. Ainaro survey at Subago. 254

Figure 11.6. Views towards Manatuto from the remains of the Sau Huhun fortification, showing its defensive position. 255

Figure 11.7. Sau Huhun fortification. 256

Figure 11.8. Iliheu Tatua hill. 256

Figure 11.9. Mapulu Ro Malae. 258

Figure 11.10. Maiana tomb. 259

Figure 11.11. Ili Kere Kere, a small overhang on a sheer cliff face in the Tutuala area with stone wall and dancers. 260

Figure 11.12. Map showing the location of identified fort sites on Kisar island. 265

Figure 11.13. The view from Loi Puru Ula looking north (left) towards the Pur Pura Negeri Lama (KSR 49—indicated), and the view from the Pur Pura Negeri Lama south towards Loi Puru Ula (KSR 68 and 69). 266

Figure 11.14. The Pur Pura Negeri Lama (KSR 49) showing the significant heights of the walls (A, D); extensive stonework (B) and chambers within the main wall dividing the headland (C). 267

Figure 11.15. Fallen megalithic standing stones from the old Pur Pura village complex (KSR 50), located within the Pur Pura Negri Lama fortifications (KSR 49). 267

Figure 11.16. Cave (KSR 54) (A) below the Pur Pura Negri Lama containing carved timber post (B). 268

Figure 11.17. Loi Puru Ula 1 (KSR 68) fortified rock-shelter with altar (A: viewer's left) and rock wall from base of cliff to the lip of the shelter floor, forming a staircase for access to the site (A: viewer's right). The rock-shelter has a commanding view of the plain below (B). 269

Figure 11.18. Loi Puru Ula 2 (KSR 69) showing the paved extended shelter floor (A) and stone wall with gate separating the different shelters along the terrace (B). 270

Figure 11.19. Nomaha Negeri Lama (KSR 72) view from plain looking north-northwest to the hilltop where the fortification is located (A), and the view of the stone wall looking north (B). 271

Figure 11.20. Jawalang Selatan Kota Lama 1 (KSR 81) showing stone wall with entrance (A) and the commanding view of the plain to the south-southeast (B). 271

Figure 11.21. Sokon (KSR 87) fortification showing stone walls following the ridge (A) with 'z'-shaped constructions (B, in detail). 272

Figure 11.22. Jawalang Selatan Kota Lama 2 (KSR 106). 273

Figure 11.23. Map showing the location of identified fort sites on the islands of Wetang and Babar Besar. Sites are numbered based on Kealy et al. (2018) (see also Table 11.4). 275

Figure 11.24. Kukeweble Negeri Lama (#61) showing the high (A), thick (B) surrounding wall constructed of a mix of medium to very large stones (C). In the centre of the Negeri Lama was a circular stone altar under the shade of a Banyan tree (D). 276

Figure 11.25. Wulua Negeri Lama (#48) showing narrow stone staircase leading to the gateway on the cliff edge (A), and stone arrangements surrounding the gateway with its commanding view over the plain below (B). 277

Figure 11.26. Wulyeni Negeri Lama (#56) showing stone stair for entrance (A), circular stone wall (B and D), and stone tools located inside (C). 277

List of tables

Table 2.1. Radiocarbon dates from Macapainara from Squares A, C and D.	18
Table 2.2. Distribution of Macapainara glass and tradeware.	22
Table 2.3. Frequency of Macapainara stone artefacts across three excavation squares relative to spit.	29
Table 2.4. Macapainara raw material frequency.	29
Table 2.5. Macapainara frequency of conchoidal fracture variables.	29
Table 2.6. Macapainara summary of characteristic edge modification variables.	30
Table 2.7. Macapainara NISP recorded by square and spit for the three trenches that produced vertebrate remains during the 2008 excavations.	32
Table 2.A1. Macapainara tradeware.	43
Table 2.A2. Macapainara representative shellfish data (Square D, NISP and MNI).	46
Table 3.1. Radiocarbon and thermoluminescence dates from Ira Ara.	55
Table 3.2. Vertebrate fauna from Ira Ara, Units 1, 2 and 3.	60
Table 3.3. Molluscan fauna from the Ira Ara site, Unit 1.	61
Table 4.1. Vasino radiocarbon dates.	74
Table 4.2. Vasino earthenware pottery weights by square (g).	77
Table 4.3. Vasino earthenware vessel forms.	78
Table 4.4. Vasino stone artefact assemblage.	82
Table 4.5. Vasino stone artefact types.	83
Table 4.6. Vasino modification characteristics counts.	83
Table 4.7. Vasino functional attributes of perforated discs.	84
Table 4.8. Vasino number of individual specimens (NISP) of vertebrate taxa recovered.	85
Table 4.9. Vasino top 10 shell taxa by weight (g).	89
Table 4.10. Vasino top 10 shell taxa by MNI.	90
Table 5.1. Leki Wakik Test Pit B earthenware sherd external surface colour by spit.	117
Table 5.2. Leki Wakik tradeware sherd typology distribution.	118
Table 5.3. Leki Wakik major mollusc taxa and habitat by spit. Counts shown are MNI.	119
Table 5.4. Leki Wakik vertebrate NISP and unidentified specimens by spit.	121
Table 5.A1. Leki Wakik excavated material weights (in grams except as noted).	130
Table 5.A2. Leki Wakik radiocarbon results.	132
Table 6.1. Macapainara radiocarbon dates.	138
Table 7.1. Locations (north to south) surveyed in South Sulawesi for historical sites.	155

Table 7.2. Chronologically dated hilltop sites in parts of South Sulawesi with reliable rainfall. 160

Table 7.3. Chronologically dated hilltop sites in drought-prone parts of South Sulawesi. 161

Table 7.4. South Sulawesi non-hilltop fortifications in locations near hilltop fortifications. 163

Table 7.5. Fortifications in Makassar and its hinterland (excluding Kale Goa). 163

Table 7.6. Other Makasar and Bugis non-hilltop fortifications. 164

Table 7.7. Non-Bugis non-hilltop fortifications in Luwu Regency. 164

Table 8.1. Geographical details of the four surveyed Buton forts. 192

Table 10.1. Proto-Malayo-Polynesian reconstructions around walls and their building. 239

Table 10.2. Austronesian languages with #lutuR 'stack, pile up stones'. 240

Table 10.3. Austronesian languages with #lutuR 'fence, man-made barrier'. 240

Table 10.4. Austronesian languages with #lutuR 'stone wall'. 240

Table 10.5. Papuan languages with #lutuR 'stone wall'. 241

Table 11.1. Summary data on fortified sites in West Sumba. 250

Table 11.2. Summary data on fortified sites in Timor-Leste, numbered by district and corresponding to Figure 11.4. 260

Table 11.3. Summary data on fortified sites in Kisar. 273

Table 11.4. Summary data on fortified sites in the Babar Island group. Numbers follow full list of survey localities from Kealy et al. (2018: Table 1). 278

1

Forts and fortifications in Wallacea

Sue O'Connor, Andrew McWilliam and Sally Brockwell

Introduction

This volume documents a common phenomenon found throughout the islands of Wallacea, east of the Wallace Line in the Indonesian archipelago: the fortified hilltop settlement. Historically, fortified settlements have been a common built form across the archipelago. The great naturalist Alfred Wallace (1869), during his survey of the region between 1854 and 1862, and later Henry Forbes (1885) in the mid-1880s, made frequent references to these structures that were in wide use due to the continuing prevalence of hostilities across the region. In the century and more since these records however, the provenance and forms of these remarkable built structures have been largely overlooked by contemporary researchers, and many of these impressive structures are now subject to neglect and erosion, reclaimed by forest regrowth, or repurposed for contemporary construction needs. One possible reason for the scant research attention paid to fortified settlements is their low archaeological visibility and remoteness from contemporary settlements.

The present volume seeks to redress this gap in the record by presenting a selection of research papers on the archaeology and ethnohistory of fortified settlements across the archipelagic region known as Wallacea, offering new perspectives on their origins and purpose, structural forms and defining features. Given the scale and extent of fortifications found in varying degrees of integrity across the island chains from Bali to Maluku and Sulawesi to West Papua, the current collection represents a preliminary set of findings and observations that can form the basis for further investigations and more sustained heritage considerations.

In discussing the concept of 'fortified settlements', we are referring in the main to strategically located, piled stone structures within a broadly similar set of constituent and locational characteristics (see Lape 2006). Most of the fortified settlements we have observed are located in inaccessible places: on hilltops or cliff sites with precipitous drop-offs on one or more sides and masked by dense vegetation. Sections of the forts typically feature massive stone walls up to 4 m high and 1 m thick, which demarcate the defensive perimeters of the structures. From an archaeological perspective, these steeply incised crags look uninviting for human habitation, and lack in situ water sources and arable land where crops might be cultivated. In other places, the sites of former fortified settlements are located close to contemporary villages or within seasonal swidden farmland, and many have had their stone walls extensively quarried for use in house foundations, base material for roads or as garden perimeter walls against feral pig incursions. In some cases, only vestiges of the defensive walls remain with scatters of earthenware sherds or porcelain tradeware attesting to their earlier occupation.

Some of the settlements we discuss in this volume have been occupied in living memory and have rich oral histories recalling their mythic and historical significance. They form important material markers of ancestral origins and renown for the contemporary descendants of these earlier settlers. As the ancestral dwellings of a contemporary lineage they often house the graves of ancestors and other significant focal structures, reinforcing their status as places of veneration that are visited regularly and where sacrificial ceremonies are performed.

The present collection draws on a series of surveys undertaken to prospective locations in the islands of eastern Indonesia. They include surveys undertaken since 2000 by Pannell, O'Connor, McWilliam, Brockwell, Lape and Chao in Timor-Leste; Bulbeck, Caldwell, Hasanuddin and Somba in Sulawesi; Brockwell, O'Connor and Tanidjuro in Sumba; and O'Connor and Kealy in Kisar Island. There are many other prospective locations and island sites where fortification was prevalent. Forbes' (1885) account indicates that they extended as far east as Tanimbar Island (*Timor Laut*) in southern Maluku, but further research is likely to dramatically expand their distribution across the region.

To date we have recorded over 30 indigenous fortified sites and excavated six forts in different places in Timor-Leste, while Bulbeck and others have recorded systematically a series of stone forts in Sulawesi. On the island of Sumba, Brockwell and O'Connor visited a range of fortified villages, and recorded the graves, internal features and fortified walls, as did Kealy and O'Connor in Babar and Kisar (Figure 1.1). But, as in many areas of the region, sensitivities among contemporary descendants of the former residents over ground disturbance, mostly relating to the continuing ancestral and spiritual significance of the sites, precluded the possibility of excavation. The preliminary results of our surveys and excavations on Timor and Sulawesi Islands form the body of research materials for this volume and begin the process of more systematic documentation into the distribution and variability of fortified locations throughout the archipelago.

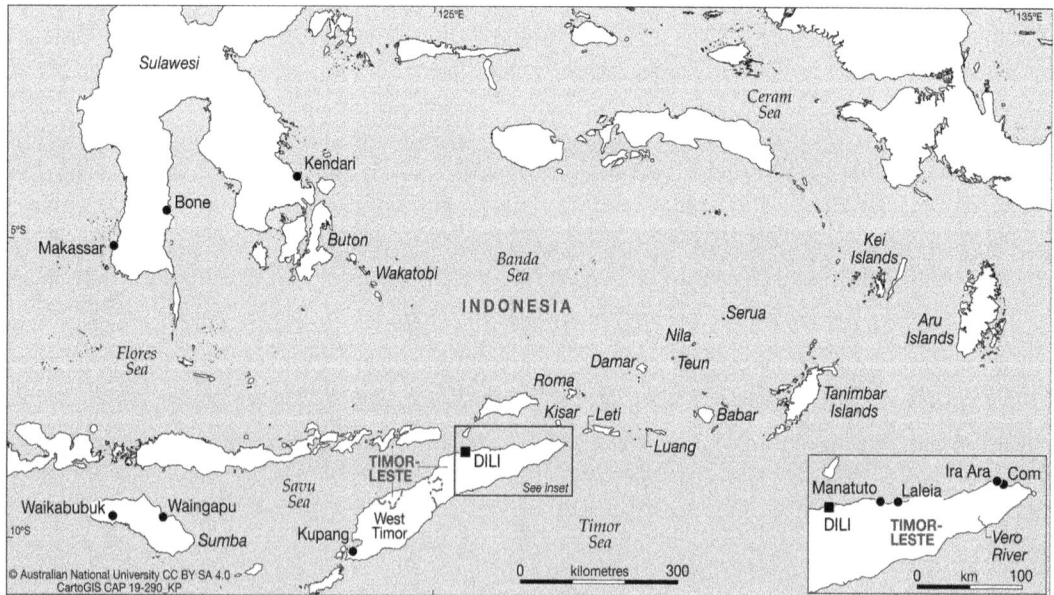

Figure 1.1. Map of study area.
Source: CartoGIS ANU.

Defining fortification in Wallacea

During his travels in Portuguese Timor during the 1880s, the redoubtable British naturalist Henry Forbes undertook journeys into the interior of the island with a view to collecting plant specimens for scientific documentation. Travelling in a cavalcade of Timorese ponies laden with stores, he made several observations about the people and lands he engaged with, which speak to the unsettled political climate of the time.

> From our elevated position the whole country within the sweep of the eye was of a most singular conformation being entirely composed of knife-edges, peaks and precipitous slopes of deep valleys. It surprised me to observe that it was the most inaccessible peaks and isolated crags that were crowned by dwellings, hidden from sight generally among groves of trees. It was easy to see that I was travelling in a lawless land where every man's hand was against his neighbour and where therefore every man was constantly and restlessly on the outlook. (1885:432)

Later he visited the residence of a local headman (*Dato*) whose camp (Figure 1.2) was located in a strategic, defensive site:

> Entering through a high-barred gateway, we found the homestead to consist of eight to ten well built houses … Surrounded by a high stone wall surmounted by a cactus hedge and built on a rocky buttress jutting out over a precipitous gorge. It was unapproachable except on the one side by which we entered. (1885:434)

Forbes's description applied to the upland territory of Lequidoi in the Mambai-speaking district of Ailieu, but it highlights two common features of Portuguese Timor at the time: namely, the instability and threats of armed attacks by rivals, and equally the prevalence of strategic, fortified settlements located on precipitous cliffs and hilltops. Defensive fortified settlements, it seems, was the preferred and prevailing pattern of residence across much of rural Portuguese Timor.

Figure 1.2. The stronghold of Sauo.
Source: H.O. Forbes (1885: facing 434).

The Dutch geographer F.J. Ormeling, in his 1956 volume on the geography of Timor, also made specific mention of the existence of fortified settlements. He noted that rocky outcrops and hilltops 'provide[d] a natural refuge for the mountain folk. There the people build their fortified mountain villages; there they lay in wait for the enemy' (1956:35). There is a strong continuity here with the description of Henry Forbes.

Figure 1.3. Massive limestone rubble walls, Vero Valley, with Andrew McWilliam.
Source: Photo courtesy of Sue O'Connor.

Many of the fortified sites identified in Timor-Leste exhibit several common characteristics, taking into account variations created by site topography and terrain. Forts with more massive walls usually have gateways and narrow meandering passageways, through which people entering were required to pass. In our surveys, the only well-preserved examples of these gateways were located in forested areas well away from contemporary settlements and had avoided the pattern of stone recycling due to their distance away from population centres (Figure 1.3).

Access to the fortified sites may have been guarded from above. The walls on the larger structures are sometimes slitted, indicating that weaponry was probably used to guard the entrances. The thickness of the walls, which are constructed as parallel dry stone ramparts and filled with the coralline rubble that litters much of the landscape of far eastern Timor, suggests that the occupants were defending themselves from more than just spears or even muskets. In the case of the latter, wooden palisades or simple barriers may have sufficed. The massive density of some of the walls suggests that they were built as defence against artillery (cannon) attack, which has also been indicated by oral narratives recorded from local custodians of the sites (see Chapter 6, this volume). An additional element of the stone walls that assisted in their protective strength was the extensive planting of cacti outside, atop and inside the perimeter walls, providing an additional defensive barrier (see McWilliam 2000:465).

In Timor-Leste, gateways to fortified sites typically open onto an internal walled space (in Fataluku: *laca*), which is said to be the area where visitors were inspected or greeted. These spaces are often shaped in a semicircular format. Oral accounts, together with the mapping of the internal features of the fortifications, indicate that the settlements also contained circumscribed ceremonial spaces where dancing and communal feasting took place (F: *sepu*) and areas where ancestral graves are now located.

Figure 1.4. Grave and sacrificial platform at Masui.
Source: Photo courtesy of Andrew McWilliam.

Figure 1.5. Manatuto.
A (above): Skulls on platform looking towards Mt St Antonio with stone altar in foreground, 1913. B (below): Modern-day view of Mt St Antonio with telecommunications tower.

Source: Photo A by António Nascimento Leitão, courtesy of Natural History and Science Museum of University of Porto, register number MHNC-UP-FCUP-IA-AF-775. Photo B courtesy of Sue O'Connor.

Many forts also include distinctive sacrificial stone platforms and/or altar stones, some of which are marked with standing stones or carved wooden posts (F: *ete uru ha'a* and or *sikua*) (Figure 1.4). Like ancestor graves these structures remain highly significant sites of sacrificial veneration for customary owners of the former settlements and are carefully avoided unless ritual activities are intended.

Our survey of a hilltop settlement within the perimeter of the current town of Manatuto indicates that at least some of these platforms were previously used in headhunting rituals (Figure 1.5). Today there is little to be seen on the site of the former settlement; however, our guide noted that, several years prior to our visit in 2010, he had seen a stone 'altar' with human skulls lying scattered around its base. The location where he found the altar is clearly the same spot as that in the 1913 Portuguese photograph in Figure 1.5. This figure reveals more than 30 skulls lined up on a wooden frame above a stone platform (note also the cactus growing on the perimeter of the upper hilltop). The image likely records the success of punitive raids against rebellious Timorese groups in the interior, possibly during or associated with the last great rebellion against Portuguese rule in Timor, the war of Manufahi and the ruler Boaventura (1911–1912), in which Manatuto participants acted as loyal militias and reservists (*arrarais* and *moradores*) for their colonial Portuguese allies (see Roque 2010). As the photo was taken in 1913, this festival of heads (*Festival das Cabeças*) clearly represents a Portuguese-sanctioned activity – so not directly related to the origins of fortification but evidence that inter-communal violence was common until the early twentieth century. Today in this location there are small stone houses with stone bases, walled yards and gardens, which have no doubt recycled the stone from the platform and walls of the fortified settlement of Sau Huhun at Manatuto (see Chapter 11).

According to oral accounts, residential and ritual houses were built within the walls of the fortified dwellings, and historical records indicate that they were in the style of elevated, four-posted structures consistent with the classic Austronesian built designs (see Hauser-Schaublin 1989:13). Oral traditions also indicate that gardening and other subsistence-related activities took place outside the walls on the lower slopes, while domestic animals, such as cattle and buffalo, would be herded into the enclosures in times of threat or imminent attack. Surprisingly, all fortified sites that we have recorded lie some distance from freshwater sources, with nearest springs or creeks sometimes being kilometres distant.

Why were settlements fortified?

Decisions to construct defensive fortifications against the threat of attack and violent conflict have been a recurring feature of human settlements from earliest antiquity. The reasons and proximate causes that precipitate and sustain fortification, however, have long been the subject of debate and speculation. Among the array of reasons put forward include struggles over limited resources, the desire to control strategic locations, or a response to repeated incursions or invasion by foreign forces.

Archaeologists have somewhat conflicting views regarding the drivers of fortification. Lape and Chao (2008; cf. also Field 2008) have linked the emergence of fortifications in the Indo-Pacific region with a period of rapid climate change, reduced rainfall and environmental fluctuations beginning about AD 1000, leading to resource unpredictability and inter-group conflict driven by competition for fertile land and resources. These arguments are reviewed in detail in this volume by Bulbeck and Caldwell (Chapter 7). On the other hand, O'Connor et al. (2012) have argued that where such structures have been reliably dated in Island Southeast Asia, it has been shown that most were constructed well after this period, with a peak of fort building occurring in the fifteenth to seventeenth centuries AD; much later than the climate change model would allow. Instead, they suggest that the late onset of fortification, coupled with findings from anthropological and historical research, indicates that a range of external social and economic factors may have been more significant catalysts for the onset of fort-building (see also Chapter 6, this volume). McWilliam (Chapter 6, this volume) discusses the trade in sandalwood from the island of Timor, and how exchanging sandalwood for value goods, such as iron, ceramics and later muskets and gunpowder, must have led to inequalities in wealth. The introduction of maize and the expansion of wet rice (*sawah*) cultivation at the time of Dutch and Portuguese colonisation may have allowed for new levels of agricultural productivity, supporting higher population densities and more opportunities for surplus production and its control. The regional trade in slaves may also have played a significant role, particularly in the seventeenth and eighteenth centuries AD, corresponding with the rise in Dutch colonial demand for labour in places like the nutmeg plantations on Banda Island in neighbouring Maluku. Slaves were often acquired as a result of inter-polity raiding, and this may in turn have accelerated the process of fortification and alliance. Populations without physical, geographical or warrior protection would have been particularly vulnerable to raiding parties.

Kingdoms, princedoms, chiefdoms?

Historical sources are also far from unanimous about the scale and complexity of autonomous rule that should be ascribed to the polities in the different islands of Wallacea, or even within single islands. Hägerdal (2012:52), for example, points out that the Dutch and Portuguese sources of the seventeenth and early eighteenth centuries use the term kings (*reis, koningen*) to describe the local leaders, and kingdoms (*reinos, rijken*) to describe the areas they ruled. He argues this translation of the local concepts has exaggerated their importance, given the size of the local domains and the overall population of Timor at the time. He also points out that there were significant variations in the size and complexity of the diverse autonomous domains across the islands. The ruling domains in Java, South Sulawesi and parts of Sumatra, for example, could be as large as, and comparable in terms of population and control of goods with, European kingdoms. Conversely, hereditary rulers of political jurisdictions on islands such as Rote and Sawu were basically 'lords' of a mere few villages (Hägerdal 2012:52). For Timor, inconsistency in the sources makes it difficult to estimate the size of these autonomous domains, but overall the impression is of 'a complex of small and steadily shifting centres of power that become increasingly fragmentary the further east one goes' (Hägerdal 2012:52).

The term 'chiefdom' is arguably a more fitting concept to describe the polities represented by the remains of many of the fortified structures. The anthropologist Schulte Nordholt's (1971:403) accounts of West Timor demonstrate the importance of hereditary networks, ritual and kin relationships and marriage alliances in maintaining and extending the power and influence of rulers and their domains. The records of the Dutch United East India Company (Verenigde Oostindische Compagnie, VOC) for the pre-1900 period indicate that conflicts over the borders of these small polities were rife and rule was rarely stable (Hägerdal 2012:52). Chiefdoms typically expanded and consolidated through exclusion and incorporation (Earl 1853:281), and McWilliam (1996) has suggested that, in eastern Wallacea, this process was in part achieved by the development of ritualised forms of headhunting, which were common throughout the archipelago and used to assert and maintain political centrality between rivals (McWilliam 1996). The politics of indirect rule pursued for centuries by Dutch and Portuguese colonial power are likely to have played into the dynamics of local domain politics and inter-domain struggles for influence and favour (see also Roque 2010).

Discussion of the chapters in the volume

The volume is divided into three parts: Archaeology of Forts, Social History of Forts, and Conclusion and Future Directions.

In Part 1, we report on excavations of coastal and inland fortified and other defensive settlements in: Macapainara near the village of Com, the village of Ira Ara, and Vasino fort near the village of Moro at the eastern end of Timor-Leste (Chapters 2, 3 and 4); and Leki Wakik near the village of Laleia in north central Timor-Leste (Chapter 5) (see Figure 1.1). Chapters 2, 4 and 5 describe the excavation, chronology and analysis of assemblages of shell, animal bone and trade items from Macapainara, Vasino and Leki Wakik, built on steep hills at the eastern end of Timor-Leste, with the aim of establishing a history of settlement and subsistence at these sites. In Chapter 3, Lape et al. describe investigations at nearby Ira Ara, a fortified settlement site with human graves that provides new data on diet, trade and mortuary practices c. AD 1700. The radiocarbon dates and tradeware from these particular settlements in Timor-Leste point to occupation between the fifteenth and mid-twentieth centuries.

Oral accounts and social history relating to the use of the fortified sites in Timor-Leste and southern Sulawesi are discussed in Part 2. In Chapter 6, McWilliam argues against the position proposed by Lape and Chao (2008) that fortification is related to climatic unpredictability and social conflict over access to resources. He draws on a range of historical, ethnographic and archaeological evidence from Timor-Leste to suggest an alternative set of social drivers for processes of fortification. These factors comprise momentous changes in social conditions that coincided with the advent of Portuguese colonialism in the region from the early sixteenth century. Bulbeck and Caldwell support McWilliam's arguments in Chapter 7, where they draw together a wealth of scattered historical and archaeological evidence regarding indigenous fortifications in South Sulawesi and their sociopolitical foundations to test the theories proposed by Lape and Chao (2008) and Field (2008). Chapters 8 and 9 describe fortifications on the islands of Buton and Wakatobi in Southeast Sulawesi. In Chapter 8, Hasanuddin discusses the broader political tensions that led to fortifications in the sixteenth-century kingdom of Buton. In Chapter 9, Nani Somba describes how the development of forts on Wakatobi was triggered by the islands' strategic geographical location for maritime trade and its role as a colony of Buton. In Chapter 10, Schapper discusses fortifications in Maluku province in far east Indonesia. Using evidence from historical records and linguistics, she argues that, contra Lape and Chao (2008) and McWilliam (Chapter 6, this volume), fortified settlement-building cannot be attributed to particular climatic or socioeconomic conditions but is best understood as a cultural feature diffused on a regional level. Chapter 11 in Part 3 contains the results of surveys of fortifications undertaken in Ainaro, central Timor-Leste; Manatuto, north central Timor-Leste; Vero Valley, eastern Timor-Leste; and the eastern Indonesian islands of Sumba, Babar and Kisar. The volume concludes in Chapter 12 with an assessment of future research directions.

References

Earl, G.W. 1853. *The native races of the Indian Archipelago: Papuans*. H. Bailliere, London. doi.org/10.5962/bhl.title.101733.

Field, J.S. 2008. Explaining fortifications in Indo-Pacific prehistory. *Archaeology in Oceania* 43:1–10. doi.org/10.1002/j.1834-4453.2008.tb00025.x.

Forbes, H.O. 1885. *A naturalist's wanderings in the Eastern Archipelago: A narrative of travel and exploration from 1878 to 1883*. Sampson, Low, Marston, Searle and Rivington, London. doi.org/10.5962/bhl.title.36489.

Hägerdal, H. 2012. *Lords of the land, lords of the sea: Conflict and adaptation in early colonial Timor, 1600–1800*. KITLV Press, Leiden. doi.org/10.26530/oapen_408241.

Hauser-Schaublin, B. 1989. *Kulthäuser in Nordneuguinea*. Abhandlungen und Berichte des Staatlichen, Museums für Volkenkünde Dresden no. 43. Akademie Verlag, Berlin.

Lape, P.V. 2006. Chronology of fortified settlements in East Timor. *Journal of Island and Coastal Archaeology* 1(2):285–297. doi.org/10.1080/15564890600939409.

Lape, P.V. and C.-Y. Chao 2008. Fortification as a human response to late Holocene climate change in East Timor. *Archaeology in Oceania* 43(1):11–21. doi.org/10.1002/j.1834-4453.2008.tb00026.x.

McWilliam, A. 1996. Severed heads that germinate the state: History, politics, and headhunting in Southwest Timor. In J. Hoskins (ed.), *Headhunting and the social imagination in Southeast Asia*, pp. 127–166. Stanford University Press, Stanford.

McWilliam, A. 2000. A plague on your house? Some impacts of *Chromolaena odorata* on Timorese livelihoods. *Human Ecology* 28(3):451–469. doi.org/10.1023/A:1007061632588.

O'Connor, S., A. McWilliam, J.N. Fenner and S. Brockwell 2012. Examining the origin of fortifications in East Timor: Social and environmental factors. *The Journal of Island and Coastal Archaeology* 7(2):200–218. doi.org/10.1080/15564894.2011.619245.

Ormeling, F.J. 1956. *The Timor problem: A geographical interpretation of an undeveloped island*. T.B. Wolters, Groningen and Jakarta.

Roque, R. 2010. *Headhunting and colonialism: Anthropology and the circulation of human skulls in the Portuguese Empire 1870–1930*. Palgrave Macmillan, New York.

Schulte Nordholt, H.G. 1971. *The political system of the Atoni of Timor*. KITLV Verhandelingen 60. Martinus Nijhoff, The Hague. doi.org/10.26530/oapen_613379.

Wallace, A.R. 1869. *The Malay archipelago: The land of the orang-utan and the bird of paradise. A narrative of travel with sketches of man and nature*. 1st edition. Macmillan, London. doi.org/10.5962/bhl.title.131886.

Archaeology of forts

2

The fortified settlement of Macapainara, Lautem District, Timor-Leste

Sue O'Connor, David Bulbeck, Noel Amano Jr, Philip J. Piper, Sally Brockwell, Andrew McWilliam, Jack N. Fenner, Jack O'Connor-Veth, Rose Whitau, Tim Maloney, Michelle C. Langley, Mirani Litster, James Lankton, Bernard Gratuze, William R. Dickinson, Anthony Barham and Richard C. Willan

Introduction

The hilltop location known as Macapainara is an extensive fortified settlement complex near the modern coastal village of Com (Figure 2.1). Although the settlement is no longer occupied, families living in the modern harbour village of Com identify it as their ancestral homeland and visit the ancestral graves in the settlement to perform rituals. Macapainara is 175 m above sea level and approximately 2 km in from the northern coastline of Timor-Leste (Figure 2.1). In 2008, excavations were carried out within the walls in order to assess the nature and chronology of occupation. The phenomenon of fort building and its chronology in Timor-Leste have been examined elsewhere (Fenner and Bulbeck 2013; O'Connor et al. 2012). Here we focus on describing the excavated cultural assemblage.

The Macapainara settlement occurs over two levels. The upper level, known as Ili Vali, references the large rocky bluff on which this part of the complex is located. Ili Vali has a narrow stone entrance way, several graves made of dressed stone and several large flat circular dressed disks made of a fine-grained sedimentary rock, identified locally by the term '*batu Makassar*' (see McWilliam et al. 2012; Figure 2.2). The lower level, known as Macapainara, is surrounded by massive encircling stone walls to the north and south that are up to 3 m high and 2 m thick at the base. This area is a natural sediment trap and was selected for excavation as the part of the complex most likely to have a deep deposit. Macapainara has several graves, including one very large structure facing east–west identified as a double grave, containing the remains of the former ruler of Ili Vali/Macapainara and his close political ally (Figure 2.3) (McWilliam et al. 2012). This grave measures 3 m in length and c. 2.2 m in width. The base of the grave is constructed from shaped limestone blocks while the upper section is made from the flat slabs of dressed fine-grained sedimentary rock. At the time of our field visit a Chinese Blue and White tradeware bowl was placed on the surface (Figure 2.4).

Figure 2.1. Location of Macapainara.
Source: CartoGIS ANU.

Figure 2.2. '*Batu Makassar*' flat circular stone at Ili Vali with upright stone next to it. Both are shaped from a fine-grained sedimentary rock.
Source: Photo courtesy of Sue O'Connor.

Figure 2.3. Double grave at Macapainara.
Source: Photo courtesy of Sue O'Connor.

Figure 2.4. Chinese Blue and White tradeware.
Source: Photo courtesy of Sue O'Connor.

Senior clansmen of the contemporary settlements of Mua Pusu and Loho Matu, in the village of Com, recall in their oral histories a time when they lived at Macapainara. During this period, they were actively engaged in inter-island exchange networks, including lucrative trade in sandalwood and human slaves. According to oral histories of the area there was a strong relationship between endemic warfare, the maintenance of fortified settlements and the enslavement of rival communities. Control over the strategic anchorages of the coast enabled them to benefit from the flow of high-value trade goods, especially muzzle-loader firearms, ammunition and gunpowder, while acting as intermediaries with hinterland groups trafficking in war captives and slaves.

In the process, the coastal groups grew rich and contributed to their reputation as *Orang Kai*. This was a widely used term across the Malay trading world, including the neighbouring islands of the Moluccas, where the *Orang Kaya* represented an oligarchy of elders from small but wealthy communities who had established a 'mercantile aristocracy' (see Goodman 1998; McWilliam 2007; Villiers 1981:728–729).

Excavation at Macapainara

Macapainara was excavated over a four-week field season in July–August 2008. A wide variety of cultural materials were recovered, consistent with the oral traditions relating to the age and use of the site, including earthenware, imported tradeware and glass (comprising vessel fragments and beads). Also recovered—and less expected—were a quantity of modified flaked stone artefacts. Subsistence remains included a variety of wild and domesticated terrestrial animal species, fish, shellfish and sea urchin. Small quantities of worked shell and bone were also recovered, demonstrating that decorative items were made at the site using locally available materials. Charcoal was found throughout the excavation and was used for dating the deposit.

Excavations of three 1 x 1 m squares (A, C and D) reached a depth of c. 1.6 m, when culturally sterile sediment was encountered, showing that sediment accumulated rapidly during the period the site was occupied (Figure 2.5). Excavation occurred in arbitrary spits between 5 cm and 10 cm in thickness. All excavated sediment was dry sieved through 3 mm sieves and finds were sorted at the site. Cultural material was returned to The Australian National University (ANU) for further analysis and remains in the quarantine facility at the Department of Archaeology and Natural History.

Stratigraphy

The Macapainara deposits consist of pale grey to light grey-brown, poorly sorted, fine to medium sandy silty gravels and medium to coarse gravelly silts. There is near horizontal bedding, with grading from coarser to finer thin beds, and infrequent thin lenses. Gravel size clasts are typically 50–150 mm sub-angular to sub-rounded limestone. Angular shale clasts up to 180–260 mm occur occasionally. Throughout the sequence, gravels are matrix supported, with most elongate and planar clasts laid sub-horizontal, and showing only slight preferred orientation and no consistent dip.

Figure 2.5. South section of Squares C and D, Macapainara, showing stratigraphic units.
Source: Photo courtesy of Sue O'Connor.

There is limited pedogenic development. A modern humic topsoil (5–7 cm Ao horizon with leaf litter) has developed, capping a 15–20 cm zone with abundant modern rootlets. The stratigraphy is consistent with the sequence ages, indicating ongoing accumulation of over 1.5 m of deposit over 300 years, with numerous artefacts and dumped settlement refuse within the coarser fabric of all layers. The fine to coarse banding probably reflects episodic in-wash, bringing poorly sorted, collapsed and reworked settlement debris and refuse deposits (and possibly some reworked colluvium) short distances into the depocentre. Walls and layout of other built structures have probably confined the locus of deposition, leading to relatively fast net accumulation. The 1.5 m deep cultural sequence sits, probably unconformably, over an undulating contact onto denser, lighter yellow-brown, clayey sandy silts. This basal unit comprises a bioturbated earlier soil land surface and is largely devoid of coarser gravel clasts.

Chronology of occupation

Nine accelerated mass spectrometry (AMS) radiocarbon dates on charcoal were obtained from throughout the deposit at Macapainara (Table 2.1; Fenner and Bulbeck 2013). Only charcoal radiocarbon dates are included because the carbon reservoir offset for marine shell (ΔR) is unknown for this area. Bayesian analysis of the nine results indicates Macapainara was probably first occupied between AD 1695–1780, and likely postdates AD 1600 (97 per cent probability). It was not abandoned until the mid-twentieth century or later.

Table 2.1. Radiocarbon dates from Macapainara from Squares A, C and D.

Sample	Lab ID	Radiocarbon date (RCYBP)	Calibrated range (year AD)
A2c	WK24947	54 ± 30	1809 to 1837, 1845 to 1858, 1880 to 1922
A8c	WK24948	8 ± 30	1806 to 1840, 1842 to 1867, 1876 to 1923
A13c	WK24949	221 ± 30	1666 to 1683, 1725 to 1814 1836 to 1849, 1855 to 1879
C2c	WK24950	107 ± 30	1804 to 1923
C7c	WK24951	72 ± 30	1808 to 1839, 1844 to 1866, 1878 to 1923
C13c	WK24952	282 ± 30	1644 to 1665, 1739 to 1801
D2c	WK24953	49 ± 30	1809 to 1838, 1880 to 1922
D8c	WK24954	193 ± 37	1721 to 1897, 1920 to 1932
D15c	WK24955	93 ± 30	1806 to 1870, 1876 to 1924

Calibrations and Bayesian analysis were performed using the BCal calibration program (Buck et al. 1999) with the SHCal04 calibration curve (McCormac et al. 2004). Calibrated date ranges shown are the 95 per cent highest probability density regions.
Source: Adapted from Fenner and Bulbeck (2013: Table 1).

Methods

Glass beads and sherds

The majority (N = 11) of the total excavated glass beads and sherds were analysed from Macapainara, using laser-ablation-inductively coupled plasma-mass spectrometry (LA-ICP-MS) (see Lankton and Gratuze 2011 for more detailed methods).

Earthenware

The entire Macapainara earthenware assemblage was inspected twice by David Bulbeck, and a further petrographic analysis was undertaken by William R. Dickinson. During the first inspection, a Microsoft Access database was created to record the pottery in detail. The Access 'parent' table, 'vessel', was created to record information that went beyond the individual sherd, such as cases of multiple sherds that had evidently fragmented from the same originally deposited pot, or cases where the sherd(s) assigned to a pot were diagnostic as to the pot's original vessel form. A second Access parent table, 'sherd', allowed for observations at the level of the sherd or group of similar sherds, with links to supplementary observations in Access 'child' tables on rim, neck, shoulder, footring and basal sherds, as well as slipped sherds and decorated sherds. Not every sherd was individually recorded, and instead unslipped body sherds were classified into a 'sherd' group (e.g. 'Spit A3 "Brown", externally reduced, internally and externally smoothed, with traces of paddle and anvil manufacture'), and a representative sherd from each group was recorded in the Access database.

Over 6,600 'sherd' observations were made, whether these were observations of individual sherds, multiple sherds from the same vessel (and vessel part) found in the same spit, or a representative sherd from a 'sherd' group. Observations included the number of sherds involved, their weight to the nearest tenth of a gram, internal and external Munsell colours, and signs of surface finish. Additional observations for rim sherds included their orientation as everted, direct or inverted (following Shepard 1974); if everted, whether the rim section was short, long or indeterminate, particular rim shape characteristics, and (where possible to estimate) approximate rim diameter. Neck sherds (which often were also rim sherds) were recorded as having a profile that was sharp, rounded or indeterminate, and shoulder sherds as sharply or less sharply carinated. Footring and basal sherds were recorded according to their shape based on the variability noted during the first inspection of the assemblage.

Tradeware

The 67 tradeware sherds excavated from Macapainara were studied in detail so as to infer the probable form of the parent vessel and the parent vessel's place of manufacture (according to the categories used in the literature on trade ceramics). About three-quarters of the classifications are Chinese, and these are notified in terms of the finer categories 'Guangdong', 'Ming', 'Transitional', 'Zhangzhou' (formerly known as Swatow), 'Kraaksporselein', and 'Qing' (which includes wares dated to the Yongzheng reign). Zhangzhou wares were classified into 'Ming Zhangzhou', 'Zhangzhou' and 'Qing Zhangzhou', following the classification system developed for these wares in South Sulawesi, where Zhangzhou (Swatow) sherds abound (Bulbeck 1992). The dates for the Zhangzhou subclassifications are taken from Bulbeck (1996–97) except where finer chronological matches are available from the literature.

The term 'porcelain' is restricted to sherds with a translucent body, as determined by shining a small torch through the sherd's wall. The only true porcelain sherds excavated from Macapainara were Chinese. Three Chinese sherds and one Vietnamese sherd were also identified as 'semi-porcelain', which indicates marginal translucency and/or a pinkish rather than pure white body. Sherds from similarly high-fired vessels with a fine fabric virtually free of inclusions, but which are opaque rather than translucent—such as the so-called porcelains exported in mass from European factories during the colonial era—are identified as 'fine stoneware'. 'Stoneware', where not qualified as fine, refers to coarser fabrics that may be strongly tinted, such as the fabrics found in large, coarse stoneware jars (martavans).

Bulbeck conducted further analyses, the results of which are available in Bulbeck (2012), including fabric identification and the colour of the body and glazed surface, which was recorded using a Munsell soil colour chart. Approximate hardness of the body was tested by the 'scratch test' with a quartz crystal and, for any fabric softer than quartz, a steel knife blade. An estimate was made of the approximate percentage of the fabric composed of inclusions, primarily with reference to the exposed surface but taking into account the weathered body surface. The weights of the tradeware sherds were measured to the nearest 0.01 of a gram, the maximum body thickness recorded to 0.1 mm, and the colours of any decorations were recorded using a range of Munsell colour charts, by default the soil colour chart when a match could be found. Documentation of the sherds in Bulbeck (2012) also includes discussion of which sherds could be assigned to the same parent vessel and a description of the basis for each tradeware classification.

Stone artefacts

Stone artefact analysis involved an initial inspection and count of specimens. The quantity of artefacts is surprising in view of the historical context of the site (Table 2.1), and it is assumed that stone would have been 'abandoned as an important tool-making material at least 2,000 years ago' following the introduction of metal (Glover 1986:202). For this reason, a set of nominal variables were employed to confirm the veracity of artefact identification, following methods employed in the analysis of the Lemdubu assemblage from the Aru Islands (Hiscock 2007:210). Variables included the presence of a striking platform, bulb of percussion, negative flake scars, external initiation and flake termination; these, in combination, support artefact identification.

To establish whether cores were reduced onsite (as opposed to being imported from outside and potentially older sites), reduction variables such as core rotations, number of flake scars, and flake cortex types were recorded, following Marwick (2008). To quantify the intensity of retouched flake reduction, the Average Geometric Index of Unifacial Reduction (AGIUR) was also recorded (Kuhn 1990).

One explanation for the stone artefact assemblage at this fort site is a strike-a-light tool industry—where siliceous stone flakes are marginally retouched, usually with metal implements, for the sole purpose of creating sparks for fire-lighting (e.g. Glover and Ellen 1975:52–53). The use of strike-a-lights is widely reported from Island Southeast Asia (Brumm 2006; Glover 1986:202; Glover and Ellen 1975; Pannell and O'Connor 2005:201; Scheans et al. 1970:180; Skertchly 1890:450, 451). From these studies a set of characteristic edge modification variables were employed to test the likelihood of this function. The use of metal objects as percussors will likely create marginal concentrations of step fractures, crushing or cascading, bifacial battering, dense striations and typically minimal retouch before discard (Andrefsky 2009:196; Brumm 2006:169–170; Glover and Ellen 1977; Staperd and Johansen 1999:768). Notably, one study has shown that even when individual flakes are observed in strike-a-light activities, apparent characteristic modification variables, particularly striations, may not be present (Brumm 2006:170). Nonetheless, each artefact was examined for these characteristics.

Vertebrate faunal remains

Distinctive vertebrate elements were identified to family, genus or species using the modern comparative reference collection and digital database housed at the Archaeological Studies Program, University of the Philippines. The maximum lengths of all fragments greater than 5 mm were measured, unless they showed evidence of modern breakage, to identify any spatial and temporal variability in fragment size that might provide information on taphonomic process. Taphonomic terminology follows Piper (2006) modified from Lyman (1994). Important taphonomic and anthropic alterations, including weathering, burning, dog gnawing and butchery marks were recorded.

The criteria used for the biometric analyses of post-cranial elements follow von den Dreisch (1976). Whenever applicable, alternative measurements from diagnostic anatomical locales were used. Features that might indicate defects, for instance bone regrowth/pathologies, were also recorded. For caprine and suid teeth, a standard measurement for the length of the tooth was taken, and then the width of each molar column measured. All measurements were taken at, or as close to, the base of the enamel as possible. Since goat and pig teeth change shape as they wear, this location provides a point of reference where the analyst can be confident that all measurements of archaeological and comparative specimens will be comparable. To compensate for inter-analyst preferences, the lengths of the pig M1s and M2s were also measured at the occlusal surface (in brackets in Tables 5 and 6 of Piper and Amano 2011) so that they can be compared irrespective of which measurement has been used by other specialists. Pig ageing from molar eruption and post-cranial fusion follows Bull and Payne (1982), and molar wear scales are based on those presented by Grant (1982).

All teeth and bones with key taphonomic and anthropic modifications and other selective elements were photographed and archived using a Nikon Coolpix Digital camera. Micrographs were also taken using the same camera mounted on a Nikon C-LEDS stereomicroscope.

Invertebrate faunal remains

All shells and shell fragments were identified to the lowest possible taxonomic level through the use of ANU and Museum and Art Gallery of the Northern Territory malacology collections. Sea urchin was weighed. The shell assemblages were quantified by weight (g), minimum number of individuals (MNI) and number of identified specimens present (NISP) for each of the three excavations squares (A, C and D). Weight, MNI and NISP were calculated in an attempt to assess potential biases inherent in each. The MNI method, which quantifies one repetitive feature per taxon throughout an assemblage, avoids the fragmentation bias inherent in the NISP technique and other biases associated with the sole use of weight to quantify taxon through time (Classen 1998), and for this reason is used as the primary mode of quantification.

The repetitive features or elements selected throughout the Macapainara assemblage are: the posterior valve for chitons, apices for gastropods, and for bivalves, both left and right hinges were counted, with the greater number selected (following Classen 1998). All shell was counted and weighed within excavation spit divisions. In spits where a taxon was present, but the repetitive element was absent, the MNI is noted as '<1', to avoid overestimation of that taxon for the entire square. It should be noted that while *Turbo* sp. and *Nerita* sp. opercula were quantified during laboratory analysis, opercula counts are excluded from all aggregative calculations, to avoid inflating representation of the Turbinidae and Neritidae families. Shell reduction patterns were noted during analysis. Some species in particular showed repetitive reduction or damage patterns suggestive of their use for artefact manufacture.

Organic artefacts

The shell artefacts were photographed with a Canon digital SLR camera. Identification of manufacture and use traces was based on previous analyses of marine shell technologies (e.g. Bar-Yosef Mayer 2005; Cristiani et al. 2014; d'Errico et al. 1993; Langley and O'Connor 2015, 2016; Stiner et al. 2013; Szabó 2010; Vanhaeren et al. 2013). Bone artefacts were identified during the vertebrate faunal analysis and are described in the results, although a detailed use-wear analysis has yet to be undertaken.

Results

Glass sherds and beads

Across squares, Spits 1 to 5 produced 21 sherds from glass vessels (Table 2.2). Six representative examples were sent to James Lankton in 2009 for chemical analysis. Lankton and Gratuze (2011) report that all of them were very high in lime and alumina and moderate in magnesia. Their composition indicates they were made using oak ash as the source of flux, producing a type of glass common in Europe from the seventeenth to nineteenth centuries.

Spits 2 to 14 yielded a small assemblage of seven glass beads (2 g), of which five were sent to Lankton for chemical analysis (Figure 2.6). Four of the seven beads appear to be of Chinese production, best dated to between the sixteenth and eighteenth centuries. Two beads have tentative European parallels, while one appears to be an Indo-Pacific bead. Although the production of Indo-Pacific beads was largely wound up by AD 1200, these beads remain in circulation till today as heirloom jewellery in Timor-Leste and the Indonesian province of Nusa Tenggara Timur, including West Timor (Francis 1999:94–95). Accordingly, the Indo-Pacific bead at Macapainara could be from an heirloom, and so its identification does not necessarily contradict the sixteenth- to eighteenth-century dating suggested by the Chinese beads.

Figure 2.6. Glass and shell beads from Macapainara (sample).
Source: Photo courtesy of Mirani Litster.

Table 2.2. Distribution of Macapainara glass and tradeware.

Material	Vessel/container glass pieces			Glass beads			Tradeware sherds		
Squares	A	C	D	A	C	D	A	C	D
Spit 1	4	–	8	–	–	–	1	–	1
Spit 2	4	2	1	–	2	–	7	6	3
Spit 3	–	–	–	–	–	–	4	–	–
Spit 4	–	–	–	–	1	–	2	1	3
Spit 5	2	–	–	–	–	1	1	–	3
Spit 6	–	–	–	–	–	–	–	–	–
Spit 7	–	–	–	–	–	–	7	–	2
Spit 8	–	–	–	–	–	1	–	1	2
Spit 9	–	–	–	–	–	–	2	2	3
Spit 10	–	–	–	–	–	–	5	4	1
Spit 11	–	–	–	–	–	–	1	2	2
Spit 12	–	–	–	–	–	–	–	–	–
Spit 13	–	–	–	–	–	–	–	1	–
Spit 14	–	–	–	–	–	2	–	–	–

Source: Authors' summary.

Earthenware

Close to 1.3 per cent (32 kg) of the excavated sediment (excluding excavated rocks) constituted pottery. Square A yielded around 7 kg, Square C 11 kg and Square D 14 kg, making up between 0.9 per cent and 1.5 per cent of the excavated sediment in these squares. The upper spits tended to yield the most pottery: for instance, Spits 2 to 4 in Square A, Spits 3 to 7 in Square C and Spits 4 to 7 in Square D. Some 2.88 kg or around 9 per cent of the pottery (by weight) is decorated (e.g. Figure 2.7a–e). Square C has a lower proportion of decorated sherds. In every square, Spits 7 and 8 yielded an above-average proportion of decorated sherds. The most common form of decoration is paddle-impressed: vertical lines (1.4 kg), rectangular impressions (992 g), horizontal lines (32 g) and curvilinear lines (30 g). Rare forms of decoration include some 156 g with abstract painted decorations (see Figure 2.7b–d), incisions (horizontal, vertical, slanting and curvilinear lines; triangles, commas and chevrons, 94 g altogether), impressions (quadrilateral, rectangular and reniform, 68 g altogether), notched and appliqué corrugations (52 g), rectangular and slanting notches (13.5 g together) and vertically gouged lines (15 g). Temper types often consisted of foraminiferal calcareous grains, variably combined with a dominant element of massive terrigenous grains or limeclast calcareous grains.

The great majority of assignments of sherds to a parent vessel involved sherds from the same spit, but many assignments involving sherds from different spits were also made (Figure 2.8). Most pairs of adjacent spits in Square A contained sherds that were assigned to a single parent vessel, and the same was true for many pairs of adjacent spits (sometimes ranging across three spits) in Squares C and D. There were also several cases of the adjacent C and D Squares yielding sherds assigned to the same parent vessel.

Just over 5 per cent (1.7 kg) of the Macapainara sherdage was recorded as slipped, including 5.9 per cent (of 5.5 kg) of rim sherdage, 2.4 per cent (of 5.6 kg) of neck sherdage, 6.8 per cent (880 g) of shoulder sherdage, and 6.0 per cent (of 18.6 kg) of the body sherds. Slips were applied slightly more often to external surfaces (76 per cent, including sherds slipped on both surfaces) than internal surfaces (65 per cent, including sherds slipped on both surfaces). Red slips were dominant (62 per cent), but brown slips (11.2 per cent), black slips (13.2 per cent) and white slips (12.5 per cent) were also recorded. Red slips included a distinctive, dark red burnished slip, notable in the Vasino assemblage, but observed on just 178 g of the Macapainara sherdage, mainly in Spits 11 to 15 (158 g). Addition of resin to the applied coat often appeared to be the factor responsible for the brown-slipped effect, as sometimes observed on the black-slipped surfaces (which appeared carbonised and polished). White slipping, more characteristic of internal than external surfaces, may have been achieved by application of calcareous-rich clay.

The most commonly recorded external surface colours were grey (16.9 kg, 53 per cent) and brown (13.8 kg, 43 per cent). The grey sherds were frequently dark grey (5.2 kg, 16.3 per cent) and very dark grey (4.3 kg, 13.4 per cent), usually associated with reducing firing conditions, but also often pinkish grey (2.1 kg, 6.6 per cent), reddish grey (1.3 kg, 4.1 per cent) and light brownish grey (1.2 kg, 3.8 per cent), associated with a more oxidising firing environment. Commonly recorded variants of the brown sherds were reddish brown (3.8 kg, 27.5 per cent), light reddish brown (2.3 kg, 16.7 per cent) and greyish brown (2.7 kg, 19.6 per cent), in the last case verging on the grey sherds in their colour. Rare surface colours included black (567 g, 1.8 per cent), red (129 g, 0.4 per cent), reddish yellow (40 g, 0.1 per cent) and white (24 g, 0.1 per cent).

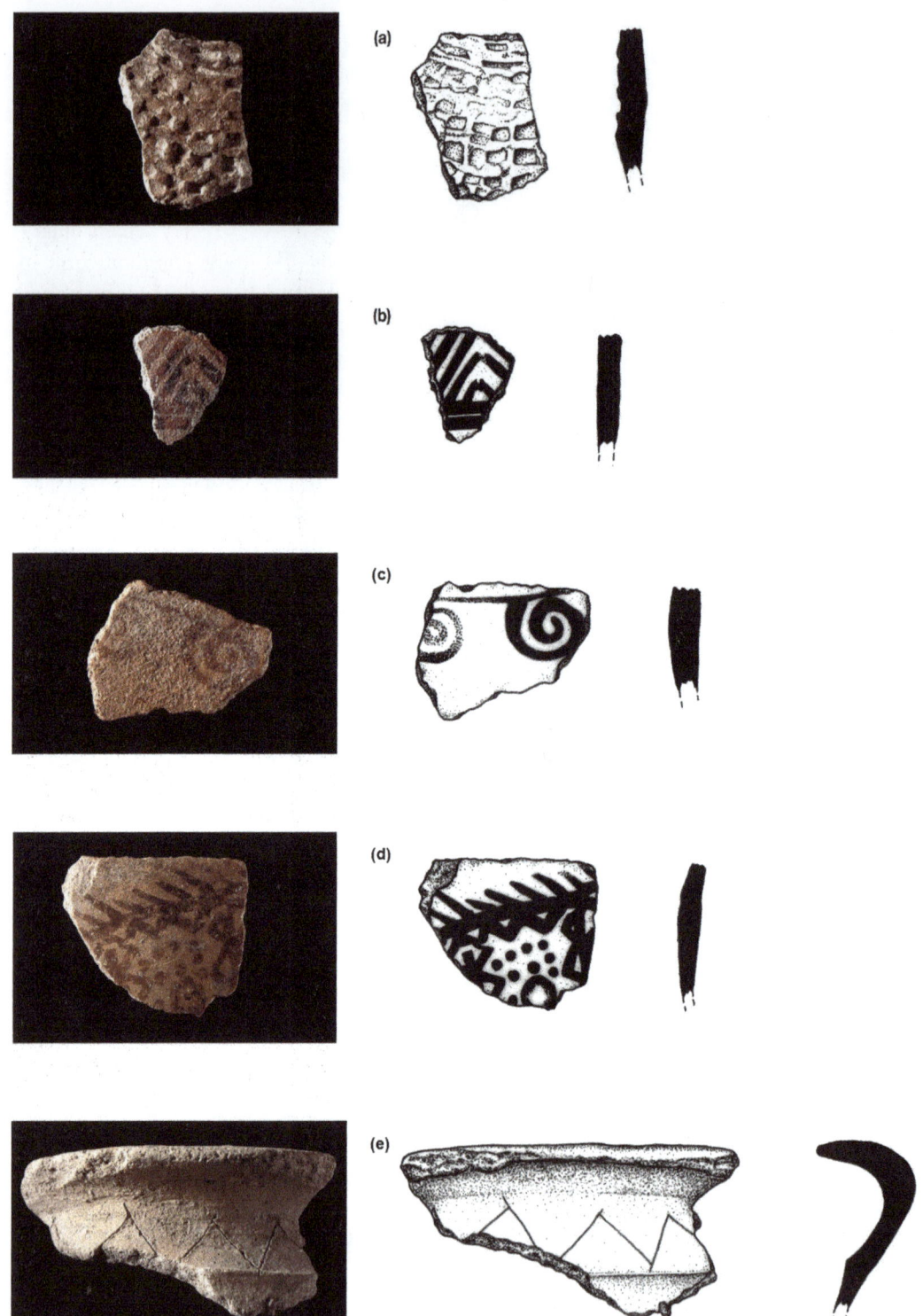

Figure 2.7. Decorated sherds from Macapainara.
Source: Photos and drawings courtesy of Virginia Das Neves.

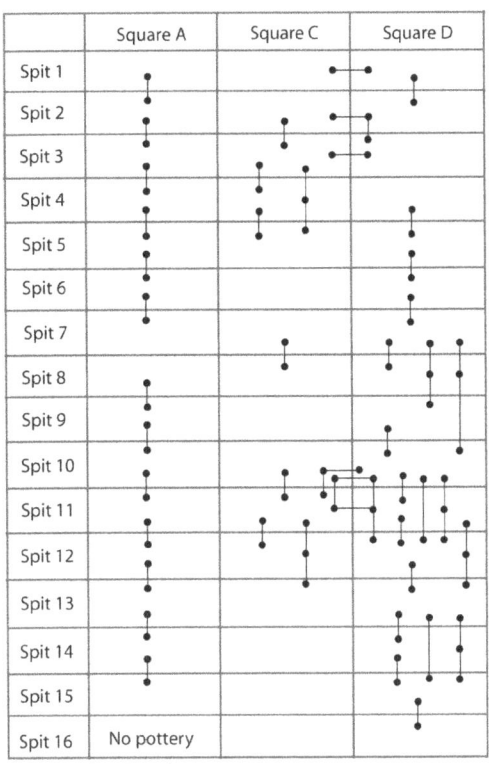

Figure 2.8. Recognised Macapainara vessels with sherds from separate spits.
Source: David Bulbeck.

The Macapainara externally red-slipped sherds accounted for most of the red-coloured sherds and also a proportion of the reddish brown (including light and dark reddish brown) sherds. In addition, 1.5 kg (4.7 per cent) of the sherds were recorded as externally self-slipped, typically associated with a reddish brown colour. The externally black-slipped, brown-slipped and white-slipped sherds were respectively associated with black or other dark colours, reddish brown or reddish grey, and whitish colours. In addition to the externally slipped and self-slipped sherds, a further 2.0 kg (6.2 per cent) of the Macapainara sherds were externally smoothed. Wiping marks were visible on both faces of approximately 12 per cent of the assemblage, external wiping marks on some 26 per cent, and internal wiping marks on some 8 per cent of the assemblage.

No wasters were recorded to indicate pottery manufacture at Macapainara itself. Blistered external and/or internal surfaces suggestive of overfiring were recorded on only 350 g (1.1 per cent) of the assemblage. The sherds appeared to be fully oxidised for 14.0 kg (43.8 per cent) of the assemblage, although surface clouds and smudges from firing were recorded on a further 4.7 kg (14.7 per cent), and evidence of grey or dark cores on a further 626 g (~2 per cent). Internally or externally reduced surfaces, occurring together or in combination with a reduced internal wall, were recorded for 13.7 kg (42.1 per cent) of the assemblage, including 1.8 kg (5.6 per cent) where the sherd was reduced entirely. The above observations in most cases would reflect firing conditions for the vessels during their manufacture, although in some cases post-manufacture exposure to heat (such as an open fire) may have left surface clouds and/or similar visual effects to earthenware vessels fired in a reducing environment.

Ceramic forms, rim shapes and manufacturing techniques

Ceramic form could be determined for 287 vessels, as well as one cylinder and five flat discs. Most or all of these ceramic products would be distinct individual items (comparable to MNIs in faunal analysis) and the true number represented by the assemblage would be much greater than 293. The majority of ceramic items were classified as jars (83 per cent) on the basis of possessing a neck and everted rim. Most of these appeared to be medium-sized jars (71 per cent of ceramic items) with a rim diameter between 11 and 19 cm. A smaller number appeared to be small jars (2 per cent of items) with a rim diameter up to 10 cm, or large jars (10 per cent of items) with a rim diameter of at least 20 cm. One use of the medium-sized jars may have been as cooking pots, although only 300 g of the Macapainara sherds preserved carbonised traces on their surfaces. The large jars were presumably used as storage vessels. Just 2 per cent of the jars appear to have been covered, and only four sherds apparently from cover handles were identified.

Apparent serving vessels with an unrestricted rim were classified as plates (6 per cent), most of which had an everted foot, and bowls (4 per cent), some equipped with a footing. Three footed vessels were identified as having a distinctly carinated shoulder and constricted rim and may have been used for the slow burning of incense or other aromatic substances. Other rare forms included two squarish boxes, two apparent stoves (large vessels lacking curvature) and six crucibles (identified by their tough earthenware fabric, apparently exposed to very high temperatures, direct pointed rim and/or small rounded chamber). The crucible fragments are important evidence for metallurgy at Macapainara.

Jar rim shape showed considerable variability. Rounded (Figure 2.9.A), semi-squared (Figure 2.9.B) and squared (Figure 2.9.C) rims were classified as furrowed if the rim end contained a distinct furrow (Figure 2.9.F) or fattened if the rim end was distinctly expanded (Figure 2.9.G). Sharp-ended rims included triangular (Figure 2.9.D) and pointed (Figure 2.9.E) varieties. Distinctly upturned rims were classified as upturned (Figure 2.9.H) regardless of their other shape details. Upturned rims accounted for around a third of the jar rims (by weight), rounded rims a quarter of the jar rims and the variety of other shapes the remainder. In relation to stratigraphy, rounded jar rims predominated in Spits 9 to 15 at Macapainara but dropped to between 9 per cent and 25 per cent in Spits 1 to 8 where the other rim shapes, notably upturned rims, increased in frequency. This rim shape variability may have been in imitation of similar rim shapes found on Chinese and Thai jars and other export ceramics (see Bulbeck 1996–97; Green et al. 1981; Harrisson 1990).

Evidence for pottery manufacturing and finishing techniques was based on the criteria in Rye (1981). Possible evidence of coil-building was observed on just one sherd. Hand modelling was recorded as the forming technique for the cylinder, disc and crucible bodies. Slab building was recorded as the forming technique for the stoves, as well as four plates and six jars. The dark red burnished vessels sometimes appeared to have been manufactured on a fast wheel, as indicated by regular, closely spaced wheel-throwing lines. Similar evidence of fast wheel manufacture was recorded on a medium-sized jar. The most commonly recorded manufacturing techniques, sometimes recorded together on the same vessel, were the use of a slow wheel, mainly at the rim and neck (3.8 kg) and the paddle-and-anvil technique, mainly on body sherds (10.9 kg). Where vessel form could be associated with these techniques it was most frequently a medium-sized jar, in line with the predominance of this vessel form in the assemblage. Therefore, the most common production procedure for the Macapainara vessels probably involved shaping the jar with a paddle applied externally (often leaving vertical paddle impressions) and an anvil held inside the wall.

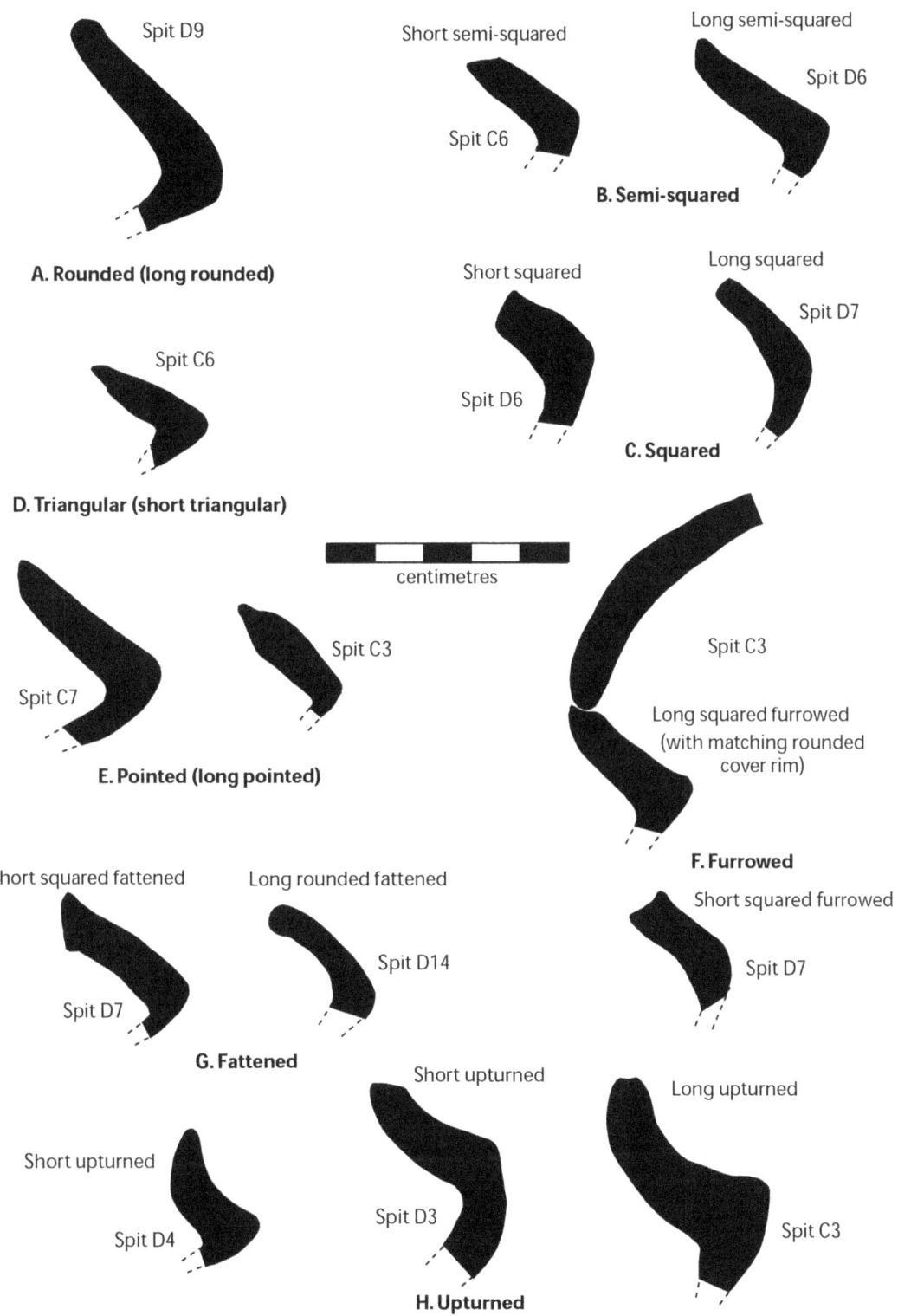

Figure 2.9. Macapainara jar rim shapes.
Source: David Bulbeck.

Tradeware

The 67 imported tradeware sherds from Macapainara (Appendix Table 2.A1), weighing 154 g in total, appear to represent 55 different vessels. Most of the sherds (52–53; c. 78 per cent) are identified as Chinese, with dates between the sixteenth and nineteenth centuries (plus three mid to late second millennium datings). Six Vietnamese sherds dated to between the fifteenth and nineteenth centuries, and possibly all as late as the seventeenth century, were recovered from Spits 3 to 7. Three European sherds dating to the eighteenth and early nineteenth centuries were excavated in the top two spits and Spit 7. The remaining classes include two Thai (Singburi) storage jars (Spits 2 and 7, sixteenth to seventeenth centuries), two Coarse Brown storage jars from Thailand or Cambodia (Spits 9 and 10, sixteenth to seventeenth centuries), and a Coarse Red jar from Vietnam (Spit 9, seventeenth to eighteenth centuries).

In addition, Square D yielded three bracelet fragments that appear to be low-fired stoneware, of European (perhaps Portuguese) or Brazilian production. Spit 4 produced a pierced bracelet segment (weight 0.35 g), and Spit 5 produced two joining fragments from a different polished ceramic bracelet (weight 1.40 g).

The entire tradeware assemblage may be dated to between the sixteenth and nineteenth centuries. Some evidence was found for increasing age of the tradeware identifications with depth, as the sherds in Spits 10 to 13 could all date to between the sixteenth and seventeenth centuries (see Appendix Table 2.A1). However, caution should be exercised when interpreting the accuracy of the tradeware dates, as they are consistently earlier than radiocarbon dates from the same level, by 57 to 178 years. The reason for this is argued to be careful handling and curation of the exotic wares, giving them a long use life before their final deposition as broken sherds at Macapainara (Fenner and Bulbeck 2013). Certainly, the tradeware identifications would be inconsistent with occupation at Macapainara any earlier than the sixteenth century, and indeed would be consistent with a seventeenth-century onset of habitation. It should be noted that most of the sherds were small, with a median weight of 0.82 g and a range of 0.15–22.73 g. While the small size of the available sherds may cast doubt on some of the individual identifications, especially those that lack diagnostic decorations, together the identifications point to a coherent assemblage dated to the quite short time frame of the sixteenth to nineteenth centuries AD.

Stone artefacts

The excavation at Macapainara recovered 392 stone artefacts distributed over the three excavation squares (Table 2.3), including flakes, flake fragments, retouched flakes, cores and a hammer stone. The majority of artefacts occur in the upper half of the sequence in all squares and their distribution follows that of other materials associated with occupation at the site (Figure 2.10). The raw material is dominated by red and cream cherts (89.5 per cent) and opaque brown chalcedonies (3.8 per cent), with a variably thin porous cortex (Table 2.4). These sources are locally available, where chert seams occur in the limestone and in secondary sources as cobbles within streams and river beds.

As noted, the quantity of stone artefacts is surprising in view of the historical context, so the variables used to establish each artefact as anthropogenic were recorded and summarised in Table 2.5. Results indicate a lower than expected frequency of these variables (see Hiscock 2007:10); however, all stone artefacts at Macapainara displayed a combination of these conchoidal variables (Table 2.5).

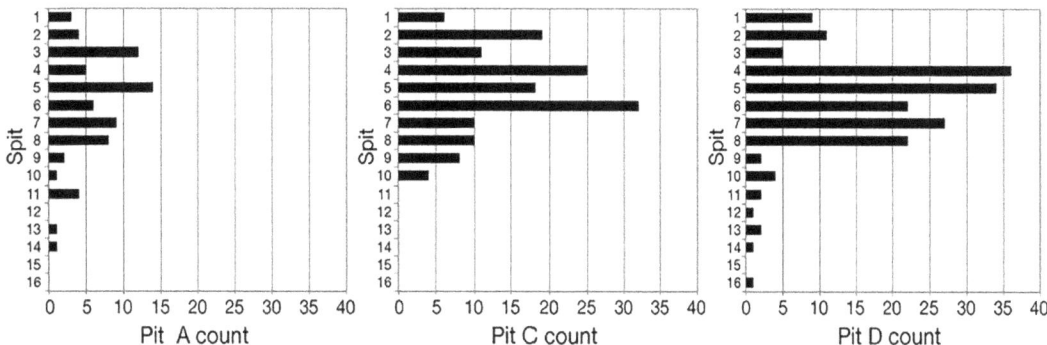

Figure 2.10. Vertical distribution of stone artefacts in each square relative to spit.
Source: Tim Maloney. Redrawn by CartoGIS ANU.

Table 2.3. Frequency of Macapainara stone artefacts across three excavation squares relative to spit.

Spit	Square A	Square C	Square D
1	3	6	9
2	4	19	11
3	12	11	5
4	5	25	36
5	14	18	34
6	6	32	22
7	9	10	27
8	8	10	22
9	2	8	2
10	1	4	4
11	4	–	2
12	–	–	1
13	1	–	2
14	1	–	1
15	–	–	–
16	–	–	1
Total	70	143	179

Source: Authors' summary.

Table 2.4. Macapainara raw material frequency.

Raw material	Frequency #	%
Chert	351	89.5
Chalcedony	15	3.8
Limestone	8	2.0
Glass	2	0.5
Quartz	1	0.3
Quartzite	1	0.3
Fine-grained sedimentary	11	2.8
Mudstone	3	0.8
Total	392	100

Source: Authors' summary.

Table 2.5. Macapainara frequency of conchoidal fracture variables.

Variable	Negative scars	External initiation	Termination	Platform present	Bulb of percussion
Frequency	349	346	317	262	238
Assemblage %	88.8	88.1	80.7	66.7	60.6

Source: Authors' summary.

The reduction sequences suggest onsite reduction and discard, rather than recycling of artefacts from older deposits predating the use of the hilltop as a fortified settlement. Cores, for example (N = 27), were identified with zero to four rotations, between two and 12 flake scars, and varied amounts of cortex. The distribution of cortex on flake dorsal surfaces also suggests onsite flake production. For example, primary flakes as well as a range of secondary flakes with cortex along either the entire lateral margin, or the proximal and distal portions, indicates that pebbles and sub-angular nodules were reduced at the site (e.g. Marwick 2008).

Of the 108 retouched flakes, few specimens exhibited invasive flaking (4.8 per cent) and none resembled reported formal tools from other Timor-Leste sites (e.g. Glover 1986; Marwick et al. 2016). Instead, retouch was predominately delivered onto the dorsal surface and restricted to medial and distal margins, where concentrations of step terminating or cascading scars accumulated on the majority of retouched flakes (73.6 per cent). These concentrations of step terminating scars are associated with low levels of flake reduction (AGIUR = 0.35), yet the increasing frequency of step terminating retouch scars is associated with increasing AGIUR values (t = 11.457, df = 40, p = <0.0005). This trend suggests that the accumulation of retouch was not a strategy to remove the build-up of step terminating scars or steep retouched edge angles, as might be expected in the maintenance of cutting or scraping tools.

This unusual modification resembles existing descriptions of strike-a-light tools, where siliceous stone flakes were marginally retouched with metal implements to purpose sparks for fire lighting (Brumm 2006; Glover 1986:202; Glover and Ellen 1975:52–53; Pannell and O'Connor 2005:201; Scheans et al. 1970:180; Skertchly 1890:450, 451). From these studies, we can expect marginal concentrations of step fractures, crushing or cascading, bifacial battering, dense striations and typically minimal retouch before discard to be a reasonable indicator of strike-a-light functions (Andrefsky 2009:196; Brumm 2006:169–170; Glover and Ellen 1977; Staperd and Johansen 1999:768). Results demonstrate that such characteristic variables occur on the majority of flakes in the assemblage (Table 2.6). Figure 2.11 illustrates two examples of step terminating scar concentrations and striations, typical of chert retouched flake margins from Macapainara.

Table 2.6. Macapainara summary of characteristic edge modification variables.

Variable	Observed	Not observed	% Flakes
Step terminating concentrations	168	60	73.6
Parallel and non-parallel striations	65	163	28.5
Bifacial battering	124	104	54.8
Crushing	118	110	51.75

Source: Authors' summary.

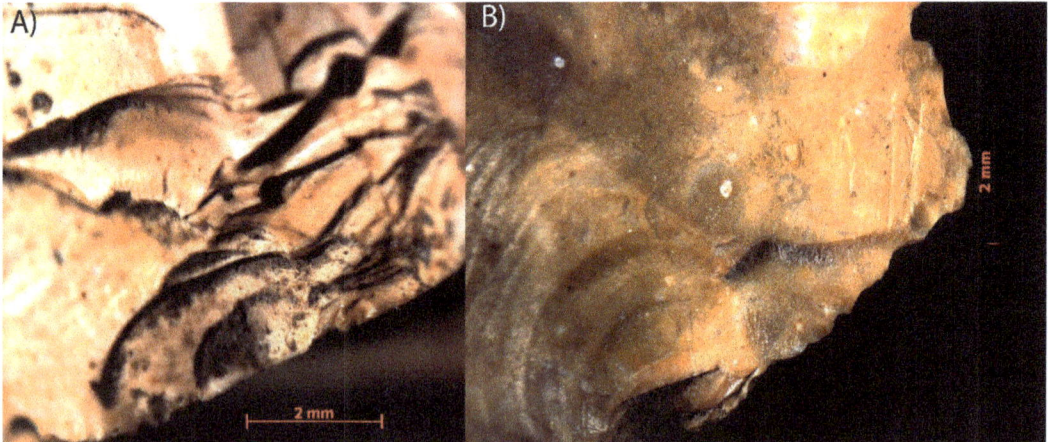

Figure 2.11. Margins of typical chert retouched flakes, thought to be strike-a-light tools.
A: Step terminating scar concentration; B: Parallel striations emerging from marginal scars.
Source: Photos courtesy of Tim Maloney.

In summary, the Macapainara lithic assemblage indicates that cores were reduced at the settlement to produce small, thick and squat-shaped flakes suitable for use as strike-a-lights.

Vertebrate faunal remains

Most of the vertebrate faunal remains from Macapainara were recovered from D Square, with much of it only slightly weathered (Figure 2.12). A total of 239 fragments of bone were identified to taxon, with mammals accounting for 65.27 per cent (N = 156) of all identified vertebrate remains, with smaller amounts of fish (N = 73, 30.54 per cent), reptile (N = 8, 3.34 per cent) and bird (N = 1, 0.4 per cent) (Table 2.7).

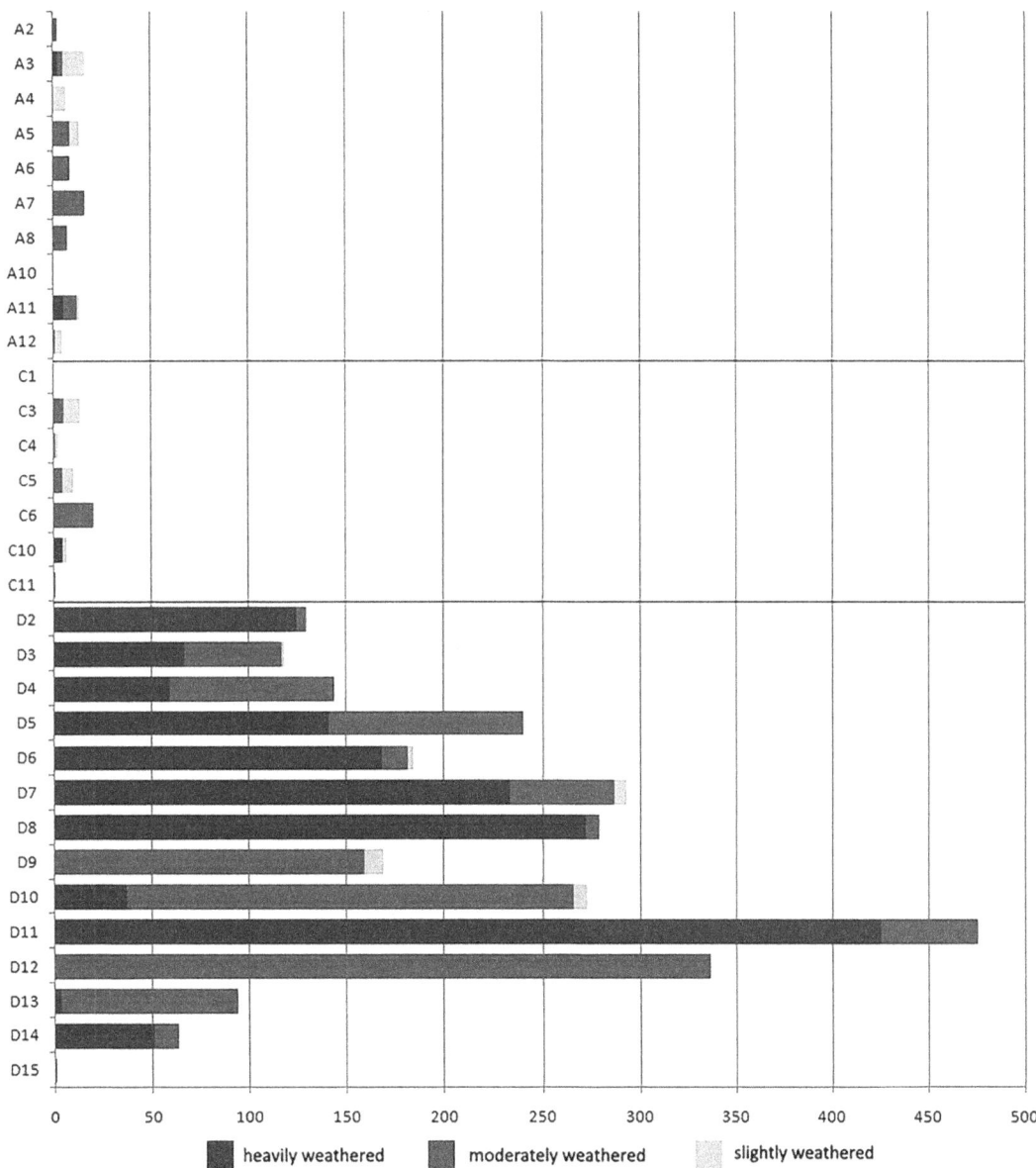

Figure 2.12. Distribution of Macapainara vertebrate faunal remains, and associated weathering (NISP).
Source: Noel Amano Jr and Philip Piper. Redrawn by CartoGIS ANU.

Sixty-three fragments of Bovinae were recorded from all depths within Square D as deep as Spit 14. Of these, three were identified as belonging to cattle *Bos* sp. and no specimens of the water buffalo *Bubalus bubalis* were recorded. Numerous long bone fragments classified as 'large mammal' are probably also Bovinae, especially below Square D Spit 6 where this is the only large mammal identified in the zooarchaeological record. Fragments of most high meat-yielding body parts such as the humerus, scapula and pelvis, and those of lower utility like the phalanges, are all represented, suggesting that whole carcasses were being dressed at the site. Very few skeletal elements of Bovinae useful for ageing were recovered from Macapainara. A moderately worn (Grant Stage F) lower left M1 from Square D Spit 11 and an upper left *Bos* sp. dp4 from D Spit 10 were probably from a young adult, and a fragmented, heavily worn upper right M3 fragment (middle tooth column) is probably from an individual greater than four years of age (Grigson 1982).

Table 2.7. Macapainara NISP recorded by square and spit for the three trenches that produced vertebrate remains during the 2008 excavations.

Square/layer	Taxon										
	Teleosteii*	Serpentes	Gekkonidae	Aves	*Phalanger o.*	Rodentia	*Canis f.*	*Equus f.c.*	*Sus s.*	Bovinae	*Capra h.*
A2	-	-	-	-	-	-	-	-	-	-	-
A5	-	-	-	-	-	-	-	-	-	-	-
A7	-	-	-	-	-	-	-	-	-	-	-
C3	-	-	1	-	-	-	-	-	-	-	-
C4	-	-	-	-	-	-	-	-	-	-	-
C6	-	-	-	-	-	-	-	-	-	-	-
D2	-	-	-	-	-	-	2	-	5	1	-
D3	2	-	-	-	-	-	-	-	2	1	1
D4	2	-	-	-	-	1	1	1	3	1	-
D5	6	-	-	-	-	-	4	1	22	2	-
D6	5	-	-	-	-	-	2	-	11	4	1
D7	23	-	-	-	-	-	1	-	3	13	-
D8	14	-	-	-	1	-	3	-	3	8	-
D9	6	4	-	-	-	-	-	-	2	8	-
D10	4	3	-	-	-	-	1	-	7	3	-
D11	-	-	-	1	-	-	-	-	6	16	-
D12	-	-	-	-	-	-	-	-	1	4	-
D13	-	-	-	-	-	-	-	-	1	1	4
D14	7	-	-	-	-	-	-	-	-	1	3
D15	-	-	-	-	-	-	-	-	-	-	-

* D4 = 1 Siluriformes; D5 = 1 Elasmobranch; D6 = 2 Diodontidae; D7 = 1 Lutjanidae, 1 Serranidae, 1 Scaridae, 6 Diodontidae; D8 = 3 Diodontidae; D9 = 1 Serranidae.
Square A produced no faunal remains that could be identified to family or lowest taxonomic level.
Phalanger o. = *Phalanger orientalis*; *Equus f.c.* = *Equus ferus caballus*; *Sus s.* = *Sus scrofa*; *Capra h.* = *Capra hircus*; *Canis f.* = *Canis familiaris*.
Source: Authors' summary.

Stages of epiphysial fusion suggest Bovinae of a variety of ages are represented in the assemblage. Two metapodial fragments with fused distal ends recovered from Square D Spit 6 represent individuals more than two to three years old (Silver 1970; Schmid 1972). An unfused distal tibia from Square D Spit 10 is from an individual less than two years old and an unfused acetabulum recovered from Square D Spit 9 suggests a juvenile individual less than six months old. A left tibia with fused proximal epiphysis from Square D Spit 11 represents the oldest bovine in the assemblage and is from an individual that is more 42 months old.

Pig bone was as common in the assemblage (NISP = 66, 27.6 per cent of identified elements) as fragments of Bovinae and was also recovered from all depths in Square D. The majority of the pig elements identified were tooth fragments (N = 52), albeit with only six complete teeth recorded. Based on canine morphology, both male and female individuals are represented in the assemblage. A loose unerupted lower right M1 from Square D Spit 2 and an unworn dp3 from Square D Spit 11 represent an individual not older than four to eight months. An unworn upper right M2 from Square D Spit 5 and an unworn upper central incisor from Square D Spit 2 are probably also from subadult individuals. Two complete isolated dp4s with roots (Grant Stage B and J respectively), demonstrating that they were not naturally shed, from Square D Spits 6 and 11 were from individuals of less than 12–18 months (Bull and Payne 1982). Notably no M3s were recorded in the assemblage, suggesting that most of the pigs were of young age when they were slaughtered.

Nine fragments of caprine bone were recorded in the Macapainara assemblage. Only the domestic goat *Capra hircus* has been introduced to Timor-Leste and all remains positively identified to *Capra/Ovis* are taken to be goat. Sheep are known to have been introduced to the region only in the very recent past. All but a single subterminal phalange from Square D Spit 3 were fragments of tooth. It is notable that the majority of the goat remains (N = 7) were recorded in the deeper spits of Square D Spits 13 and 14. Only two fragments were found higher in the sequence, a moderately worn upper right M2 recorded from Square D Spit 6 and a fused subterminal phalanx from Square D Spit 3. At least two individuals could be identified based on eight complete teeth recovered. A lower right P2 worn almost to the pulp cavity was recovered from Square D Spit 14, a moderately worn upper left M1 (Grant Stage E) and a lower left M1 (Grant Stage D) from Square D Spit 13 were all probably from adult individuals (Table 8 in Piper and Amano 2011). The four measurable teeth from Macapainara fall within the size range of a selection of goat molars held at the University of the Philippines Archaeological Studies Program (UP-ASP).

A total of 14 dog elements from at least two individuals were identified. Of the 10 dog teeth recovered, only three specimens could be measured due to the fragmentary nature of the other elements. A partially damaged lower left M1 from Square D Spit 6 measured 18.52 mm in length and 14.67 mm in breadth. This element is comparable in size to the M1s of the Southeast Asian dog specimens maintained at UP-ASP (average L = 18.83 mm, average W = 14.03 mm). A dog distal humeral shaft from Square D Spit 2 had a medio-lateral width of 22.78 mm and an antero-posterior depth of 15.15 mm, which is relatively small in comparison to a dataset held in the UP-ASP zooarchaeological laboratory of 43 individuals (average M-L = 29.83 mm, average A-P = 22.16 mm). A moderately worn lower right M2 from Square D Spit 6 (Figure 12 in Piper and Amano 2011) had a length of 12.15 mm and maximum breadth of 11.51 mm. This M2 is significantly larger than those maintained in the UP-ASP reference collection (average L = 9.59 mm, average B = 11.23 mm). No butchery was recorded on the dog bones.

Two horse bones were recorded in the assemblage. A heavily weathered basal phalanx from Square D Spit 5 exhibited the pathological modification non-articular periostosis. Non-articular periostosis is not uncommon in modern horses and has even been recorded in *Equus conversidens* from the Pleistocene (Scott and Rooney 2001). It is characterised by lesions related to the avulsion of ligaments from their bony attachments resulting normally from irregular and jerky movements of the affected leg segment (Rooney and Robertson 1996). Such instability usually results from misplacement of the foot on the surface (Scott and Rooney 2001). This appears to have been exacerbated in this specimen from Macapainara because the basal phalange itself is malformed, with one distal condyle missing its medial or lateral margins making the bone asymmetrical. A fragmented distal articular end of a horse metacarpal was also recorded in Square D Spit 4.

Nine fragments of terrestrial wild vertebrates were identified at Macapainara. Snake vertebrae (N = 7) were recovered from Square D Spit 9 and Square D Spit 10, a gecko vertebra in Square C Spit 3 and two phalanges tentatively identified as from the northern common cuscus (*Phalanger orientalis*) from Square D Spit 7 and Square D Spit 8. The only rodent bone, the proximal end of an ulna from D4, has a similar size and morphology to that expected for a commensal species. A fragment of the right tarsometatarsus from a chicken-sized bird was identified from Square D Spit 11 but it lacks the diagnostic spur that develops in *Gallus gallus*.

Of the 73 fragments of fish recorded in the assemblage, 17 could be identified to subclass or family. The majority of the bones were either undiagnostic vertebrae or spines. Fish remains were recorded at all depths. A serrated pectoral spine, probably from a catfish (order Siluriformes) was recovered from Square D Spit 4 (Figure 15c in Piper and Amano 2011). The distinctive, robust dermal spines of pufferfish (Diodontidae) were identified (N = 11) in Square D Spits 7 and 8 (Figure 15d in Piper and Amano 2011), and the anterior portions of grouper (Serranidae) and snapper (Lutjanidae) dentary bones were found in Square D Spit 7, as well as a pharyngeal plate of a parrotfish (Scaridae) (Figure 15b in Piper and Amano 2011). An anterior fragment of a grouper left maxilla was recorded in Square D Spit 14 and a shark or ray (elasmobranch) vertebra was recovered from Square D Spit 5.

Invertebrate faunal remains

Square A contained 16.3 kg of shell comprised of 65 taxa (Figure 2.13), 38 of which were identified to species, 18 to genus and 10 to family or greater. The dominant species throughout time, based on MNI counts, were, in descending order; *Turbo bruneus, Angaria delphinus, Tectus fenestratus, Trochus maculatus, Rochia nilotica, Nassarius arcularia, Nerita plicata, Nerita albicilla, Lambis* sp., and *Vasum turbinellum*. The dominant family groups through time, based on MNI counts, were, in descending order: Turbinidae, Tegulidae, Trochidae, Neritidae, Strombidae, Haliotidae, Conidae, Nassariidae and Angariidae. Square A also returned 88.3 g of sea urchin, from Spits 2–13.

Square C contained 19.9 kg of shell (Figure 2.13). A total of 79 taxa were identified for Square C, 52 of which were identified to species, 17 to genus and 11 to family or greater. The dominant species throughout time, based on MNI counts, were, in descending order: *Turbo bruneus, Turbo chrysostomus, Tectus fenestratus, Trochus maculatus, Rochia nilotica, Angaria delphinus, Nassarius arcularia, Nerita albicilla, Cymbiola vespertilio*, and *Haliotis* sp. The dominant family groups through time, based on MNI counts, were, in descending order: Turbinidae, Trochidae, Tegulidae, Neritidae, Strombidae, Haliotidae, Conidae, Nassaridae and Angariidae.

Square D contained 26.0 kg of shell (Figure 2.13). A total of 74 taxa were identified for Square D, 48 of which were identified to species, 18 to genus, and 9 to family or greater (see Appendix Table 2.A2). The dominant species throughout, based on MNI counts, were, in descending order: *Turbo bruneus, Tectus fenestratus, Trochus maculatus, Turbo chrysostomus, Rochia nilotica, Angaria delphinus, Nassarius arcularia, Nerita albicilla, Nerita plicata* and *Haliotis* sp. The dominant family groups through time, based on MNI counts, were, in descending order: Turbinidae, Tegulidae, Trochidae, Neritidae, Haliotidae, Nassariidae, Angariidae, Conidae and Strombidae.

Several of the *Turbo*, *Tectus* and *Angaria* shells exhibited a single hole flaked into their body whorl, along with a minimal amount of chipping localised around the aperture (see examples in Figure 2.14 C–D). On most of these shells, no further signs of modification were observed, and thus it seems that this treatment of the shells was most probably for food processing.

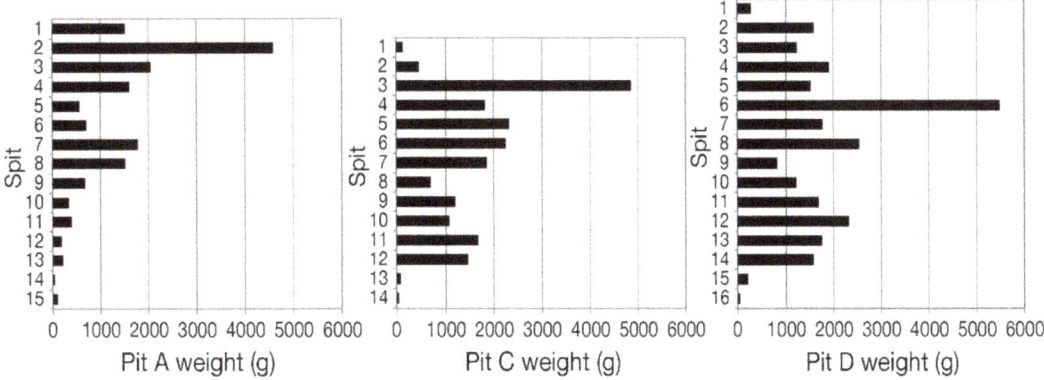

Figure 2.13. Total shell weight from Macapainara Squares A, C and D (g).
Source: Mirani Litster.

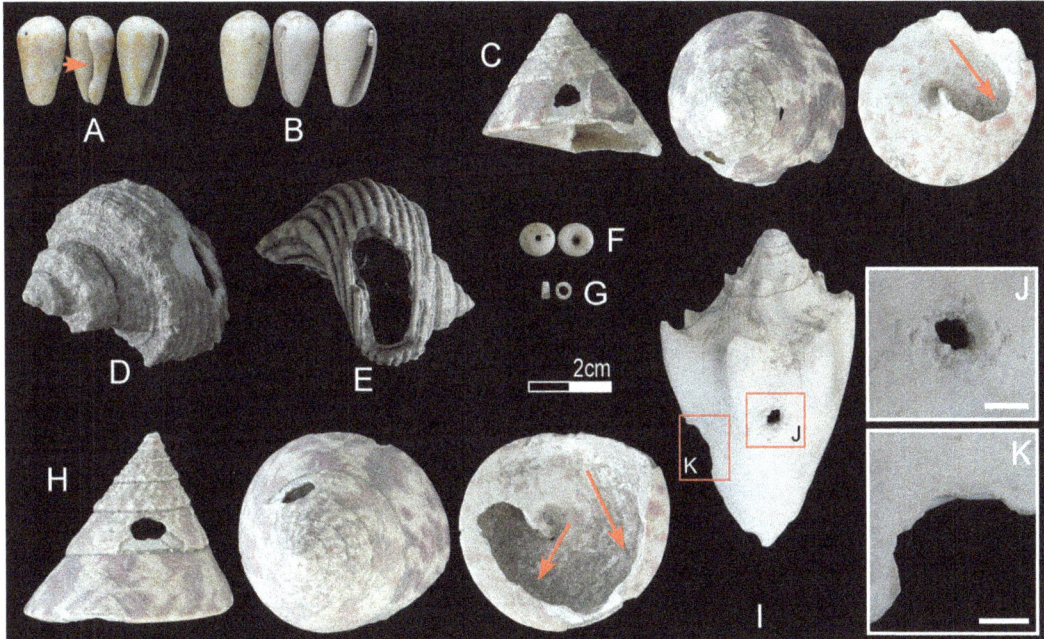

Figure 2.14. Worked and utilised sea shells from Macapainara.
A and B: Juvenile cone snails used as beads, red arrow indicates worn lip from stringing; C and H: *Rochia nilotica* shells with single perforation in spire and worked base (indicated by red arrows); D and E: *Turbo* shells with single perforation; F: *Conomurex* shell apex exhibiting extreme rounding as polish from use; G: Scaphopod bead; I-K: *Cymbiola vespetilio* shell with perforation and notched lip. Scale bars = 5 mm.
Source: Photos courtesy of Michelle Langley.

Mollusc habitat

With the exception of the few individuals of *Melanoides tuberculata*, all of the Macapainara molluscs identified to species level are reef, rocky shore, or sand and sea grass associated taxa. The north coast of Timor-Leste is comprised of the Baucau Limestone formation: a series of terraces that alternate between in situ coral reef and calcarenite, demarcating the stages of Timor's uplift from the Pleistocene onwards (Audley-Charles 1968). The limestone reef fringes the coastline and the fore reef plunges abruptly to the continental shelf. The intertidal reef flat is littered with dead corals and other rubble, with small patches of sand and sea grasses. The near absence of bivalves in the Macapainara mollusc assemblage reflects the relative paucity of bivalves in the molluscan fauna of Timor-Leste due to the lack of depositing shores. There is a distinct paucity of mangroves along the north coast of Timor-Leste, and the few forests that do exist are small in size and sparse (Alongi 2009:537). No mangrove habitats occur today within a 10 km radius of Macapainara. The absence of mangrove-associated taxa in the Macapainara assemblage is therefore not surprising.

Five complete *M. tuberculata* shells were recovered from the Macapainara excavation (two from Square A, both Spit 15; two from Square C, one from Spit 8, the other from Spit 11; one from Square D Spit 10). *M. tuberculata* is a freshwater gastropod that can tolerate brackish conditions. It is predominantly a burrowing species and mainly feeds on algae. The individuals range from 0.1 to 0.2 g in mass, and from 0.9 to 2.1 cm in shell length (from apex to columella base). Given the small number of *M. tuberculata*, their small size and the lack of other freshwater shells in the assemblage, it seems likely that they entered the site as an incidental by-product of another activity, such as water collection, or plant gathering.

Several of the marine molluscs also occur in very low numbers and individual shells are of small size. These may have been brought ashore incidentally attached to pieces of substrate or other shells. For example, *Nassarius pauper* is a common predator of corals, and if live corals or other resources were collected from the reef these taxa may have been collected incidentally. *Drupella cornus* and *Mipus* sp. also fall into this category.

Since habitat preference, or tolerance, can differ markedly within Molluscan families, genera and occasionally species, given the different levels of identification for the Macapainara assemblage it is impossible to ascribe precise habitat ranges to all taxa, especially fragments identified only to family or genus level.

In summary, the majority of the Macapainara shell assemblage was collected for consumption, and from the rock and reef platform directly to the north of the site. Based on MNI, *Turbo bruneus* is the dominant species across all three squares and through time, while Turbinidae, Tegulidae, Trochidae, Angariidae and Neritidae are the dominant family groups. *Turbo bruneus* is a large gastropod that is a popular item of contemporary local cuisine. Trochidae, Tegulidae and even small *Nerita* sp. are also still collected for consumption. Focus seems to have been on the larger species from the families Turbinidae and Trochidae, although even relatively small Nerite species were regularly collected. Nerites are available at the upper reaches of the intertidal zone so are available for collection even at high tide.

Organic artefacts

Shell

Anthropogenic traces reflect both the alteration of shells to access the animal inside (as outlined above), as well as more extensive working to create ornamental and utilitarian technologies.

Evidence for the selection of *Turbo*, *Rochia* and *Tectus* shells, possibly for making fishhooks, beads or similar small items, is found in extensively flaked whorls (Figure 2.15 A–D). Examples from Square C Spit 8 and Square D Spit 6 show sectioning via indirect percussion was also used to reduce the shell (Figure 2.15 B–C). The remnants of an extremely large and heavily worked *Turbo* (Figure 2.15 A) similarly indicates that this genus was targeted for tool manufacture, as was *Nautilus pompilius*. For this latter species, several siphuncle pieces displaying anthropogenic flaking up to their edges, as well as some 35 g of outer shell fragments, were identified, though no preforms, finished tools or ornaments of any of these raw materials were found.

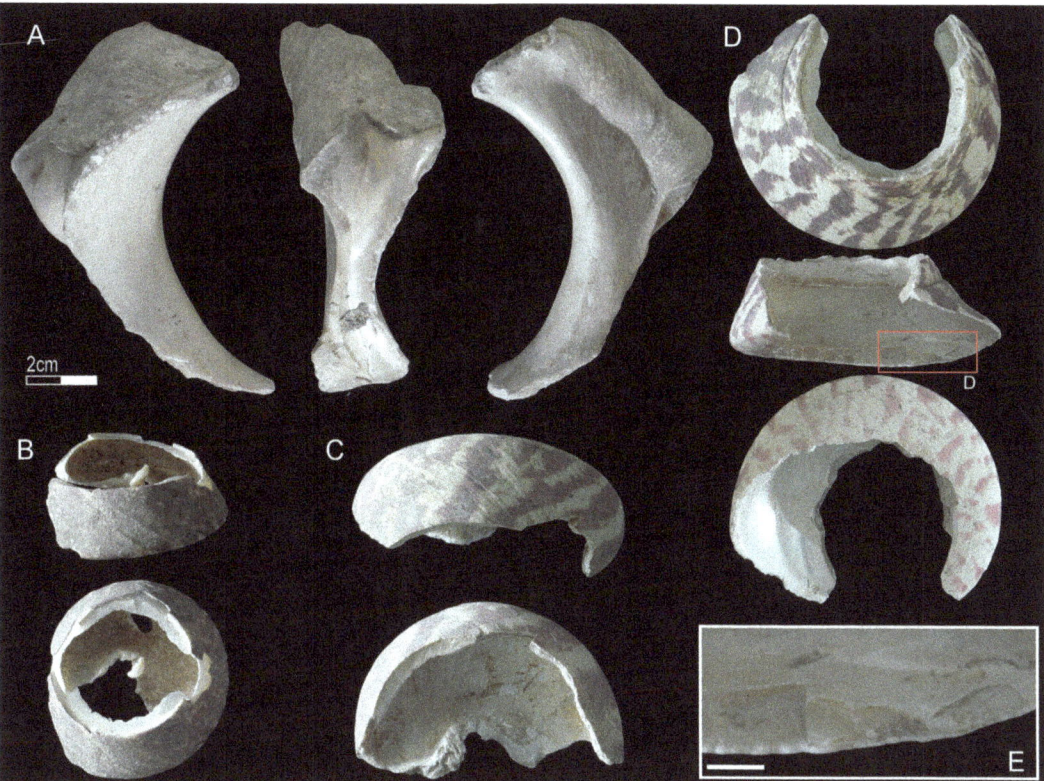

Figure 2.15. Worked *Rochia*, *Tectus* and *Turbo* shells.

A: Remnant of large and extensively worked *Turbo* shell; B: *Tectus pyramis* shell exhibiting sawn sections; C: *Rochia nilotica* shell exhibiting sawn sections; D and E: Body of a *Rochia nilotica* shell with anterior and posterior sections reduced by consecutive flaking. Scale bar = 5 mm.

Source: Photos courtesy of Michelle Langley.

Another gastropod, a *Cymbiola vespetilio* (Figure 2.14 I), exhibits numerous impact marks (localised pitting) around a single small puncture (Figure 2.14 J). These marks indicate that a sharp point was repeatedly struck against its surface in order to pierce the shell body. A notch is also found in the outer lip (Figure 2.14 K), suggesting that the shell suffered repeated stress to this localised area. This combination of perforation and notch implies that it was strung in some manner, perhaps being used as a weight or ornament.

Also found (Square A Spit 4) were three *Conomurex luhuanus* tops, their bodies flaked away and a hole driven through their centre to create a kind of large bead (Figure 2.16 A–C). Comparison of these artefacts with ethnographic material finds that they are likely spindle whorls—identical specimens continue to be used in the region today. Comparison of the Macapainara *Conomurex* with the ethnographic example shown in Figure 2.16 found that, while the former had their body removed roughly via percussion and the latter was finished off to a smooth and horizontal plane by grinding, all are of similar size and weight, and their central perforations exhibit similar characteristics such as size, edge rounding and cross-section. Interestingly, another three *Conomurex* were found one spit above, and are of similar size. Two of these examples have begun to be reduced with targeted direct flaking into their lip.

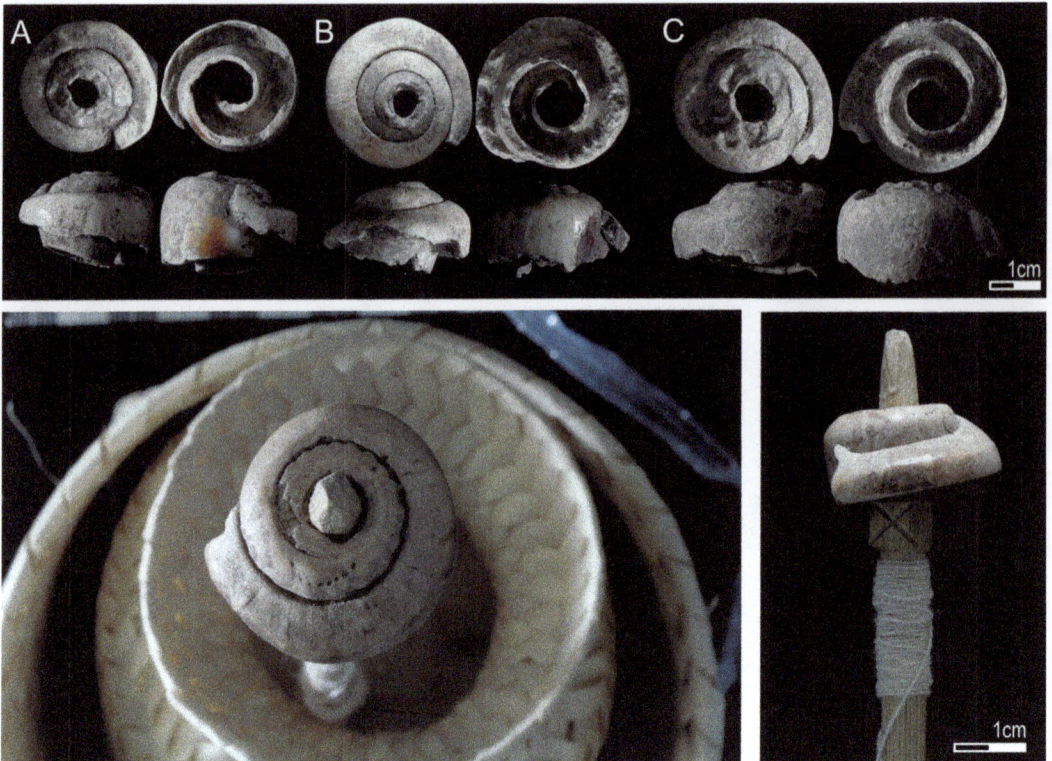

Figure 2.16. *Conomurex luhuanus* shell spindle whorls.

A–C: Spindle whorls recovered from Macapainara; Bottom left and right: Ethnographically collected *Conomurex luhuanus* spindle whorl from Timor-Leste. Used to spin cotton.

Source: Photos courtesy of Michelle Langley.

Finally, four shells appear to be items of personal ornamentation. Two are juvenile strombids (Figure 2.14 A and B), the hole in their posterior extremity the result of natural beach-wash abrasion, though one exhibits significant wear from being strung on its outer lip (Langley and O'Connor 2016). A third, also made on a *Conomurex*, though this time only its top, shows significant rounding and polish accrued through wear (Figure 2.14 F) (Langley and O'Connor 2015). Finally, a short length of scaphopod was identified (Figure 2.14 G). Ethnographic observations of the working of these shells for beads from northwestern Australia found that creating sections requires a sharp and directed tap with a hard object (such as a knife), and thus, its form may be deliberately determined (Balme et al. 2018).

Figure 2.17. Bone artefacts.

A: Polished tooth ornament recovered from D4; B: Spatula-shaped bone tool from D5; C: Drilled fish vertebrae.

Source: Photos A–B courtesy of Noel Amano Jr; Photo C courtesy of Michelle Langley.

Bone

An ornament made of tooth was recovered from Square D Spit 4 (Figure 2.17 A). It is heavily polished and ground on three sides and has a 1.91 mm circular hole 4 mm from the intact edge. It has a maximum length of 10.95 mm and a maximum depth of 2.56 mm. The hole appears to be worn, suggesting that the ornament was strung.

A spatula-shaped bone tool was recovered from Square D Spit 5 (Figure 2.17 B). It measured 45.75 mm in length, with a maximum width of 17.17 mm and a thickness of 3.54 mm. The tool was flat with a cortical bone surface evident on one side and medullary on the other. The wide end was ground in a sloping manner from the cortical surface to make a sharp rounded edge. There was no real attempt to give the tool a high polish, although both sides have been ground. The wider end is rough and pitted from use.

Conclusions

Our survey and excavation results from Macapainara indicate that the fortified structure was occupied for domestic living and was also the site of ritual and symbolic activities. Oral accounts of the ethnohistories of the area indicate that a significant population formerly lived within the settlement. Certainly, the diversity and quantity of earthenware and tradeware suggests cooking and consumption of food and the storage of perishables and water. Stone strike-a-lights were made onsite, presumably as fire starters and remained an essential component of Fataluku travelling kit until well into the twentieth century. The presence of a number of shell spindle whorls indicates fibre production and probably also weaving took place within this domestic space.

The settlement served as a locus from which a variety of subsistence pursuits were carried out across a broad geographic area encompassing grazing lands, marine reefs and rock platforms and forest. All excavation areas contained abundant earthenware pottery, animal bones and a wide variety of marine shellfish. While some of the shellfish were clearly transported for reduction into decorative and utilitarian items, the larger proportion seems to have been for subsistence. Domestic species contributed most of the protein in the diet and comprise predominantly cattle and pigs; however, some wild animals such as cuscus were hunted and fish were brought back from the coast, albeit in small numbers. Horse was also present, and these were important commodities during the sixteenth to eighteenth centuries AD in Timor (Gunn 2010).

Based on current evidence from the radiocarbon dates, Macapainara was occupied during the seventeenth to nineteenth centuries AD. Most of the glass, glass beads and tradewares can also be dated to this period, although the tradewares would also allow for initial occupation as early as the sixteenth century. The sixteenth to nineteenth centuries coincide with the advent and expansion of European colonial activities in the region, and mesh well with local *ratu* oral history which recounts the occupation at Macapainara as a time when local raiding was rife and they were engaged in slaving and the sandalwood trade.

References

Alongi, D.M. 2009. Paradigm shifts in mangrove biology. In G. Perillo, E. Wolanski, D. Cahoon and M. Brinson (eds), *Coastal wetlands: An integrated ecosystem approach,* pp. 615–640. Elsevier, Amsterdam.

Andrefsky, W. Jr 2009. *Lithics: Macroscopic approaches to analysis.* Cambridge Manuals in Archaeology. 2nd edition. Cambridge University Press, New York.

Audley-Charles, M. 1968. *The geology of Portuguese Timor*. Burlington House, London.

Balme, J., S. O'Connor and M.C. Langley 2018. Marine shell ornaments in north western Australian archaeological sites: Different meanings over time and space. In M.C. Langley, M. Litster, D. Wright and S. May (eds), *The archaeology of portable art: Southeast Asia, Pacific, and Australian perspectives*, pp. 258–273. Routledge, London. doi.org/10.4324/9781315299112-16.

Bar-Yosef Mayer, D.E. 2005. The exploitation of shells as beads in the Palaeolithic and Neolithic of the Levant. *Paléorient* 31:176–185. doi.org/10.3406/paleo.2005.4796.

Branyan, L., N. French and J. Sandon. 1989. *Worcester Blue and White porcelain 1751–1790: An illustrated encyclopaedia of the patterns*. Barrie and Jenkins, London.

Brown, R.M. 2004. The Ming gap and shipwreck ceramics in Southeast Asia. Unpublished PhD thesis, University of California, Los Angeles.

Brumm, A. 2006. Fire-making using a stone 'strike-a-light' in the Soa Basin of Flores, Indonesia. *Bulletin of the Indo-Pacific Prehistory Association* 26:168–170.

Buck, C., G. Boden, A. Christen and G. James 1999. BCal online radiocarbon analysis tool. bcal.shef.ac.uk. Accessed 10 September 2010. doi.org/10.11141/ia.7.1.

Bulbeck, D. 1996–97. The Bronze–Iron Age of South Sulawesi, Indonesia: Mortuary traditions, metallurgy and trade. In F.D. Bulbeck and N. Barnard (eds), *Ancient Chinese and Southeast Asian Bronze Age cultures*. Volume II, pp. 1007–1076. Southern Materials Center, Taipei.

Bulbeck, D. 2012. Tradeware and glass sherds, and beads and other ornaments excavated at Macapainara and Vasino, East Timor, in 2008. Unpublished report to the Department of Archaeology and Natural History, The Australian National University, Canberra. (Available from the author.)

Bulbeck, F.D. 1992. A tale of two kingdoms: The historical archaeology of Gowa and Tallok, South Sulawesi, Indonesia. Unpublished PhD thesis. The Australian National University, Canberra.

Bull, G. and S. Payne 1982. Tooth eruption and epiphysial fusion in pigs and wild boar. In B. Wilson, C. Grigson and S. Payne (eds), *Ageing and sexing animal bones from archaeological sites*, pp. 55–71. British Series 109. British Archaeological Reports, Oxford.

Classen, C. 1998. *Shells*. Cambridge University Press, Cambridge.

Cristiani, E., R. Farbstein and P. Miracle 2014. Ornamental traditions in the Eastern Adriatic: The Upper Palaeolithic and Mesolithic personal adornments from Vela Spila (Croatia). *Journal of Anthropological Archaeology* 36:21–31. doi.org/10.1016/j.jaa.2014.06.009.

d'Errico, F., P. Jardón-Giner and B. Soler-Mayor 1993. Critères à base expérimentale pour l'étude des perforations naturelles et intentionnelles sur coquillages. In P.C. Anderson (ed.), *Traces et fonction: Les gestes retrouvés—Actes du Colloque Internationale de Liège*, pp. 243–254. Éditions Eraul, Liège.

Fenner, J.N. and D. Bulbeck 2013. Two clocks: A comparison of ceramic and radiocarbon dates at Macapainara, East Timor. *Asian Perspectives* 52(1):143–156. doi.org/10.1353/asi.2013.0005.

Francis, P. Jr 1999. *Beads of the world: A collector's guide with revised price references*. 2nd edition. Schiffer Publishing, Atglen, PA.

Frasché, D.F. 1976. *Southeast Asian ceramics ninth through seventeenth centuries*. The Asia Society, Washington D.C.

Glover, I. 1986. *Archaeology in Eastern Timor, 1966–67*. Terra Australis 11. Department of Prehistory, Research School of Pacific Studies, The Australian National University, Canberra.

Glover, I.C. and R.F. Ellen 1975. Ethnographic and archaeological aspects of a flaked stone collection from Seram, eastern Indonesia. *Asian Perspectives* 18(1):51–60.

Glover, I.C. and R.F. Ellen 1977. A further note on flaked stone material from Seram, eastern Indonesia. *Asian Perspectives* 20(2):236–240.

Godden, G.A. 1974. *British pottery: An illustrated guide.* Barrie and Jenkins, London.

Goodman, T. 1998. The *sosolot* exchange network of Eastern Indonesia. In J. Miedema, C. Ode and R.A.C. Dam (eds), *Perspectives on the bird's head of Irian Jaya: Proceedings of the conference, Leiden, 13–17 October 1997*, pp. 421–454. Editions Rodopi B.V., Amsterdam.

Grant, A. 1982. The use of tooth wear as a guide to the age of domestic ungulates. In B. Wilson, C. Grigson and S. Payne (eds), *Ageing and sexing animal bones from archaeological sites*, pp. 91–108. British Series 109. British Archaeological Reports, Oxford.

Green, J., R. Harper and S. Prishanchittara 1981. *The excavation at the Ko Kradat wrecksite, Thailand, 1979–1980.* Western Australian Museum Department of Maritime Archaeology, Perth.

Grigson, C. 1982. Sex and age determination of some bones and teeth of domestic cattle: A review of the literature. In B. Wilson, C. Grigson and S. Payne (eds), *Ageing and sexing animal bones from archaeological sites*, pp. 7–23. British Series 109. British Archaeological Reports, Oxford.

Gunn, G.C. 2010. *Historical dictionary of East Timor.* Scarecrow Press, Lanham.

Guy, J.S. 1986. *Oriental trade ceramics in South-East Asia: Ninth to sixteenth centuries.* Oxford University Press, Oxford.

Harrisson, B. 1990. *Pusaka: Heirloom jars of Borneo.* Oxford University Press, Oxford.

Harrisson, B. 1995. *Later ceramics in South-East Asia sixteenth to twentieth centuries.* Oxford University Press, Oxford.

Hiscock, P. 2007. Artefacts on Aru: Evaluating the technological sequences. In S. O'Connor, M. Spriggs and P. Veth (eds), *The archaeology of the Aru Islands, Eastern Indonesia*, pp. 205–234. Terra Australis 22. ANU Press, Canberra. doi.org/10.22459/ta22.2007.10.

Kuhn, S. 1990. A geometric index of unifacial reduction for stone tools. *Journal of Archaeological Science* 17(5):585–593. doi.org/10.1016/0305-4403(90)90038-7.

Langley, M.C. and S. O'Connor 2015. 6,500-year-old *Nassarius* shell appliqués in Timor-Leste: Technological and use wear analyses. *Journal of Archaeological Science* 62:175–192. doi.org/10.1016/j.jas.2015.06.012.

Langley, M.C. and S. O'Connor 2016. An enduring shell artefact tradition from Timor-Leste: *Oliva* bead production from the Pleistocene to Late Holocene at Jerimalai, Lene Hara, and Matja Kuru 1 and 2. *PLoS ONE* 11(8):e0161071. doi.org/10.1371/journal.pone.0161071.

Lankton, J. and B. Gratuze 2011. Glass samples from Timor and Papua New Guinea: LA-ICP-MS chemical compositional analysis. Unpublished report.

Li, J. 2010. Qing dynasty ceramics. In Li Zhiyan, V.L. Bower and H. Li (eds), *Chinese ceramics from the Palaeolithic Period through the Qing Dynasty*, pp. 459–533. Yale University Press, New Haven.

Lyman, R.L. 1994. *Vertebrate taphonomy.* Cambridge University Press, Cambridge.

Macintosh, D. 1977. *Chinese Blue and White porcelain.* David and Charles, London.

Marwick, B. 2008. What attributes are important for the measurement of assemblage reduction intensity? Results from an experimental stone artefact assemblage with relevance to the Hoabinhian of Mainland Southeast Asia. *Journal of Archaeological Science* 35:1189–1200. doi.org/10.1016/j.jas.2007.08.007.

Marwick, B., C. Clarkson, S. O'Connor and S. Collins 2016. Early modern human technology from Jerimalai, East Timor. *Journal of Human Evolution* 101:45–64. doi.org/10.1016/j.jhevol.2016.09.004.

McCormac, F.G., A.G. Hogg, P.G. Blackwell, C.E. Buck, T.F.G. Higham and P.J. Reimer 2004. Shcal04 Southern Hemisphere Calibration, 0–11.0 Cal Kyr BP. *Radiocarbon* 46(3):1087–1092. doi.org/10.1017/s0033822200033014.

McWilliam, A. 2007. Harbouring traditions in East Timor: Marginality in a lowland entrepôt. *Modern Asian Studies* 41(6):1113–1143. doi.org/10.1017/s0026749x07002843.

McWilliam, A., D. Bulbeck, S. Brockwell and S. O'Connor 2012. The cultural legacy of Makassar stone in East Timor. *The Asia Pacific Journal of Anthropology* 13(3):262–279. doi.org/10.1080/14442213.2012.674054.

O'Connor, S., A. McWilliam, J.N. Fenner and S. Brockwell 2012. Examining the origin of fortifications in East Timor: Social and environmental factors. *The Journal of Island and Coastal Archaeology* 7(2):200–218. doi.org/10.1080/15564894.2011.619245.

Pannell, S. and S. O'Connor 2005. Toward a cultural topography of cave use in East Timor: A preliminary study. *Asian Perspectives* 44(1):193–206. doi.org/10.1353/asi.2005.0011.

Phan, H.L., N. Đình Chiến, N. Quang Ngọc 1995. *Bat Trang ceramics 14th–19th centuries*. Gio Publishers, Hanoi.

Piper, P.J. 2006. A taphonomic assessment of the small vertebrate remains from the cave site of Liang Bua, Flores Eastern Indonesia. Unpublished report for Pusat Arkeologi Nasional Indonesia (ARKENAS).

Piper, P.J. and N. Amano 2011. A report on the animal remains from the 2008 excavations at Macapainara, East Timor. Unpublished report. The Australian National University, Canberra. hdl.handle.net/1885/111566. Accessed 17 March 2020.

Rinaldi, M. 1989. *Kraak porcelain: A moment in the history of trade*. Bamboo Publishing, London.

Rooney, J.R. and J.L. Robertson 1996. *Equine pathology*. Iowa State University Press, Ames.

Rye, O.S. 1981. *Pottery technology: Principles and reconstruction*. Taraxacum, Washington D.C.

Satō, M. 1981. *Chinese ceramics: A short history*. Translated into English and adapted by K. Hanaoka and S. Barberi. John Weatherhill, New York/Tokyo.

Scheans, D.J., K.L. Hutterer and R.L. Cherry 1970. A newly discovered blade tool industry from the central Philippines. *Asian Perspectives* 13:179–181.

Scheurleer, D.F.L. 1974. *Chinese export porcelain: Chine de commande*. Faber and Faber, London.

Schmid, E. 1972. *Atlas of animal bones*. Elsevier, Amsterdam.

Scott, E. and J. Rooney 2001. Non-articular periostosis of a proximal phalanx of *Equus conversidens*. *PaleoBios* 21(2):12–14.

Scott, R.E. 1992. Archaism and invention: Sources of ceramic design in the Ming and Qing dynasties. In G. Kuwayam (ed.), *New perspectives on the art of ceramics in China*, pp. 80–98. Far Eastern Art Council, Los Angeles County Museum of Art, Los Angeles.

Shepard, A.O. 1974. *Ceramics for the archaeologist*. Carnegie Institution Publications, Washington D.C.

Silver, I.A. 1970. The ageing of domestic animals. In D.R. Brothwell and E.S. Higgs (eds), *Science in archaeology: A survey of progress and research*, pp. 250–268. Thames and Hudson, London.

Skertchly, S.B.J. 1890. On fire-making in North Borneo. *The Journal of the Anthropological Institute of Great Britain and Ireland* 19:445–452. doi.org/10.2307/2842488.

Staperd, D. and L. Johansen 1999. Flint and pyrite: Making fire in the stone-age. *Antiquity* 73:765–777. doi.org/10.1017/s0003598x00065510.

Stiner, M., S.L. Kuhn and E. Gülec 2013. Early Upper Paleolithic shell beads at Üçağizili Cave I (Turkey): Technology and the socioeconomic context of ornament life-histories. *Journal of Human Evolution* 64:380–398. doi.org/10.1016/j.jhevol.2013.01.008.

Szabó, K. 2010. Shell artefacts and shell-working within the Lapita Cultural Complex. *Journal of Pacific Archaeology* 1:115–127.

Vanhaeren, M., F. D'errico, K. Van Niekerk, C. Henshilwood and R.M. Erasums 2013. Thinking strings: Additional evidence for personal ornament use in the Middle Stone Age at Blombos Cave, South Africa. *Journal of Human Evolution* 64:500–517. doi.org/10.1016/j.jhevol.2013.02.001.

Villiers, J. 1981. Trade and society in the Banda Islands in the sixteenth century. *Modern Asian Studies* 15(4):723–750. doi.org/10.1017/s0026749x0000874x.

von den Driesch, A. 1976. *A guide to the measurement of animal bones from archaeological sites*. . Bulletin No. 1. Peabody Museum of American Archaeology and Ethnology, Cambridge, Massachusetts.

Young, C.M., M.-F. Dupoizat and E.W. Lane (eds) 1982. *Vietnamese ceramics*. Southeast Asian Ceramics Society, Singapore.

Appendices

Table 2.A1. Macapainara tradeware.

Square/ spit	Classification	Date	Form	Vessel part	Fabric	Elucidatory comparisons in the ceramics literature
A/1	Transitional cf. Jiajing	Mid-17th century	Bowl	Lower body	Fine stoneware	Bowl from the c. 1643 'Hatcher recovery' (Harrisson 1995: Colour Plate 16)
A/2	Ming/ Transitional	16th-17th centuries	Bowl	Body	Fine stoneware	None (sherd lacks decorations)
A/2	Singburi (Thailand)	16th-17th centuries	Large jar	Shoulder	Stoneware	Unglazed variant of Harrisson's (1990) 'Sawankhalok' jars, actually made mainly in Singburi, till the early 18th century (Brown 2004)
A/2	Zhangzhou (plainware?)	17th century	Bowl/ plate	Base	Stoneware	Swatow plainware/celadon ('3G/VI'), Bulbeck (1992:560–564, 569)
A/2	Zhangzhou blue-and-white 'pseudomorph'	Late 17th century	Bowl	Lower body	Stoneware	Harrisson (1995: Plate 79)
A/2	Early Qing red overglaze decorated	Late 17th – early 18th century	Tile	Border	Fine stoneware	Related to the tiles made in China, based on their Dutch prototype, during the reign of Emperor Kangxi (Scheurleer 1974:56, 99)
A/2	Early Qing blue-and-white	Early 18th century	Bowl	Footring	Fine stoneware	Batik pattern (Harrisson 1995:79, 80) in the lavender tone characteristic of early 18th-century Chinese Blue and White (Macintosh 1977:77, 83)

Square/spit	Classification	Date	Form	Vessel part	Fabric	Elucidatory comparisons in the ceramics literature
A/2, A/3 (4 sherds)	Qing (Yongzheng) copper spotted underglaze	Early 18th century	Jarlet	Basal rim, body	Porcelain	Illustrated wares with underglaze red but no underglaze blue are dated to the Yongzheng reign, 1723–1735 (Satō 1981: Fig. 302; Li 2010: Fig. 9.4)
A/3	Vietnam monochrome	16th–17th centuries	Closed vessel	Body	Stoneware	Frasché (1976: Fig. 108); see also Frasché (1976:97–99)
A/4	Vietnam monochrome	16th–17th centuries	Bowl	Body	Stoneware	Frasché (1976:99, 137)
A/4	Transitional blue-and-white	17th century	Bowl	Body	Porcelain	May match the late Transitional (Shunhzi) covered bowl illustrated by Satō (1981: Fig. 290)
A/5	Transitional/Qing blue-and-white	17th–18th centuries	Bowl/cup	Rim	Porcelain	None (decoration is undiagnostic)
A/7	Vietnam monochrome	15th–17th centuries	Lime pot	Handle fragment	Stoneware	Young et al. (1982: Plates 182, 183); Phan et al. (1995: Plate 61)
A/7	Ming blue-and-white	16th century	Bowl/plate	Base abutting footring	Stoneware	Clear, strong blue coloration and greenish tinged glaze suggest late Ming (cf. Macintosh 1977)
A/7	Singburi (Thailand)	16th–17th centuries	Large jar	Body	Stoneware	Black glazed variant of Harrisson's (1990) 'Sawankhalok' jars, actually made mainly in Singburi, till the early 18th century (Brown 2004)
A/7	Qing celadon	Late 17th – early 18th century	Jar	Cover rim	Stoneware	Most plausible parallel are early Qing vessels made in imitation of 13th–14th-century celadons but covered with a pale celadon glaze (see Scott 1992)
A/7	Qing whiteware	17th – early 18th centuries	Closed vessel	Shoulder	Porcelain	Features consistent with 17th- to early 18th-century whiteware (cf. Bulbeck 1992: Tables B-29, B-31)
A/7	European painted blue-and-white	Mid-18th century	Tallish vessel	Body	Low-fired stoneware	Mid-18th-century Worcester blue-and-white 'porcelain' (cf. Branyan et al. 1989:44, 75, 79, 93, 148, 201, 206)
A/7 (7)	Qing monochrome	18th–19th centuries	Jarlet	Body/cover facet	Semi-porcelain	Pink semi-porcelain body, as found among Chinese Qing monochromes (Bulbeck 1992: 551)
A/9 (1)	Coarse Brown (Thailand/Cambodia)	16th–17th centuries	Jar	Shoulder	Stoneware	Harrisson (1990: Plates 149, 150)
A/9 (2)	Coarse Red (Vietnam)	17th–18th centuries	Jar	Body	Stoneware	Harrisson (1990: 39, Plates 106–114)
A/10 (3 sherds)	Ming Zhangzhou blue-and-white	16th century	Dish	Lower body	Stoneware	Harrisson (1995: Plate 43)
A/10	Brittle (South China/Vietnam)	16th century	Jar	Body	Stoneware	Harrisson (1990)
A/10	Late Ming blue-and-white	Late 16th – early 17th century	Plate	Footring	Porcelain	Features consistent with Wanli wares (Scheurleer 1974:49)
A/11	Ming green overglaze	Early 16th century	Jarlet	Shoulder	Porcelain	Hongzhi porcelain bowl (Satō 1981: Fig. 250)

Square/ spit	Classification	Date	Form	Vessel part	Fabric	Elucidatory comparisons in the ceramics literature
C/2	Qing Zhangzhou blue-and-white	Late 17th – early 18th century	Jar	Body	Stoneware	Qing Swatow ('2C/II'), Bulbeck (1992:564)
C/2 (4 sherds)	Qing whiteware	18th century	Bowl	Rim	Semi-porcelain	Features consistent with 18th-century whitewares (cf. Bulbeck 1992:577, Tables B-18, B-31)
C/2	Qing blue-and-white	Late 18th century	Closed vessel	Body	Fine stoneware	Qianlong flask (SatĐ 1981: Fig. 300)
C/4	Early Qing blackware	Early 18th century	Closed vessel	Body	Stoneware	Closest match found is the 'iron rust' blackwares of the early 18th-century Yongzheng reign (Li 2010:489)
C/8	Zhangzhou plain	17th century	Open vessel	Base	Fine stoneware	Swatow plainware ('4G/VI'), Bulbeck (1992:564)
C/9	Ming blue-and-white	16th century	Plate	Rim	Fine stoneware	Guy (1986: Fig. 71)
C/9	Ming/Transitional blue-and-white	16th–17th centuries	Bowl	Rim	Porcelain	Unwavering, thick blue line slightly below rim tip is found with many 16th- and 17th-century bowls and dishes (see Guy 1986; Harrisson 1995)
C/10	Guangdong blackware	Mid-2nd millennium	Jar	Body	Stoneware	Guangdong jar with Temmoku-like glaze (Harrisson 1990)
C/10	Ming Zhangzhou blue-and-white	16th century	Open vessel	Base	Fine stoneware	Ming Swatow ('4D/VI'), Bulbeck (1992: 564)
C/10	Zhangzhou plain	17th century	Plate	Base	Fine stoneware	Swatow plainware ('4C/VI'), Bulbeck (1992: 564)
C/10	Zhangzhou celadon	17th century	Bowl/plate	Body	Fine stoneware	Swatow plainware/celadon ('4G/VI'), Bulbeck (1992:560–64, 569)
C/11 (2 sherds)	(Ming) Zhangzhou (plainware?)	16th–17th centuries	Bowl/plate	Body	Fine stoneware	Swatow '5C/VI', Ming Swatow or Swatow (cf. Bulbeck 1992:564)
C/13	Guangdong blackware	Mid-late 2nd millennium	Jar	Body	Stoneware	Guangdong jar with Temmoku-like glaze (Harrisson 1990)
D/1	European printed blue-and-white	Early 19th century	Plate	Base	Stoneware	Godden (1974: Fig. 305), 'an underglaze-blue printed adaptation of Chinese export-market porcelain'
D/2	Early Qing blue-and-white	Early 18th century	Bowl/plate	Base	Semi-porcelain	Batik pattern (Harrisson 1995:79, 80) in early 18th-century lavender tone (Macintosh 1977:77, 83)
D/2	European creamware	Late 18th century	Teapot/tureen	Cover	Fine stoneware	Creamware teapots and tureens are characteristic of late 18th-century British pottery (Godden 1974)
D/2	Vietnam blue-and-white	19th century	Tea tray	Base	Stoneware	Phan et al. (1995: Plate 209)
D/4	Ming blue-and-white	Late 16th century	Plate	Rim	Fine stoneware	Harrisson (1995: Plate 2)
D/4	Guangdong brownware	Mid-late 2nd millennium	Jar	Shoulder	Stoneware	Guangdong jar (Harrisson 1990)
D/4	Vietnam brownware	18th century	Vase	Shoulder	Stoneware	Phan et al. (1995: Plate 149)
D/5	Vietnam ivory ware	17th–19th centuries	Vase	Body	Semi-porcelain	Phan et al. (1995: Plates 96, 157, 194)

Square/spit	Classification	Date	Form	Vessel part	Fabric	Elucidatory comparisons in the ceramics literature
D/5	Qing blue-and-white	Late 18th century	Bowl	Cavetto	Porcelain	Orange-peel effect to dead white glaze, and dark grey decorations, typically late 18th century (Scheurleer 1974:32; Macintosh 1977:83)
D/5	Qing monochrome	19th century	Bowl	Cavetto	Stoneware	Moulded 'utility' ware (cf. Harrisson 1995:101-102)
D/7	Vietnam monochrome	16th-17th centuries	Lime pot	Handle fragment	Low-fired stoneware	Phan et al. (1995: Plate 61)
D/7	Late Ming blue-and-white	Late 16th - early 17th century	Jar	Body	Porcelain	Finely graded washes of blue typical of Wanli wares (Macintosh 1977:6), especially c. 1600 jar illustrated by Harrisson (1995: Plate 7)
D/8	Kraaksporselein blue-and-white	Late 16th - early 17th century	Plate	Footring	Stoneware	Rinaldi (1989: Plates 70, 89)
D/8	Kraaksporselein blue-and-white	Late 16th - early 17th century	Plate	Rim	Porcelain	Rinaldi (1989: Plates 85-86, 90)
D/9 (3 sherds)	Guangdong blackware	19th century	Jar	Body	Stoneware	Imitation gusi Guangdong jars (cf. Harrisson 1990:53, Plate 156)
D/10	Coarse Brown (Thailand/Cambodia)	16th-17th centuries	Jar	Body	Stoneware	Harrisson (1990)
D/11	Ming Zhangzhou blue-and-white	16th century	Dish	Base	Stoneware	Ming Swatow ('5D/IV'), Bulbeck (1992:564)

Sources: See references throughout table.

Table 2.A2. Macapainara representative shellfish data (Square D, NISP and MNI).

Taxon	1	2	3	4	5	6	7	8	9	10	11	12	13	14	15	16	Total
Chiton sp.	<1	<1	1	3	1	1	1	1	<1	1	3	-	2	1	-	-	15
Patella sp.	-	-	6	3	9	8	6	1	-	1	-	3	4	-	-	-	41
Haliotis crebrisculpta	-	-	-	-	-	-	-	-	2	-	1	1	-	1	-	-	5
Haliotis varia	-	4	1	10	8	16	14	-	-	-	-	-	-	-	-	-	53
Haliotis sp.	<1	-	-	5	-	5	-	2	2	2	2	<1	3	<1	-	-	21
Trochus maculatus	1	2	7	17	1	49	8	11	5	6	16	4	4	7	<1	<1	138
Trochus sp.	-	6	<1	2	-	<1	-	<1	3	4	5	<1	<1	6	<1	<1	26
Tectus fenestratus	-	6	3	11	-	44	13	5	-	5	43	26	28	48	6	3	241
Rochia nilotica	1	8	8	10	<1	9	5	5	2	2	14	15	7	4	1	<1	91
Monodonta labio	-	-	-	1	-	<1	-	-	-	-	-	-	-	-	-	-	1
Turbo argyrostomus	-	-	-	-	-	-	-	1	-	-	-	-	-	-	-	-	1
Turbo bruneus	7	11	18	22	58	82	35	52	6	11	35	29	12	15	2	-	395
Turbo chrysostomus	-	14	4	3	21	28	8	11	2	-	5	9	6	7	1	-	119
Turbo reevei	-	-	-	-	-	-	-	1	-	-	-	-	-	-	-	-	1
Turbo sp.	-	-	4	<1	4	5	-	1	2	8	14	5	<1	4	<1	1	48
Turbo spp. opercula	21	27	14	53	3	66	51	27	13	10	15	7	15	19	2	1	344
Lunella cinerea	-	-	-	-	1	-	-	1	-	-	1	-	1	-	-	-	4
Bellastraea squamifera	-	5	1	2	-	<1	4	-	-	-	1	6	2	1	1	-	23
Angaria delphinus	1	6	5	6	-	27	8	9	-	4	3	5	4	8	1	1	88
Nerita albicilla	-	<1	4	6	-	28	15	6	3	1	6	1	3	2	2	-	77

Taxon	1	2	3	4	5	6	7	8	9	10	11	12	13	14	15	16	Total
Nerita exuvia	-	-	-	<1	-	5	1	2	1	2	1	-	-	-	-	-	12
Nerita plicata	1	1	2	9	-	25	7	7	2	-	-	-	-	1	-	-	55
Nerita polita	-	1	1	2	<1	6	7	-	1	4	2	1	6	4	1	-	36
Nerita undata	-	-	-	-	-	2	8	7	1	-	-	-	4	-	-	-	22
Nerita sp.	-	-	<1	-	1	<1	-	2	<1	<1	<1	2	6	<1	<1	-	11
Nerita spp. opercula	-	-	-	-	-	-	1	-	-	-	-	-	-	-	-	-	1
Cerithium nodulosum	-	-	-	-	-	2	1	-	-	-	-	1	-	-	-	-	4
Melanoides tuberculata	-	-	-	-	-	-	-	-	-	-	1	-	-	-	-	-	1
Conomurex luhuanus	-	-	-	1	5	6	2	4	-	-	-	-	-	4	1	-	23
Lentigo lentiginosus	-	-	-	1	-	-	-	-	-	-	2	-	2	-	-	-	5
Canarium labiatum	-	-	-	-	-	-	-	-	-	-	-	-	-	1	-	-	1
Lambis sp.	<1	1	2	2	2	3	<1	1	1	2	2	1	1	1	1	<1	20
Naticidae sp.	-	1	-	-	-	-	-	-	-	-	-	-	-	-	-	-	1
Cypraea tigris	-	-	1	<1	-	1	6	5	<1	1	<1	2	<1	-	1	-	17
Cypraea sp.	<1	4	1	3	3	1	<1	<1	2	1	3	1	1	<1	-	<1	20
Lyncina vitellus	-	-	2	5	-	8	4	3	2	3	1	1	3	2	<1	<1	34
Drupa sp.	-	-	-	-	1	-	-	-	-	-	-	-	-	-	-	-	1
Thais aculeata	-	-	-	-	-	-	-	1	-	-	-	-	-	-	-	-	1
Mancinella armigera	-	-	-	-	-	3	-	1	-	-	-	-	-	-	-	-	4
Menathais tuberosa	-	-	-	-	-	-	-	-	1	1	-	-	-	-	-	-	2
Thais sp.	-	-	-	-	-	-	-	<1	-	-	-	-	-	-	-	-	-
Muricidae sp.	-	-	-	-	-	-	-	1	-	-	3	-	-	-	-	-	4
Mipus erosus	-	-	-	-	-	-	-	-	-	-	-	-	-	1	-	-	1
Pollia fumosa	-	<1	-	<1	-	1	<1	<1	-	-	-	-	1	-	<1	-	2
Pollia sp.	-	-	-	-	1	-	-	-	-	-	-	1	-	1	-	-	3
Nassarius arcularia	-	2	2	8	14	16	13	8	3	-	-	1	6	6	-	-	79
Nassarius pauper	-	-	-	-	-	-	-	-	-	1	-	-	-	-	-	-	1
Nassariidae sp.	-	-	-	-	-	1	-	-	-	-	-	-	-	-	-	-	1
Latirolagena smaragdulus	-	-	-	-	-	2	-	-	1	-	<1	1	2	2	-	-	8
Latirus sp.	-	-	-	-	-	-	-	-	-	-	-	-	-	1	-	-	1
Vasum ceramicum	-	1	-	-	-	-	-	-	-	-	-	-	-	-	-	-	1
Vasum turbinellus	-	-	-	2	-	11	3	4	-	-	3	1	<1	1	-	-	25
Vasum sp.	-	-	-	-	-	-	<1	-	-	1	-	-	-	-	-	-	1
Nebularia coffea	-	-	-	-	1	-	-	1	-	-	-	-	-	-	-	-	2
Olividae sp.	-	-	-	1	-	1	-	2	-	-	-	-	<1	-	-	-	4
Harpa sp.	-	-	-	-	-	-	-	-	-	-	-	-	<1	-	-	-	-
Cymbiola vespertilio	-	3	3	5	1	4	2	3	1	3	1	2	1	1	-	-	30
Conus canonicus	-	-	-	-	-	1	-	-	-	-	-	-	-	-	-	-	1
Conus litteratus	-	-	2	2	-	6	1	4	<1	4	1	1	<1	2	1	-	24
Conus marmoreus	-	-	1	-	-	5	<1	1	1	<1	<1	-	1	<1	-	-	9
Conus omaria	-	-	1	-	-	-	-	-	-	-	-	-	-	-	-	-	1
Conus pennaceus	-	-	-	-	-	1	-	-	-	<1	-	-	-	-	-	-	1
Conus striatus	-	-	-	2	-	<1	<1	-	<1	-	<1	-	<1	<1	<1	-	2
Conus sp.	1	1	3	2	1	5	2	1	<1	-	<1	-	1	<1	<1	<1	17
Terebra felina	-	-	-	-	-	<1	-	-	-	-	-	-	-	-	-	-	-
Bullidae sp.	-	-	-	-	-	2	2	<1	-	-	-	1	<1	1	-	-	6
Hippopus hippopus	-	2	-	1	1	1	1	2	1	-	<1	<1	1	-	-	<1	10

Taxon	1	2	3	4	5	6	7	8	9	10	11	12	13	14	15	16	Total
Tridacna crocea	1	3	1	2	1	3	3	-	-	<1	<1	<1	1	<1	<1	<1	15
Tridacna sp.	-	-	1	<1	-	-	-	-	-	-	-	-	-	-	-	-	1
Periglypta puerpera	-	-	-	-	-	-	-	1	-	-	-	-	-	-	-	-	1
Veneridae sp.	-	-	-	-	-	-	-	-	-	-	-	1	-	-	-	-	1
Bivalvia sp.	-	-	-	-	1	1	1	<1	-	-	-	-	<1	<1	-	-	3
Nautilus sp.	1	-	<1	-	<1	1	<1	<1	-	-	<1	<1	<1	-	-	-	2
Total MNI	35	109	99	202	139	491	234	195	58	79	183	129	128	152	21	6	2260

Source: Authors' summary.

3

The Ira Ara site: A fortified settlement and burial complex in Timor-Leste

Peter V. Lape, John Krigbaum, Jana Futch, Amy Jordan and Emily Peterson

Introduction

Much of the archaeological research to date conducted in Timor-Leste has focused on Pleistocene and early Holocene sites with an orientation toward questions of initial human settlement and migration (e.g. O'Connor 2007; O'Connor et al. 2002) or the rich rock art record in the region (Lape et al. 2007; O'Connor 2003; O'Connor and Oliveira 2007). Recently there has been a growing interest in investigating the many fortified and/or hilltop settlements that date to the post-AD 1000 era (Chao 2008; Lape 2006; Lape and Chao 2008). These are of interest because of the prominent role they play in contemporary Timorese concepts of history, sacred practice, land tenure and identity, as well as the potential they hold to understand past social conflict and landscape use. This latter issue resonates with the recent history of violent conflict in Timor-Leste as well as current struggles to resolve land tenure and land use by contemporary Timorese individuals and institutions (Fitzpatrick 2002, 2010; Pannell 2006; McWilliam 2008).

Although archaeological research on these sites is still in its formative stages, having commenced only since 2003, attempts have been made to explain the chronological and spatial patterns of fortified sites. A model proposed by Lape and Chao (2008) predicts that initial fortification building in a given region will be located at the boundaries of resource-rich and resource-poor areas during times of drought. According to the model, these initial fortified settlements should have appeared when drought frequency and severity increased significantly, such as when El Niño–related droughts affected Timor. Thus, the model predicts that the earliest fortifications will appear in these areas during the twelfth to fourteenth centuries AD, when El Niño Southern Oscillation frequency doubled (compared with previous centuries). Fortification building after this initial resource-triggered phase may be caused by other reasons related to social processes, and the model does not predict the timing and location of these activities. Preliminary tests of this model on dated fortified sites in the Lautem and Manatuto districts of Timor-Leste were supportive. Investigations of this pattern based on the published literature in the wider tropical Pacific region did not strongly confirm the theory (Field and Lape 2010). However, more work is needed to test the model in Timor-Leste and other regions. Well-dated sites, particularly of the initial wall construction, are a crucial requirement for this line of investigation.

The Ira Ara site is located adjacent to a regionally important permanent freshwater spring, which should have flowed even during times of severe drought. According to the model, the Ira Ara area should show a higher than average concentration of fortified sites, the oldest of which should date to the twelfth to fourteenth century AD. Unfortunately, we were not able to definitely date the initial construction of the walling at Ira Ara, and so this site cannot be used as an additional test of the Lape and Chao (2008) model without additional excavation and dating. However, the site is of interest because of the human burials contained in it. Two of these burials were partially excavated and will be discussed in this paper. These are the only burials excavated and analysed from Timor-Leste to date and they provide an initial glimpse into late precolonial burial practices that include an analysis of associated grave goods and insight into past diet using human bone chemistry.

Site description

Ira Ara is the name of a small settlement located in the Lautem district of eastern Timor-Leste (Figure 3.1). The name (literally 'water source' or 'water roots' in the Fataluku language, a non-Austronesian language spoken in the Lautem district) refers to a large freshwater spring and an associated *tei*, or spirit dweller, around which the village is organised. Just to the north of the spring pool is a large circular mound approximately 60 m in diameter. The mound consists of a limestone outcrop that has been built up and expanded by humans with dry stacked limestone boulders and sediment fill to create a roughly circular walled platform about 3 m higher than the natural surface on the south and west sides. The north and east sides of the outcrop are unmodified cliffs, the tops of which extend about 6–10 m above the surrounding landform, which slopes down to the sea. We located the site in a 2004 survey of water sources in the Lautem area. At that time, the south and west stone walls and fill were being dug away by local residents to provide material for terracing around a small church and chapel just west of the spring (Figure 3.2). We recorded fragments of human bone in the scattered fill and in situ exposures of graves in these cut sections of the mound. On top of the mound were several stone platforms similar in size and construction to graves in Tutuala area fortified sites. Part of one of the platforms on the southern edge of the mound was probably carried away during the recent wall deconstruction. Local residents were aware that their digging was exposing and disturbing graves. They reported that prior to 1999, Indonesian authorities had forced them to build the church and chapel using stone and fill from the site. It is unclear whether these activities continued after Indonesian withdrawal in 1999.

In 2005, we returned with a small University of Washington field school and asked for permission to excavate in non-burial portions of the mound and in the area associated with the previously disturbed burials. Local permissions were complicated by the fact that seven *ratu* (clan) territories converged on the mound and the boundaries were unclear in the area of the graves. Over the course of two weeks of excavations, permissions were granted and revoked several times as different clan leaders were consulted and boundaries re-evaluated. Ultimately we were able to designate three formal units (Figure 3.1) and partly excavated a 50 cm x 2 m pit in a non-burial area of the mound (Unit 1) plus portions of two disturbed burials (Unit 2, Burial 1 and Unit 3, Burial 2).

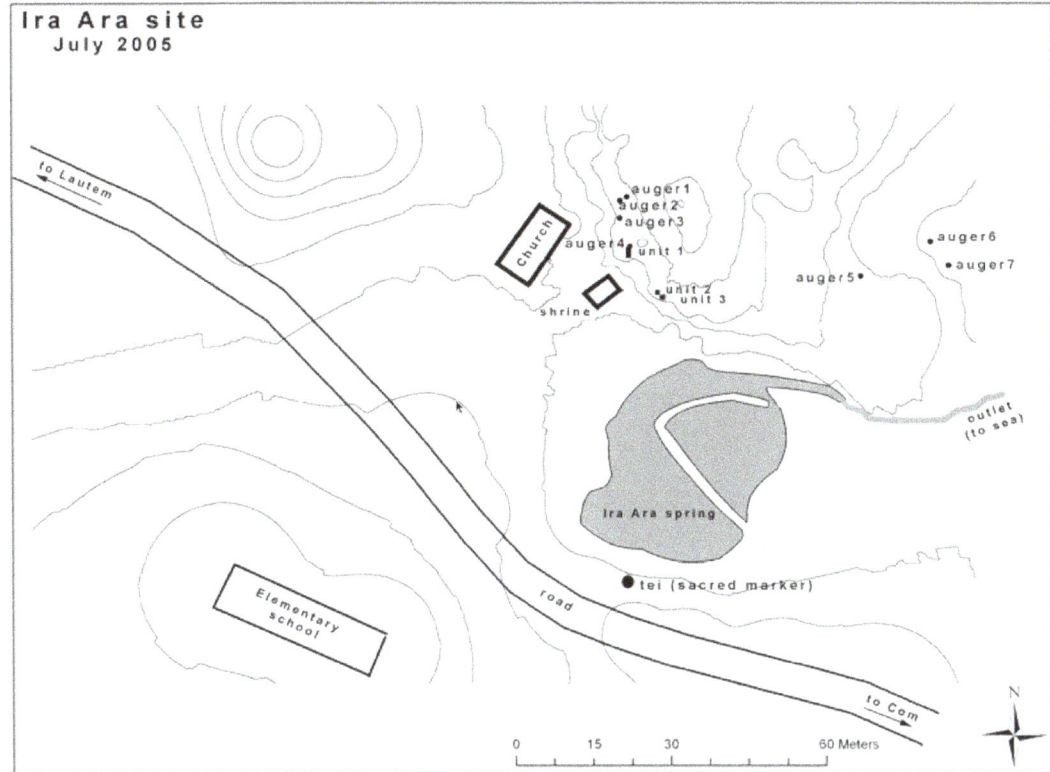

Figure 3.1. Map of the Ira Ara site.
Source: Peter V. Lape.

Figure 3.2. Ira Ara south mound edge showing disturbed section, July 2005.
Source: Photo courtesy of Jana Futch.

Abandoned walled village sites (*lata*) are places of high cultural importance in much of Lautem. They often contain the graves of ancestors, whose names are sometimes remembered by local residents (for detailed ethnographic analyses of Fataluku cultural geography, see McWilliam 2007a, 2007b, 2007c, 2008; Pannell 2006; Pannell and O'Connor 2005). Local residents remember these sites as villages once inhabited by a single or, in rare cases, multiple *ratu*. Previous archaeological excavations confirm that these are usually occupation sites containing a wide range of artefacts and faunal remains (Chao 2008; Lape 2006; Lape and Chao 2008). These sites are frequently associated with or enclose *tei*, which are glossed as 'sacred' equivalent to the Tetum term *lulik*, but also mean 'spirit being', and are usually marked with stone or carved wood posts (*sikua*). Contemporary people continue to visit *tei*, provide sacrificial food during ritually important events, and maintain the *sikua*. The Ira Ara *tei* is located on the south side of the spring pool and is marked by a *sikua* made from an upside-down tree stump with roots, symbolising the 'root' (*ara*) aspect of the spring (Figure 3.3). The stone burial platforms on top of the mound are known locally as grave markers, but the ancestors buried in the largely destroyed southernmost platform are thought to be from a *ratu* that was extirpated during an inter-clan battle in the past. There are members of this *ratu* currently living in Ira Ara, but they are recent immigrants from another part of Lautem and not considered direct descendants of those buried in the mound. This may explain why the burial platform and the human remains under it were disturbed, and why we were ultimately allowed to excavate the remains. Under normal circumstances, burial platforms in Lautem are well maintained and disturbance of any kind (archaeological or otherwise) is prohibited.

Figure 3.3. The Ira Ara *sikua*, with spring pool and mound in background, July 2004.
Source: Photo courtesy of Peter V. Lape.

Given the short time frame for excavations, which was further shortened by delays during permission negotiations, our excavation strategy was focused on identifying an occupation chronology for the mound, initial wall construction date, and documentation of disturbed burials. Very shallow sediments in eastern Timor-Leste coupled with high levels of forest disturbance and erosion make it difficult to find intact, stratified deposits at open sites, so excavations were preceded by auguring to identify areas of the mound with the deepest intact fill. Unit 1, located in the non-burial portion, was excavated in the area of deepest sediments, but it still only extended to a maximum depth of 51 cm before hitting limestone bedrock. The entire central portion of the mound was comprised of exposed limestone devoid of sediment, with earthenware and seventeenth- to nineteenth-century tradeware sherds scattered about the rock surface. This area may have once been covered with sediment that later eroded away, leaving the denser artefacts behind, though it is also possible that there was never much sediment here. The two burials identified were located on the eroding and disturbed southern edge of the mound. We were only able to recover the cranium associated with Burial 1, and just the left portion of the upper body associated with Burial 2 from the pelvis to the cranium (Figures 3.4 and 3.5). All excavated deposits were dug with trowels and dry screened through 4 mm mesh. Pits were backfilled immediately after excavations and, in the case of the two burials, local residents constructed a rock retaining wall to hold backfill in the grave areas after we finished excavation. All collections were brought to the University of Washington for analysis on loan from the Ministry of Culture of Timor-Leste. Human remains (except small samples destroyed by analysis) were returned to the leader of the *ratu* associated with the burials in November 2006 for reburial, presumably at the same site.

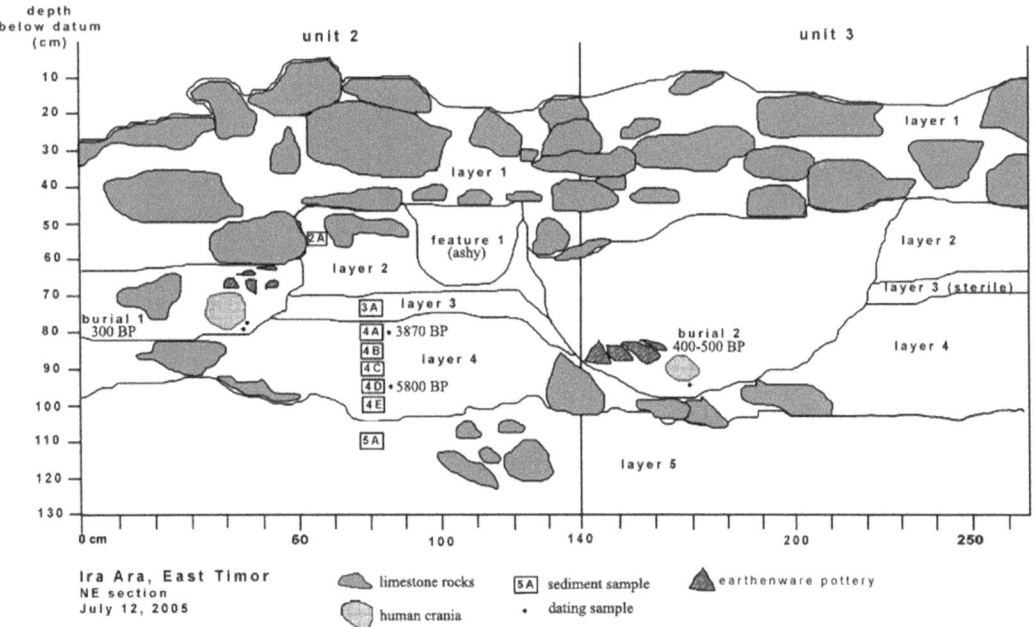

Figure 3.4. Ira Ara northeast section of Units 2 and 3 (Burials 1 and 2).
Source: Peter V. Lape.

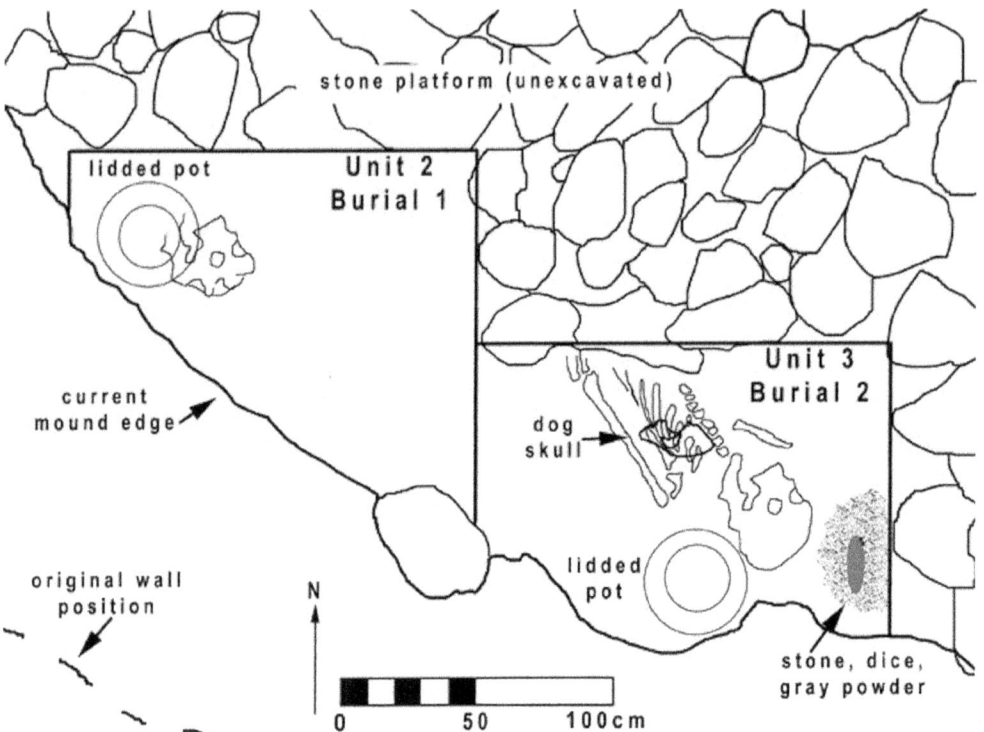

Figure 3.5. Plan view of Ira Ara Burials 1 and 2.
Source: Peter V. Lape.

Site chronology

As discussed above, precise dating of the initial construction of fortified sites is needed to test the model proposed by Lape and Chao (2008). However, shallow and disturbed sediments in fortified sites in the Lautem area have made precise dating of the construction and occupation of these sites difficult (Lape 2006). Further complicating this is the flat radiocarbon calibration curve known to exist at the time during which many of the sites were built. Unfortunately, we did not encounter well-stratified undisturbed cultural deposits at the Ira Ara site. We obtained six radiocarbon dates and two thermoluminescence dates from the Ira Ara site (Table 3.1). Six of these eight dates were from the burials that were dug after the initial wall construction and showed the best promise for dating the burials themselves. The other two dates were from undisturbed occupation layers below the burials that appear to predate the wall construction and give an indication as to pre-fortification use of the site (Figure 3.4). We did not expose stratigraphic contexts that were suitable for dating the initial wall construction. We also did not conduct any direct dating of Unit 1, as it lacked stratigraphic integrity. As part of an ongoing project to evaluate the relationship between luminescence and radiocarbon dates in the region, we paired two sets of luminescence/C14 dates from earthenware sherds with sooting on their exterior surfaces plus an additional associated charcoal C14 sample. Both of these sets of dates fell within the uncertainty range of their respective paired and associated samples. Three dates from Burial 1 all had relatively large uncertainties of ±200 years. Although the C14 results from Burial 2 suggest a somewhat older date compared to Burial 1, the luminescence date had a smaller uncertainty that placed it in the late seventeenth century AD, roughly contemporaneous with Burial 1. Neither burial contained complete tradeware vessels as grave goods, although there were a small number of fragments of seventeenth-century AD tradeware in the burial fill also suggesting seventeenth century or later burial dates.

Table 3.1. Radiocarbon and thermoluminescence dates from Ira Ara.

Sample number	Lab number	Layer/association	Material	Radiocarbon age (BP)	13C/12C ratio	C14 2 sigma calibrated or luminescence age	Basis for luminescence age
02B1011004	Beta-214263	burial 1/directly under cranium	marine shell	190 +/- 40	+0.3 ‰	AD 1650-1810	-
02B1017001	Beta-214264	burial 1/soot from burial pot	charcoal	60 +/- 40	-24.0 ‰	AD 1680-1740 AD 1800-1930 AD 1950-1960	-
022B057004	UW-1675	burial 1/burial pot lid fragment	earthenware	-	-	AD 1630-1690	TL/IRSL/OSL
03B2000037	Beta-21465	burial 2/human ulna	bone	150 +/- 50	-12.0 ‰	AD 1440-1650	-
03B2147005	Beta-21466	burial 2/soot from burial pot	charcoal	300 +/- 40	-24.2 ‰	AD 1470-1660	-
03B2147005	UW-1676	burial 2/burial pot fragment	earthenware	-	-	AD 1390-1690	TL
024A061900	Beta-230699	unit 2/layer 4A	marine shell	3870 +/- 40	+0.8 ‰	2560-2360 BC	-
024D091900	Beta-230700	unit 2/layer 4D	marine shell	5800 +/- 40	+1.7 ‰	4830-4660 BC	-

Source: Authors' summary.

Two C14 dates on marine shell were obtained from an exposed but undisturbed section of Layer 4 (Figure 3.4). Both burial pits cut into Layers 3 and 4, but Layer 4 appears to have been deposited prior to the wall construction layers. Thus, wall building must have happened after the deposition of Layer 4 (5800–3870 cal BP) and before Burial 2 (500 cal BP). It is possible that this large range could be reduced with additional excavation targeting Layer 2 in an area outside of burial disturbance.

No pottery was observed in Layer 4, even though the upper portion falls within the age when pottery is found at other sites in Timor and eastern Indonesia. However, we only cleared portions of a section and did not excavate this layer completely, so conclusions are subject to further evaluation. The date of the lower part of Layer 4 (5800 cal BP) suggest the site was attractive to people (probably because of the spring) prior to the so-called Southeast Asian Neolithic (4000–2000 BP), and that the site has further potential to reveal landscape use in this period (Spriggs 2000, 2003; Spriggs et al. 2003). Relatively large numbers of lithic artefacts, found in all excavation units at the site (probably redeposited from older layers by the burial disturbance or washed in from higher elevation portions of the mound), also suggest a long occupation chronology for the site, predating the seventeenth-century AD age of the burials when metal would have been widely available and lithic tool using traditions had presumably ended.

Human burials

The two burials identified in the field and partially recovered were adjacent to each other and covered by a single stone platform, the remnants of which extended north into the intact mound (Figure 3.5). The Burial 2 skeleton was extended and oriented north–south with the head to the south, away from the coastline and toward the spring pool. Based on the observed cranial position of Burial 1, this skeleton was similarly oriented. The grave pits were lined with limestone boulders. Both graves had been exposed in section from the south, and both crania were exposed when we began excavation in 2005. The Burial 1 cranium was very fragmented, probably as a result of recent exposure and disturbance by roots and rock boulder fill above. Associated human remains recovered from Burials 1 and 2 were studied with respect to inventory and life history parameters, including age and sex criteria, observed pathologies and stable isotope analysis. Scoring and procedures for age and sex estimation followed Bass (2005) and Buikstra and Ubelaker (1994).

Burial 1 (young adult female)

Only portions of the cranium were recovered of this individual, which included two portions of the upper jaw (maxilla) with right teeth in situ, portions of both right and left temporal bones, including the left zygoma (cheek bone), and a full complement of loose, slightly worn teeth. The right temporal fragment observed helps to identify Burial 1 as a young female and the mastoid process is slight in volume with a score of 1 (ordinal scale 1 to 5), which also suggests female, making the sex estimation of this individual quite secure, and consistent with the overall gracile nature observed in the preserved cranial fragments. The left temporal fragment lacks the mastoid process and petrous portion, but includes the squamous portion and an articulated zygoma. The squamous exhibits a fresh suture along its anterior margin (spheno-temporal suture), which suggests an age of young adulthood, probably 20–30 years. The left temporal fragment also shows evidence of pathology, with pitted and reactive bone associated along the inferior distal margin of the zygoma, at the distal site of origin of the masseter muscle. The masseter is a major chewing muscle, and this individual would have felt pain during chewing based on this observation. A curious localised, bowl-shaped wear pattern on the occlusal surface of the left upper first molar (LM1) and lower molars (LM1 and LM2) was observed in association with this feature. The LM1 and LM2 were quite heavily worn; LM3 was unworn, but exhibited a single, gross (extreme) dental caries along the distal portion of the cemento-enamel junction. Some noteworthy staining, reddish in colour, was also observed on anterior and posterior teeth of this individual that can likely be attributed to the chewing of betel nut. Staining was patchy rather than ubiquitous across the preserved dentition; however, it is informative to couple the extreme localised tooth wear with the pathology observed on the zygoma and the staining observed on portions of the dentition.

With the full complement of teeth present in this young adult female, those teeth associated with alveolar bone (principally the right maxilla (RM3-RM2; RM1-RI1), but also a small mandibular fragment (LM2)) showed no evidence of pathology. Similarly, teeth showed no signs of dental caries except for the gross caries in the LM3. Wear scores were recorded and show slight wear generally, albeit moderate wear on the molars associated with the left side of the individual's jaw. Non-metric features of the molars included the presence of a large hypocone and the absence of a metaconule, Carabelli's cusp and enamel extensions. In addition, no shovelling of the incisors was observed and all premolars had a single root.

Burial 2 (young adult female)

Burial 2 is better represented skeletally than Burial 1, with portions of the lower jaw (mandible), upper vertebrae, and left trunk and upper arm recovered during excavations. Postcranially, the upper thorax was preserved with both scapulae and clavicles represented, including the glenoid fossa of the left scapula, which articulated with a near-complete (95 per cent) humerus. Portions of the manubrium and the body of the sternum were also present.

The mandible was preserved in two parts, with most associated dentition present. RM3 to RI1 were in situ, LI1 to LP1 were loose, and LM2 and LM3 were in situ, in a smaller fragment. The second left premolar and first molar (LP2 and LM2) were not observed. Well-defined non-carious buccal pits were present on RM1 and LM2. All teeth scored for dental wear were lightly worn, and with the eruption and partial wear of the third molars, young adult age is supported. Similar to Burial 1, only one dental caries was observed with Burial 2, with her LM3, although this was of moderate size and situated on the occlusal surface of the tooth. Dental calculus was light. Remnant evidence of dental staining was present along occlusal aspects of the molars and incisors, although this too was slight to moderate in incidence.

With respect to the left scapula, five fragments were examined and a scapular notch was deemed absent. The only metric readily obtained from the gracile pieces was with the glenoid cavity, which had a vertical diameter of 35 mm, and is in the possible female size range according to Bass (2005:123). The overall gracile character of the shoulder girdle, however, may be coupled with a metric from the near-complete right clavicle. Its maximum length was 136.5 mm, which equates to female in Bass (2005:131), and the midshaft circumference was 35 mm. The medial epiphysis shows complete union (>20 years), and there is a pronounced conoid tubercle. The left clavicle is missing its medial end but shows evidence of a pronounced bilateral groove along the conoid tubercle. The left humerus, near complete, was measured for maximum length (299 mm), maximum/minimum midshaft diameter (18.85/14.412 mm), vertical humeral head diameter (43.16 mm), epicondylar breadth (54.91 mm) and articular width (42.21 mm). No septal aperture was present and there was a moderate bicipital groove present. The gracile nature of the limb bones, including the humeral head diameter and epicondylar breadth, and the clavicle support a female sex designation for Burial 2.

The preserved vertebrae were similarly gracile and, overall, moderately well preserved. All seven cervical vertebrae were preserved, although the axis, atlas and C7 were only represented by partial centra (bodies). Otherwise, all cervical and thoracic vertebrae T1 to T8 were represented by both centra and respective neural arches. Corresponding ribs with the preserved thoracic vertebrae include both right and left 1st and 2nd ribs and principally left 3rd–7th ribs. This is consistent with the field notes and recordings of Burial 2 in situ and subsequent recovery of her partial skeleton.

Isotopic analysis

Stable isotope ratio analysis is now routine to help situate individuals with respect to their presumed diet versus that observed from other lines of evidence in the archaeological record. Shellfish remains present in the Ira Ara site, and the site's proximity to the coast suggests that marine foods, for example, played a significant role in the local diet, as it has for over 30,000 years, as represented in eastern Timor-Leste cave assemblages (O'Connor et al. 2002; Veth et al. 2005). A pilot study examining the tooth enamel from each of the two burials was conducted to assess the nature of diet consumed by the individuals represented at the site, which has the potential to reveal other types of foods consumed by people there that are not represented in the archaeological record.

Ratios of light stable isotopes of carbon and nitrogen are especially useful in reconstructing the dietary regimes of past peoples; however, such analyses require good preservation of bone collagen. The radiocarbon date on bone collagen obtained from the bone seems to have produced a reasonable $\delta^{13}C$ value (−12.0‰) through the analysis supplied by Beta Analytic (Table 3.1). Such a value suggests that C4 plants (which would have principally included millet and/or sugarcane) and perhaps marine foods were major food sources. This is corroborated by bulk analyses of the tooth enamel from the two left lower third molars (LM3) from Burials 1 and 2. These two teeth were sampled for stable isotope ratio analysis of the tooth enamel. Here we focus on the $\delta^{13}C$ values from analysis of cleaned 'bulk' tooth enamel, with Burial 1 averaging −7.3‰ and Burial 2 averaging −6.4‰, yielding a population average of −6.9‰. These $\delta^{13}C_{en}$ results are not comparable directly with the $\delta^{13}C_{co}$ value of −12‰ from the C14 analysis as they derive from different tissues. The isotope ratio derived from the bone collagen fraction is biased towards the protein portion of the diet (which has a fractionation offset from consumed 'protein' of c. 5‰). In contrast, the fractionation offset from diet for tooth enamel is closer to −9.4‰ (Ambrose et al. 1997). What this translates to for the Ira Ara findings is that the maritime-based diet we are observing was clearly supplemented by C4 cultigens most likely millet, and not simply ^{13}C enriched through the consumption of marine-based foods. Marine foods, however, were clearly a component of the diet, and these may have included a variety of invertebrate and vertebrate foods, including perhaps higher trophic/pelagic species.

Grave goods

Burial 1 had an intact earthenware pot and lid (Figure 3.6) immediately right of the cranium, which contained sediment and the bones of a small bird, probably an immature chicken (*Gallus gallus*). Five brass/bronze earrings were found associated with the fragmented cranium.

Burial 2 also contained a small-lidded pot to the immediate left of the cranium, which was quite similar in size and form as that found in Burial 1, but it was fragmented and did not contain intact fill. Two unusual ivory dice and a groundstone artefact were located right of the cranium, the latter tentatively identified by local informants as a knife sharpener (Figure 3.7). A white powder, identified as calcite, was associated with the groundstone and ivory dice. It may have been related to chewing of betel nut, which is common in Ira Ara today, and may have been responsible for the staining and erosion of the teeth in both burials as described above.

Figure 3.6. Earthenware pot from Ira Ara Burial 1.
Source: Peter V. Lape.

Figure 3.7. Ira Ara Burial 2 showing position of groundstone artefact and fragmented earthenware pot and lid.
The dog cranium was 3 cm above the chest area, and the dice were immediately adjacent to the groundstone artefact. Both were removed prior to this photo.
Source: Photo courtesy of Peter V. Lape.

The dice were six-sided and somewhat irregular in shape (Figure 3.8). They had unusual numbering, with four through eight pips, plus eight and nine (missing the five and six pips present on standard dice). Local informants were unfamiliar with this type of dice, and we have been unable to find similarly numbered examples of dice in the published literature. The cranium of a dog (*Canis familiaris*) was located above the chest area, presumably buried with this individual. No post-cranial dog remains were recovered and no other grave goods were found in this burial, though it should be noted that we were only able to excavate to the bottom of the stone-lined grave pit in the area associated with the cranium of Burial 2.

Figure 3.8. Dice from Ira Ara Burial 2.
Source: Peter V. Lape.

Fauna

Excavations at Ira Ara did not expose well-stratified undisturbed cultural deposits, and animal bones recovered were generally poorly preserved and fragmentary. Results presented here therefore represent the presence of animal species from mixed stratigraphic contexts representing several thousand years of human use of the site. As such, our analysis simply shows animal species present in the assemblage. A total of 309 bones were analysed from all three excavation pits, of which 206 were identified to family level or better (Table 3.2). Animal taxa present at Ira Ara include several human introductions, some thought to be quite recent. Conspicuously absent were rat and bat species, which are prevalent in other Timorese sites, though this may be simply a result of a small and poorly preserved faunal sample.

Table 3.2. Vertebrate fauna from Ira Ara, Units 1, 2 and 3.

Taxon	Present	Absent
Phalanger orientalis	X	-
Sus scrofa	X	-
Galliformes	X	-
Cervus timorensis	X	-
Capra hircus	X	-
Canis familiaris	X	-
Paradoxurus herphroditus	X	-
Bos taurus	X	-
Bubalus bubalis	X	-
Equus	X	-
Fish	X	-
Felis silvestris	X	-
Rattus exulans	-	X
Mega and Microchiroptera	-	X
Macaca fascicularis	-	X

Source: Authors' summary.

With respect to invertebrate remains, shellfish were also represented in all excavation units. However, only the shell from Unit 1 was analysed, since Unit 1 appeared to have less chance of mixed deposit than lower Layers 3 and 4, which had been disturbed by the two burials. Although Unit 1 was not directly dated, the presence of small amounts of tradeware in the Unit 1 context suggest a post-AD 1200 age for this deposit.

A total of 562 marine shell specimens were recovered from this unit, of which 216 were identifiable to at least the family level (Table 3.3). Although sample size is quite small, there is considerable diversity in the molluscan faunal assemblage. The 216 identified specimens represent 16 families, 19 genera and 20 species, forming a range of taxa from an intertidal reef flat. The most abundant taxa include *Rochia nilotica*, *Turbo* sp., *Tridacna* sp., *Trochus maculatus*, *Cypraea* spp., *Hippopus hippopus* and *Conomurex luhuanus*, and these large bivalves and gastropods dominate the assemblage. Four families, Trochidae, Tegulidae, Turbinidae and Tridacnidae, together account for 65 per cent of the identified specimens.

The abundance of these large-bodied, high-ranked taxa indicates that the occupants of Ira Ara had access to a rich coral reef patch for foraging. The same taxa are also abundant in many shell assemblages at other Timor-Leste sites, including both fortified hilltop settlements of similar age in the Manatuto region (Chao 2008), and cave sites in Tutuala (O'Connor et al. 2002) and Baucau (E. Glover 1986; I. Glover 1986), with evidence for occupation since the terminal

Pleistocene or early Holocene. Due to the mixed nature of the deposits and small sample size, little can be said about diachronic patterning in shellfish use at Ira Ara itself, but qualitative similarity between this assemblage and those from much older prehistoric sites is consistent with the pattern observed by both Emily Glover (1986) and O'Connor et al. (2002): that there is very little evidence for change over time in the availability and exploitation of coral reef habitats in Timor-Leste.

Table 3.3. Molluscan fauna from the Ira Ara site, Unit 1.

Taxon	NISP	%
GASTROPODA		
HALIOTIDAE		
Haliotis sp.	5	2.3
TROCHIDAE		
Trochus maculatus	19	8.8
Trochus sp.	11	5.1
TEGULIDAE		
Rochia nilotica	30	13.9
TURBINIDAE		
Turbo chrysostomus	5	2.3
Turbo setosus	4	1.9
Turbo spp.	23	10.6
HIPPONICIDAE		
fam. Hipponicidae	3	1.4
NERITIDAE		
Nerita costata	3	1.4
Nerita polita	5	2.3
Nerita undata	3	1.4
STROMBIDAE		
Conomurex luhuanus	13	6.0
CYPRAEIDAE		
Cypraea spp.	15	6.9
MITRIDAE		
VOLUTIDAE		
fam. Volutidae	4	1.9
CONIDAE		
Conus litteratus	3	1.4
Conus spp.	5	2.3
BIVALVIA		
TRIDACNIDAE		
Hippopus hippopus	15	6.9
Tridacna crocea	3	1.4
Tridacna maxima	8	3.7
Tridacna sp.	20	9.3

Taxa representing <1% of the total assemblage are omitted. These include: *Angaria delphinus*, *Turbo bruneus*, *Nerita albicilla*, *Nerita plicata*, *Nerita* sp., *Lambis lambis*, *Strombus* sp., Naticidae, *Nassarius* sp., Fasciolaridae, *Mitra mitra*, *Conus marmoreus*, Terebridae and Polyplacophora.

NISP: Number of individual specimens.

Source: Authors' summary.

Lithic artefacts

Timor is located in an area heavily trafficked by various long-distance traders and has been part of the greater Indian and Chinese trade patterns since AD 100–200 (Chao 2008; Lape 2000; Reid 1993). This incorporation into a world economy brought major changes to the material culture of Timor, including a replacement of lithic artefacts with those of metal. The accepted date for the introduction of metal to Timor is also around 2000 BP (I. Glover 1986:203). Ian Glover (1986:202) notes: 'Flint is used occasionally for strike-a-lights in Timor today and … was abandoned as an important tool-making material at least 2000 years ago'. It was therefore unexpected to find chipped stone artefacts (except for strike-a-lights) at Ira Ara, given the probable seventeenth-century AD date of the burials. However, 186 lithic artefacts were recovered from the three excavation pits, representing a variety of artefact types; only two of these artefacts showed evidence of use as strike-a-lights (Figures 3.9, 3.10).

The majority of these artefacts are made of chert, a material locally present in cobble form. No obsidian artefacts were present, though they show up in older cave assemblages in the Lautem area (Ambrose et al. 2009). This collection of tools and debitage shows great similarity to the assemblages described by Ian Glover (1986; Ellen and Glover 1974) as Neolithic. He divides flakes with secondary working into six categories: tanged points, side scrapers, other scrapers, flaked adzes, burins and miscellaneous (1986:34). While no tanged points or flaked adzes were identified in the Ira Ara site, the remaining artefact types were present here. In addition, Ira Ara contained notched and tipped flakes; Ian Glover places notched tools in the 'scraper' category. He believes it is:

> most probable that these artefacts were woodworking tools. The fact that so many are notched suggests that they were used for small, cylindrical objects such as digging sticks, bows, spears, or blow guns. (I. Glover 1986:35)

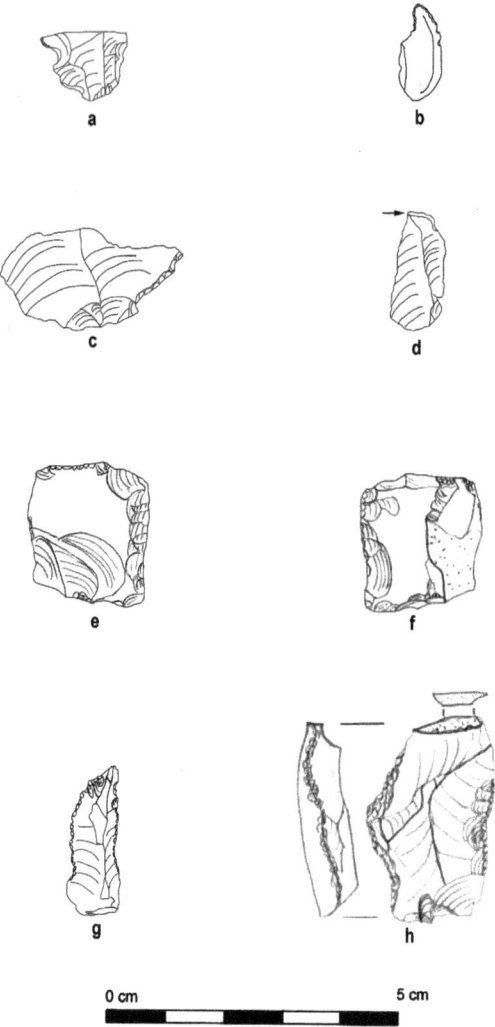

Figure 3.9. Selected lithic artefacts from Ira Ara.
A: Retouched flake with notch and tip (0102183400);
B: Retouched flake with tip (022A036800a); C: Retouched flake with tip (022A033800e); D: Burin (02B2043800d);
E: Flake scraper, ventral view (022B043800a); F: Flake scraper, dorsal view (022B043800a); G: Retouched flake (001133400); H: Core used as 'strike-a-light' (00000003510).
Source: Peter V. Lape.

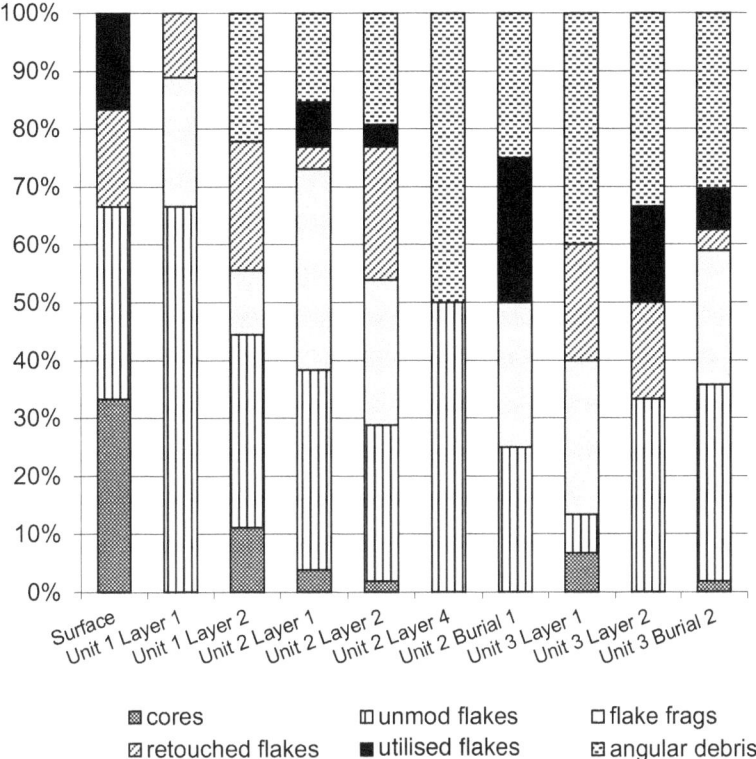

Figure 3.10. Relative frequency of lithic artefact types from Ira Ara.
Source: Authors' summary.

The lithic artefacts do not appear to have a random distribution throughout the different units, with 87 per cent of all artefacts found in the burial fill. The similar distribution of artefacts between the two burials may indicate that they were buried at about the same time or, more likely, the lithic assemblages are from earlier occupations that eroded from higher elevations on the mound and/or were mixed from deeper layers into the burial fill during inhumation.

Discussion

The Ira Ara site adds important new information about fortified settlements in Timor-Leste, and particularly about seventeenth-century AD burial practices. It does not allow conclusive testing of the resource-dependent model for initial fortification building as described in Lape and Chao (2008). To adequately test that model, a complete survey of fortified settlements in the Ira Ara region would need to be completed, with each site's initial fortification building episode securely dated. The earliest sites should date to times of increasing drought frequency and be located at the boundary of resource-rich and resource-poor areas. We would expect the Ira Ara site to be one of these earliest sites, given its location next to a large permanent water source in an otherwise dry area. Local informants recall that this spring has always flowed, even during severe droughts such as those experienced during major El Niño events in 1982–83 and 1997–98. Dates for the initial wall building at Ira Ara must be prior to the burials and after the deposition of Layer 4 (between 3800 cal BP and 500 cal BP). Without further excavation, it is impossible to date the initial wall building more precisely, and thus the model cannot yet be tested. Dating the fortified period at Ira Ara is complicated by occupation and use of the site in the mid-Holocene, prior to fortification building. Future excavations at the site should focus on narrowing this date range by excavating in areas of non-burial disturbance to find the Layer 2/3 interface, or by dating material immediately under the lowest course of limestone rocks used to build the walls, in the few areas not yet destroyed by recent activity.

The faunal and lithic assemblages are difficult to interpret, given that most were from burial fill and thus are likely from mixed contexts. Intriguing results that call for further examination are the lack of rats and bats in the fauna, and the presence of a diverse range of lithic artefacts. Neither would be expected in intact second millennium AD assemblages, but both are probably the result of stratigraphic disturbance and taphonomic processes.

Burial practices at the site are similar to metal age burials in other parts of Island Southeast Asia, with the presence of lidded pots, grave goods and jewellery. Notably absent are beads and tradeware vessels, which are common in many late metal age burials in the region (cf. Bellwood 1997). Many late Neolithic and early metal age burials in Indonesia and the Philippines are jar burials, though this practice may have changed in the later metal age, perhaps replaced by sacrificial animal burial in smaller jars as seen in Burial 1 (Simanjuntak et al. 2006). Local informants reported ongoing or remembered traditions of burying the dead with an offering of rice and baby chickens in small pots. Analyses of a small and fragmentary sample of human bone limits our ability to draw large conclusions. However, results from isotopic analysis show the probable inclusion of C4 plants, most likely millet, in the local diet. This might be the result of large-scale forest clearance and reliance on millet as a substitute perhaps for rice by the seventeenth century. This pattern of subsistence might be expected for people relying on a mix of marine and agricultural resources and calls for further research into palaeoenvironmental conditions and subsistence practices during this time period.

Acknowledgements

The authors wish to thank the following institutions and individuals for their contributions: Ministerio da Educacao, Cultura, Juventude e Desporto, Timor-Leste, Dr Armindo Maia, Virgilio Simith, Cecila Assis, Abílio da Conceição Silva, Horacio da Costa, the *Xefe de Suco*, *ratu* leaders and people of Ira Ara and Moro villages, Nuno Vasco Oliveira, Sue O'Connor, Sally Brockwell, Andrew McWilliam, Sandra Pannell, Chin-yung Chao, James Taylor, Robert Wood, Brooke Avery, Randy Hert, Kass Bessert and two anonymous reviewers. Thanks also to Richard Willan (Museum and Art Gallery of the Northern Territory) who updated the section on molluscan fauna.

References

Ambrose, S.H., B.M. Butler, D.B. Hanson, R.L Hunter-Anderson and H.W. Krueger 1997. Stable isotopic analysis of human diet in the Marianas Archipelago, Western Pacific. *American Journal of Physical Anthropology* 104(3):343–361. doi.org/10.1002/(sici)1096-8644(199711)104:3<343::aid-ajpa5>3.0.co;2-w.

Ambrose, W., C. Allen, S. O'Connor, M. Spriggs, N. Oliveira and C. Reepmeyer 2009. Possible obsidian sources for artefacts from Timor: Narrowing the options using chemical data. *Journal of Archaeological Science* 36(3):607–615. doi.org/10.1016/j.jas.2008.09.022.

Bass, W.M. 2005. *Human osteology: A laboratory and field manual.* 5th edition. Missouri Archaeological Society, Columbia.

Bellwood, P. 1997. *Prehistory of the Indo-Malaysian Archipelago.* University of Hawai'i Press, Honolulu.

Buikstra, J.E. and D.H. Ubelaker (eds) 1994. *Standards for data collection from human skeletal remains*. Arkansas Archeology Survey Research Series 44. Fayetteville Arkansas Archeological Survey, Fayetteville.

Chao, C.-Y. 2008. A microregional approach to the social dynamics in the late prehistoric Manatuto, East Timor, 11th–18th century. Unpublished PhD thesis. University of Washington, Seattle.

Ellen, R.F. and I.C. Glover 1974. Pottery manufacture and trade in the Central Moluccas: The modern situation and the historical implications. *Man* (n.s.) 9:353–379. doi.org/10.2307/2800690.

Field, J. and P. Lape 2010. Paleoclimates and the emergence of fortifications in the tropical Pacific islands. *Journal of Anthropological Archaeology* 29:113–124. doi.org/10.1016/j.jaa.2009.11.001.

Fitzpatrick, D. 2002. *Land claims in East Timor*. Asia Pacific Press, Canberra.

Fitzpatrick, D. 2010. The relative resilience of property: First possession and order without law in East Timor. *Law and Society Review* 44(2):205–238. doi.org/10.1111/j.1540-5893.2010.00402.x.

Glover, E. 1986. Prehistoric utilisation of tropical reef molluscs in East Timor, Indonesia. *Journal of Conchology* 32:151–165.

Glover, I. 1986. *Archaeology in Eastern Timor, 1966–67*. Terra Australis 11. Department of Prehistory, Research School of Pacific Studies, The Australian National University, Canberra.

Lape, P.V. 2000. Contact and colonialism in the Banda Islands, Maluku, Indonesia. *Bulletin of the Indo-Pacific Prehistory Association* 20:48–55.

Lape, P.V. 2006. Chronology of fortified settlements in East Timor. *Journal of Island and Coastal Archaeology* 1(2):285–297. doi.org/10.1080/15564890600939409.

Lape, P.V. and C.-Y. Chao 2008. Fortification as a human response to late Holocene climate change in East Timor. *Archaeology in Oceania* 43(1):11–21. doi.org/10.1002/j.1834-4453.2008.tb00026.x.

Lape, P.V., S. O'Connor and N. Burningham 2007. Rock art: A potential source of information about past maritime technology in the Southeast Asia-Pacific region. *International Journal of Nautical Archaeology* 36(2):238–253. doi.org/10.1111/j.1095-9270.2006.00135.x.

McWilliam, A. 2007a. Austronesians in linguistic disguise: Fataluku cultural fusion in East Timor. *Journal of Southeast Asian Studies* 38(2):355–375. doi.org/10.1017/s0022463407000082.

McWilliam, A. 2007b. Harbouring traditions in East Timor: Marginality in a lowland entrepôt. *Modern Asian Studies* 41(6):1113–1143. doi.org/10.1017/s0026749x07002843.

McWilliam, A. 2007c. Looking for Adê: A contribution to Timorese historiography. *Bijdragen tot de Taal-, Land- en Volkenkunde* 163(2/3):221–238. doi.org/10.1163/22134379-90003684.

McWilliam, A. 2008. Fataluku healing and cultural resilience in East Timor. *Ethnos* 73(2):217–240. doi.org/10.1080/00141840802180371.

O'Connor, S. 2003. Nine new painted rock art sites from East Timor in the context of the Western Pacific region. *Asian Perspectives* 42(1):96–128. doi.org/10.1353/asi.2003.0028.

O'Connor, S. 2007. New evidence from East Timor contributes to our understanding of earliest modern human colonisation east of the Sunda Shelf. *Antiquity* 81:523–555. doi.org/10.1017/s0003598x00095569.

O'Connor, S. and N. Oliveira 2007. Inter- and intra-regional variation in the Austronesian painting tradition: A view from East Timor. *Asian Perspectives* 46(2):389–403. doi.org/10.1353/asi.2007.0014.

O'Connor, S., M. Spriggs and P. Veth 2002. Excavation at Lene Hara Cave establishes occupation in East Timor at least 30,000–35,000 years ago. *Antiquity* 76:45–50. doi.org/10.1017/s0003598x0008978x.

Pannell, S. 2006. Welcome to the Hotel Tutuala: Fataluku accounts of going places in an immobile world. *The Asia Pacific Journal of Anthropology* 7(3):203–219. doi.org/10.1080/14442210600965158.

Pannell, S. and S. O'Connor 2005. Toward a cultural topography of cave use in East Timor: A preliminary study. *Asian Perspectives* 44(1):193–206. doi.org/10.1353/asi.2005.0011.

Reid, A. (ed.) 1993. *Southeast Asia in the early modern era: Trade, power, and belief.* Cornell University Press, Ithaca.

Simanjuntak, T., M. Hisyam, B. Praesyo and T.S. Astiti (eds) 2006. *Archaeology: Indonesian perspective: R.P. Soejono's festschrift.* International Center for Prehistoric and Austronesian Studies, Indonesian Institute of Sciences, Menteng, Jakarta.

Spriggs, M. 2000. Out of Asia: The spread of Southeast Asian Pleistocene and Neolithic maritime cultures in Island Southeast Asia and the Western Pacific. *Modern Quaternary Research in Southeast Asia* 16(V–VI):51–76.

Spriggs, M. 2003. Chronology of the Neolithic transition in Island Southeast Asia and the Western Pacific: A view from 2003. *The Review of Archaeology* 24(2):57–80.

Spriggs, M., S. O'Connor and P. Veth 2003. Vestiges of early pre-agricultural economy in the landscape of East Timor: Recent research. In A. Källén and A. Karlström (eds), *Fishbones and glittering emblems: Proceedings from the EurASEEA Sigtuna Conference*, pp. 49–58. Museum of Far Eastern Antiquities, Stockholm.

Veth, P., M. Spriggs and S. O'Connor 2005. Continuity in tropical cave use: Examples from East Timor and the Aru Islands, Maluku. *Asian Perspectives* 44(1):180–192. doi.org/10.1353/asi.2005.0015.

4

Excavations at the site of Vasino, Lautem District, Timor-Leste

Sally Brockwell, Sue O'Connor, Jack N. Fenner, Andrew McWilliam, Noel Amano Jr, Philip J. Piper, David Bulbeck, Mirani Litster, Rose Whitau, Jack O'Connor-Veth, Tim Maloney, Judith Cameron, Richard C. Willan and William R. Dickinson

Introduction

This chapter explores the archaeology and ethnohistory of one of the distinctive fortified settlements in the eastern part of Timor-Leste. In 2009, a team from The Australian National University (ANU), together with local people, partially excavated the site of Vasino, located close to the north coast of Timor-Leste, above the modern village of Moro-Parlamento (Figure 4.1). The site had been fortified with large stone walls and the aim was to provide more data on when, how and why these fortifications were used in the region. Two related questions guided the research. First, when was the main period of fort construction initiated? Secondly, what were the prevailing environmental and social conditions of those times?

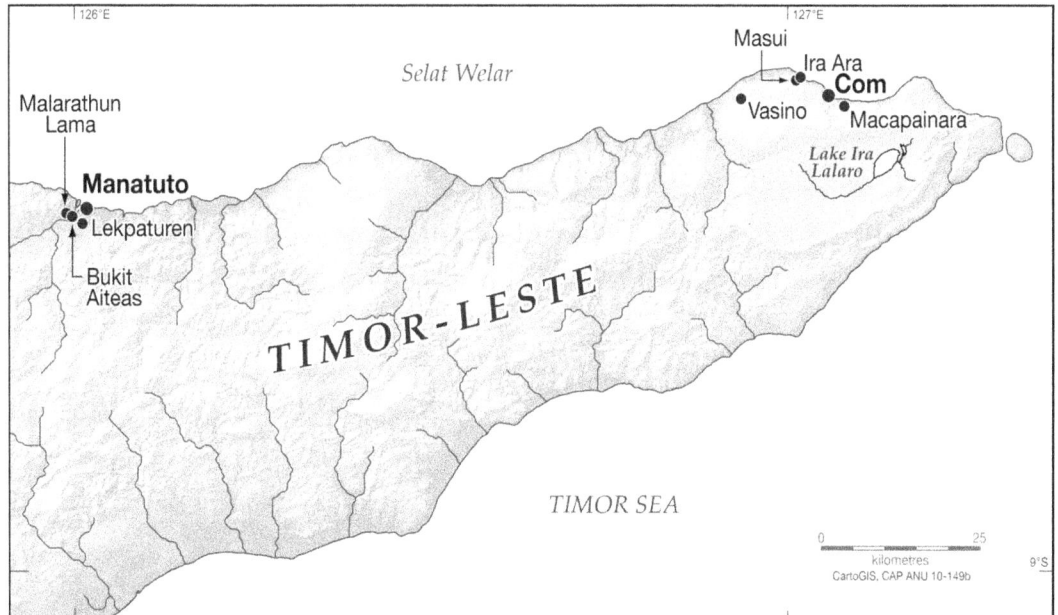

Figure 4.1. Location of Vasino and other fortified sites in Timor-Leste.
Source: CartoGIS ANU.

Vasino site location and layout

Vasino was identified during fieldwork in 2008. It was noted at the time that the site was fortified with stone walls similar to those at Macapainara (see Chapter 2, this volume) with large stones on the outside, infilled with smaller rubble. There were also prickly pear plants (*Opuntia* sp.), an exotic species from the Americas commonly used in Timor to deter intruders (Figure 4.2), and graves laid with so-called *batu Makassar*, large flat stones, said by the locals to have come from the eponymous Makassar (Figure 4.3; McWilliam et al. 2012). Vasino is a two-level site about 2 km inland from the northern shore, and 40 km from the eastern shore of Timor-Leste, within Lautem Province. It is located on a hilltop at an elevation of about 240 m. It is covered with moderately dense vegetation, primarily small trees and shrubs. While well known to local people, this site is not currently used for occupation or agriculture.

Figure 4.2. Vasino walls and prickly pear.
Source: Photo courtesy of Andrew McWilliam.

Figure 4.3. Vasino *batu Makassar* grave.
Source: Photo courtesy of Andrew McWilliam.

The lower level has a nearly flat surface that encompasses an area of ~1950 m². It is bordered on the west by a high, steep cliff, while stone walls and shorter cliffs line its north and south edges (Figure 4.4). This level contains two stone structures with standing stone markers, which local informants identified as graves, as well as a carved wooden pole (*tei* or *ete uru ha'a*) of current sacred significance (Figure 4.5). Its eastern boundary is a 3–5 m high cliff, which also forms the western boundary of the upper level.

The upper level gently slopes from the south down to the north. It covers ~2740 m², with a 2–4 m deep natural gully with steep sides along its eastern side. The gully is about 5 m wide along the northern portion of the upper level and widens considerably as it continues south. To the east of the gully is a rising slope that eventually crests on a hill that overlooks the site. The northern boundary of the upper level is protected by a slope with a series of stone walls, which we have termed the 'Back Entrance'. This area also has a stone wall that projects to the northeast for about 23 m from the site and then turns at a right angle and continues for another 40 m to the northwest. The function of this wall is unclear, but it may have a defensive role in protecting the northern hill slope from attack. The upper level has one stone structure identified as a grave, and another, circular structure 15 m in diameter, which local informants identified as a water buffalo corral (*loho*). The latter seems unlikely since there is no gap in the large stone walls that could have functioned as an entrance.

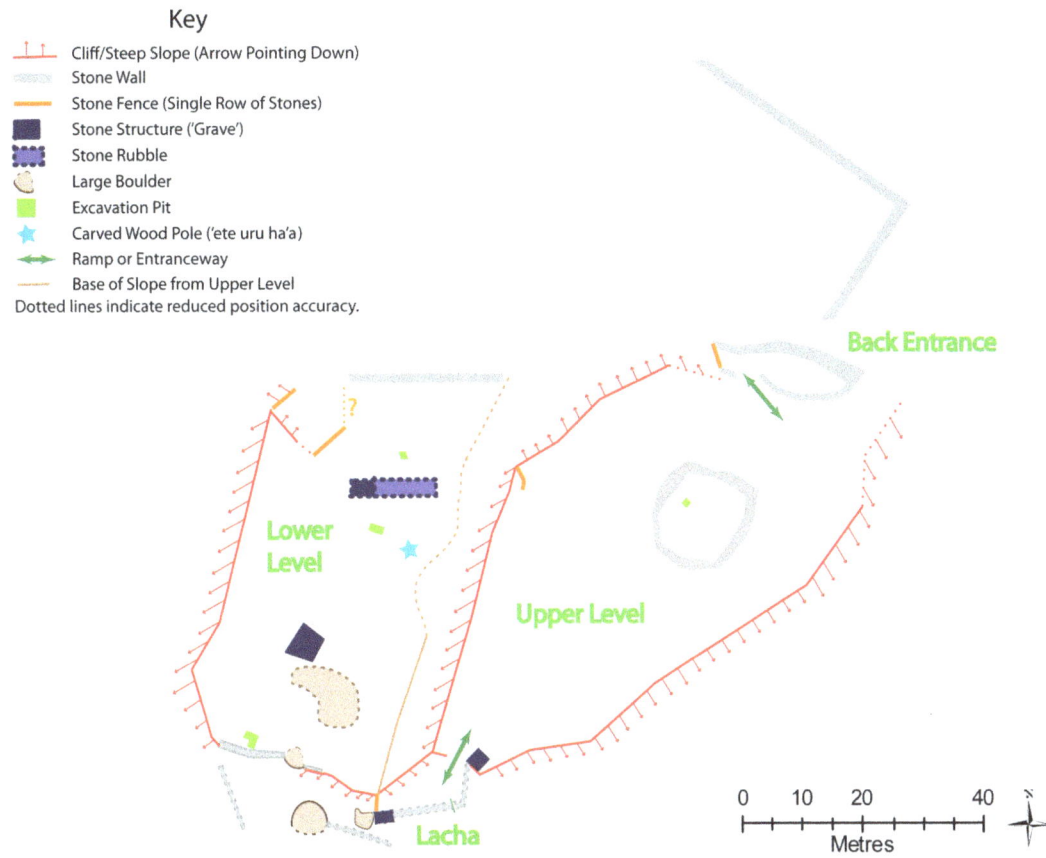

Figure 4.4. Vasino plan of fortifications and features.
Source: Jack Fenner.

Figure 4.5. Vasino carved wooden pole (*tei* or *ete uru ha'a*).
Source: Photo courtesy of Andrew McWilliam.

Vasino's two levels are joined on the south side by a stone wall-lined *laca*, an internal walled space that is said to be where visitors were greeted. A grave structure is located within the *laca* at a pinch point between natural stone cliffs about midway along the slope between the two levels. Outside the *laca*, the ground slopes gently down to the south and east.

Excavation

To identify activity areas and determine the chronology of the site, eight 1 m squares were excavated within the walled enclosure, seven on the lower level and one on the upper level (Figure 4.4). The excavations reached depths of between ~50 and 120 cm. Excavation squares were located according to a number of factors: free of trees and other vegetation that could not be cleared by machete; no associated sensitive cultural features (e.g. graves); potential depth of deposit; and, in the case of Squares E, F and G, close to and under a wall feature at the edge of the site.

Squares of 1 x 1 m were laid out and excavated in 5–20 cm spits by trowel, according to finds and conditions within each square. In situ charcoal and shell samples were taken where possible for radiocarbon dating. Bulk sediment samples were taken from each spit for potential palynological and other sediment analyses. The sediment from each spit was weighed so volumes could be calculated for comparisons between spits, and dry sieved through 3 mm mesh onto the spoil heap.

Rocks were taken from the sediment, weighed separately and discarded onto the spoil heap. Sieve contents were sorted into basic categories onsite (pottery, shell, stone artefacts, bone, charcoal, seeds). Any remaining sediment was weighed and discarded onto the spoil heap. Finds were then taken to the village of Moro, where they were washed and shell was categorised roughly into biological taxa. Cultural material was subsequently analysed in detail according to methods outlined below.

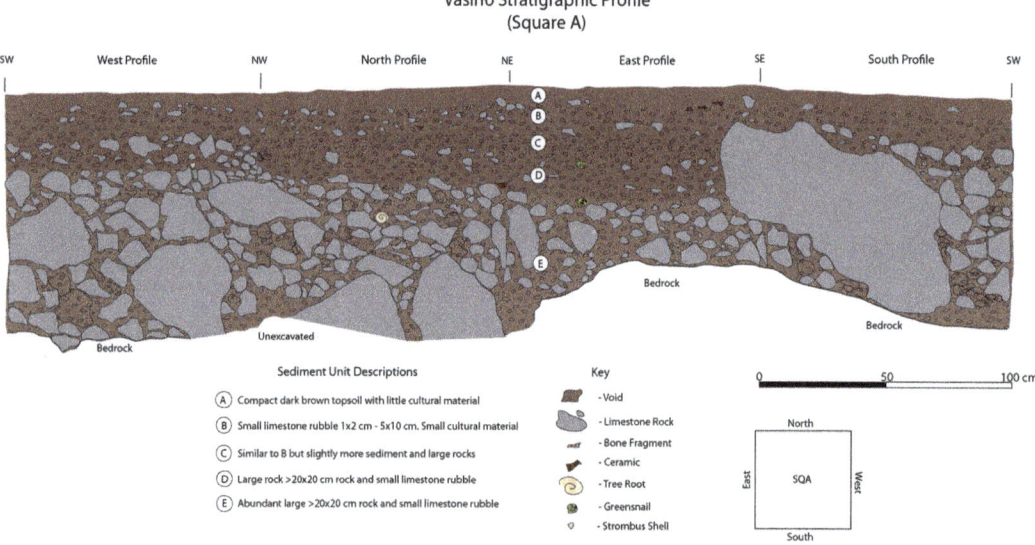

Figure 4.6. Vasino Square A section drawing.
Source: Tim Maloney.

Square A was located near a wall close to the northern end of the site in a locale clear of vegetation that appeared to have a good depth of deposit. The square reached a depth of 94 cm before bedrock or large rocks were encountered that covered the entire base (Figure 4.6). The deposits were excavated in six spits. In Spit 1, the sediment was very compact but became looser with depth and contained small stones. It contained shell, pottery, bone, stone, seeds and charcoal throughout. Some red slip and painted pottery was present. Both shell and pottery were broken into small pieces, but these became larger and increasingly dense in the middle of the deposit. In Spit 4, an undressed *batu Makassar* (12.5 x 12.5 cm) was located on the northern wall of the deposit; the sediment contained large rocks and there were not many finds. In Spit 5, the sediment was less organic and consisted mostly of small rocks. An extremely large rock, 40–50 kg, was removed from the centre of this spit. Most of the sediment in Spit 6 (80 per cent) consisted of small rocks. The cultural material decreased towards the base of the deposit where it was dominated by land snails and there was only one small piece of pottery. The large rocks removed from Spit 4 onwards resulted in large spit depths.

Square C reached a depth of 54 cm before bedrock was encountered (Figure 4.7). There were four spits. Finds included shell, pottery, bone, stone, seeds and charcoal. There were few finds in the top spit but by Spit 3, a dense concentration of pottery and bone became apparent. The base of Spit 3 was dominated by large immovable rocks on the northern and southwestern walls. Finds decreased in the last spit, which was dominated by land snails. Large rocks appeared throughout the deposit and their removal resulted in uneven spit depths.

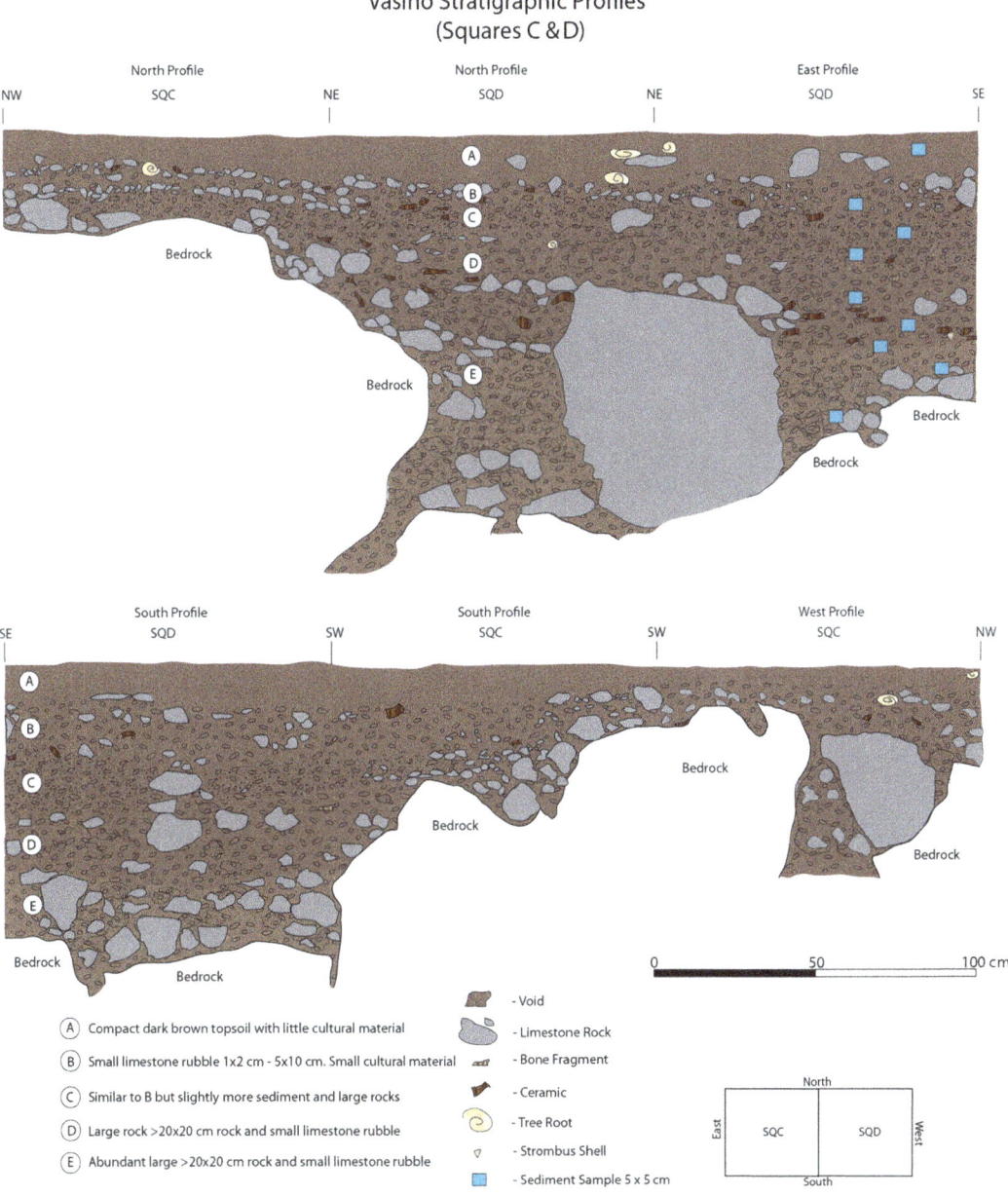

Figure 4.7. Vasino Squares C and D section drawing.
Source: Tim Maloney.

Square D was an extension of Square C and was excavated to avoid the large rocks encountered in Square C. It reached a depth of 120 cm, at which point bedrock was reached. It contained 10 spits (Figure 4.7). Finds included shell, pottery, bone, stone, seeds and charcoal. The top layer of deposit consisted of clumping, clayey sand that was dark in colour and contained little cultural material or rock. Spit 2 contained looser sediment with more small and medium rocks. The frequency of both finds and rocks increased with depth, and by Spits 3–5, large amounts of pottery, bone and marine shell were being recovered. There were more small rocks in Spits 5 and 6. There was a hearth with some charcoal in the centre of the northern wall of Spit 6. The number of small rocks in the sediment increased in Spit 7, while cultural material decreased from then onwards. By Spit 8, the sediment was much rockier though there was still marine shell present. Spit 9 marked the beginning of the land snail horizon. The removal of large rocks in Spit 10 made this a large spit. Square D was disturbed by two large potential rodent holes in the northeast corner in Spit 3, and in Spit 10 another hole appeared on the northwest wall of the trench.

Square E was located on the southern end of the site near to a fortress wall. It was 51 cm deep curtailed by a base of large rocks. There were six spits (Figure 4.8). Finds included shell, pottery, bone, stone, seeds, charcoal and a perforated disc (discussed below). Spit 1 consisted of hard compacted soil with no rocks, and there were relatively few finds and no charcoal. However, the soil of Spits 2–4 was dark and humic, and there was a dense concentration of cultural material, especially pottery and bone. Spit 3 contained more rocks, which decreased by Spit 4. In Spit 5, large immovable rocks were apparent in the corners and the centre of the trench, with much less pottery; here the land snail horizon began. Spit 6 contained mostly land snail, with few other finds.

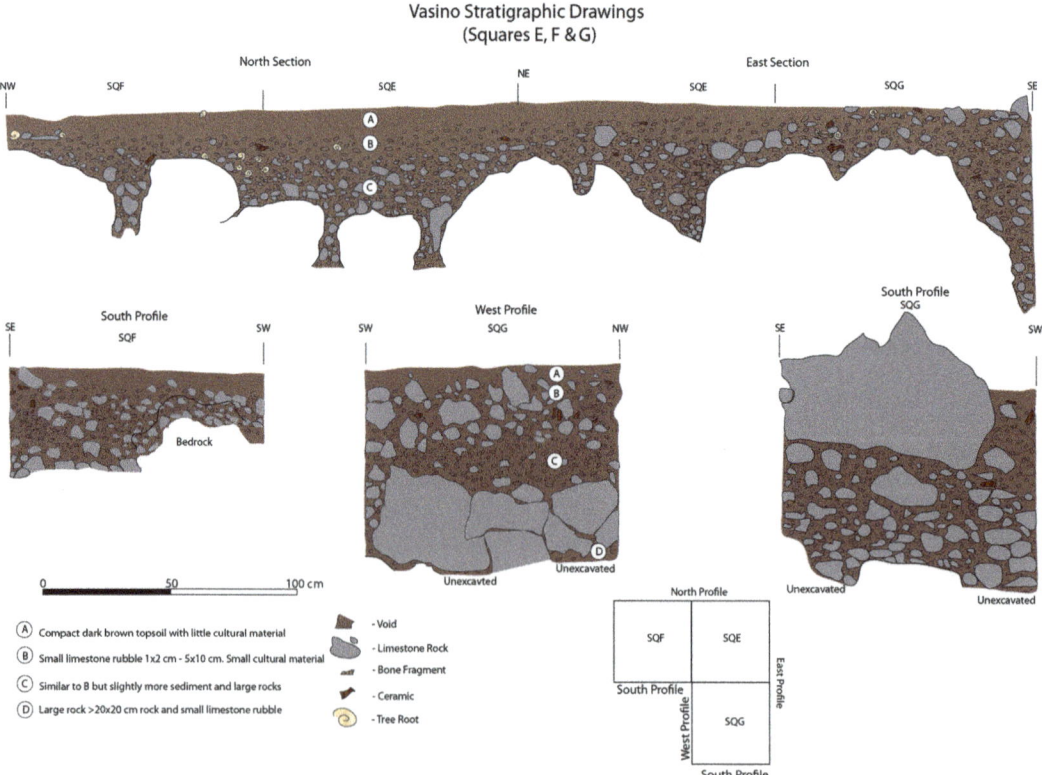

Figure 4.8. Vasino Squares E, F and G section drawing.
Source: Tim Maloney.

Square F was adjacent to the east wall of Square E. It was 38 cm deep and contained four spits (Figure 4.8). The base was rocky. Finds included shell, pottery, bone, stone, seeds and charcoal. The first spit was a hard compacted layer, disturbed by tree roots. The second spit contained many rootlets, a large rock began to appear on the western wall, much pottery was found and there was a pig's tusk and a perforated disc (discussed below). Spit 3 also contained large amounts of pottery and bone, with an increased amount of marine shell and the deposits becoming increasingly rocky on the western wall. The fourth spit was very rocky, with large amounts of pottery still apparent and an increase in the number of stone artefacts. Land snail increased towards the base where there were fewer finds.

Square G was adjacent to the south wall of Square E, immediately next to the fortress wall (Figure 4.8). It was 68 cm deep and contained seven spits. The base was covered in large rocks. Finds included shell, pottery, bone, stone, seeds and charcoal. The top spit contained many finds, including large amounts of pottery. The large number of finds continued until Spit 4, though it was increasingly rocky. In Spit 5, the number of finds decreased and large rocks dominated the western and southern walls. By Spit 6, land snail was dominant, though there was still some pottery. Spits 6 and 7 were larger and contained higher quantities of rock and land snail.

Square H was located in the upper level of Vasino (Figure 4.4). It was situated on a flat earth base in the side of a rocky hill. It was 38 cm deep and contained four spits. The base was reached at bedrock. Finds included shell, pottery, bone, stone, seeds and charcoal. Spits 1 and 2 consisted of hard compacted soil with some rocks and contained many stone artefacts, some pottery and shell. By Spit 3, bedrock dominated the western half of the square. A large hearth appeared at the top of Spit 4 and came directly down onto bedrock at the base of the spit (Figure 4.9).

Although there were differences between the squares, the general impression we gained from the excavations was that a top layer with few finds and much land snail was followed by a dense cultural layer containing shell, pottery, bone, stone, seeds and charcoal, followed by a third layer coming down onto bedrock that was again dominated by land snail.

Figure 4.9. Vasino Square H: photo of section.
Source: Photo courtesy of Sally Brockwell.

Radiocarbon and chronology

Twenty-six AMS (accelerator mass spectrometry) radiocarbon dates have been obtained for Vasino (Table 4.1, Figure 4.10). Samples for dating were not point-positioned during excavation, so all samples were derived from sieve residue. Six dates obtained from *Turbo bruneus* marine mollusc shell appear to be unreliable: their $\delta^{13}C$ values vary widely, duplicate measurements of the same shell (ANU19913 and ANU19914) produced very different radiocarbon dates, and most dates are much younger than charcoal dates from the same spits. The latter problem could be partially explained by a local marine radiocarbon offset (ΔR), but it would require a local offset of about 1000 years for the earliest dates to correspond with charcoal-based dates from the same spits. Given the nature and severity of these problems, shell radiocarbon data are not included in any of the Vasino date estimates.

Table 4.1. Vasino radiocarbon dates.

Square	Spit	Material	Lab ID	$\delta^{13}C$[1]	Radiocarbon date (RCYBP)	Calibrated range (year AD; 95% range)[2]
A	2	Charcoal	ANU12626	-27.3	510 ± 20	1420 to 1452
A	3	Charcoal	ANU12627	-27.4	590 ± 20	1327 to 1337, 1391 to 1428
A	3	Shell	ANU19909	7.0	2190 ± 35	79 to 257
A	5	Charcoal	ANU12710	-21.1	1180 ± 30	886 to 991
A	5	Shell	ANU19910	1.3	2205 ± 35	63 to 242
A	6	Charcoal	ANU12629	-25.0	670 ± 30	1299 to 1395
C	2	Charcoal	ANU12635	-26.5	410 ± 30	1454 to 1511, 1573 to 1621
C	3	Charcoal	ANU12636	-25.4	430 ± 20	1450 to 1502, 1591 to 1614
C	4	Charcoal	ANU12637	-26.8	420 ± 20	1452 to 1506, 1586 to 1618
D	1	Charcoal	ANU12638	-28.9	130 ± 20	1692 to 1727, 1806 to 1870, 1876 to 1920
D	2	Charcoal	ANU12709	-14.4	960 ± 30	1037 to 1186
D	2	Shell	ANU19911	2.7	850 ± 35	1420 to 1524
D	4	Shell	ANU19912	8.0	1275 ± 35	1048 to 1218
D	7	Charcoal	ANU12639	-28.8	200 ± 20	1662 to 1701, 1721 to 1809
D	7	Shell	ANU19913	8.4	2345 ± 35	101 BC to 86
D	7	Shell	ANU19914	-2.8	1115 ± 35	1213 to 1336
D	10	Charcoal	ANU12630	-28.5	490 ± 20	1426 to 1458
E	2	Charcoal	ANU12631	-27.2	Modern	~1974
E	6	Charcoal	ANU12631	-27.2	380 ± 20	1477 to 1627
F	2	Charcoal	ANU12633	-28.6	90 ± 20	1701 to 1722, 1810 to 1837, 1880 to 1921
F	4	Charcoal	ANU12619	-24.8	400 ± 20	1457 to 1512, 1547 to 1566, 1568 to 1622
G	1	Charcoal	ANU12620	-26.7	Modern	~1983
G	7	*Celtis* sp. nut case	ANU12625	-10.5	360 ± 30	1484 to 1638
G	7	Charcoal	ANU12621	-26.9	210 ± 20	1658 to 1693, 1727 to 1805
H	1	Charcoal	ANU12623	-25.6	320 ± 20	1508 to 1583, 1619 to 1649
H	4	Charcoal	ANU12624	-25.0	170 ± 20	1672 to 1743, 1798 to 1819, 1825 to 1893, 1922 to 1933

Notes:

1 ANU Radiocarbon Lab $\delta^{13}C$ values are not directly comparable with $\delta^{13}C$ values obtained using IRMS (isotope-ratio mass spectrometry) for stable isotope analysis.

2 Calibrated using BCal (Buck et al. 1999) and the SHCal04 calibration curve (McCormac et al. 2004).

Source: Jack Fenner.

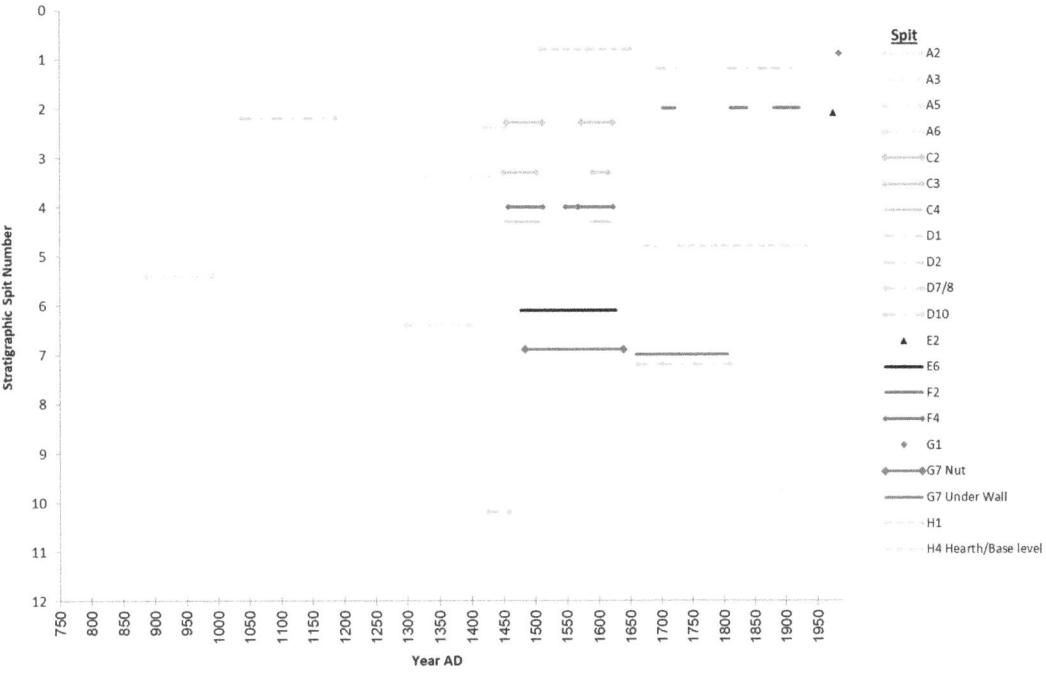

Figure 4.10. Vasino radiocarbon dates (excludes shell-based dates).
Source: Jack Fenner.

As discussed in the Excavation section, there was no visible stratigraphy at Vasino so we cannot rely on this indicator when assessing square disturbance and, in the absence of micromorphology or other forms of sediment analysis, we must use date inversions. The dates for Square D in particular indicate a large inversion in Spit 2 or 7 (Table 4.1), so Square D dates are excluded from site chronology estimations. Also, Square A Spit 5 shows a major inversion with a date that is substantially earlier than those from Spit 3 above it or Spit 6 below it; in fact, the Spit 5 date is earlier than any other date from the site. The Spit 6 date is in line with what would be expected based on the dates from Spit 2, so the problem may be related solely to the Spit 5 date. We nevertheless took the conservative approach and excluded the dates from both Spits 5 and 6 from Vasino date estimates.

The only other date inversion is between Spits 1 and 4 of Square H. This square contains lots of burnt material, which may be derived from a hearth that spanned multiple spits. Nevertheless, the Square H dates are recent enough that they are unlikely to affect overall site dating (although they are the only dates available for the upper level of the site). Except for Square D, there were no burrows or other disturbances visible during excavation, so all other dates are considered valid. Excluding the six shell dates, four dates from Square D and two dates from Square A, a total of 14 reliable dates remain. Two of these, however, are from near-surface samples that postdate AD 1950 and are therefore excluded.

Bayesian analysis of radiocarbon dates can contribute to determining the start of occupation at Vasino by providing a quantitative estimation of the probability that site occupation (as identified by radiocarbon dates) was later than a specific date. Essentially it combines the probability distributions of all calibrated radiocarbon dates and then uses this distribution to estimate the site occupation probabilities. The method is discussed elsewhere (Fenner and Bulbeck 2013); in this analysis all Bayesian estimates are performed using the BCal online Bayesian radiocarbon analysis tool (Buck et al. 1999).

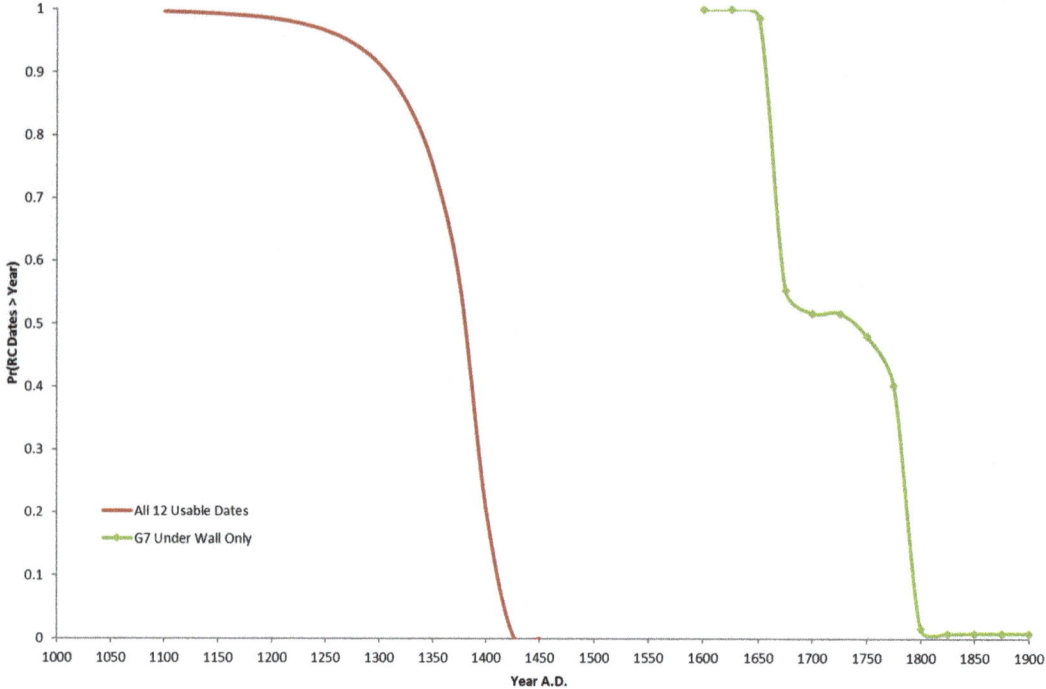

Figure 4.11. Vasino Bayesian model.
Source: Jack Fenner.

Using the Bayesian approach results in an estimate of a 91 per cent probability that Vasino dates to later than AD 1300, a 75 per cent probability that it is later than AD 1350, a 50 per cent probability that it is later than AD 1375, a 20 per cent probability that it is later than AD 1400, and a 0 per cent probability that it is later than AD 1425 (Figure 4.11). The initial site occupation thus most likely falls in the second half of the fourteenth century.

As the basal spits of the excavated squares all came down onto bedrock with decreasing amounts of cultural material and increasing quantities of land snail, it was concluded that the basal dates mark initial site occupation. However, it is important to note that this analysis is considered likely to date the start of occupation at Vasino, rather than start of fortifications. There is only one radiocarbon date directly related to the start of fortifications: ANU12621 is from charcoal obtained from under the site perimeter wall adjacent to Square G at Spit 7. This date is more than 250 years later than the initial site occupation date (Figure 4.11) and would, if used alone, indicate that fortifications started much later than previously suggested.

Post-excavation methods and results

Earthenware pottery

Just over 50 kg of earthenware pottery was recovered (Bulbeck 2011). Owing to time constraints, most of the plain pottery was recorded just for its weight, and only rim and decorated sherds were all recorded in terms of their sherd counts and detailed observations (see below). Base sherds were also recorded when they could be related to rim sherds, as well as one identified handle to a cover, but no spouts were observed. The textbook source used for general observations was Shepard (1974), and the source used for identifying firing and other manufacturing methods was Rye (1981). Shepard's textbook outlines a geometric system for classifying any vessel form, including allowance for contour complexities such as pedestals, which can then be applied to the pottery assemblage under analysis. Also owing to time constraints, illustrations and photographs of the Vasino decorated sherds were not prepared, but they are similar to their Macapainara counterparts (see Chapter 2, this volume).

Where undertaken, detailed observations included rim shape and (where possible to estimate) vessel form and approximate rim diameter, any decorations, signs of surface finish and manufacturing technique, and internal and external Munsell colours (for further explanation, see Chapter 2, this volume). This was done for all of the pottery from Spits 4 and 5 of Square A and Spits 2 to 5 of Square G, in the former case because the fabric of the pottery appeared generally different from the other spits, and in the latter case because the generally large size of the sherds made it feasible to assign a large proportion of the sherds to the original vessels from which they had come. In these latter cases, the assignment of vessel form is more secure than when it is based just on rim form, but even here the vessel form identifications are based primarily on rim characteristics. The general description of the Vasino pottery in the following paragraphs is based on the 11.96 kg (24 per cent of the assemblage) recorded in detail.

The majority of vessels were apparently formed using the paddle-and-anvil technique and finished on a slow wheel. Approximately 6 per cent of the pottery is decorated (Table 4.2), usually in the form of paddle-applied impressions, mainly faint vertical lines (2.3 kg) but also faint horizontal lines (105 g) and sharp rectangular impressions (46 g). A rare form of decoration involved the use of a reddish clay-based paint to create dots, lines and other curvilinear shapes, recorded on 88 g of the total assemblage. Other rare forms of decoration included notched corrugations (125 g), pinched and appliqué nubbins (65 g), incised, impressed and gouged lines (102 g together), wheel-thrown horizontal lines (62 g), and single examples of a punched hole, cord-marking and an appliqué medallion.

Table 4.2. Vasino earthenware pottery weights by square (g).

Square	Decorated sherd weight	Total sherd weight	Percentage decorated
A	46.6	1,444.4	3.2
C	440.5	7,310.5	6.0
D	1,500.6	20,616.2	7.3
E	115.6	6,793.9	1.7
F	96.5	5,573.5	1.7
G	707.2	7,458.6	9.5
H	13.3	1,113.5	1.2
Total	2,920.3 (88.3 g painted)	50,310.6	5.8

Source: David Bulbeck.

Based on the tightly knit and low-porous nature of the fabric, most of the assemblage appears high-fired by earthenware standards, occasionally bordering on stoneware (cf. Rye 1981). The temper of the Vasino sherds consists of foraminiferal calcareous grains, sometimes combined with a dominant element of massive terrigenous grains, or limeclast calcareous grains (occasionally mixed with foraminiferal calcareous grains). These temper additions led to the white speckling visible macroscopically on most of the Vasino (as well as Macapainara) sherds (Dickinson 2011). The external surface was usually coloured brown (6.8 kg), especially reddish brown (4.0 kg), and otherwise grey (4.7 kg), often pinkish or reddish grey (2.1 kg). Rare surface colours included dark red (325 g), usually associated with a distinctive slipped and burnished variety of ware, as well as black (122 g), recorded on some highly reduced sherds, pink (6 g), white (6 g) and reddish yellow (5 g). External surface finishing included smoothing (5.7 kg) and polishing (20 g), as well as self-slipping (256 g) and the application of a red slip (359 g), black slip (15 g) or white slip (11 g). Even the 5.6 kg of sherds that did not clearly have these surface finishing effects showed some attention to finish, in the form of external wiping marks on around 40 per cent of them.

Vessel form could be determined for 287 vessels (Table 4.3). Most or all of these vessels would be distinct vessels (comparable to the 'estimated vessel equivalents' of Orton and Tyers 1991) even if the real number of vessels represented by the assemblage may be much greater than 287. The great majority were classified as jars (91 per cent), comparable to Shepard's (1974) Fig. 21(h) structural class, based on possessing a neck and everted rim. Most of these appear to be medium-sized jars (83 per cent of vessels) with a rim diameter between 11 and 18 cm where it could be estimated (vessel height estimates unfortunately unavailable). Most of the medium-sized jars have thin rims and rounded lips, but even these show considerable variability. Other jars have thick short rims, while a very unusual variant observed on two sherds from Square D Spit 6 involves lobed rims resulting from the great variability of rim thickness and shape observable on a single sherd. A small number of jars have squarish rims (Figure 4.12). Only a small number of jars appeared to be large (7 per cent of vessels) with a rim diameter of 20 cm or more, or small jars (1 per cent of vessels) with a rim diameter up to 10 cm. One use of the medium-sized jars may have been as cooking pots, based on their similarity to the *periuk* cooking pots so commonly recorded for Indonesian pottery assemblages (Santoso 1995), although only one Vasino sherd was recorded to have carbonised traces (on an interior surface). The large jars were presumably used as storage vessels. Very few of the jars (2 per cent) appear to have been covered with lids, and only one sherd, which appears to be a cover handle, was identified.

Table 4.3. Vasino earthenware vessel forms.

Vessel form	Number recorded	Average rim diameter (cm)	Rim diameter range (cm)	Distribution in site
Cup	4	10.5	8-13	C2, E2, E4, G6
Plate	11	14.0	13-19	D3, D4, E3, F2, F3, G1, G4, H1, H3
Bowl	7	23.3	17-30	C1, D3, D4, D5, D6, E4, F2, F3
Constricted vessel	4	Not recordable	Not recordable	C2, E3, G4
Small jar	4	10	10	C4, D6, G2, G3
Medium-sized jar	235	14.9	11-18	C3, C4, D2, D3, D4, D5, D6, D7, D8, D9, E2, E3, E4, E5, F1, F2, F3, F4, G1, G2, G3, G4, G5, G6, H1, H2
Medium-sized covered jar	5	12.8	11-15	D2, D4, D5, D6
Large jar	15	22.0	20-24	A3, C1, C2, C3, C4, D2, D3, D5, D6, G3, G4
Large covered jar	1	23	23	D6
Stove	1	Not recordable	Not recordable	D6

Source: David Bulbeck.

Apparent serving vessels were classified as cups (1 per cent), small vessels similar in shape to Shepard's (1974) Fig. 20(l) structural class, plates (4 per cent), comparable to Shepard's Figs 20(a) and 21(a) structural classes, and bowls (2 per cent), comparable to Shepard's Fig. 20(m) structural class. The plates, with a rim form suggestive of a shallow unrestricted vessel, may include some covers to jars, but even so the great majority of jars would have lacked covers. There were few bowls but most of these were a distinctive type of vessel with a burnished red-slipped surface and neatly finished foot (Figure 4.13). The only other identifiable vessel type with a similar surface treatment was the collection's single large covered jar, from Square D Spit 6 (Figure 4.13). The red burnished sherd selected as an example of these fine wares for petrological analysis was identified as '*Telepunu*' temper, distinguished by limeclast calcareous grains (Dickinson 2011). Finally, three vessels had rims suggestive of a constricted vessel form, and one sherd apparently from a stove, based on the lack of curvature along the rim ledge, was recorded.

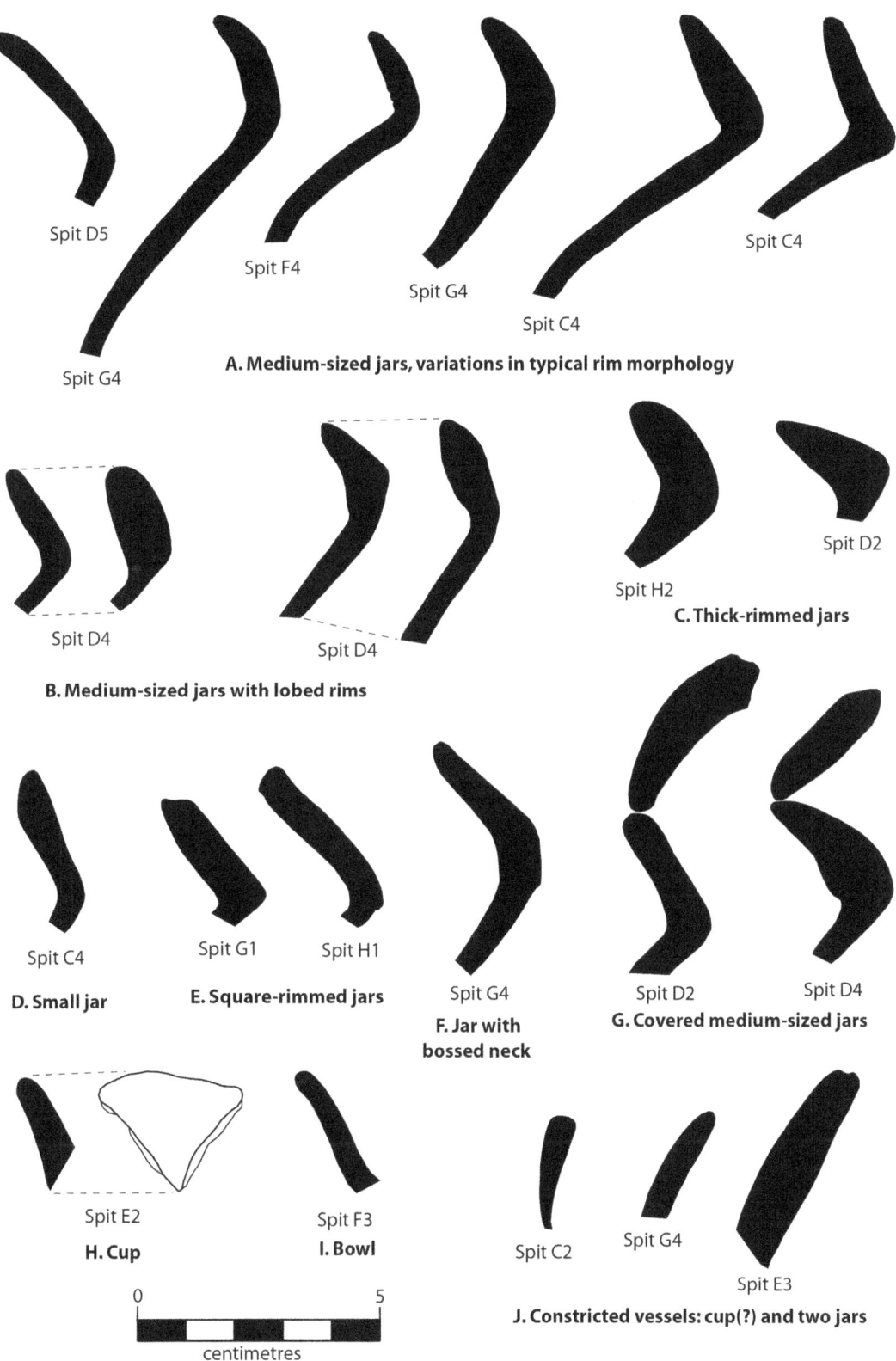

Figure 4.12. Vasino earthenware pottery rims.
Source: David Bulbeck.

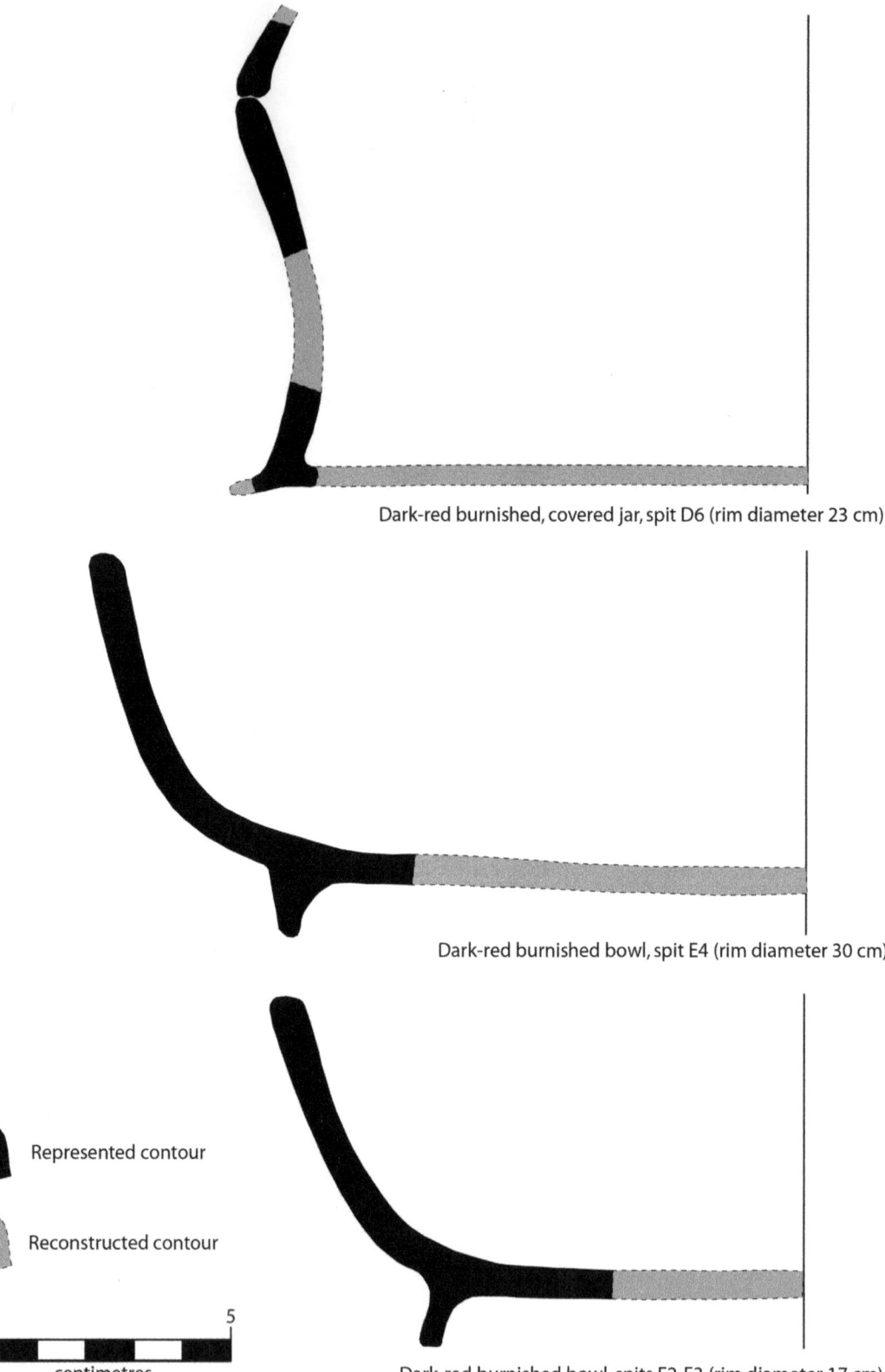

Figure 4.13. Vasino earthenware reconstructible contours.
Source: David Bulbeck.

The dark red burnished vessels, including the large covered jar and footed bowls, appear to have been manufactured on a fast wheel as indicated by regular, closely spaced wheel-throwing lines. Similar evidence of fast wheel manufacture was recorded on four sherds from medium-sized jars. The most commonly recorded manufacturing techniques were the use of a slow wheel (120 vessels) and the paddle-and-anvil technique (213 vessels), sometimes on the same vessel. Where vessel form could be determined, it was most frequently a medium-sized jar, as expected given the predominance of this vessel form in the collection. Evidence of coil-building was not observed and evidence for hand modelling as the only forming technique was recorded for just a cup, a plate, the stove and eight of the medium-sized jars. The typical production procedure for the Vasino vessels therefore probably involved shaping the jar with a paddle applied externally (often leaving vertical impressions) and an anvil held inside the wall, and the neck and rim finished on a slow wheel.

No wasters were recorded to indicate pottery manufacture at Vasino itself. Blistered surfaces suggestive of overfiring were recorded on only 88 g of the nearly 12 kg of Vasino sherds recorded in detail. The sherds appeared to be fully oxidised for 4.2 kg of the recorded total, although surface clouds and smudges from firing were recorded on a further 3.9 kg of the assemblage, and evidence of internally reduced walls included dark cores on a further 947 g of the assemblage. Internally or externally reduced surfaces, occurring together or in combination with a reduced internal wall, were recorded for 2.9 kg of the assemblage, including 327 g where the sherd was reduced entirely. The above observations in most cases would reflect firing conditions for the vessels during their manufacture, although in some cases post-manufacture exposure to heat (such as an open fire) may have left surface clouds or an apparently reduced surface.

Imported tradewares

Tradewares are high-fired ceramics, often with patterns, that have been imported from Mainland Asia, starting around the tenth century, usually of Chinese origin (Habu et al. 2017: 154). They are of much finer quality than earthenware. Only three tradeware sherds were recovered from Vasino. These were examined to identify possible manufacture locations according to categories presented in the literature on trade ceramics in the region (Bulbeck 2012; Frasché 1976; Guy 1986; Harrisson 1995; Li 2010).

One sherd weighing 1.13 g has been identified from Square C Spit 2. Externally it has a glossy black glaze (Munsell 5YR 2/1) and has a very dark grey body and internal surface (N 3/-). The body is a stoneware harder than quartz with small, sparse inclusions that include dark and (rarer) light-coloured specks. It is decorated with a vertically aligned mat impression. With its lack of a curved surface and thickness of merely 4.8 mm, the sherd is likely to be from a box. It may be from a Qing black monochrome, in view of the achievements of Chinese potters in producing 'mirror black' wares with a tinge of red in the glaze during the late seventeenth and early eighteenth centuries (Li 2010).

Two tradeware sherds, almost certainly from the same vessel, were recovered from Square F Spit 1. Together they weigh 6.38 g, and probably come from near the base of a martavan, a large pottery jar used especially for domestic storage of water or food (Merriam-Webster 2018). Externally the rough, unglazed surface is very dark greyish brown (10YR 3/2) and internally there is a smooth and sheeny, dark brown glaze (7.5YR 3/2). The body, which is a stoneware softer than iron, is black (10YR 2/1). Sharp-edged white grains (perhaps quartz) dominate the inclusions, along with occasional gleaming black specks. The best match is the Brittleware that is particularly a feature of the ceramics from the sixteenth century Brunei capital of Kota Baru (Harrisson 1990). However, this specimen may date to a later time.

Stone artefacts

The aim of the lithics analysis was to describe the morphology of flakes, cores and debris and examine flaking strategies and investigate why flaked lithic material occurs in the Vasino fort site—a post-tradeware context. A central aim of this analysis was to test the model that flaked lithic artefacts were associated with strike-a-light activities, where siliceous stone flakes are marginally retouched, usually with metal implements, for the sole purpose of creating sparks for fire lighting (e.g. Glover and Ellen 1975:52–53). Flaked lithic artefacts used as strike-a-lights have been observed elsewhere in the region from similar archaeological contexts, after regional trade networks were importing metal goods (Brumm 2006; Bulbeck and Caldwell 2000:23, 32; Glover 1986:202; Glover and Ellen 1975; Lape et al. this volume; Scheans et al. 1970:180; Skertchly 1890:450, 451).

Analysis of stone artefacts at Vasino followed the methods outlined in Maloney (2011). In order to ensure accurate identification of flaked lithic artefacts, in an archaeological assemblage of post-tradeware and metal goods where lithic artefacts were superficially unexpected, diagnostic attributes that recognise controlled human blows were recorded. This methodology was applied to lithic assemblages from the Aru Islands by Hiscock (2007:211), where attributes were recorded that evidenced culturally modified lithic materials as anomalous in their reconstructed geomorphic context (Bryan and Schnurrenberger 1985:139). A set of nominal variables were employed following Hiscock (2007:211). Variables included the presence of a striking platform, bulb of percussion, negative flake scars, external initiation and flake termination; in combination, these support artefact identification. To identify strike-a-light technology, a set of variables outlined in O'Connor et al. (Chapter 2, this volume) were followed, based on observations of this practice throughout Island Southeast Asia (Brumm 2006; Glover 1986:202; Glover and Ellen 1975; Scheans et al. 1970:180; Skertchly 1890:450, 451). Variables include marginal concentrations of step fractures, crushing or cascading, bifacial battering, dense striations and typically minimal retouch before discard (Andrefsky 2009:196; Brumm 2006:169–170; Glover and Ellen 1975).

The stone artefact assemblage from Vasino is small (Table 4.4) and sparsely distributed throughout the deposit. A total of 74 flaked stone artefacts were recovered, including flakes, flaked pieces, retouched flakes and cores (Table 4.5). An additional four manuport sedimentary pebbles, exotic to the geomorphic context but without any modification, were recovered, as well as one small ground limestone piece.

Table 4.4. Vasino stone artefact assemblage.

Spit	A	C	D	E	F	G	H	Total
1	1	5	1	1	0	5	16	29
2	2	2	2	1	0	3	11	21
3	0	0	4	0	3	0	9	16
4	0	1	3	1	1	0	0	6
5	0	-	0	0	-	0	-	0
6	1	-	2	1	-	1	-	5
7	-	-	2	-	-	0	-	2
8	-	-	0	-	-	-	-	0
9	-	-	1	-	-	-	-	1
10	-	-	0	-	-	-	-	0
Total	4	8	15	4	4	9	36	80

Note: A dash indicates that the spit level was not excavated. Spits are not stratigraphically aligned (i.e. Spit A1 may be a different stratigraphic level than C1).

Source: Tim Maloney.

Table 4.5. Vasino stone artefact types.

Class	Count	Assemblage percentage
Flake (× 10 mm)	19	24
Flake (< 10 mm)	4	5
Flaked piece	22	28
Retouched flake	12	15
Flake broken	7	9
Manuport (pebble)	4	5
Core single platform	3	4
Core multiple platform	2	3
Broken retouched flake	2	3
Core bidirectional	1	1
Primary flake	1	1
Debitage flake	1	1
Ground surface	1	1
Total	79	100

Source: Tim Maloney.

Chert is the dominant raw material (90 per cent) and was reduced from small rounded nodules or cobbles with rounded and porous cortex. Chert nodules and cobbles are found close to Vasino. This material appears similar to those varieties described by Glover and Ellen (1975:55) and Glover (1986), used in strike-a-light industries, although, in contrast, flakes in the Vasino assemblage retained a higher frequency of cortex (N = 33).

Fifty-five artefacts (~70 per cent) displayed edge modification consistent with strike-a-light use-wear (Table 4.6). These flakes are typically lightly retouched, with bifacial battering on isolated sections of the margins, and small step terminating scars with striations emerging from them (N = 21).

Table 4.6. Vasino modification characteristics counts.

Modification characteristic	Edge modification scars	Bifacial battering	Step fracture concentration	Crushing concentration	Striations parallel	Striations non-parallel
Count	55	34	47	24	18	21
Percentage of assemblage	69.6	43.0	59.5	30.4	22.8	26.6
Percentage of modified flakes	98.2	60.7	50.9	21.8	32.1	37.5

Source: Tim Maloney.

This form of modification resembles existing descriptions of strike-a-light tools (see Chapter 2, this volume), where siliceous stone flakes were marginally retouched with metal implements to produce sparks for fire ignition (Brumm 2006; Glover 1986:202; Glover and Ellen 1975:52–53; Scheans et al. 1970:180; Skertchly 1890:450, 451). From these observations we can expect marginal concentrations of step fractures, crushing or cascading, bifacial battering and dense striations to be a reasonable indicator of strike-a-light functions and use-wear (Andrefsky 2009:196; Brumm 2006:169–170; Glover and Ellen 1975). Results demonstrate that such characteristic variables occur on the majority of flakes in the assemblage (Table 4.6), with bifacial battering and step fracture concentrations being most prevalent.

The perforated discs

Two ambiguous perforated discs were recovered, most likely either beads or spindle whorls. Disc 1 was excavated from Spit 2 in Square F, at a depth of 8 cm where it was found in association with large quantities of pottery. Disc 2 was excavated from Spit 3 in Square E at a depth of 20 cm along with large numbers of similar finds.

The material composition of both discs was tested with 10 per cent hydrochloric acid (HCl). The reaction indicated that both artefacts were made from limestone. A further attribute analysis was conducted to establish function. As Table 4.7 indicates, Disc 1 measured 29 mm in diameter and was 5 mm in height. It weighed 2.8 g. As it was less than half of its original size, its original weight was estimated to have been 5.9 g. It was discoid in shape with raised sections on the upper surface around the central perforation. No use-wear marks were discernible on the central perforation. Disc 2 was also discoid in shape. It measured 21 mm in diameter and 10 mm in height. Its central perforation measured 2 mm. It weighed 2.2 g. Because it was broken and essentially half of its original size, its original weight was estimated to have been about 4.5 g. No use-wear marks were discernible on the central perforation. Disc 2 was far more weathered than Disc 1.

Table 4.7. Vasino functional attributes of perforated discs.

Item	Context	Material composition	Diameter (mm)	Central perforation (mm)	Height (mm)	Weight (g)	Shape	Comments
1	F2	limestone	21	2	10	2.2	discoid	broken 1/2
2	E1	limestone	29	8	5	2.8	discoid	broken <1/2

Source: Judith Cameron.

Both discs from Vasino were made from limestone. The material composition of artefacts is frequently indicative of function. Tools, for example, are usually made from more durable, common materials than ornaments, but some materials are ambiguous and in such cases identification is more complicated. Although stone is commonly used for beads, research into Southeast Asian spindle whorls indicates that, while pottery is the predominant material used for spindle whorls in the Southeast Asian archaeological record, stone spindle whorls have also been found in the region (Cameron 2013). However, the stone whorls that have been excavated from Neolithic sequences are much larger in size and heavier, being made to spin coarse, strong fibres. In terms of size, the Vasino discs lie just within the range of spindle whorls but they are also within the range of beads. The shape of the discs is more diagnostic. In India, for example, stone has been chosen for beads since the prehistoric period onwards, especially beads of the same shape as Disc 1. The size of central perforations is a more critical attribute. While the central perforation of Disc 2 lies within the range of spindle whorls, the central perforation of Disc 1 is far too narrow to take a spindle, the other component of the hand spindle. When these functional attributes are considered, with the absence of use-wear, the weight of evidence suggests that it is more likely that the discs from Vasino are beads rather than spinning tools.

Vertebrate faunal remains

This section is based on the full and detailed report of the Vasino vertebrate analysis by Amano and Piper (2011). A total of 3023 bone fragments were recovered from Vasino during the 2009 excavation. Of these, 1495 (49.5 per cent) were from Square D, 490 (16.2 per cent) from Square C, 377 (12.5 per cent) from Square G, 262 (8.7 per cent) from Square F, 212 (7 per cent) from Square E, 94 (3.1 per cent) from Square A, and 93 (3 per cent) were from Square H (Figure 4.14). No vertebrate remains were recovered from Square B. The bones tended to be slightly concentrated in Spits 3 and 4, especially in Square C, D and E, and in the subsurface layers in Squares F, G and H. Differential weathering of some skeletal elements, especially in Squares C and D, suggests they have been subjected to little, if any, post-depositional reworking since their burial.

All vertebrate remains collected from the 2009 excavations of Vasino were examined in this study. The maximum lengths of all fragments greater than 5 mm were measured, unless they showed evidence of modern breakage, to identify any spatial and temporal variability in fragment size that might provide information on taphonomic process. Taphonomic terminology follows Piper (2003), modified from Lyman (1994). Important taphonomic and anthropogenic alterations, including weathering, burning, dog gnawing and butchery marks were recorded, and the location and orientation of human-derived bone modifications (e.g. cut and chop marks) were recorded in detail.

Distinctive vertebrate elements were identified to family, genus or species using the modern comparative reference collection and digital database housed at the Archaeological Studies Program, University of the Philippines. The criteria used for the biometric analyses of post-cranial elements follow von den Dreisch (1976). Whenever applicable, alternative measurements from diagnostic anatomical locales were used. Features that might indicate defects, for instance bone regrowth/pathologies, were also recorded. All teeth, bones with key taphonomic and anthropic modifications and other selective elements were photographed and stored in the university digital archive using a Nikon Coolpix Digital camera. Micrographs (microscopy images) were also taken and archived using the same camera mounted on a Nikon C-LEDS stereomicroscope.

For caprine and suid teeth, a standard measurement for the length of the tooth was taken, and the width of each molar column measured. All measurements were taken at, or as close to, the base of the enamel as possible. Since goat and pig teeth change shape as they wear, this location provides a point of reference where the analyst can be confident that all measurements of archaeological and comparative specimens will be comparable. To compensate for inter-analyst preferences, the lengths of the pig M1s and M2s were also measured at the occlusal surface (Piper and Amano 2011: Tables 5 and 6) so that they can be compared irrespective of which measurement has been used by other specialists. Pig ageing from molar eruption and post-cranial fusion follows Bull and Payne (1982), and molar wear scales are based on those presented by Grant (1982).

Table 4.8. Vasino number of individual specimens (NISP) of vertebrate taxa recovered.

Class	Order	Family	Taxon	Common name	NISP
Teleostei (Infraclass)				Bony fish	11
	Perciformes	Serranidae	Serranidae	Grouper	1
Reptilia	Squamata	Serpentes (Suborder)	Serpentes	Snake	1
	Testudines	Chelonioidea	Chelonioidea	Sea turtle	1
Mammalia	Primates	Cercopithecidae	*Macaca fascicularis*	Long-tailed macaque	4
	Carnivora	Canidae	*Canis familiaris*	Domestic dog	8
	Artiodactyla	Suidae	*Sus* sp(p). (domestic)	Domestic pig	94
		Bovidae	*Capra aegagrus hircus*	Domestic goat	87
		Bovidae	Bovinae (Subfamily)	Cattle/buffalo	65
		Cervidae	*Rusa* cf. *timorensis*	Sunda sambar	5

Source: Noel Amano and Philip Piper.

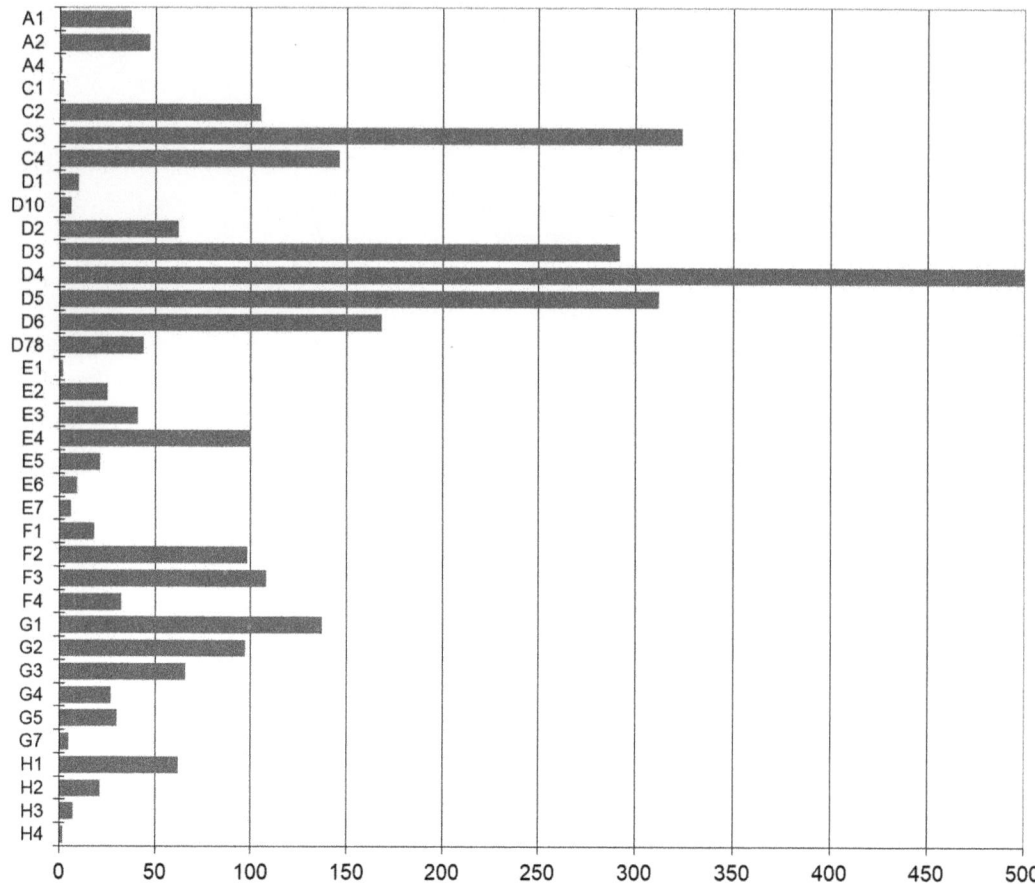

Figure 4.14. Vasino distribution of vertebrate remains Squares A–H (NISP).
Source: Noel Amano Jr and Philip Piper.

The identification of the bone assemblage was severely limited by its fragmentary nature, and of the 2980 bones recovered, just 277 (9.3 per cent) bone fragments could be identified to family or a higher taxonomic level (Table 4.8).

Mammals account for 94.9 per cent (N = 263) of all the identified vertebrate remains, with a few fish (N = 12; 0.4 per cent) and reptile (N = 2; 0.07 per cent) bones also recovered. More than 77 per cent of the identified remains were recovered from Squares C and D. The mammal remains in Vasino were dominated by pig, goat and large bovine, cattle or buffalo. No differences in the frequencies of the three major taxa could be discerned through time at Vasino.

Human teeth were recorded from Square G, including two incisors from Spit 2, and an upper molar from Spit 4.

In total, five fragments of deer were recorded throughout the archaeological sequences, all from the D Square, the lowest at Spit 5. The remains are most likely to be from the Javan Rusa (*Rusa timorensis*), which is the only deer species introduced to Timor.

It was not possible to distinguish whether the 65 fragmentary bovine remains represented in the archaeological record belonged to either the genus *Bos* or *Bubalus*. The significance of this is discussed below. The majority of these remains were teeth (32.3 per cent), followed by ribs (18.5 per cent) and vertebral fragments (12.3 per cent). Ageing data are scarce for bovines, but the evidence from teeth and post-cranial remains suggests that they were probably from relatively young individuals of less than 28–32 months of age (Silver 1970).

In total, 94 fragments of pig (*Sus* sp(p).) were recovered, the majority of which consisted of loose teeth. The results indicate that majority of the specimens (mandibular or maxillary) recovered did not exceed 18–22 months of age at death, with most probably slaughtered within the first 12–18 months of life (Bull and Payne 1982; Habermehl 1975). The age profile established from the dentition is supported by a number of unfused post-cranial elements recovered.

Eighty-seven fragments of caprine bone were recovered from Vasino from the topsoil (G1) to the lowest levels in Square D Spit 6. Although the remains of sheep and goats are difficult to distinguish in the archaeological record, the domestic goat (*Capra aegagrus hircus*) is the only taxon to be introduced into Island Southeast Asia (discussed below) until very recently (Fenner et al. 2017), and all the caprine remains from Vasino are considered to come from this taxon. Teeth were the most common goat remains recovered (37.9 per cent considering complete elements and 57.5 per cent including fragments).

Hillson (2005) noted that there is considerable variation in the eruption timing of the teeth of different domestic goat breeds, but the moderately to heavily worn nature of the M1s and M2s, and worn M3s, in the Vasino collection would suggest that several individuals probably exceeded 24 months in age at death (Moran and O'Connor 1994). Records of at least two dp4s and lightly worn M1s indicates the additional presence of some subadult individuals. Overall, the dental analysis of the Vasino caprine assemblage suggests goats from a relatively young age to quite old were being slaughtered on the site. The predominantly fused postcranial elements support the age profile derived from the dentition and indicate that the majority of goats were probably kept for at least two years before they were slaughtered.

It is not possible to distinguish with any absolute certainty in the Vasino assemblage whether the pig species represented is the domestic Eurasian wild boar (*Sus scrofa*) or the Sulawesi warty pig (*Sus celebensis*), a translocated wild species present on Timor (i.e. Clason 1986), or a hybrid of both. However, comparisons of tooth measurements with *Sus scrofa* specimens from Mainland Asia suggest that the specimens from Vasino show considerable size diminution over their wild progenitors. The measurements are also significantly smaller compared to those from *Sus celebensis*. The predominance of juvenile and subadult pigs in combination with size reduction is a good indication that the pigs from Vasino represent a managed, domestic population.

A total of eight dog bones from at least two individuals (based on two right mandibular M3s) were recorded.

Reptiles were represented by just two bone fragments: a single sea turtle phalanx recovered from Square G Spit 3, and a snake vertebra recorded in Square E Spit 2.

Twelve fish bones were recorded. The elements included several cranial fragments and a few vertebra and spines. Only one element was identified to the family level, a left maxillary fragment from a grouper (Serranidae) in Square D Spit 6.

Invertebrate faunal remains

Shells and shell fragments were identified to the lowest possible taxonomic level, using the Archaeology and Natural History (ANU) reference collection, in conjunction with a range of literary sources, including Cernohorsky (1972, 1978) and Hinton (1972). An attempt at identification was made for every shell fragment and no suppositions of 'edibility' of species were imposed during analysis (following Szabó 2009:186). In order to avoid inaccuracy, the dominant species within each sample was not assumed where a shell fragment only possessed the morphology definitive for genus level.

The shell assemblages were quantified by weight (g), minimum number of individuals (MNI) and number of identified specimens present (NISP). MNI was calculated by the same repetitive feature throughout the Vasino assemblage; the posterior valve for chitons, apices for gastropods, and for bivalves both left and right hinges were counted, with the greater number selected for each square (following Szabó 2009:187). It should be noted that while *Turbo* sp. and *Nerita* sp. opercula were quantified during laboratory analysis, opercula counts are excluded from all aggregative calculations presented (Whitau 2011) to avoid inflating representation of the Turbidae and Neritidae families. The condition of shells and shell fragments, including evidence of artefact manufacture if any, was also noted during quantification.

Weight, MNI and NISP were all employed as each quantification method has its own inherent bias. Larger, denser molluscs, such as *Tridacna* sp., rank high on a comparative weight scale, although there are fewer individual fragments. Smaller shells of lower density, particularly *Melanoides* sp., which is a freshwater gastropod, tend to sit on the lower rungs of a comparative weight scale, even though it is the most dominant taxon in terms of both MNI and NISP. The cultural transformations that create and distort the assemblage can also create biases, particularly where the repetitive element selected for MNI counts is concerned. In the Vasino mollusc assemblage, although Trochidae was among the most dominant taxa in terms of weight and even NISP, it had very low MNI counts. This is because the apices were the repetitive element for all gastropods, and very few examples of the Trochidae family were uncovered with their spires intact. This bias is probably produced by people removing the spire of *Trochus* and *Tectus* species to extract the flesh for consumption.

The total shell weight from the Vasino assemblage was 6453.77 g. Of this, the marine shell weight was 4795.29 g and the terrestrial gastropod weight was 1658.48 g (Table 4.9). A total of 58 taxa (excluding opercula) were identified. By weight, *Turbo bruneus* and the Turbinidae were the most dominant taxon and family group, respectively. The top five species by weight were, in declining order: *Turbo bruneus*, *Hippopus hippopus*, *Clypeomorus batillariaeformis*, *Tridacna crocea* and *Cypraea* sp. (Table 4.9; Figure 4.15). The top family groups by weight, in declining order, were: Turbinidae, Cardiidae, Tegulidae, Arcidae and Neritidae. By MNI and NISP counts, *Melanoides* sp. and Thiaridae were the most dominant taxon and family group respectively. The total MNI was 1159 (Table 4.10). The top five taxa by MNI count were, in declining order: *Melanoides* sp., *Clypeomorus batillariaeformis*, *Turbo bruneus*, *Nerita albicilla* and *Cypraea* sp. (see Table 4.10; Figure 4.15). The top five family groups by MNI count were, in declining order: Thiaridae, Potamididae, Turbinidae, Neritidae and Arcidae. The total NISP was 2329. The top five taxa by NISP count were, in declining order: *Melanoides* sp., *Turbo bruneus*, *Chiton* sp., *Clypeomorus batillariaeformis* and *Pollia fumosa*. The top five family groups by NISP count were, in declining order: Thiaridae, Turbinidae, Tegulidae, Potamididae and Chitonidae. However, the dominance of *Melanoides* sp. in Square H means that it is over-represented in the Vasino excavations as a whole. If Square H is excluded, *Turbo bruneus* and *Clypeomorus batillariaeformis* become the dominant taxa by NISP.

Table 4.9. Vasino top 10 shell taxa by weight (g).

Square	Spit	Turbo bruneus	Hippopus hippopus	Clypeomorus batillariaeformis	Tridacna crocea	Cypraea sp.	Conus sp.	Nerita albicilla	Rochia nilotica	Strombus sp.	Thiaridae
A	1	26.60	2.60	-	2.20	3.22	-	-	-	-	-
A	2	2.84	2.60	-	-	1.54	-	-	-	-	-
A	3	10.08	-	18.30	3.26	-	1.70	7.68	-	-	0.88
A	4	30.81	18.95	89.50	3.14	-	5.90	54.04	-	-	1.89
A	5	7.32	-	5.16	5.83	-	-	23.82	-	-	1.25
A	6	-	-	-	-	-	-	-	-	-	0.50
C	1	19.53	-	-	-	-	-	-	-	-	-
C	2	40.13	-	5.25	1.39	10.08	0.37	-	-	-	-
C	3	62.40	-	7.13	-	4.72	14.98	-	19.07	-	-
C	4	20.36	-	8.06	-	1.25	11.41	-	-	-	-
D	1	-	-	-	6.98	-	1.66	-	-	-	-
D	2	32.25	-	8.22	-	2.20	0.70	-	-	-	-
D	3	40.00	-	13.40	13.81	3.02	17.80	-	-	-	-
D	4	110.90	-	11.97	0.80	3.91	-	-	1.58	3.83	-
D	5	73.73	-	-	-	13.05	2.10	-	16.45	68.47	-
D	6	36.22	41.79	25.13	44.44	5.10	13.11	5.01	5.24	19.65	-
D	7	4.40	51.43	-	-	0.20	-	-	-	1.35	-
D	8	-	-	2.84	-	6.46	-	2.17	-	-	-
D	9	-	-	1.50	-	-	-	0.80	-	-	0.58
E	1	2.12	-	-	-	-	2.49	-	-	-	-
E	2	8.38	-	-	0.88	7.78	12.50	-	-	-	-
E	3	6.52	-	-	-	-	30.05	2.09	-	-	-
E	4	15.99	-	-	-	6.13	-	1.92	-	2.92	0.35
E	5	-	-	-	-	0.85	-	7.53	-	-	1.24
E	6	-	-	-	-	-	-	2.91	-	-	1.75
E	7	25.80	2.60	-	0.20	3.22	-	-	-	-	-
F	1	-	-	-	-	-	-	-	-	-	-
F	2	24.87	7.94	-	-	4.47	-	-	-	18.61	
F	3	32.57	-	-	-	20.69	-	-	-	7.14	0.96
F	4	2.07	-	2.83	-	-	-	-	-	-	0.25
G	1	9.93	-	-	-	16.72	13.12	-	19.70	-	-
G	2	49.77	-	-	9.96	22.90	1.61	-	-	-	1.58
G	3	20.08	43.44	-	28.94	24.95	1.57	-	-	-	-
G	4	18.39	23.32	-	-	6.51	4.36	-	-	-	-
G	5	19.96	-	-	-	-	-	7.96	-	-	-
G	6	-	-	-	-	-	-	31.68	-	-	7.50
G	7	-	-	-	-	-	-	-	-	-	3.12
H	1	13.70	8.99	-	3.36	2.14	-	6.60	-	-	23.90
H	2	25.57	5.50	-	35.83	2.86	18.22	3.80	13.76	-	34.40
H	3	27.74	79.62	1.00	24.10	5.43	22.98	12.79	64.10	6.87	34.22
H	4	2.92	-	-	-	-	-	-	-	-	9.65
Total		823.95	288.78	200.29	185.12	179.40	176.63	170.80	139.90	128.84	124.02

Source: Mirani Litster.

Table 4.10. Vasino top 10 shell taxa by MNI.

Square	Spit	Thiaridae	Clypeomorus batillariaeformis	Turbo bruneus	Nerita albicilla	Cypraea sp.	Pollia fumosa	Barbatia obliquata	Chiton sp.	Nerita plicata	Nerita polita	Conus sp.	Anadara antiquata
A	1	-	-	5	-	<1	6	-	-	-	-	-	1
A	2	-	-	1	-	<1	<1	1	<1	-	-	-	<1
A	3	2	15	2	3	-	2	-	<1	-	-	1	-
A	4	7	75	8	21	-	<1	-	<1	3	6	1	-
A	5	3	4	<1	7	-	-	-	<1	-	1	-	-
A	6	1	-	-	-	-	-	-	-	-	-	-	-
C	1	-	-	2	-	-	-	-	-	-	-	-	-
C	2	-	4	6	-	2	1	<1	1	-	-	<1	<1
C	3	-	5	11	-	<1	<1	1	-	-	1	<1	<1
C	4	-	5	2	-	1	<1	2	-	-	-	<1	1
D	1	-	-	-	-	-	-	-	-	-	-	<1	-
D	2	-	5	4	-	1	1	-	-	-	-	<1	-
D	3	-	7	7	-	2	2	1	1	-	<1	1	1
D	4	-	10	15	-	3	3	3	1	-	1	-	1
D	5	-	-	9	-	3	1	3	-	1	1	2	2
D	6	-	18	2	2	<1	1	4	-	3	1	2	1
D	7	-	-	1	-	<1	-	1	-	-	-	-	-
D	8	-	2	-	1	1	-	1	-	-	-	-	-
D	9	1	1	-	1	-	-	-	-	1	1	-	1
E	1	-	-	1	-	-	<1	-	-	-	-	<1	-
E	2	-	-	1	-	1	-	2	<1	-	-	<1	1
E	3	-	-	1	1	-	-	2	-	-	-	1	-
E	4	1	-	1	1	3	<1	1	<1	-	-	-	1
E	5	3	-	-	3	<1	1	-	-	-	-	-	-
E	6	2	-	-	1	-	-	-	<1	-	-	-	-
E	7	-	-	5	-	1	8	-	-	-	-	-	1
F	1	-	-	-	-	-	-	<1	-	-	-	-	-
F	2	-	-	4	-	1	1	1	-	-	<1	-	<1
F	3	4	-	4	-	5	1	1	<1	1	-	-	-
F	4	1	2	1	-	-	-	-	-	-	-	-	-
G	1	-	-	2	-	3	<1	<1	<1	-	-	1	<1
G	2	2	-	4	-	3	<1	3	-	-	-	<1	-
G	3	-	-	2	-	7	2	2	-	-	-	<1	-
G	4	-	-	1	-	2	-	<1	-	-	-	1	-
G	5	-	-	3	3	-	-	-	-	-	-	-	-
G	6	26	-	-	11	-	-	-	-	-	-	-	-
G	7	4	-	-	-	-	-	-	-	-	-	-	-
H	1	71	-	5	2	1	1	1	7	-	<1	-	-
H	2	111	-	6	1	<1	<1	1	11	2	<1	2	-
H	3	113	<1	4	4	1	<1	-	6	<1	2	1	-
H	4	24	-	1	-	-	-	-	1	<1	-	-	-
Total		376	153	121	62	41	31	31	28	11	14	13	11

Source: Mirani Litster.

As the heavy weight of some of the marine shells skewed the results, MNI was used for interpretation. The majority of identified taxa were lower intertidal species associated with rocky reef, which can be accessed 2 km north of Vasino. Two taxa (*Nerita planospira* and *Geloina* sp.) are associated with mangrove forests, one taxon (Thiaridae) with freshwater environments and seven taxa (*Patella* sp., *Nerita plicata*, *Nerita* sp., *Cerithium* sp., *Cerithidea* sp., Arcidae, Ungulinidae and *Gafrarium* sp.) with mixed habitat zones (Figure 4.16). Terrestrial gastropod counts were also included, as proportions of land snails can sometimes reflect periods of lower occupation density.

The assemblage provides little evidence for shell artefact manufacture. With the exception of heavily reduced *Nautilus* sp. fragments, there is only one convincing example of shell reduction, a *Turbo chrysostomus* shell from Square G Spit 3. This particular *T. chrysostomus* is mostly whole, with only the outer lip missing from the mouth. A hole in the shape of an irregular trapezoid has been cut from the body whorl. This irregular shape, coupled with reduction marks on the anterior surface, clearly point towards human production likely to remove the flesh, since gastropod predation, which is initiated from the posterior surface, leaves a perfectly circular hole.

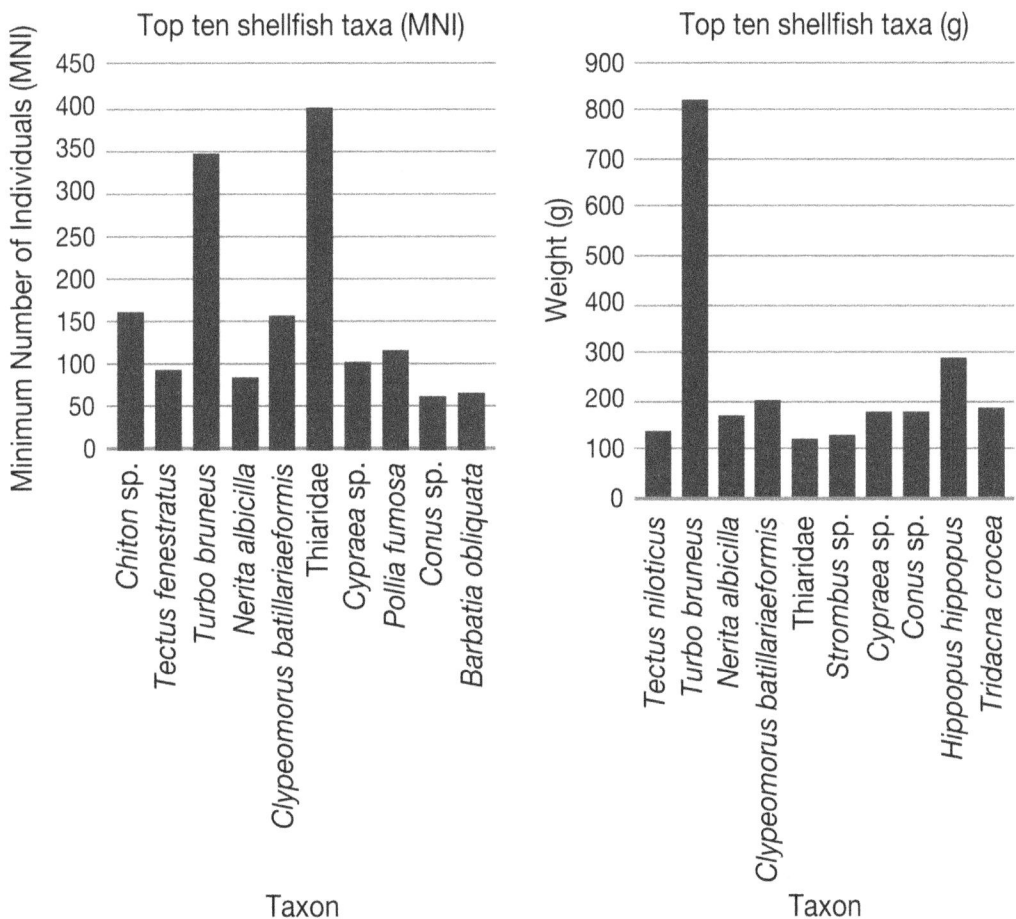

Figure 4.15. Vasino top 10 shell taxa by MNI and weight (g).
Source: CartoGIS ANU.

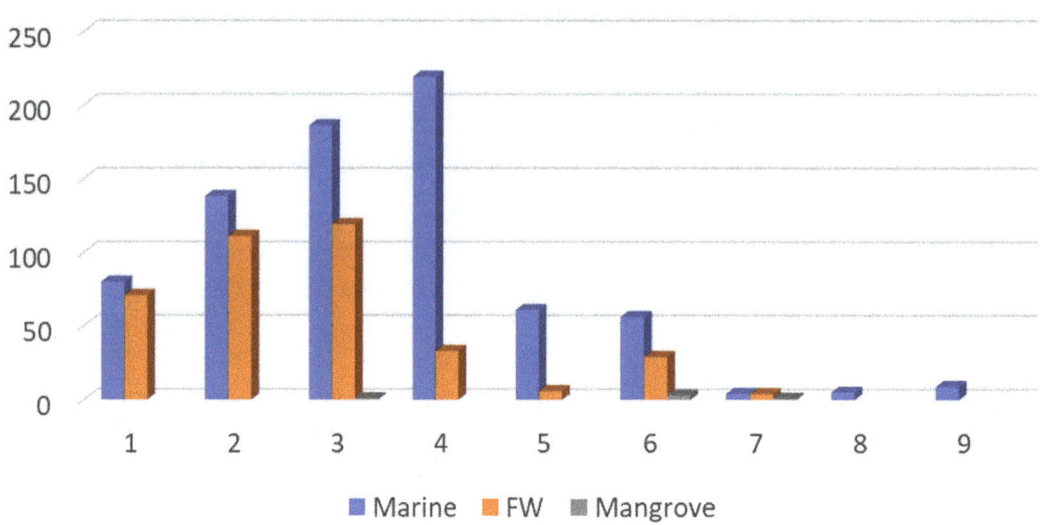

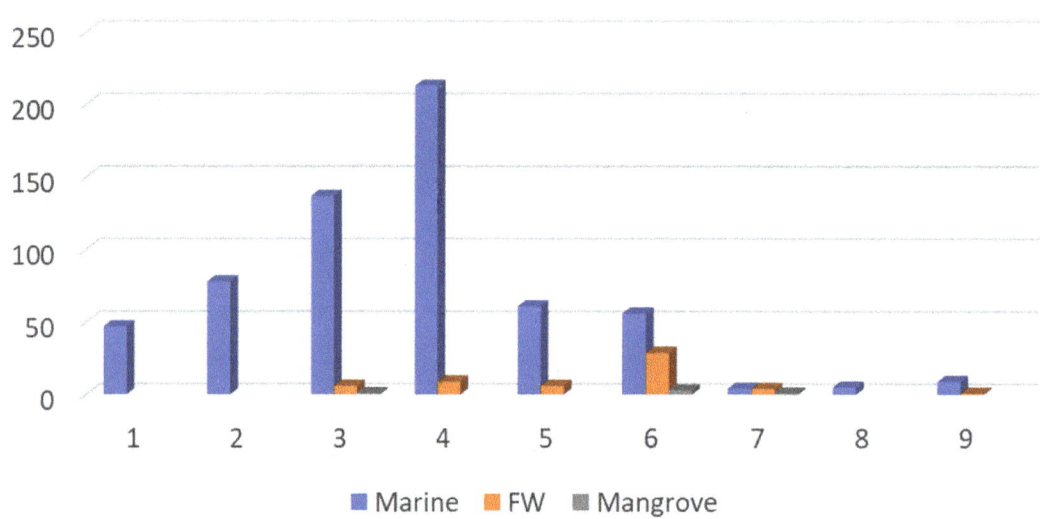

Figure 4.16. Vasino shellfish habitat by MNI (FW=Freshwater).
Source: Rose Whitau.

Discussion

The Vasino earthenware assemblage is dominated by jars with everted rims of diameter generally varying between 11 and 18 cm and rounded bodies. These earthenware vessels have a form suitable for use as cooking pots but direct evidence for such use (in the form of carbonised accretions) is minimal. Larger jars and covered jars may have been used for storage. The majority of vessels were apparently formed using the paddle-and-anvil technique and finished on a slow wheel. There is considerable variability in jar rim form, which may be related to the three separate manufacturing locales, as suggested by the three temper types identified from petrological analysis, although any matching exercise between temper type and vessel form has not been possible. Around 7 per cent of the identifiable vessels appear to have been serving vessels, including a distinctive group of dark red burnished bowls of up to 30 cm rim diameter. Around 6 per cent of the assemblage shows signs of decoration, mainly vertical paddle-impressed designs but including a small number of sherds with painted dots and curvilinear motifs. No wasters were found, therefore we conclude that all pottery has been brought into the site. Unlike the site of Macapainara at Ili Vale near the port of Com (see Chapter 2, this volume) there is minimal tradeware (and no glass or metals).

There were few formal artefact types, apart from a small quantity of strike-a-light flints. We conclude that the two limestone perforated discs are most probably beads similar to ones recorded prehistorically in India. Generally, those associated with elites are hard stone forms rather than that represented at Vasino. The softer limestone is relatively simpler to work with a small knife. There was little shell artefact manufacture, except for heavily reduced *Nautilus* sp. fragments, and only one convincing example of shell reduction, a *Turbo chrysostomus* shell.

During excavation, rodent burrows and other disturbances were recorded in Squares A and D, and along with inversions in the radiocarbon dates within different stratigraphic horizons we suggest that the spatial and temporal integrity of archaeological materials recovered from these squares has been compromised (Jack Fenner pers. comm. 2011). Analysis of the bone assemblages suggests that only minimal reworking might have occurred to the majority of the faunal remains, but the authors suggest that the chronological results presented here for the presence and absence of particular taxa within these squares should be treated with some caution. Nevertheless, the initial occurrence of the major identified taxa in Square D (pig, Bovinae and goat) is supported by their early fifteenth-century AD presence in other squares and spits, strengthening the interpretive results of this study (see below for details). It is intriguing to note that Squares C and D are located close to the most sacred places at Vasino, according to local informants: the *tei* and the graves of ancestors. The bone assemblage was certainly densest at this location and it is possible that this could have been the location of animal sacrifices in the past. Even in 2009, it was at this location that the local inhabitants chose to sacrifice animals in a ceremony to close the excavations (Jack Fenner pers. comm. 2011).

The complete absence of some wild animals, such as the northern common cuscus (*Phalanger orientalis*) and common palm civet (*Paradoxurus hermaphroditus*), and the scarcity of deer, macaque, turtle and snake suggests that hunting did not play a major role in the diet of the inhabitants of Vasino and they relied more heavily on domestic animals. This could be a result of restricted movement due to the need for security, although it is obvious that people had to leave the fort to fetch water, garden and collect shellfish.

The vertebrate faunal remains indicate that the inhabitants of Vasino primarily maintained populations of domestic pigs, goats and probably cattle throughout the fifteenth to seventeenth centuries AD, although the faunal analysis was unable to determine whether the bovine remains were of corralled domestic stock or hunted feral animals (Amano and Piper 2011:27). The present subsistence strategy of maintaining herds of pigs dominated by juveniles and subadults and herds of goats and bovines is a relatively good analogy for the economy of the inhabitants of Vasino. Sue O'Connor (pers. comm. 2011) reported that contemporary human communities in Timor-Leste maintain herds of goats up to 50 individuals that range freely during the day under the watchful eye of a shepherd and are penned at night. Individual households possess perhaps one or two sows and several individuals, ranging from piglets to young adults. Large herds of cattle and buffaloes are also seen and these are often owned by the community. This description fits relatively well with the zooarchaeological evidence and suggests these systems of animal management are perhaps of some antiquity.

Cattle or buffaloes are recorded throughout the archaeological sequence at Vasino. Glover (1986) placed the introduction of Bovinae to Timor at around 1500 BP, but this is very uncertain and concrete evidence for the remains of introduced cattle across Island Southeast Asia is rare.

Van den Bergh et al. (2009) report that diagnostic remains of cattle (presumably *Bos* or *Bubalus*) were only recovered from the upper 50 cm of deposit at Liang Bua cave on Flores and correspond to dates within the last 500 years. They argued that Bovinae were probably introduced by the Portuguese to Flores. The new records from Vasino indicate that cattle were also present in Timor by the fourteenth or fifteenth century AD. The dates, the complete absence of glass and the almost complete absence of tradeware from Vasino also suggest that the introduction of cattle to Timor likely predates European contact. It was not possible to build up a confident age profile for the Bovinae from Vasino and it is therefore not possible to determine whether the remains are those of corralled domestic stock or hunted feral animals (Amano and Piper 2011:27). However historic accounts mention the dependence of Timorese on water buffaloes as work animals, particularly for rice agriculture (cf. Dampier 1703). There are also historical records of feral buffalo being hunted on Timor. For example, William Dampier (1703: 170), who visited the north coast of Timor in 1699, noted: 'Their plantations are very mean; for they delight most in hunting; and here wild buffaloes and hogs enough, though very shy, because of their so frequent hunting'.

The archaeological research at Vasino has clearly demonstrated that goats were present in Timor by the early to mid-fifteenth century AD (Fenner et al. 2017). Zooarchaeological records of goat are scarce throughout Mainland and Island Southeast Asia, and the exact origins and timing for the introduction of the goat to Island Southeast Asia remains unresolved (Amano and Piper 2011). *Capra/Ovis* appears in the zooarchaeological record of China at 4000 cal. BP but only in small numbers (Jing and Flad 2002) and no goat bones as early as this have yet been recorded in Neolithic sites in the Philippines, Vietnam (e.g. Piper et al. 2009, 2010) or Thailand (Kijngam 2011). A recent study of animal bones from the Batanes Islands in the northern Philippines recorded goat in deposits postdating the earlier half of the first millennium AD, and the goat seems to succeed some of the earliest evidence for the introduction of Chinese porcelain on the islands (Piper et al. 2013). Patterns of long-distance Chinese trade began to emerge in the latter part of the first millennium BC and early centuries AD and then intensified towards the mid– late first millennium AD, and this latter period appears to coincide with the first appearance of the goat on the Batanes Islands. In Indonesia, Morwood et al. (2008:1785, Table 2a) recorded a single Capridae bone in Spit 21 at Song Gupuh in eastern Java slightly above a C^{14} date of 2180±120 cal. BP (WK14648). This latter identification needs further verification. However, the earliest securely dated goats in the Indonesian archipelago are from Bali, probably imported from South Asia, and dated to c. 200 cal. BC. Isotopic analyses indicated that these early goats in Bali had likely been imported from South Asia and possibly represented some of the earliest introduced caprines to the Southeast Asian region (Fenner et al. 2017).

In Timor itself, Glover (1986: 205) reported that *Capra/Ovis* remains first appear in the archaeological sequence in the cave of Uai Bobo 2, in Horizon VII (5000–6000 BP) and Horizon IX (3500–4000 BP). These dates for goat on Timor are almost certainly too old. An explanation for these early records of goat on Timor might be that a common contemporary use of caves is for goat herding pens (Sue O'Connor pers. comm. 2010). This practice is possibly of some antiquity and caused considerable disturbance and reworking of goat bones into old deposits. Glover (1986:205) did, however, also note that goat bones were only recovered in quantity at Uai Bobo 1 Horizon V and at Uai Bobo 2 in Horizon X, which are dated to about 1400–1800 and 2000–2500 BP respectively. This is a much more realistic timing for the presence of goat on Timor (Amano and Piper 2011). The dates for the presence of goats from Vasino fit neatly with the fifteenth and sixteenth-century AD accounts of Antonio Pigafetta, the chronicler of Magellan who noted that: 'In [Timor], and nowhere else, is found white sandalwood, besides ginger, swine, goats, rice … wax, and other things, and parrots of divers sorts and colours' (1969:141).

Pig bones were recovered throughout the archaeological sequences at Vasino. The age profile of the pigs suggests that these are more likely to be domestic stock maintained around the fortified site rather than hunted animals. Glover (1986:197) has argued that in his excavations the pig was consistently the earliest introduced animal to Timor, between 5000 and 4000 cal. BP. A recent review by Piper (2017) has demonstrated that pig introduction to Island Southeast Asia was more likely to have been between 3500 and 4000 BP.

The presence of bones with dog gnawing and digestion indicate that dogs likely roamed freely around the site (Amano and Piper 2011). The relative scarcity of dog bones and the absence of butchered dog bone leave the question of dogs in the diet of Timorese open to further research, but recent studies into Neolithic subsistence in southern Vietnam (Piper et al. 2014, 2017) and the northern Philippines (Piper et al. 2013) have confirmed that dogs were eaten during antiquity in Island Southeast Asia. Glover (1986) found two canines in his excavation of Bui Ceri Uato in Timor that morphometrically fall outside the range of those of typical Melanesian and Southeast Asian dogs. He also found a mandible that has a 'groove' in the lingual side of the canine alveolus 'which is characteristic of the dingo but not of the Melanesian dog' (1986:205). The teeth recovered from Vasino fall within the size range of those of modern-day Southeast Asian dogs (from the measurements of at least 43 individuals). Also, alveolar distances in the mandible recovered from Square D Spit 6 were not significantly different from those of native Philippine dogs kept in the University of the Philippines Archaeological Studies Program Zooarchaeology collection. It is possible that the remains reported by Glover (1986) represent a different population from the Vasino dogs. Currently, the oldest known canid remains on Timor are from a dog burial excavated from the cave Matja Kuru 2 and directly dated to 2967±50 BP (uncalibrated; WK-10051) suggesting a long history of domestic dogs on the island (Veth et al. 2005).

The absence of murid remains in the assemblage is also notable. Giant rats have been reported in pre-Neolithic layers in Timor (Hawkins et al. 2017a, 2017b; Veth et al. 2005). Aplin (2010) recovered the remains of several giant rats from caves in Timor-Leste, one identified as a new species of the genus *Coryphomys* dated to 1000 years BP. In his excavation of four cave sites in Timor-Leste (Lie Siri, Bui Ceri Uato, Uai Bobo 1 and Uia Bobo 2), Glover (1986) recovered more than 90,000 murid bones, mostly from *Rattus exulans* and *Melomys*. The location of Vasino on a hilltop and its intensive occupation by people could account for the rarity in endemic murid remains (though commensal taxa might be expected), and the presence of scavenging dogs could also have influenced preservation. It is also possible that many of the large endemic species were extinct before the development of the Vasino fortification in the fourteenth–fifteenth centuries AD.

Very few fish bones were recovered, which at face value might imply that fish and fishing played a very minor role in the diet of the inhabitants of Vasino. However, Piper et al. (2009) have argued that the presence of free-ranging dogs could have a severe impact on the preservation of fish bone in archaeological sites. For example, Jones (1984, 1986) found that between 85 per cent and 100 per cent of identifiable fish bone elements were lost when skeletons were fed to dogs. These experiments demonstrate just how easily fish bones are digested by dogs and this could render fishing as part of the subsistence strategy almost invisible in the archaeological record.

The majority of identified shellfish taxa were intertidal species associated with rocky reef, one taxon (Thiaridae) from freshwater environments, a small quantity from mangrove forests and seven taxa associated with mixed habitat zones (Figure 4.16). Terrestrial gastropods were also present. The presence of these species indicates exploitation of inshore marine, estuarine and freshwater habitats all found nearby today. Surprisingly, even large species such as *Tridacna* and *Hippopus* were carried inland to the upland settlement. Optimal foraging literature suggests that such large species will be harvested and the shell discarded on the reef (Bird et al. 2002, 2004). However the clam shell is quite reduced and it is possible it was brought back to be used for manufacturing shell artefacts rather than for the meat content, although no shell artefacts were found.

Conclusion

The Bayesian analysis indicates that the initial occupation of Vasino most likely falls in the second half of the fourteenth century. The implications of this chronology for the beginning date and drivers of fortifications in Timor are discussed in McWilliam (Chapter 6, this volume; c.f. also Fenner and Bulbeck 2013; O'Connor et al. 2012). Only one radiocarbon date related directly to the start of fortifications at Vasino. As it is more than 250 years later than the overall site occupation date, it would, if used alone, indicate that fortifications started much later than previously suggested. The naturally defensive position of the site, however, suggests that defence from attack was a consideration from the initial start of occupation, and that this single date may well relate to reworking or extension of the site perimeter wall along the *laca* rather than to the initial start of fortifications. Local informants estimate that the site has been abandoned for the last 200 years (Andrew McWilliam pers. comm. 2009). The archaeology appears to endorse this information as the top spits were virtually sterile of artefacts and dominated by land snail.

The overall impression of the society living at Vasino, in the 500-odd years that it was occupied from the mid-fourteenth century, is that the people had a lifestyle not dissimilar from that of Timorese subsistence farmers today and in the recent past, tending domestic animals and gardens within a similar environment (McWilliam and Traube 2011). However, unlike their modern-day counterparts, they conducted little or no hunting or fishing, with wild resource exploitation limited to some shellfish gathering. Vasino society during the time frame recorded by the excavations appears to be rather insular, albeit with some limited outside contact (pottery was brought in), but virtually no trade items, such as tradeware and glass, unlike their neighbours at Macapainara during the same time frame (Chapter 2, this volume). The lack of tradeware suggests that the inhabitants were focused on domestic activities and did not engage in trade with outsiders, unlike the inhabitants of Macapainara or Leki Wakik (see Chapters 2 and 5). This may be due to the fact that there was no good harbour near to Vasino. However, this isolation, limited movement and lack of hunting for wild animals may also be the result of the necessity for security. The position of Vasino on a hilltop and the construction of its massive fortified walls indicate that the inhabitants faced some kind of aggressive threat, the likely nature of and reasons for which are explored in McWilliam (Chapter 6, this volume).

References

Amano, N. and P.J. Piper 2011. A report on the animal remains from the 2009 archaeological excavation at Vasino in East Timor. Unpublished report. The Australian National University, Canberra. hdl.handle.net/1885/111565. Accessed 19 March 2020.

Andrefsky, W. 2009. The analysis of stone tool procurement, production and maintenance. *Journal of Archaeological Research* 17: 65–103. doi.org/10.1007/s10814-008-9026-2.

Aplin, K. 2010. Quaternary murid rodents of Timor part I: New material of *Coryphomys buehleri Schaub*, 1937, and description of a second species of the genus. *Bulletin of the American Museum of Natural History* 341:1–80. doi.org/10.1206/692.1.

Bird, D.W., J.L. Richardson, P.M. Veth and A.J. Barham 2002. Explaining shellfish variability in middens on the Meriam Islands, Torres Strait Australia. *Journal of Archaeological Science* 29:457–469. doi.org/10.1006/jasc.2001.0734.

Bird, D.W., R. Bliege Bird and J.L. Richardson 2004. Meriam ethnoarchaeology: Shellfishing and shellmiddens. *Memoirs of the Queensland Museum, Cultural Heritage Series* 3(1):183–197.

Brumm, A. 2006. Fire-making using a stone 'strike-a-light' in the Soa Basin of Flores, Indonesia. *Bulletin of the Indo-Pacific Prehistory Association* 26:168–170.

Bryan, A.L. and D. Schnurrenberger 1985. A contribution to the study of the naturefact/artifact controversy. In M.G. Plew, J.C. Woods and M.G. Pavesic (eds), *Stone tool analysis: Essays in honor of Don E. Crabtree*, pp. 133–159. University of New Mexico Press, Albuquerque.

Buck, C., G. Boden, A. Christen and G. James 1999. BCal online radiocarbon analysis tool. bcal.shef.ac.uk. Accessed 14 February 2018. doi.org/10.11141/ia.7.1.

Bulbeck, D. 2011. Vasino earthenware pottery. Unpublished report to the Department of Archaeology and Natural History, The Australian National University, Canberra. (Available from the author.)

Bulbeck, D. 2012. Tradeware and glass sherds, and beads and other ornaments excavated at Macapainara and Vasino, East Timor, in 2008. Unpublished report to the Department of Archaeology and Natural History, The Australian National University, Canberra. (Available from the author.)

Bulbeck, D. and I. Caldwell. 2000. *Land of iron: The historical archaeology of Luwu and the Cenrana Valley. Results of the Origin of Complex Society in South Sulawesi Project (OXIS)*. Centre for South-East Asian Studies, University of Hull, Hull.

Bull, G. and S. Payne 1982. Tooth eruption and epiphysial fusion in pigs and wild boar. In B. Wilson, C. Grigson and S. Payne (eds), *Ageing and sexing animal bones from archaeological sites*, pp. 55–71. British Series 109. British Archaeological Reports, Oxford.

Cameron, J. 2013. The spinning tools from Sunget, Anaro and Savidug. In P. Bellwood and E. Dizon (eds), *4000 years of migration and cultural exchange: The archaeology of the Batanes Islands, Northern Philippines*, pp. 115–121. Terra Australis 40. ANU E Press, Canberra. doi.org/10.22459/ta40.12.2013.07.

Cernohorsky, W.O. 1972. *Marine shells of the Pacific II*. Pacific Publications, Sydney.

Cernohorsky, W.O. 1978. *Tropical Pacific marine shells*. Pacific Publications, Sydney.

Clason, A.T. 1986. The faunal remains of Paso in Northern Sulawesi, Indonesia. In *Proceedings of the International Congress of Zooarchaeology*, pp. 35–62. La Pensée Sauvage, Grenoble.

Dampier, W. 1703. *A new voyage round the world; describing particularly, the Isthmus of America, several coasts and islands in the West Indies, the Isles of Cape Verd, the passage by Terra del Fuego, the South Sea Coasts of Chile, Peru, and Mexico, the Isle of Guam, one of the Ladrones, Mindanao and other Philippine and East India Islands near Cambodia, China, Formosa, Luconia, Celebes etc., and New Holland, Sumatra, Nicobar Isles, the Cape of Good Hope, and Santa Hellena: Their soil, rivers, harbours, plants, fruits, animals, and inhabitants: their customs, religion, government, trade etc.* Volume 1. Knapton, London. doi.org/10.5962/bhl.title.135457.

Dickinson, W. 2011. Petrological report on pottery from East Timor. Unpublished report. Department of Archaeology and Natural History, The Australian National University, Canberra.

Fenner, J.N. and D. Bulbeck 2013. Two clocks: A comparison of ceramic and radiocarbon dates at Macapainara, East Timor. *Asian Perspectives* 52(1):143–156. doi.org/10.1353/asi.2013.0005.

Fenner, J.N., R.K. Jones, P.J. Piper, M. Llewellin, M.K. Gagan, B. Prasetyo and A. Calo 2017. Early goats in Bali, Indonesia: Stable isotope analyses of diet and movement. *The Journal of Island and Coastal Archaeology* 13(4):563–581. doi.org/10.1080/15564894.2017.1325421.

Frasché, D.F. 1976. *Southeast Asian ceramics, ninth through seventeenth centuries.* The Asia Society, Washington D.C.

Glover, I. 1986. *Archaeology in Eastern Timor, 1966–67.* Terra Australis 11. Department of Prehistory, Research School of Pacific Studies, The Australian National University, Canberra.

Glover, I. and R.F. Ellen 1975. Ethnographic and archaeological aspects of a flaked stone collection from Seram, Eastern Indonesia. *Asian Perspectives* 18(1):51–60.

Grant, A. 1982. The use of tooth wear as a guide to the age of domestic ungulates. In B. Wilson, C. Grigson and S. Payne (eds), *Ageing and sexing animal bones from archaeological sites*, pp. 91–108. British Series 109. British Archaeological Reports, Oxford.

Guy, J.S. 1986. *Oriental trade ceramics in South-East Asia: Ninth to sixteenth centuries.* Oxford University Press, Oxford.

Habermehl, K.H. 1975. *Die Alterbestimmung bei Hausund Labortieren.* Paul Parey, Berlin.

Habu, J., P. Lape and J. Olsen 2017. *The handbook of East and South East Asian archaeology.* Springer Ebook, New York. doi.org/10.1007/978-1-4939-6521-2.

Harrisson, B. 1990. *Pusaka: Heirloom jars of Borneo.* Oxford University Press, Oxford.

Harrisson, B. 1995. *Later ceramics in South-East Asia: Sixteenth to twentieth centuries.* Oxford University Press, Oxford.

Hawkins, S., S. O'Connor, T. Maloney, M. Litster, S. Kealy, J. Fenner, K. Aplin, C. Boulanger, S. Brockwell, R. Willan, E. Piotto and J. Louys 2017a. Oldest human occupation of Wallacea at Laili Cave, Timor-Leste, shows broad-spectrum foraging responses to late Pleistocene environments. *Quaternary Science Reviews* 171:58–72. doi.org/10.1016/j.quascirev.2017.07.008.

Hawkins, S., S. Samper Carro, J. Louys, K. Aplin, S. O'Connor and Mahirta 2017b. Human palaeoecological interactions and owl roosting at Tron Bon Lei, Alor Island, Eastern Indonesia. *The Journal of Island and Coastal Archaeology* 13(3):371–387. doi.org/10.1080/15564894.2017.1285834.

Hinton, A. 1972. *Shells of New Guinea and the central Indo-Pacific.* Jacaranda Press, Port Moresby.

Hiscock, P. 2007. Artefacts on Aru: Evaluating the technological sequences. In S. O'Connor, M. Spriggs and P. Veth (eds), *The archaeology of the Aru Islands, Eastern Indonesia*, pp. 205–234. Terra Australis 22. ANU Press, Canberra. doi.org/10.22459/ta22.2007.10.

Jing, Y. and R.K. Flad 2002. Pig domestication in ancient China. *Antiquity* 76:724–732. doi.org/10.1017/s0003598x00091171.

Jones, A.K.G. 1984. Some effects of the mammalian digestive system on fish bones. In N. Desse-Berset (ed.) *Second Fish Osteoarchaeology Meeting, Paris: Centre National de la Recherche Scientifique*, pp. 61–65. Monographies Techniques 16. Centre de Recherches Archeologiques, Paris.

Jones, A.K.G. 1986. Fish bone survival in the digestive systems of pig, dog and man. In D. Brinkhuizen and A. Clason (eds), *Fish and archaeology*, pp. 53–61. International Series 294. British Archaeological Reports, Oxford.

Kijngam, A. 2011. The mammalian fauna. In C.F.W. Higham and A. Kijngam (eds), *The origins of the civilization of Angkor. Volume IV: The excavation of Ban Non Wat: The Neolithic occupation*, pp. 189–196. The Fine Arts Department, Bangkok.

Li, J. 2010. Qing dynasty ceramics. In L. Zhiyan, V.L. Bower and H. Li (eds), *Chinese ceramics from the Palaeolithic period through the Qing Dynasty*, pp. 459–533. Yale University Press, New Haven. doi.org/10.1353/cri.2012.0038.

Lyman, R.L. 1994. *Vertebrate taphonomy*. Cambridge University Press, Cambridge.

Maloney, T. 2011. Stone artefacts of Macapainara and Vasino, Timor-Leste. Unpublished report. Department of Archaeology and Natural History, College of Asia and the Pacific, The Australian National University, Canberra.

McCormac, F.G., A.G. Hogg, P.G. Blackwell, C.E. Buck, T.F.G. Higham and P.J. Reimer 2004. Shcal04 Southern Hemisphere Calibration, 0–11.0 Cal Kyr BP. *Radiocarbon* 46(3):1087–1092. doi.org/10.1017/s0033822200033014.

McWilliam, A.R. and E.G. Traube (eds) 2011. *Land and life in Timor-Leste: Ethnographic essays*. ANU E Press, Canberra. doi.org/10.22459/lltl.12.2011.

McWilliam, A., D. Bulbeck, S. Brockwell and S. O'Connor 2012. The cultural legacy of Makassar stone in East Timor. *The Asia Pacific Journal of Anthropology* 13(3):262–279. doi.org/10.1080/14442213.2012.674054.

Merriam-Webster Dictionary 2018. Entry for 'martaban'. www.merriam-webster.com/dictionary/martaban. Accessed 25 July 2018.

Moran, N.C. and T.P. O'Connor 1994. Age attribution in domestic sheep by skeletal and dental maturation: A pilot study of available sources. *International Journal of Osteoarchaeology* 4:267–285. doi.org/10.1002/oa.1390040402.

Morwood, M.J., T. Sutikna, E.W. Saptomo, K.E. Westaway, Jatmiko, A.D. Rokus, M.W. Moore, D.Y. Yuniawati, P. Hadi, J.-X. Zhao, C.S.M. Turney, K. Fifield, H. Allen and R.P. Soejono 2008. Climate, people and faunal succession on Java, Indonesia: Evidence from Song Gupuh. *Journal of Archaeological Science* 35:1776–1789. doi.org/10.1016/j.jas.2007.11.025.

O'Connor, S., A. McWilliam, J.N. Fenner and S. Brockwell 2012. Examining the origin of fortifications in East Timor: Social and environmental factors. *The Journal of Island and Coastal Archaeology* 7(2):200–218. doi.org/10.1080/15564894.2011.619245.

Orton, C.R. and P.A. Tyers 1991. Counting broken objects: The statistics of ceramic assemblages. *Proceedings of the British Academy* 77:163–184.

Pigafetta, A. 1969. *Magellan's voyage: A narrative account of the first circumnavigation*. Yale University Press, New Haven and London.

Piper, P.J. 2003. Rodents, reptiles and amphibians: The palaeoecological and taphonomic study of small vertebrate remains from archaeological settlement sites. Unpublished PhD thesis. University of York, York.

Piper, P.J. 2017. The origins and arrival of the earliest domestic animals in Mainland and Island Southeast Asia: A developing story of complexity. In P. Piper, H. Matsumura and D. Bulbeck (eds), *New perspectives in Southeast Asian and Pacific prehistory*, pp. 251–272. Terra Australis 45. ANU Press, Canberra. doi.org/10.22459/ta45.03.2017.15.

Piper, P.J. and N. Amano 2011. A report on the animal remains from the 2008 excavations at Macapainara, East Timor. Unpublished report. The Australian National University, Canberra. hdl.handle.net/1885/111566. Accessed 19 March 2020.

Piper, P.J., F.Z. Campos and H.-C. Hung 2009. A study of the animal bone recovered from Pits 9 and 10 at the site of Nagsabaran in northern Luzon, Philippines. *Hukay* 14:47–90.

Piper, P.J., F.Z. Campos, D.N. Kinh and N. Amano 2010. A report on the animal remains from the 2009 archaeological excavations at An Son, Duc Hoa, District, Vietnam. Unpublished report. University of the Philippines, Manila.

Piper, P.J., N. Amano, H.-Y. Yang and T.P. O'Connor 2013. The terrestrial vertebrate remains. In P. Bellwood and E. Dizon (eds), *4000 years of migration and cultural exchange: The archaeology of the Batanes Islands, Northern Philippines*, pp. 169–199. Terra Australis 40. ANU Press, Canberra. doi.org/10.22459/ta40.12.2013.10.

Piper, P.J., F.Z. Campos, D.N. Kinh, N. Amano, M. Oxenham, B.C. Hoang, P. Bellwood and A. Willis 2014. Early evidence for pig and dog husbandry from the Neolithic site of An Son, Southern Vietnam. *International Journal of Osteoarchaeology* 24:68–78. doi.org/10.1002/oa.2226.

Piper, P.J., K.T.K Nguyen, T.K.Q. Tran, R. Wood, C.C. Castillo, A. Weisskopf, F. Campos, N.K. Dang, C. Sarjeant, A.S.B. Mijares, M. Oxenham and P. Bellwood 2017. The Neolithic settlement of Loc Giang on the Vam Co Dong River, southern Vietnam and its broader regional context. *Archaeological Research in Asia* 10:32–47. doi.org/10.1016/j.ara.2017.03.003.

Rye, O.S. 1981. *Pottery technology: Principles and reconstruction*. Taraxacum, Washington, D.C.

Santoso, S. 1995. *Tradisi Gerabah di Indonesia dari Masa Prasejarah hingga Masa Kini*. Himpunan Keramik Indonesia, Jakarta.

Scheans, D.J., K.L. Hutterer and R.L. Cherry 1970. A newly discovered blade tool industry from the central Philippines. *Asian Perspectives* 13:179–181.

Shepard, A.O. 1974. *Ceramics for the archaeologist*. Carnegie Institution Publications, Washington D.C.

Silver, I.A. 1970. The ageing of domestic animals. In D.R. Brothwell and E.S. Higgs (eds), *Science in archaeology: A survey of progress and research*, pp. 283–302. Praeger Printing, New York.

Skertchly, S.B.J. 1890. On fire-making in North Borneo. *The Journal of the Anthropological Institute of Great Britain and Ireland* 19:445–452. doi.org/10.2307/2842488.

Szabó, K. 2009. Molluscan remains from Fiji. In G. Clark and A. Anderson (eds), *The early prehistory of Fiji*, pp. 183–211. Terra Australis 31. ANU E Press, Canberra. doi.org/10.22459/ta31.12.2009.08.

van den Bergh, G., H. Meijer, R. Awe Due, M. Morwood, K. Szabó, L. van den Hoek Ostende, T. Sutikna, E. Saptomo, P. Piper and K. Dobney 2009. The Liang Bua faunal remains: A 95kyr sequence from Flores, East Indonesia. *Journal of Human Evolution* 57(5):527–537. doi.org/10.1016/j.jhevol.2008.08.015.

Veth, P., S. O'Connor and M. Spriggs 2005. Continuity in tropical cave use: Examples from Timor-Leste and the Aru Islands, Maluku. *Asian Perspectives* 44(1):180–192. doi.org/10.1353/asi.2005.0015.

von den Driesch, A. 1976. *A guide to the measurement of animal bones from archaeological sites*. Bulletin No. 1. Peabody Museum of American Archaeology and Ethnology, Cambridge, Massachusetts.

5

The site of Leki Wakik, Manatuto District, Timor-Leste

Jack N. Fenner, Mirani Litster, Tim Maloney, Tse Siang Lim, Stuart Hawkins, Prue Gaffey, Sally Brockwell, Andrew McWilliam, Sandra Pannell, Richard C. Willan and Sue O'Connor

Introduction

Leki Wakik is a large hilltop site with several large stone walls and circular stone arrangements located within the Manatuto district in the central region of Timor-Leste. It is similar to other hilltop sites in the area whose function and occupation time frame have been subject to debate (e.g. Lape and Chao 2008; O'Connor et al. 2012). In August 2011, a team from The Australian National University (ANU) supported by Timorese workers mapped the site and excavated five test pits intended to assess site use and occupation time frame. A substantial artefact assemblage was recovered that includes lithics, earthenware pottery, ceramics and faunal remains, which provides evidence of the use of the site and the surrounding landscape and, particularly, whether unusual circular stone arrangements demarcate special activity or occupation areas. A series of radiocarbon dates from an unusual area surrounded on three sides by large stone walls provide chronological context for the site.

We begin by discussing Leki Wakik's location within the landscape and its general layout and surface configuration. We then review historical and ethnological information about the site. Subsequent sections describe our excavation and analysis methods, followed by a detailed review of the results, including excavation pit stratigraphy and associated chronology (where available), and the cultural material assemblage of lithics, earthenware, tradeware ceramics, invertebrate faunal remains (mostly mollusc shell) and vertebrate faunal remains. We then use this information to characterise the site, beginning by identifying patterns that span multiple artefact classification types and continuing with a consideration of whether Leki Wakik should be classified as a fortified site in the context of other Timor-Leste fortified sites. The concluding section summarises our assessment of the site.

Site location and layout

Leki Wakik is located near the eastern border of Manatuto district in eastern Timor-Leste (Figure 5.1). The Banda Sea coastline is approximately 750 m to the north of the site, while the Laleia River is about 500 m to the east.

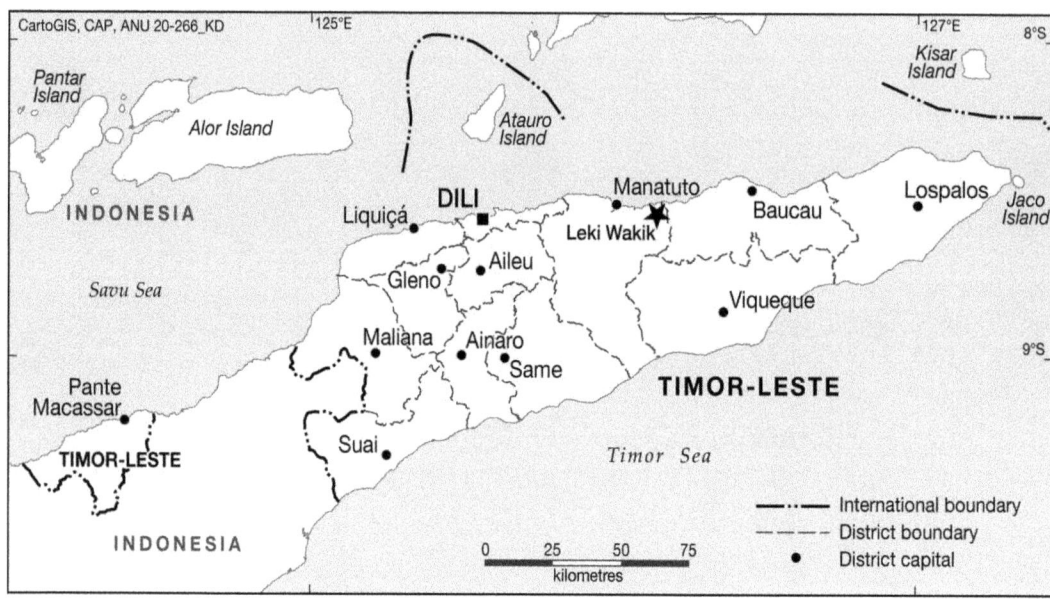

Figure 5.1. Timor-Leste map showing the location of Leki Wakik.
Source: CartoGIS ANU, modified by Jack Fenner.

Taking the natural hill slope edges as site boundaries, Leki Wakik covers about 39,000 m² (Figure 5.2). This enormous area appears to be partitioned into three or four sectors; most notably, stone walls partition off arms of the site in the northwest and northeast. If these arms are excluded, the central area covers about 31,000 m² and includes a large, very flat area in the north and a smaller southern area that generally slopes gently down to the northeast. The slope is most noticeable starting just to the west of the datum (Figure 5.2), but even within that area the slope is less than 10 degrees. It is unclear whether the site occupants would have considered the southern portion to be a separate area from the northern three-quarters of the site, but both portions include stone circles, which suggests that the site at least extends across the entire central area.

While slopes outside the site were not measured, site boundaries shown as thick black lines in Figure 5.2 mark areas where the land slopes steeply down outside the site. In most of these areas, it is possible but difficult to walk directly up the slope. The northern edge was not precisely mapped due to modern vegetation obstructions, but the dotted line is a reasonable approximation; the slope outside the site is steep in this area as well. The perimeter marked in purple is considered moderate slope; an adult can walk directly up the slope outside the site with moderate effort. Similarly, the low slope area to the west of the site can be walked with little effort.

There are four prominent stone walls extant within the site: two large, partially collapsed walls that partition off the northeastern and northwestern arms of the site, a large wall that extends in from the site boundary in the southeast and partially encloses a flat area, and a small, low wall in the southern portion with no apparent function. About 7.5 m south of the latter wall is an alignment of single stones running roughly parallel to it for about half its length; this could be a recent feature or it could be the surface remnant of a larger wall.

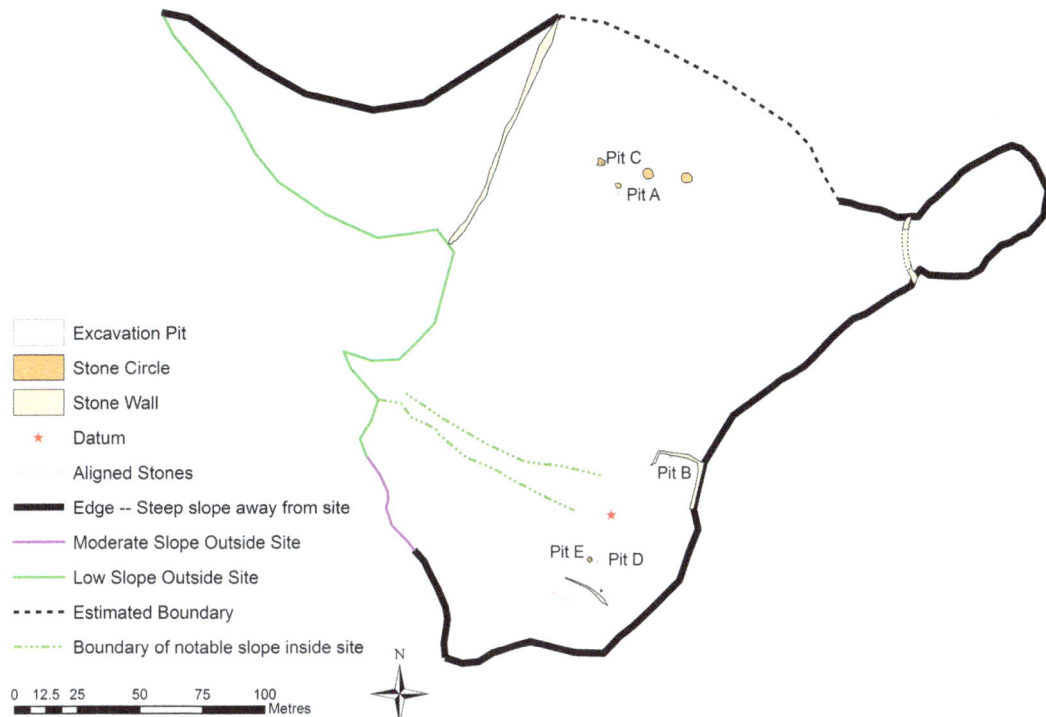

Figure 5.2. Leki Wakik site plan view.
Source: Jack Fenner.

At first, the two prominent walls that partition the site's arms in the north appear to be defensive in nature. They are thick walls; while generally a maximum of about 1 m high today, they originally would have been substantially higher. Neither wall contains a visible gap or entryway. The defensive nature of the walls, however, becomes unclear when considering the overall site layout. The northeast wall partitions off a relatively small area that otherwise is bounded by some of the steepest slopes around the site. The wall thus protects the northeast arm from the rest of the site (or vice versa) rather than providing protection from a force attacking the site from outside. More significantly, the northwest wall peters out in an area with low slope; a force coming from the west could easily go around it. We will revisit this issue when discussing site function below. We also note that there are several very large prickly pear cacti (*Opuntia elatior*) standing over 2 m tall growing along the wall in the northwest, which present formidable though geographically constrained barriers. This invasive weed, however, was introduced to Timor-Leste in the early twentieth century (McWilliam 2000:465) and thus was not present during most of Leki Wakik's occupation.

There are six roughly circular piles of stone within Leki Wakik: four clustered in the central north of the site and two in the southeast (Figure 5.2). In the north, the two westernmost stone piles are 2.0 to 2.6 m in diameter while the two eastern piles are larger, at 4.0 to 4.5 m in diameter. In the south, there is a small stone circle (0.8 m diameter) located about 2 m north of the internal stone wall and a larger circle (2.1 m diameter) 12 m to its northwest. Test pits were placed inside stone circles in the north (Pit C) and the south (Pit E; Figure 5.3). For comparative purposes, test pits were also excavated just outside of stone circles in the north and south (Pits A and D, respectively). An additional test pit (Pit B) was excavated within the southeastern area partially enclosed by a substantial stone wall.

Figure 5.3. Leki Wakik circular stone arrangements.

Top: Stone circle in southern portion of the site showing Pit E position in 2011; Bottom: Large stone circle in northern portion of the site in 2010.

Source: Top photo courtesy of Jack Fenner, bottom photo courtesy of Sally Brockwell.

Figure 5.4. Typical view of Leki Wakik in August 2011.
The view is looking northeast from the vicinity of Test Pit E. Surface stones are present throughout the site and do not appear to be artefacts.
Source: Jack Fenner.

No clearly modern structures were present at the site. While the area is likely browsed regularly by goats (goats were twice herded across the site during the excavation period), there does not appear to have been cultivation or other large-scale recent anthropogenic or natural disturbance to the site. The present vegetation consists largely of grass clumps and occasional low trees. Trees are more abundant along the northern boundary of the site and on the hillslopes outside the site. Stones are abundant on the surface (Figure 5.4).

Historical context

Portuguese colonial archives offer no direct information about Leki Wakik, but the area lies within the former boundaries of the 'minor' kingdom (*reino*) of Laleia on the northern coast of Timor, and midway between the politically powerful indigenous domains of Manatuto and Vemasse that were early and prominent ports for maritime trade (McWilliam 2007). They share the common language of Galóli. During the late sixteenth and early seventeenth centuries, an intense rivalry developed between Portuguese, Dutch, Makassarese (from Sulawesi) and Chinese traders for access to the highly lucrative white sandalwood trade (Boxer 1948; Gunn 1999). Control over the supply and export of sandalwood by the Timorese coastal political domains bestowed upon them significant wealth and political autonomy. Trade in other desirable commodities also flourished, including the sale of war captives as slaves to work in the spice plantations of Banda and Batavia and commercial exchanges of guns and ammunition, textiles, beeswax, Chinese ceramics and other tradeware (McWilliam 2007).

In the nineteenth century, the *Regulo* (ruler) of Laleia, along with the rulers of neighbouring Manatuto and Vemasse districts, formed an alliance with the Portuguese Colonial Government as military auxiliaries (*arrarais*) and reservists (*moradores*), and were active in the numerous bloody pacification campaigns against rebellious kingdoms in the interior of Timor (Davidson 1994). These campaigns were usually led by Portuguese military officers and featured mass looting and destruction of the opposition's defensive settlements accompanied by headhunting and the enslavement of women and children (Roque 2010). There is also evidence (Joliffe 1978:35) that late nineteenth- to early twentieth-century attempts by the Portuguese government to pacify the local people resulted in intense indigenous rebellion against the colonial regime (see also Pannell 2006:205).

According to contemporary residents of Laleia, a modern village about 3 km to the south, Leki Wakik is regarded as a 'sacred' (*lulik*) place—specifically an area containing a sacred marker, which was the focus of local offerings. It may have been a large black slab stone located on the northeastern arm of the site near the north side of the wall (Figure 5.5). It is a fine-grained sedimentary rock and has been worked into a circular or wheel shape with a longest dimension of 54 cm, a width of 42 cm and a height of about 10 cm. Similar stones have been found at Macapainara (see Chapter 2, this volume) and elsewhere in Timor-Leste (McWilliam et al. 2012). The name of the site, Leki Wakik, refers to an ancestral 'giant', and reflects the mythological traditions associated with it and nearby cultural heritage sites (for example, a nearby site is said to have a 'footprint' of the 'giant'). Leki Wakik may be the site of the old settlement and key historical stronghold for the Galóli-speaking settlers of the territory. We also recorded another former village site, Bai Hohon, located nearby, closer to the beach area, which had a number of graves. Local informants stated that Bai Hohon and Leki Wakik were of the same antiquity.

Figure 5.5. Leki Wakik large black slab stone considered sacred by Laleia villagers.
Source: Photo courtesy of Sally Brockwell.

Methods

Magnetometry

Magnetometry was employed on 4 to 7 August 2011 across three grids to assist in selecting the locations for test pit excavations. It was performed using a Geometrics G-856AX proton precession magnetometer. The magnetometry grids were laid out using tape measures, with the corners subsequently mapped using a total station. Magnetic field intensity samples were taken at 1 m intervals. Transects were performed in a single direction and a single corner of the grid was sampled at the end of each transect to record fluctuations in background magnetism. Data were downloaded from the instrument and corrected for diurnal variation and other background magnetism fluctuations. While in the field, a basic magnetic field map was prepared using MagMap2000 software. Subsequent to fieldwork, the data were georeferenced using total station data and the maps shown in this report were created using ArcGIS 10.3.

Excavation and mapping

Five 1 x 1 m test pits were excavated in arbitrary 5 cm spits. Sediment was separated from large rocks, and both the sediment and rocks weighed using a hand scale. Depths were measured using string levels from an arbitrary local datum point. In Pit B, significant artefacts and charcoal samples encountered while excavating were point-positioned. Due to time constraints, in the other pits only charcoal retained for dating purposes was point-positioned. Sediment was dry screened through 1.5 mm screens, and basic sorting was performed onsite. Sediment bulk samples were obtained from each spit, and the basal level of each spit was drawn and photographed. Sediment colours were recorded using Munsell soil colour charts, and pH estimated using simple barium sulphate pH dye kits. Excavation continued until culturally sterile sediment or bedrock was reached. A metal detector was used to scan below the final layer of each pit to check for remaining metallic artefacts; none were encountered (and only a single metallic artefact was found during excavations). At the end of excavation the stratigraphy of pit walls were drawn, then a plastic bag containing a short note giving basic excavation details was placed at the bottom of each pit and the pit refilled. Artefacts were washed and dried (to conform with Australian quarantine protocols) prior to packing and shipment to ANU.

Due to the intense sunlight at the site, plastic shades were erected over each test pit, resulting in a series of shallow, approximately 10 cm diameter modern postholes surrounding each pit. The site was mapped using a Leica TPS800 total station and GPR111 prism. Total station data were georeferenced using a basic Garmin GPS receiver.

Lithics

Stone artefact analysis involved an initial inspection and count of specimens, following the methods outlined in O'Connor et al. (Chapter 2, this volume).

Earthenware pottery

Earthenware weights were recorded for each square, and all sherds were examined from Square B, after Shepard (1974) and White and Henderson (2003). The following characteristics were recorded: sherd type (body/rim/base), paste (fine/medium/coarse), weight (to the nearest tenth of a gram), thickness (mm), length (maximum dimension in mm), width (mm), forming technique (if it could be discerned), angle, articulation and stance of the rim, exterior surface treatment and evidence for surface treatment, surface lustre (plain, dull, bright), exterior surface Munsell colour, whether the surface was oxidised or reduced, exterior decoration type and variety, exterior use-wear or damage (sooting, abrasion, pitting, spalling, scratching etc.), interior surface treatment and evidence for treatment, interior surface lustre (plain, dull, bright), interior surface forming evidence, interior surface Munsell colour, whether the interior surface was oxidised or reduced, evidence for interior use-wear and whether the core was oxidised or reduced.

Tradeware ceramics

High-fired glazed ceramics at Leki Wakik are classified as tradeware ceramics and were analysed using a macroscopic (visual) comparative analysis. A Canon EF 100mm f/2.8 Macro USM lens was used to take photo-macrographs (up to 1:1 magnification) of both exterior and interior surfaces as well as fabric cross-sections of the sherds. These photo-macrographs allowed for a finer resolution of diagnostic details that are otherwise difficult to observe and record with the naked eye. Forty-seven metric and non-metric variables were recorded. Non-metric data (i.e. provenance, vitrification level, fabric texture, fabric, glaze colours and others) were assessed based on the analyst's (Tse Siang Lim) knowledge and familiarity with high-fired glazed ceramics produced in China and Mainland Southeast Asia. This data should be treated as preliminary and, hence, should not be used in comparisons with other high-fired glazed ceramics outside of the Leki Wakik assemblage without caution.

As per standard taxonomical practice in the analysis of high-fired glazed ceramics, the Leki Wakik sherds have been preliminarily classified according to typologies based on their respective glaze and body colours and, in the case of Polychrome and Blue and White sherds, glaze colour-decoration combination. Additional information on tradeware ceramic analysis methods is provided in Supplement 1.

Invertebrate faunal remains

Marine and freshwater shells and shell fragments were identified to the lowest taxonomic level possible using the ANU Archaeology and Natural History (ANH) and the Museum and Art Gallery of the Northern Territory malacology collections. The names were standardised to conform with the current listing on the online database, the World Register for Marine Species. The shell assemblages were quantified by weight (g), minimum number of individuals (MNI) and number of identified specimens (NISP). The MNI method quantifies one repetitive feature per taxon throughout the assemblage, thereby avoiding the inflation associated with fragmentation commonly seen when using NISP counts (Classen 1998); for this reason, it is the primary mode of quantification used in the analysis.

The MNI was calculated through the use of the same non-repetitive element for each taxon, which included the aperture for the two *Stenomelania* species, the spires for all other gastropods, the posterior valve for chitons, and the siphon for *Nautilus* species. Both the left and right hinges were counted for bivalves with the greater number selected per square. *Turbo* sp. was quantified during laboratory analysis; however, opercula counts are excluded from aggregative family calculations to avoid inflating Turbinidae quantities. Shell and shell fragment condition and evidence for cultural modification were noted during quantification.

Vertebrate faunal remains

Vertebrate skeletal elements were identified to the lowest taxonomic level possible by comparison with reference material held at the ANU ANH Osteology reference collection. Large bovids were further distinguished based on size and morphological comparison of teeth using photographic references provided by Phil Piper. Bones were quantified using NISP and weight (g) to compensate partially for biases of fragmentation; MNI was not assessed using bones due to issues of interdependence and assemblage aggregation of large fauna and its overemphasis of rare species (Lyman 2008).

Taphonomic indicators of pre- and post-depositional processes were assessed to distinguish cultural butchery practices from natural post-mortem bone surface modifications. Green fracture patterns were assessed based on fracture shape using a schematic designed by Sadek-Kooros (1975) whereby obtuse, helical (spiral), and acute fracture angles with smooth fracture surfaces are considered fresh fractures (often the result of butchery) while irregular fracture shapes with rough surfaces are considered post-depositional breaks (Coil et al. 2017). The data were crosschecked by observing bone surface marks such as tooth, percussion, and trampling marks to confirm the agent of bone breakage (e.g. Galán et al. 2009). Weathering and root etching were also observed based on morphologies described by Behrensmeyer (1978), but only the presence or absence of severe degradation (more than stage 3) was recorded. Burning was estimated based on a colour scale of 0–5 (Stiner et al. 1995), whereby blackened carbonised bone is 3 and calcined bones are 4–5. This was crosschecked for other bone-burning morphologies such as shrinkage and surface structure (Shipman et al. 1984).

Results

Magnetometry

Two magnetometry grids were positioned within the northern and southern stone circle areas, while the third was placed such that it spanned the partially fenced-in area in the southeast of the site (Figure 5.6). The resulting magnetic field maps show several commonalities.

First, all three show linear patterns aligned with one of the grid axes. These patterns correspond closely to the linear sampling transects and are very likely to be sampling artefacts, perhaps related to a changing background magnetic field. While diurnal variation was accounted for by sampling a single location at the start of each transect and subsequently applying an appropriate correction factor, minor fluctuations that occur during each transect itself cannot be accounted for with this method. Likewise, instrument variation or alignment differences amongst transects could produce anomalous linear features. Second, the range of magnetic field variation is low in all grids. For instance, the range of magnetic field variation across all of Grid 1 (after adjusting for diurnal variation) was 10.0 nanoTeslas; the Grid 1 diurnal variation itself was over 25 nanoTeslas. This provides further indication that much of the magnetic variation was due to fluctuations in the noise rather than signals of archaeological relevance. Finally, the grids do not show clear magnetic anomalies in areas with above-ground stone circles (Grids 1 and 2) or stone walls (Grid 3). This suggests that these stone features are not magnetically active and that magnetometry likely would not reveal the presence of similar features buried below the surface. There are a few areas within the grids that display interesting or suggestive patterns, such as the green area in the west of Grid 2, which seems to bend and interrupt a red area. However, no sharp, clearly anthropogenic patterns are displayed, and whether the patterns in these suggestive areas are truly significant cannot be determined without extensive excavation. Therefore, the magnetometry data were disregarded, and the positioning of excavation pits based on other factors, such as assessment of the function of the stone circles and the unusual walled-in area in the southeast of the site.

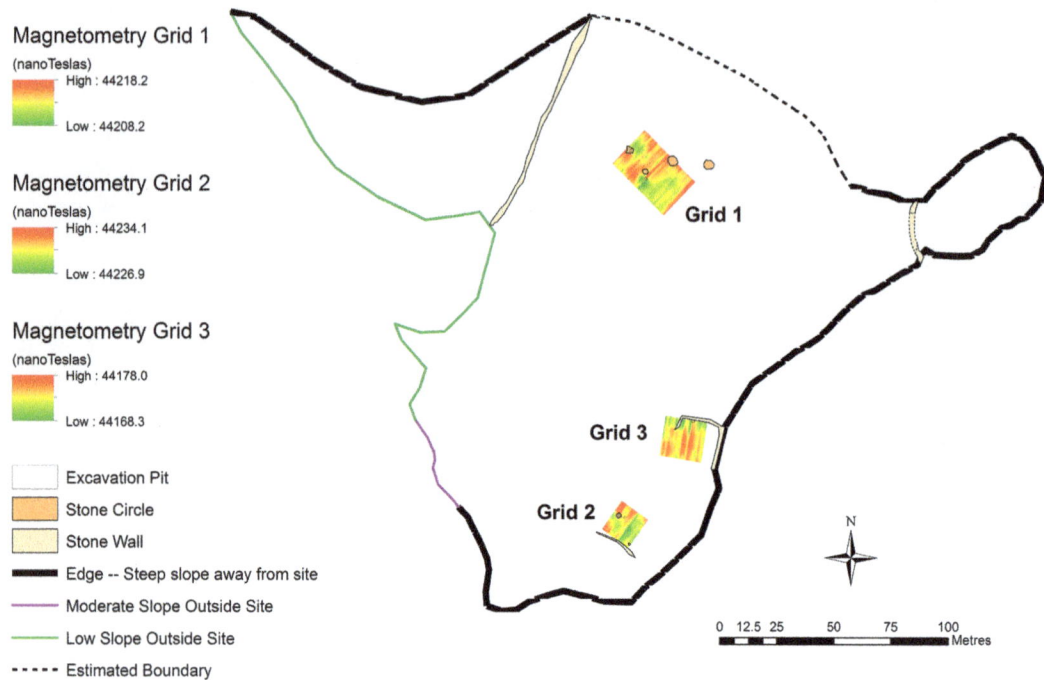

Figure 5.6. Leki Wakik magnetometry grid locations.
Source: Jack Fenner.

Excavation and survey

Appendix Table 5.A1 shows the weights of sediment, stone and each artefact type recovered during excavations; Supplement 2 contains more detailed artefact data. We will briefly review the stratigraphy and other relevant aspects of each excavation pit in this section, and then present the results of more detailed artefact analyses in subsequent sections.

Test Pit A

Test Pit A was located in the northern portion of the site (Figure 5.2), and was about 12 m southeast of Test Pit C (Figure 5.7). It was about 1.4 m south of a stone circle, in an area with thin vegetation—mostly dry grass—and highly compacted surface sediment. Eight spits were excavated and two stratigraphic units (SU) were revealed. SU 1 is a grey brown, fine sandy silt, which is poorly sorted. SU 2 is a red brown, fine sandy silt, and is poorly sorted, with angular gravel and cobbles (Figure 5.8). Mollusc shell was found in all SUs, and in all spits except Spit 8, while earthenware was located in Spits 2 to 5 and 7. Tradeware ceramics were limited to the uppermost spits and SU 1. A small amount of concrete was found in Spit 2, and bone and coral were largely confined to the upper four spits.

The stratigraphy shows several intrusions by SU 1 into SU 2 (Figure 5.8); these may be postholes and/or animal burrows. Stratigraphic disturbance is also supported by accelerator mass spectrometer (AMS) radiocarbon analysis of a charcoal sample from Spit A7 (the lowest cultural layer in Test Pit A), which produced a modern date (Appendix Table 5.A2). Unfortunately, the sample was not piece-plotted and it is unknown whether it derived from one of the deep intrusions by SU 1.

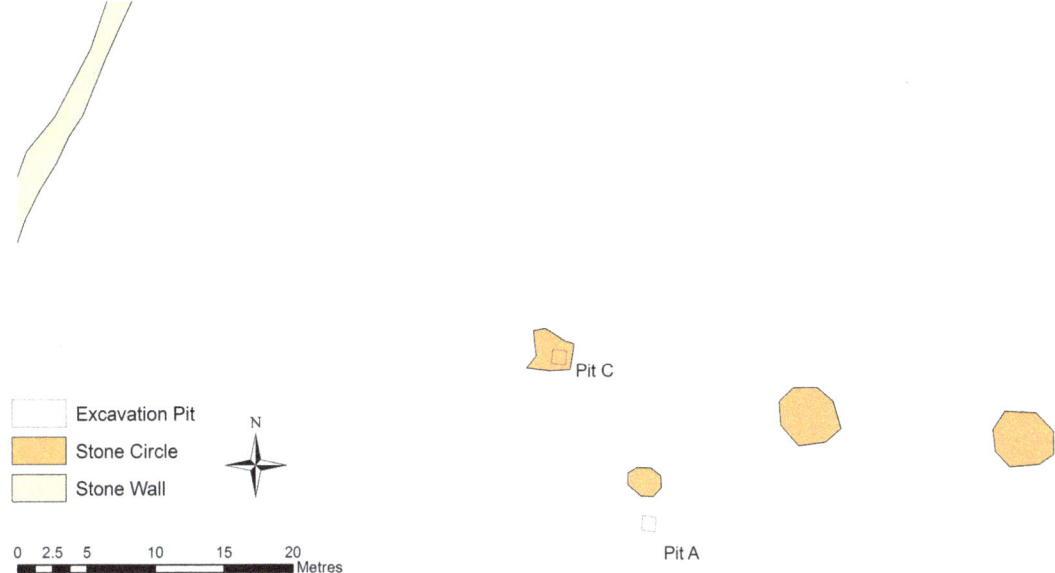

Figure 5.7. Leki Wakik Test Pits A and C in the northern area of site.
Source: Jack Fenner.

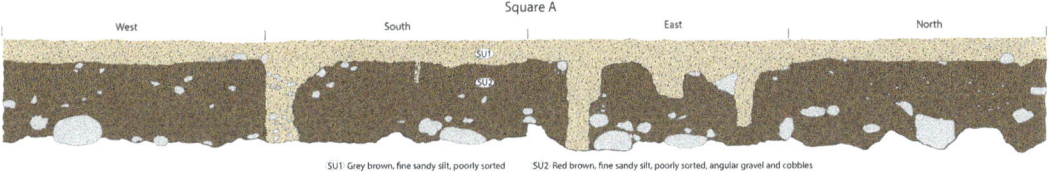

Figure 5.8. Leki Wakik Test Pit A section drawing.
Source: Tim Maloney.

Test Pit B

Test Pit B was located near the eastern edge of the site boundary (Figure 5.2), adjacent to a stone wall (Figure 5.9). The surface contained sparse grass and several large stones. The excavation revealed five SUs within 14 spits. This represents substantially more artefact-bearing sediment accumulation than is present in other Leki Wakik test pits, probably due to build-up along the adjacent stone wall. SU 1 is a fine, well-sorted brown silt of moderate compaction (Figure 5.10). It contained abundant animal bone and earthenware pottery, as well as marine, freshwater and terrestrial mollusc shell and small amounts of tradeware ceramics (Table 5.A1). Active bioturbation was observed in the southeastern corner.

The second SU is a fine brown silt, well sorted, with loose to moderate compaction. This extended generally from about 10 cm in depth to 40–50 cm. This layer included the majority of the cultural materials, including mollusc shell, bone, lithics and ceramics.

The third SU is composed of poorly sorted silt and gravel, and had loose to moderate compaction. Most classes of cultural material were found in this layer, except for terrestrial gastropod shell, which stops at SU 2. SU 4 refers to a small lens of pale brown fine silt with gravel, which is well sorted, and well compacted (Figure 5.10). SU 5 is a gravel with silt, which is poorly sorted and of moderate compaction. This SU contained marine and freshwater shell, crustacean, charcoal, earthenware pottery and a very small number of lithics in Spits 10 and 11. No cultural material was found in Spit 13.

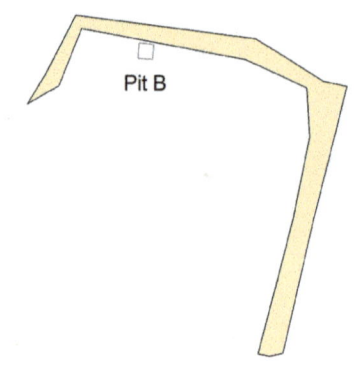
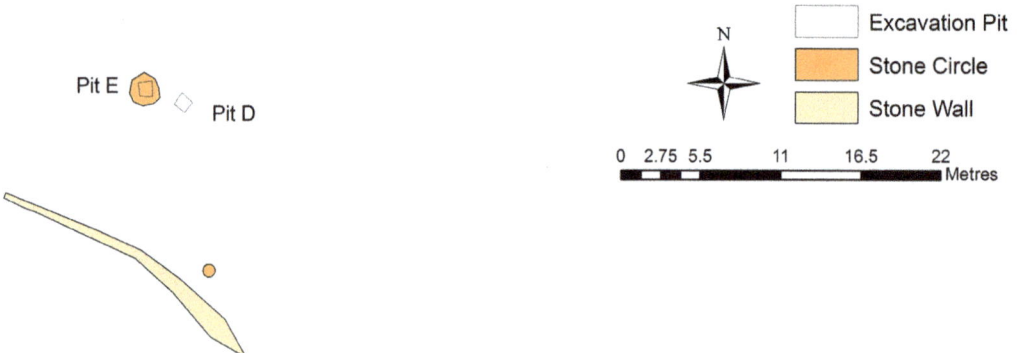

Figure 5.9. Leki Wakik southeastern excavation area.
Source: Jack Fenner.

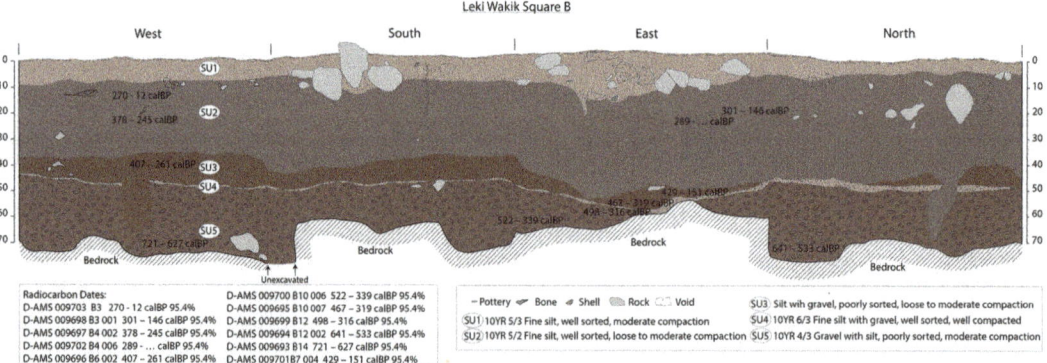

Figure 5.10. Leki Wakik Test Pit B profile drawing.
Source: Tim Maloney.

Eleven AMS radiocarbon dates were obtained for Test Pit B (Table 5.A2; Figure 5.11). Six of the dates were obtained from various marine shells with the remainder from charcoal, which has not been identified to species. Unfortunately, the marine shell ΔR calibration offset is unknown for Timor-Leste, so the shell dates have large uncertainties and are not further discussed here. The charcoal dates are in stratigraphic order and indicate that SU 2 dates to the seventeenth to nineteenth centuries AD, while SU 4 dates to the late fifteenth to mid-seventeenth centuries AD (Figure 5.11).

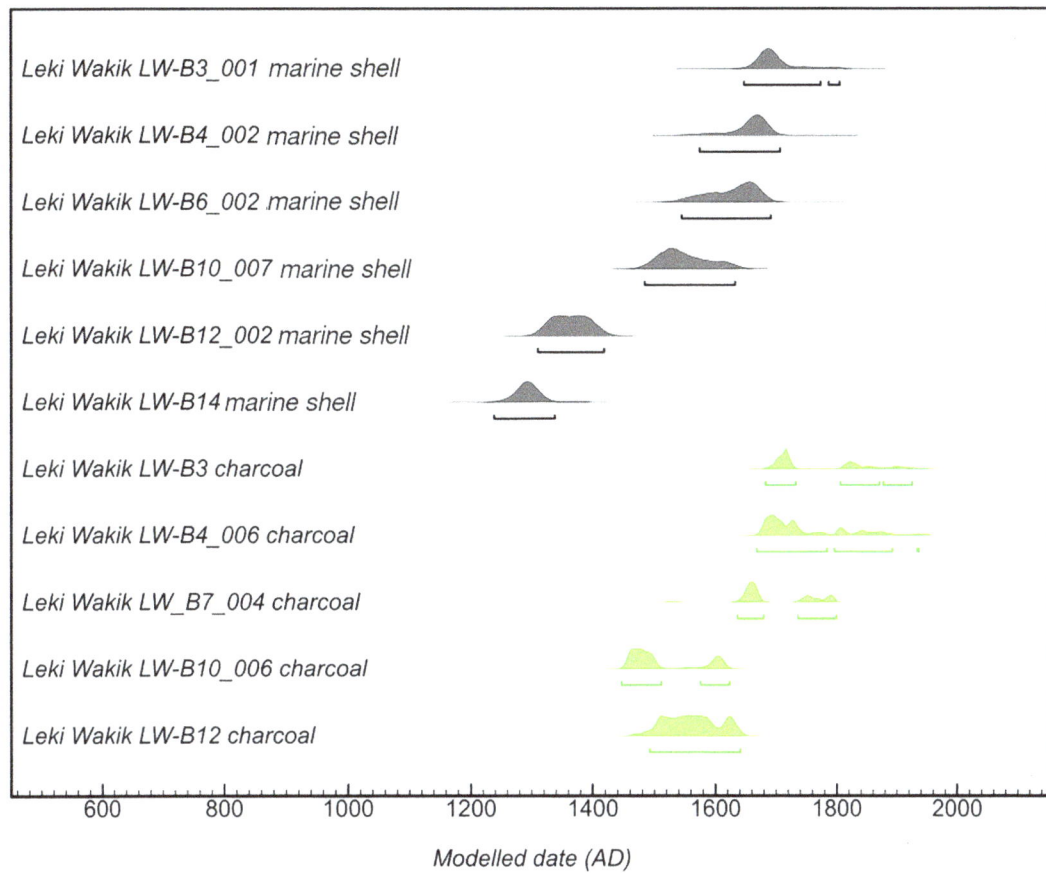

Figure 5.11. Leki Wakik Test Pit B calibrated marine shell and charcoal radiocarbon dates.
Source: Jack Fenner. See Table 5.A2 for calibration information.

Test Pit C

Test Pit C was located in the northern portion of the site (Figure 5.2) and was about 12 m northwest of Test Pit A (Figure 5.7). It was placed inside a 2.0 to 2.4 m diameter stone circle, and contained shell, coral, charcoal, artefactual stone, earthenware pottery, tradeware ceramics and metal (Table 5.A1). Two SUs and seven spits were excavated with metal found in the uppermost SU along with coral of an unknown type. All other cultural materials were found throughout both SUs. SU 1 is a fine, poorly sorted sandy silt while SU 2 is similar but darker in colour (Figure 5.12).

An attempt to date charcoal from Spit 1 was unsuccessful, as the sample did not survive the lab's pre-treatment processes. It may, in fact, have been a black mineral-enriched clay rather than charcoal.

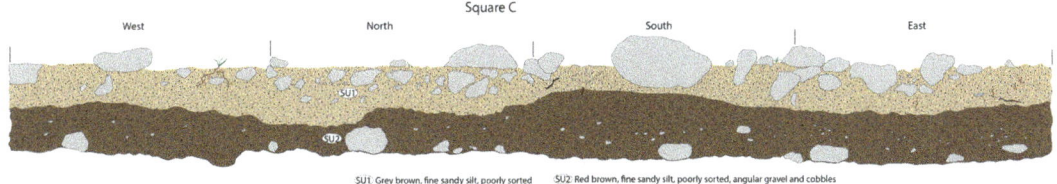

Figure 5.12. Leki Wakik Test Pit C section drawing.
Source: Tim Maloney.

Test Pit D

Test Pit D was located in the southern portion of the site (Figure 5.2), and was about 1.5 m southeast of Test Pit E (Figure 5.9). The surface was covered with light grey silty sand with patches of dry grass, and slopes gently down towards the south. Test Pit D contained marine and freshwater shell, terrestrial gastropod shell, crustacean, urchin, coral, charcoal, artefactual stone, earthenware and tradeware (Table 5.A1). No radiocarbon dating has been attempted for Test Pit D.

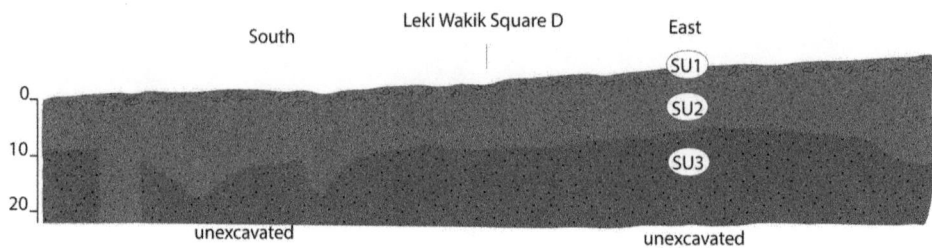

Figure 5.13. Leki Wakik Test Pit D section drawing.
Source: Tim Maloney.

Due to time constraints, profiles were only drawn for the south and east walls (Figure 5.13). Three SUs were noted, including a thin uppermost layer of gravel and larger stones. Five spits were excavated until culturally sterile sediment was reached. Marine, terrestrial and freshwater shell was found in all units and spits. Stone and earthenware were also found throughout the excavation. Tradeware was only recovered from Spit 2.

Test Pit E

Test Pit E was located in the southern portion of the site (Figure 5.2), and was about 1.5 m northwest of Test Pit D (Figure 5.9). It was placed inside a 2.1 m diameter stone circle. It contained marine and freshwater shell, terrestrial gastropod shell, crustacean, coral, seeds, charcoal, artefactual stone, earthenware and tradeware (Table 5.A1). No cultural material was found in its top spit, which consisted entirely of rocks and was slightly above the surrounding ground surface. No radiocarbon dating has been attempted for Test Pit E.

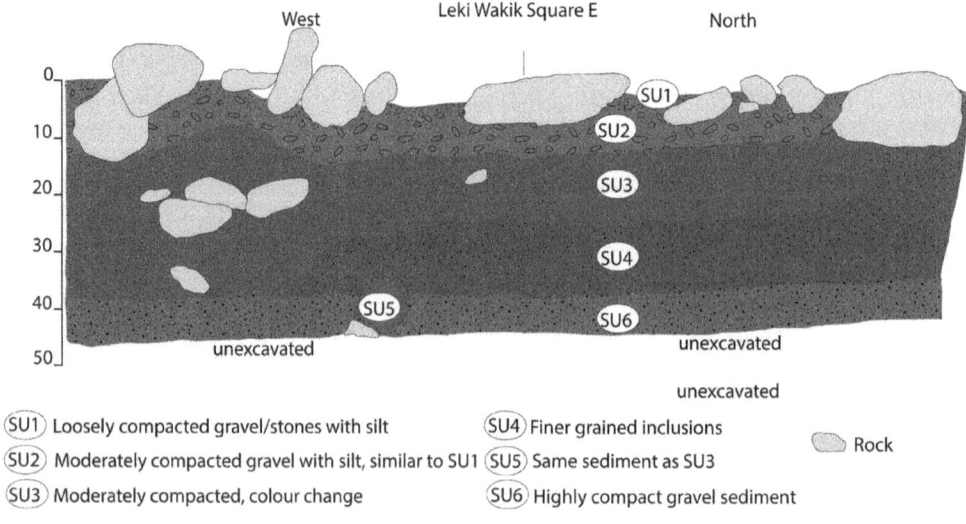

Figure 5.14. Leki Wakik Test Pit E section drawing.
Source: Tim Maloney.

Due to time constraints, profiles were only drawn for the west and north walls of Test Pit E (Figure 5.14). The majority of cultural material was found in Spits 4 (44 per cent) and 5 (30 per cent). Earthenware, terrestrial gastropod and shell were present in all spits, apart from Spit 1, with stone, seed and charcoal found in most. The greatest artefact weight was associated with marine and freshwater shell, followed by earthenware. Terrestrial gastropods were most numerous in Spits 1–5, with lower weights in Spits 6–7. Crustacean, coral, artefactual stone and tradeware were all found in minimal quantities in Spits 4–6.

Artefact analyses

All artefacts recovered during excavation were sorted by primary classification type and analysed as described in the Methods section. The results of these analyses for each artefact type are provided in the following subsections, with a subsequent section considering artefact patterns across classification types.

Lithics

A total of 32 stone artefacts were recovered across the excavation squares, consisting of flakes and flake fragments made either of chert or other fine grain sedimentary stone (Figure 5.15, Table 5.A1). These flakes are anomalous in their geological context so are undoubtedly artefacts, but it is unclear what they were used for. No lithic artefacts exhibited signs of use and cannot be described as strike-a-lights, in contrast to lithics from Macapainara and Vasino (see Chapters 2 and 4 in this volume).

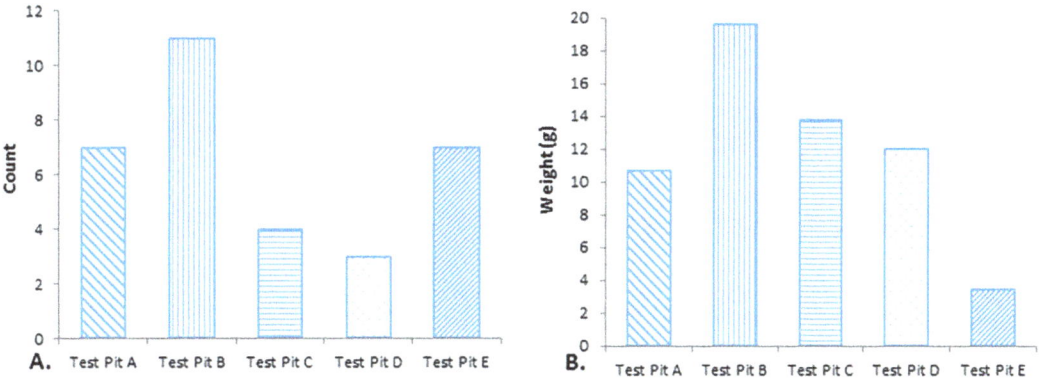

Figure 5.15. Leki Wakik lithics counts (A) and weights (B) by test pit.
Source: Jack Fenner.

Earthenware pottery

Earthenware was the second most abundant material (by weight) returned from excavations at Leki Wakik, with 4.7 kg recovered. Test Pit C contained the most, weighing 2045.1 g, while Test Pit A had the least, weighing 186.8 g. Despite extending considerably deeper than the other pits, Test Pit B contained a similar earthenware sherd weight (815.9 g) as Test Pits D (877.5 g) and E (732.7 g) (Table 5.A1).

As noted previously, detailed analysis was performed on earthenware sherds from Test Pit B. Results of this analysis are presented in Supplement 2 and summarised here. The majority were undecorated body sherds with only nine (2.2 per cent) classified as rim sherds, and two (0.5 per cent) as shoulders. Nine sherds were decorated with reddish clay-based paint or a black paint used to create abstract decorations (e.g. Figure 5.16). These are comparable to those also present in small quantities at Macapainara (Chapter 2, this volume) and Vasino (Chapter 4, this volume). The remaining decorated sherds were paddle-impressed with lines.

Slips were recorded on 49 sherds (12 per cent of all sherds). They were applied more often to external surfaces than internal surfaces with only six sherds recorded with internal slippage. Red slips dominated (N = 32), with other slips including black slip (N = 8), brown slip (N = 6) and small amounts of white slip (N = 2). White slipping likely involved the application of calcareous-rich clay. External colour was recorded on all sherds and classified by Munsell colour groups. The most common colours are grey (N = 114, 28 per cent) and brown (N = 98, 24 per cent). Red was recorded on 73 sherds (18 per cent), while 68 were black (17 per cent), 36 were reddish brown (9 per cent), 18 were pink (4 per cent), four were recorded as reddish yellow and one as white (Table 5.1).

Wiping marks were apparent on one sherd. Burnishing was also apparent on one black sherd, perhaps through the use of a pebble. Four completely reduced sherds contained carbonised residues on the internal surface, indicating likely cooking at the site. Constituting 99.5 per cent of the site assemblage, 410 sherds showed evidence of dark or grey cores, pointing to reduced firing conditions. Vessels were likely mostly formed through an external application of a paddle against an anvil held against the interior wall. Sometimes paddle impressions can be discerned.

Figure 5.16. Leki Wakik examples of decorated sherds.

The top three have an iron oxide abstract design (paint applied). The bottom two have paddle-impressed lines. The label is the spit in which the sherd was found.
Source: Mirani Litster.

Figure 5.17. Leki Wakik rim type 1.
Source: Mirani Litster.

Table 5.1. Leki Wakik Test Pit B earthenware sherd external surface colour by spit.

	Grey	Black	Red	Reddish brown	Brown	Reddish yellow	Pink	White	Total
Test Pit B									
1	4	-	1	-	-	-	-	1	6
2	16	-	-	18	-	-	-	-	34
3	14	18	10	12	10	4	1	-	69
4	2	13	8	6	4	-	6	-	39
5	20	4	1	-	14	-	3	-	42
6	-	1	5	-	3	-	-	-	9
7	11	-	12	-	8	-	3	-	34
8	10	14	10	-	23	-	3	-	60
9	25	6	16	-	19	-	2	-	68
10	7	4	9	-	12	-	-	-	32
11	2	-	1	-	-	-	-	-	3
12	3	7	-	-	5	-	-	-	15
13	-	-	-	-	-	-	-	-	0
14	-	1	-	-	-	-	-	-	1
Total	114	68	73	36	98	4	18	1	412

Source: Authors' summary.

The entire assemblage was fragmentary and ceramic form could not be discerned (unlike at Macapainara and Vasino). Test Pit B sherds were small, with an average thickness of 4.5 mm taken at a central point of the sherd. Nine rim sherds were identified, and one discernible rim sherd type can be seen (Figure 5.17). It is a long rounded, brown rim with an everted lip. Examples were found in Spits B2, B4, B7 and B12. No discernible differences associated with colour, surface treatment or decoration could be seen between SUs.

No wasters are recorded in the Test Pit B assemblage (or observed in the whole ceramics assemblage from Leki Wakik), indicating pottery manufacture likely did not occur at this location.

Tradeware ceramics

The high-fired glazed ceramics assemblage at Leki Wakik includes 44 sherds weighing a total of 276.4 g. Six sherds were recovered from Test Pit A, 15 from Test Pit B, 21 from Test Pit C and one each from Test Pits D and E (Table 5.2; dashes in the table indicate zero sherds). Thirty-six have been classified as Chinese, with the remaining sherds also consistent with Chinese origin. Eleven are attributed to the Ming Dynasty (1386–1644), with a further 13 also likely associated with same dynasty. Dating for the other sherds is uncertain or very broad. The colour of the glaze and the type of decoration suggests that a white sherd in Test Pit A Spit 1 is likely to be a Chinese ceramic from the Dehua (德化 Dé Huà) kiln complex in Fujian Province. Detailed discussion of the ceramic assignments and other tradeware results is provided in Supplement 1.

Table 5.2. Leki Wakik tradeware sherd typology distribution.

Test Pit	Spit	Brown	Green	White	Qing Bai	Blue and White	Polychrome	Brown and white	Light and dark green	Undiagnostic	Spit total
A	1	-	-	1	-	1	2	-	-	-	4
A	2	-	-	-	-	-	2	-	-	-	2
B	2	-	-	-	-	1?	1?	-	-	1	1
B	3	-	-	-	-	1?	1?	-	-	1	1
B	4	1	-	-	-	1?	1?	-	-	1	2
B	6	-	-	-	-	-	1	-	-	-	1
B	7	1	1	-	-	1	-	-	-	-	3
B	8	-	-	-	-	2	-	-	-	-	2
B	9	1	-	-	-	-	-	-	-	-	1
B	10	-	-	-	-	2	-	-	-	-	2
B	11	-	-	-	-	2	-	-	-	-	2
C	1	-	1	1	-	1	-	1	-	-	4
C	2	-	-	-	-	3 (+2?)	1 (+2?)	-	1	2	7
C	3	-	-	-	-	5	2	-	-	-	7
C	4	-	-	-	-	1?	1 (+1?)	-	-	1	2
C	5	-	-	-	-	1?	1?	-	-	1	1
D	2	-	1	-	-	-	-	-	-	-	1
E	4	-	-	-	1?	-	-	-	-	1	1
Total		3	3	2	0 to 1	17 to 24	9 to 16	1	1	8	44

Note: Possible type attributions for undiagnostic sherds are suggested within parentheses. Spits without tradeware ceramics are omitted.
Source: Authors' summary.

Invertebrate faunal remains

Recovered Leki Wakik marine and freshwater mollusc shell weight totals 4.8 kg across all test pits and includes 81 different taxa. Detailed assemblage data are provided in Table 5.A1 and Supplement 2 and are summarised here. Test Pit A contained a total shell weight of 907.4 g with a NISP of 769 and an MNI of 197. Test Pit B yielded 1325.6 g of shell (NISP = 543; MNI = 219). Test Pit C contained 973.39 g shell but only a NISP of 210 and an MNI of 88. Test Pit D contained the least shell by weight, with 526.8 g and a NISP of 423 and an MNI of 177. Test Pit E contained a shell weight of 1046.8 g, reaching a NISP of 461 and an MNI of 196.

Major marine and freshwater mollusc taxa for Leki Wakik included, in descending order (by MNI): *Stenomelania* sp. 1, *Tarebia granifera*, *Turbo* sp., *Trochus* sp., *Stenomelania* sp. 2, Cypraeidae, *Conus* sp., *Turbo chrysostomus*, *Gibberulus gibberulus gibbosus*, *Thiara scabra* and *Turbo argyrostomus*. Major family groups in descending order (by MNI) include Thiaridae, Turbinidae, Trochidae, Cypraeidae, Conidae and Strombidae.

Various habitats are represented (Table 5.3; dashes in the table indicate zero shells). Very minor contributions are from mangrove habitat species, which included *Terebralia palustris* (all test pits), *T. sulcata* (Test Pit A) and *Geloina* sp. (Test Pits A and E). No mangrove habitat shells were found below Spit 5 in any test pit. Freshwater species, likely sourced from the Laleia River, are more abundant than mangrove species (by all counts) and found throughout all squares in most spits. This included four species of small Thiaridae, common in other assemblages in Timor-Leste, including two unidentified but different species of *Stenomelania*—referred to here as *Stenomelania* sp. 1 and *Stenomelania* sp. 2. Also, *Thiara scabra* and *Tarebia granifera* were found. Additionally, one freshwater neritid is present in the assemblage: *Septaria* cf. *luzonica*. However, most species were from marine habitats from both reef and rocky intertidal areas and found throughout most spits in all squares.

Table 5.3. Leki Wakik major mollusc taxa and habitat by spit. Counts shown are MNI.

	Freshwater habitats			Marine habitats			
	Stenomelania sp. 1	*Tarebia granifera*	*Stenomelania* sp. 2	*Conus* sp.	*Trochus* sp.	Cypraeidae	*Turbo* sp.
Test Pit A							
Surface	-	-	-	-	-	<1	-
1	36	19	7	8	<1	1	<1
2	22	20	7	3	2	2	2
3	-	2	-	3	4	2	2
4	1	-	-	<1	<1	1	<1
5	-	-	-	<1	1	<1	-
6	1	-	-	-	<1	-	<1
7	-	-	-	-	<1	-	-
8	-	-	-	-	-	-	-
Total	60	41	14	14	7	6	4
Test Pit B							
1	1	-	-	-	-	-	-
2	2	2	1	<1	<1	1	<1
3	4	2	7	1	1	1	1
4	7	1	2	<1	1	<1	<1
5	4	8	9	2	-	2	-
6	1	8	4	1	1	1	1
7	9	1	5	<1	<1	<1	1
8	1	15	1	1	1	1	3
9	12	6	3	<1	<1	<1	<1
10	5	3	2	1	2	1	<1
11	8	5	1	1	1	1	1
12	2	1	-	-	-	-	-
13	-	-	-	-	-	-	-
14	-	1	<1	-	-	-	-
Total	56	53	35	7	7	8	7
Test Pit C							
1	3	-	3	2	<1	2	<1
2	<1	-	<1	-	1	<1	2
3	1	5	1	1	1	1	1
4	4	1	4	1		1	2
5	1	2	1	-	1	1	<1
6	-	1	-	-	<1	-	<1
7	<1	1	<1	-	-	-	-
Total	9	10	9	4	3	5	5
Test Pit D							
1	20	30	8	<1	3	<1	1
2	7	3	6	-	-	-	3
3	3	2	2	-	1	1	-
4	3	-	2	-	1	-	1
5	-	-	-	-	1	-	-
Total	33	35	18	<1	6	1	5

	Freshwater habitats			Marine habitats			
	Stenomelania sp. 1	*Tarebia granifera*	*Stenomelania* sp. 2	*Conus* sp.	*Trochus* sp.	Cypraeidae	*Turbo* sp.
Test Pit E							
1	-	-	-	-	-	-	-
2	-	1	1	1	1	-	-
3	4	1	1	1	<1	-	-
4	26	21	5	1	1	2	1
5	2	3	8	1	1	2	-
6	2	<1	2	<1	1	<1	-
7	-	-	-	-	1	-	-
Total	34	26	17	4	5	4	1

Source: Authors' summary.

Potentially worked shell examples are present in the shell assemblage; they are, however, too weathered for definitive conclusions to be asserted. These included two samples of *Melo* sp. recovered from the surface of Test Pit A, one sample from Spit A3, and two samples from Spit E4. One sample of potentially worked nacre was found in Spit E5, and two cowrie shell dorsa were found in Spits B6 and C4. A *Pyrene punctata* shell was recovered from Spit B2, and one Architectonicidae from Spit E6; however, no use-wear traces were observed. These may have been intended as ornaments; they are small but very attractive shells.

Turning to the results from Test Pit B, marine and freshwater shell was commonly found between Spits 1–14 (Table 5.3). No clear temporal divide between freshwater and marine shell acquisition can be seen in this location, but the radiocarbon dates indicate that mangrove species are only represented between the seventeenth and nineteenth centuries. The type of mangrove-dwelling species present (*T. palustris, T. sulcata,* and *Geloina* sp.) points to *Avicennia, Bruguiera* or *Ceriops* mangroves, as opposed to *Rhizophora* forests (Mowat 1995).

Vertebrate faunal remains

The Leki Wakik test pits yielded 304 vertebrate bones, weighing a total of 323 g. Specimen counts by taxa are shown in Table 5.4, while Supplement 2 lists taxa assignments by weight and spit. Dashes in the table indicate zero bone. Most bone was recovered from Test Pits E (NISP = 112, weight = 89 g) and B (NISP = 106, weight = 168 g), with much smaller quantities from the other test pits.

Mammal remains dominate the bone assemblage (NISP = 288), making up 95 per cent of total NISP and 99.7 per cent by weight. Most are medium to large mammals that could only be identified to class, though some of these could also be identified as medium and large bovids (Bovidae). Mammals are also the most diverse class in the bone assemblage, with five introduced domestic or commensal taxa identified to family, genus or species including water buffalo (*Bubalus bubalis*), goat/sheep (Caprinae), dog (*Canis familiaris*), pig (*Sus* cf. *scrofa*) and rat (*Rattus* sp.). Livestock, including goats and water buffalo, play an important role in Timorese socioeconomic systems today (Población 2013), and this appears to have been no different during the occupation at Leki Wakik.

Table 5.4. Leki Wakik vertebrate NISP and unidentified specimens by spit.

Test pit and spit	Bird	Fish	Scaridae	Muraenidae	Lethrinidae	mammal	medium mammal	medium-large mammal	Bovidae	medium Bovid	large Bovid	Bubalus bubalis	Canis familiaris	Caprinae	Sus cf. scrofa	Rattus sp.	Unidentified fragments	Total
A																		
1	–	–	–	–	–	–	8	–	2	–	–	–	–	–	–	–	–	10
2	–	–	–	–	–	5	5	–	–	–	–	–	–	–	–	–	–	10
3	–	2	–	–	–	–	2	–	–	–	2	–	–	–	–	–	–	6
4	–	–	–	–	1	–	2	–	–	–	–	–	–	–	–	–	–	3
A Total	–	2	–	–	1	5	17	–	2	–	2	–	–	–	–	–	–	29
B																		
1	–	–	–	–	–	–	1	–	–	–	–	–	–	1	–	–	–	2
2	–	–	–	–	–	2	1	–	–	–	–	–	–	–	–	–	–	3
3	–	–	–	–	–	–	4	–	–	–	20	–	–	6	–	1	–	31
4	–	–	–	–	–	3	–	–	–	–	–	–	–	–	–	–	–	3
5	–	–	–	–	–	–	1	–	–	–	–	–	–	–	–	–	–	1
7	–	–	–	–	–	2	–	1	–	–	2	1	–	–	–	–	–	6
8	–	–	–	–	–	12	2	–	–	–	34	2	–	–	–	–	–	50
9	–	–	–	–	–	–	1	–	–	–	–	–	–	–	–	–	–	1
10	1	–	–	–	–	3	–	–	–	–	3	–	–	–	–	–	–	7
12	–	–	–	–	–	–	1	–	–	–	–	–	1	–	–	–	–	2
B Total	1	–	–	–	–	22	11	1	–	–	59	3	1	7	–	1	–	106
C																		
1	–	–	–	–	–	–	1	–	–	–	–	–	–	–	–	–	–	1
3	–	–	–	–	–	–	1	19	–	–	–	–	–	–	–	–	–	20
C Total	–	–	–	–	–	–	2	19	–	–	–	–	–	–	–	–	–	21
D																		
1	–	–	–	–	–	–	3	–	–	–	–	–	–	–	–	–	–	3
2	–	–	–	3	–	–	9	1	–	–	2	–	–	–	–	–	4	19
3	–	–	–	–	–	–	3	–	–	–	–	–	1	–	–	–	–	4
4	–	–	1	–	–	–	–	4	–	–	–	–	–	–	–	–	–	5
5	–	–	–	–	–	4	–	–	–	–	–	–	–	–	1	–	–	5
D Total	–	–	1	3	–	4	15	5	–	–	2	–	1	–	1	–	4	36
E																		
3	–	–	–	–	–	–	3	–	–	–	–	–	–	–	–	–	–	3
4	–	3	–	–	–	73	–	–	1	1	6	–	–	–	–	1	–	85
5	–	1	–	–	–	–	–	16	–	–	–	–	–	–	2	–	–	19
6	–	–	–	–	–	–	3	–	–	–	–	–	–	–	–	–	–	3
7	–	–	–	–	–	1	–	–	–	–	–	–	–	1	–	–	–	2
E Total	–	4	–	–	–	74	6	16	1	1	6	–	–	1	2	1	–	112
Total	**1**	**6**	**1**	**3**	**1**	**105**	**51**	**41**	**3**	**1**	**69**	**3**	**2**	**8**	**3**	**2**	**4**	**304**

Source: Authors' summary.

Three of the larger bovid teeth from Spits B7–B8 could be identified to water buffalo (*Bubalus bubalis*) based on size and shape, and the other large bovid remains (NISP = 69) distributed in Test Pits A, B, D and E probably also belong to this species. Water buffalo appear to have been introduced to Timor sometime in the last 1500 years, but likely predate Portuguese contact (Glover 1986; Amano and Piper 2011). The large bovid remains in this category consist of a crania maxilla, femur, metapodial, tibia, unidentified long bone and astragali fragments, none of which had any zones of epiphyseal fusion to record. Only two dog remains were recovered: a 2nd upper adult molar with only slight wear from Spit B12 and a calcaneus from Spit D3. Caprine remains (NISP = 8) were concentrated in Spits B1–B3 with one other caprine bone in Spit E7. These consisted of mandibular fragments, a vertebra and teeth fragments. Pig remains present in Spits D5 and E5 are a cranium fragment and two mandibular tooth fragments. A *Rattus* cranium was recovered from Spit E4, and a mandible which is small enough to be *Rattus exulans* was present in Spit B3.

Non-mammalian faunal bones and teeth are quite sparsely represented in the assemblage. A single small bird (Aves) coracoid fragment from Spit B10 was only identifiable to class. Fish remains were distributed in small quantities in Test Pits A, D and E. Three families have been identified, including Scaridae (parrotfishes), Lethrinidae (emperor fishes), and Muraenidae (moray eels). Two moray eel dentaries were in Spit D2, a scarid quadrate was present in Spit D4, and a lethrinid tooth fragment was in Spit A4. Lethrinidae are voracious benthic carnivores, Scaridae are shallow reef herbivores, and moray eels are rocky shore benthic ambush predators. These taxa are predominately inshore marine reef fishes, which can be captured without the need for a boat using a variety of methods including hand lines, fish traps and gill net techniques that are commonly used by Timorese today (McWilliam 2002).

Seventeen bovid and medium to large mammal long bones, from Test Pits A, B, D and E, exhibit clear signs of obtuse and longitudinal smooth green fracture with impact scars consistent with butchery (chopping with heavy blade) practices. These include a large bovid femur from Spit A3 and a tibia from Spit B10, both of which were longitudinally split, possibly to remove marrow and grease. The possibility that these longitudinal fresh breaks could represent helical fractures caused by dog gnawing (Haynes 1983) was considered but crosschecking of bone surfaces for tell-tale signs of dog tooth marks (scoring and punctures) indicated that this was not the case. Bone flake fragments consistent with butchery were also recovered.

Four mammal long bones or cylinders, including single specimens of a large and a medium bovid, and two medium mammal specimens exhibited signs of carnivore gnawing. These cylinders typically had clear dog tooth puncture marks, compression marks and score marks indicating dogs had chewed the epiphyses off. Weathering was light on many of the bones, though three bones from Test Pits C and E do show signs of severe weathering, with noticeably extreme cracks with eroded fissures and exfoliated surfaces. None of the fish, bird or large bovid bones showed signs of burning but a number of medium to large mammal and one bovid (size unknown) bone, from Test Pits B, C, D and E, appear to be carbonised (NISP = 19), comprising 6.6 per cent of mammal bones.

Artefact patterns across classification types

Having described the artefact attributes and patterns for each classification type, we now briefly consider artefact patterns across classification types and test pits. For this analysis, we will use depth (as represented by spit number) as a rough approximation of occupation period. That is, we will sometimes treat materials from the same spit number in different test pits as if they dated to roughly the same period. While we recognise this is hazardous in the absence of clear stratigraphic parallels, or more extensive radiocarbon dating, the patterns that emerge may help in understanding site features and indicate topics ripe for further investigation.

A few notable patterns are evident in the cumulative weight of artefacts across test pits (Figure 5.18). While most test pits increase fairly smoothly before levelling out, Test Pit B increases, and then levels out with relatively low artefact weights during Spits 5 and 6 before resuming a steep climb until Spit 10. The contrast with other spits is even more pronounced when comparing artefact weight densities across test pits (Figure 5.19). Both measures are dominated by marine shell, earthenware pottery and mammal bone weights; we will consider tradeware ceramics below, but other artefacts occur so rarely that they are of little utility for intra-site analyses. Test Pit B density by spit follows the same general pattern as other test pits through Spit 6, but then abruptly increases and artefacts continue until Spit 13. This might indicate that the sterile spits in the other test pits in fact are just interregnums in occupation and that artefacts may resume in deeper, unexcavated sediment. We note, however, that unlike the sterile layers in other test pits, Test Pit B did continue to have some artefacts in Spits 5 and 6, albeit at low weights. Alternatively, the patterns might indicate that the Test Pit B area was occupied earlier than other tested areas, with occupation intensity dropping before picking up again as the wider area was occupied. Since Test Pit B was associated with a stone wall, this might be a hint that the stone walls at the site predate the wider site occupation.

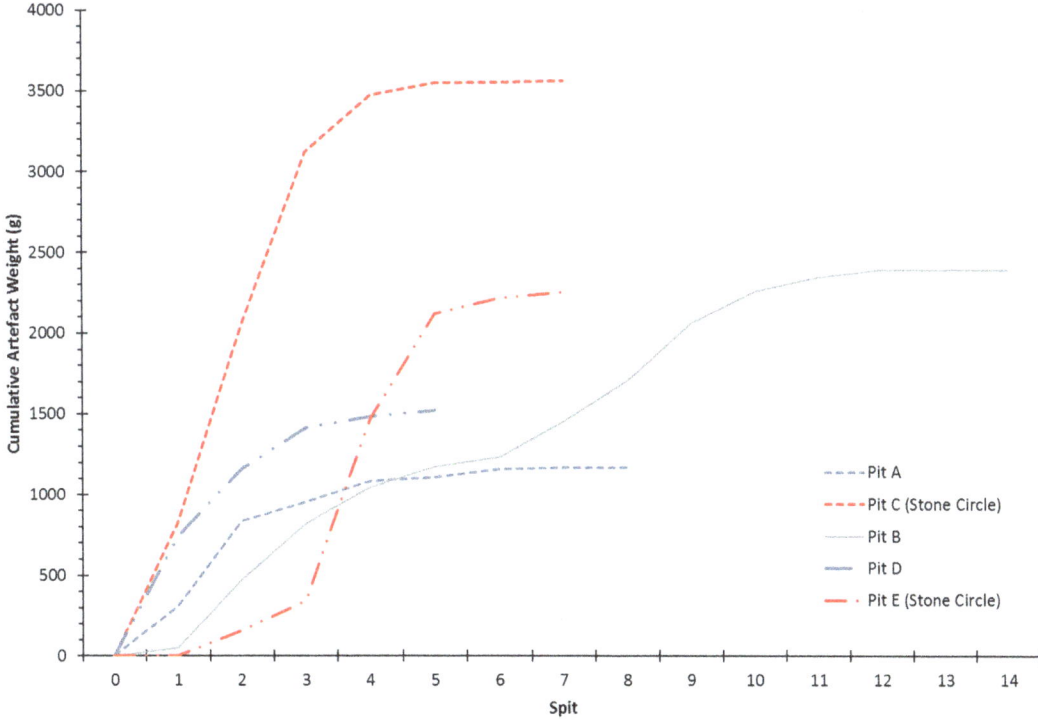

Figure 5.18. Leki Wakik cumulative artefact weight per spit.
Spit 0 is just a notional spit used to anchor the artefact curves.
Source: Jack Fenner.

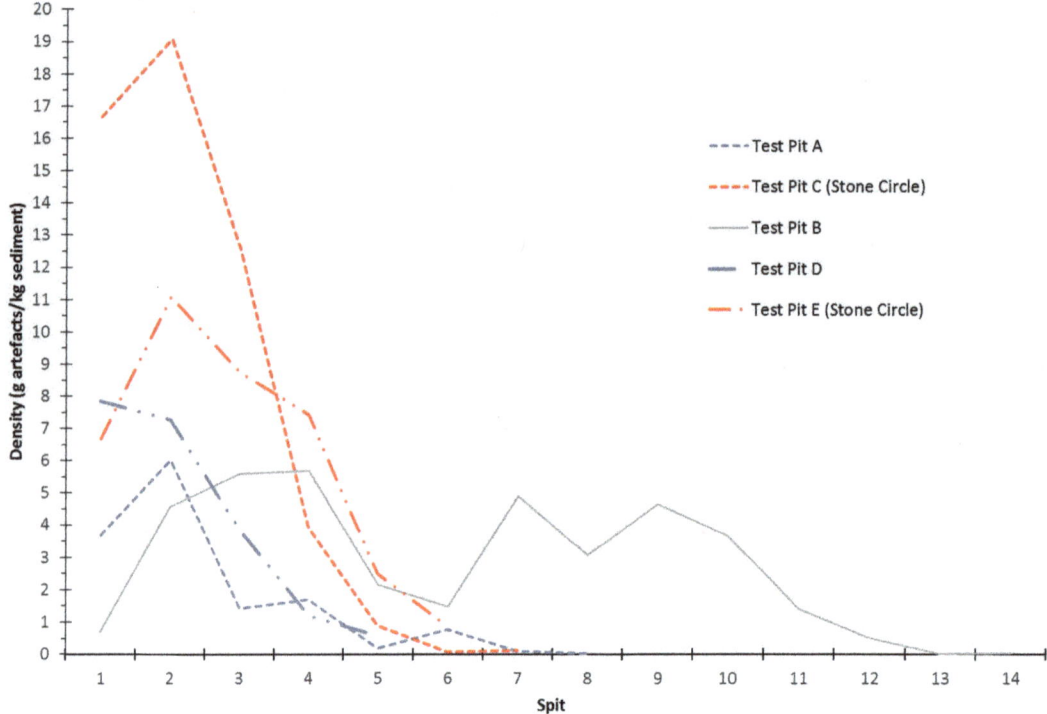

Figure 5.19. Leki Wakik artefact weight density per spit.
Density is computed as artefact weight (g)/excavated sediment weight (kg), excluding non-artefactual rocks.
Source: Jack Fenner.

A second pattern, evident in Figure 5.18 and Figure 5.19, is that the top levels of Test Pit C have higher weights and densities of artefacts than is the case for other test pits. This is due largely to a high amount of earthenware pottery in Spits 1 through 3, though marine mollusc shell is also unusually abundant in those spits (Table 5.A1). As Test Pit C is inside a stone circle, this might suggest that the stone circle areas were more densely occupied, or otherwise special places, during the relatively recent times represented by these spits. We note that Test Pit E, also located in a stone circle, has relatively high artefact weight density in its top spits, though the actual artefact weights are low (this contrast is explained by the very high abundance of non-artefactual stone in top levels of Test Pit E). Thus, there is some reason to believe that, at least during relatively recent times, the areas currently marked by stone circles were used differently to other areas.

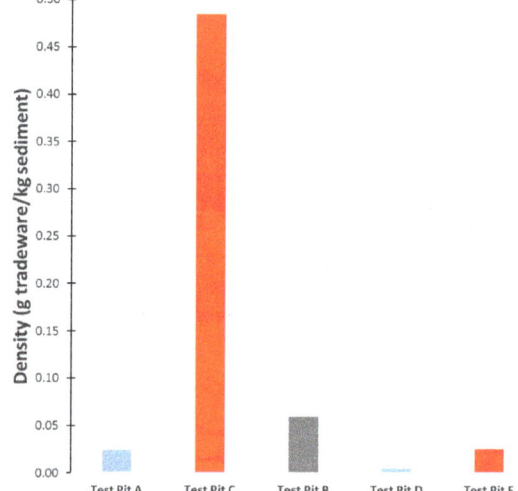

Figure 5.20. Leki Wakik tradeware density by test pit.
Red: Inside stone circle. Blue: Near stone circle.
Source: Jack Fenner.

Tradeware ceramics were a scarce, imported commodity that likely held special significance in Leki Wakik society and thus the tradeware sherd distribution within the site may indicate special or elite occupation spaces. While tradeware sherds were present in all test pits, they were concentrated in Test Pits C (48 per cent of recovered sherds) and B (34 per cent of recovered sherds) (Table 5.2). Tradeware sherds represent only about 7 per cent of the artefact weight in Test Pit C (Table 5.A1) so they are not a significant driver of its anomalously high artefact weight; instead they are another indication that the Test Pit C stone circle was a relatively special place. Test Pit E, the other stone circle site, produced only a single tradeware sherd. Test Pit B is adjacent to a large stone wall that partially encloses a relatively small area of the site, giving that area the appearance of being a special place. Its relatively high tradeware sherd count may support that assessment. It may be, however, that its abundance of tradeware is simply due to Test Pit B's much deeper excavation; relative to the amount of sediment excavated, tradeware does not appear to be especially abundant in Test Pit B (Figure 5.20).

A fortified occupation site?

A number of other hilltop sites in Timor-Leste have been interpreted as being fortified occupation sites. Sites such as Macapainara (Chapter 2, this volume), Vasino (Chapter 4, this volume) and Masui (O'Connor et al. 2012) share a number of characteristics: they are located on hilltops; are surrounded by high walls and/or cliffs (sometimes with large cacti on the perimeter); contain everyday artefacts, such as animal bone and earthenware pottery, as well as exotic tradeware ceramics; and have an initial occupation date after AD 1300, especially between 1550 and 1750 (O'Connor et al. 2012). Special dark stone slabs, usually associated with graves, are often present in fortified sites (McWilliam et al. 2012).

Leki Wakik shares all these characteristics with one significant exception: it is not surrounded by high walls or cliffs. It has two large walls positioned to cut off the central area from what we have called the northeastern and northwestern arms of the site (Figure 5.2). A third large wall runs along the perimeter for 19 m before turning in and partially enclosing a small portion of the site (including Test Pit B). However, unlike at the other sites noted above, these walls do not surround the site, spanning only about 150 m of the 775 m perimeter of the central portion of the site. Nor could the slopes around the site be considered to be cliffs; we routinely walked in zigzag fashion up the steepest slopes in the area—along the north and northeastern site boundaries—while carrying archaeological gear from the parking area. The eastern slopes could also be walked without much difficulty, and local herders routinely lead goats up the southern and western slopes. Leki Wakik is also distinguished from other hilltop sites by its size. With a central area of 31,000 m^2 it dwarfs Vasino (4690 m^2) and is more than twice the size of Masui (13,830 m^2).

With such a large perimeter, which is mostly without stone fortification and surrounded by walkable slopes, it would have taken many hundreds if not several thousand people to defend it against even a fairly small attacking force that could pick its lines of approach. If that many people were available as a defence force, one suspects that even the minor advantages of its hilltop position and short stone walls would not have been necessary. It may be that some walls were disassembled and the stone reused after the site was abandoned, though neither the existing walls nor the stone circles have gaps suggesting partial disassembly. It is possible that the occupants simply did not have enough time to build more walls before abandoning the site, but the long radiocarbon sequence from Test Pit B indicates otherwise. It is also possible that the site was simply the best defensive position available to a particular group, so they made do as best they could. However, the lack of more and better positioned walls (cutting off the northeastern arm would seem a low priority compared to fortifying low slopes elsewhere) suggests instead that at Leki Wakik defence may not have been the top priority for site occupants. Occupying the hilltop may have had other cultural or environmental attributes that were sufficient to overcome difficulties related to access and exposure on a hilltop, such as offering an opportunity for elites to demonstrate their authority and their affinity with other elites. The presence of the large black stone that receives local offerings and the overall sacred nature of the site for contemporary residents of Laleia testify to the cultural importance of the location.

Conclusions

Surface mapping and excavation of 5 m² cannot be expected to fully characterise such a large site, much less provide definitive answers to questions about site function or cultural intention. Nevertheless, our analyses do permit some tentative conclusions about the site. It clearly supported an occupation, with artefacts indicating that subsistence involved marine and freshwater resources as well as domesticated animal husbandry. Leki Wakik's occupants exploited gastropods and other shellfish from marine, estuarine and freshwater environments, though estuarine-based shells were relatively rare at Leki Wakik. There appears to be a shift towards more freshwater exploitation later in the site's history as freshwater gastropods were dominant in upper levels of Test Pits A and D and in the middle levels of E. Minor numbers of mangrove species appear for the first time in the upper levels, perhaps indicating a late formation of this ecosystem locally. The species of estuarine shellfish gathered indicates that landward rather than seaward mangrove forests were being exploited (Australian National Botanic Gardens 2019). Throughout the occupation of the site, the residents also consistently harvested marine species, which were found in all spits.

Given its location near the coast, there were surprisingly few fish remains at Leki Wakik. However, the presence of dog bones and dog-gnawed bones suggests that most discarded fish remains may have been consumed by dogs, much like they were at the Vasino fort site (Amano and Piper 2011; Chapter 4, this volume). The fish taxa that are represented are predominately inshore marine reef fishes, which can be captured without the need for a boat using a variety of methods including hand lines, fish traps, and gill net techniques that are commonly used by the Timorese today (McWilliam 2002).

Domestic livestock, including water buffalo, pigs and goats, continue to play an important role in Timorese socioeconomic systems (Población 2013). This also appears to have been the case during the occupation of Leki Wakik, which contained all these species, as well as commensal dogs and rats. It may be significant that no definitively wild mammal species' remains were found. Historical documents and local oral traditions indicate that, at times, relations between clan groups were characterised by internecine warfare and hostilities, which may have made it dangerous for hunters to pursue wild game. However, in the late nineteenth and early twentieth centuries, and particularly after the 1912 Timorese rebellion led by Dom Boaventura (the indigenous ruler of Manufahi or Same), the Portuguese introduced a program to move Timor-Leste people from 'hunter-gathering and shifting forms of agriculture to permanent gardens and other more sedentary forms of cultivation' (Fitzpatrick 2002:35), which indicates that some level of hunting was still widely practised in Timor-Leste at that time. In addition, wild game remains were recovered from the fortified sites of Macapainara and Ira Ara in the Com area to the east (see Chapters 2 and 3, this volume) and from Manatuto to the west (Lape and Chao 2008). Thus, it is surprising that wild game remains were not recovered from Leki Wakik.

At least a portion of the site must have been occupied for centuries, perhaps starting around AD 1450. The presence of tradeware from the lowest levels of the Leki Wakik excavations indicates that its occupants had some form of contact, whether direct trade or exchange, with the outside world from its formation. The lack of wasters at Leki Wakik indicates that pottery manufacture likely did not occur at this location and also implies the existence of local exchange networks. However, some of our senior male informants knew how to make pottery utensils and they recalled using locally made pottery utensils in their youth, and there is no evidence to suggest that the earthenware was imported rather than locally made at a nearby location.

Oral history and the lack of a substantial amount of historical material at the site indicate that the site was abandoned prior to the local widespread availability of Western goods. Although the site contains some stone walls and is located on a hilltop, its role as a defensive fortification is questionable. While the wall layout suggests that the area near Test Pit B partially enclosed by stone walls was a special area—perhaps an elite residence—the artefacts recovered from that pit do not seem out of the ordinary. If there was a special place revealed during excavations, it is the stone circle containing Test Pit C, which produced both an unusual abundance of artefacts and a high number of exotic tradeware sherds. In fact, both excavated stone circles yielded a higher artefact abundance than did nearby areas, indicating the stone circles mark areas of some special significance or more intensive occupation.

Supplemental material

Supplemental information is provided separately via the ANU Open Research Library and the ANU Data Commons.

Supplement 1, ANU Open Research Library:

- Lim, T.S. 2017. Report on high-fired glazed ceramics at Leki Wakik, East Timor. hdl.handle.net/1885/159483. Adobe PDF format. Unpublished report. The Australian National University, Canberra.

Supplement 2, ANU Data Commons:

- Leki Wakik artefact data sheets. dx.doi.org/10.25911/5cb55b75057a4.

Excel 2010 files in zipped format. Includes:

- LekiWakik_RecoveredMaterial_v2.xlsx
- Leki Wakik Square B Ceramics_Supps.xlsx
- Leki Wakik Shell Supplementary Information (1)_Summarised.xlsx
- LekiWakik_VertebrateData.xlsx

References

Amano, N. and P.J. Piper 2011. A report on the animal remains from the 2009 archaeological excavations at Vasino in East Timor. Unpublished report. The Australian National University, Canberra. hdl.handle.net/1885/111565. Accessed 19 March 2020.

Australian National Botanical Gardens 2019. Mangroves. Australian vegetation: Information about Australia's flora. www.anbg.gov.au/photo/vegetation/mangroves.html. Accessed 19 March 2020.

Behrensmeyer, A.K. 1978. Taphonomic and ecologic information from bone weathering. *Paleobiology* 4(2):150–162. doi.org/10.1017/s0094837300005820.

Boxer, C.R. 1948. *Fidalgos in the Far East, 1550–1770*. Martinus Nijhoff, The Hague.

Bronk Ramsey, C. 2009. Bayesian analysis of radiocarbon dates. *Radiocarbon* 51:337–360. doi.org/10.1017/s0033822200033865.

Classen, C. 1998. *Shells*. Cambridge University Press, Cambridge.

Coil, R., M. Tappen and K. Yezzi-Woodley 2017. New analytical methods for comparing bone fracture angles: A controlled study of hammerstone and hyena (*Crocuta crocuta*) long bone breakage. *Archaeometry* 59(5):900–917. doi.org/10.1111/arcm.12285.

Davidson, K.G. 1994. The Portuguese colonisation of Timor: The final stage, 1850–1912. Unpublished PhD thesis. University of Melbourne, Melbourne.

Fitzpatrick, D. 2002. *Land claims in East Timor*. Asia Pacific Press, Canberra.

Galán, A.B., M. Rodríguez, S. De Juana and M. Domínguez-Rodrigo 2009. A new experimental study on percussion marks and notches and their bearing on the interpretation of hammerstone-broken faunal assemblages. *Journal of Archaeological Science* 36:776–784.

Glover, I. 1986. *Archaeology in Eastern Timor, 1966–67*. Terra Australis 11. Department of Prehistory, Research School of Pacific Studies, The Australian National University, Canberra.

Gunn, G.C. 1999. *Timor Loro Sae: 500 years*. Livros do Oriente, Macau.

Haynes, G. 1983. Frequencies of spiral and green-bone fractures on ungulate limb bones in modern surface assemblages. *American Antiquity* 48:102–114. doi.org/10.2307/279822.

Hogg, A.G., Q. Hua, P.G. Blackwell, M. Niu, C.E. Buck, T.P. Guilderson, T.J. Heaton, J.G. Palmer, P.J. Reimer, R.W. Reimer, C.S.M. Turney and S.R.H. Zimmerman 2013. SHCal13 Southern Hemisphere calibration, 0–50,000 years cal BP. *Radiocarbon* 55:1889–1903. doi.org/10.2458/azu_js_rc.55.16783.

Joliffe, J. 1978. *East Timor: Nationalism and colonialism*. University of Queensland Press, St Lucia.

Lape, P.V. and C.-Y. Chao 2008. Fortification as a human response to late Holocene climate change in East Timor. *Archaeology in Oceania* 43(1):11–21. doi.org/10.1002/j.1834-4453.2008.tb00026.x.

Lyman, R.L. 2008. *Quantitative paleozoology*. Cambridge University Press, Cambridge.

McWilliam, A. 2000. A plague on your house? Some impacts of *Chromolaena odorata* on Timorese livelihoods. *Human Ecology* 28(3):451–469. doi.org/10.1023/A:1007061632588.

McWilliam, A. 2002. Timorese seascapes: Perspectives on customary marine tenures in East Timor. *The Asia Pacific Journal of Anthropology*, 3(2):6–32. doi.org/10.1080/14442210210001706266.

McWilliam, A. 2007. Looking for Adê: A contribution to Timorese historiography. *Bijdragen tot de Taal-, Land- en Volkenkunde* 163(2/3):221–238. doi.org/10.1163/22134379-90003684.

McWilliam, A., D. Bulbeck, S. Brockwell and S. O'Connor 2012. The cultural legacy of Makassar stone in East Timor. *The Asia Pacific Journal of Anthropology* 13(3):262–279. doi.org/10.1080/14442213.2012.674054.

Mowat, F. 1995. Variability in Western Arnhem Land midden deposits. Unpublished Masters thesis. Northern Territory University, Darwin.

O'Connor, S., A. McWilliam, J.N. Fenner, and S. Brockwell 2012. Examining the origin of fortifications in East Timor: Social and environmental factors. *Journal of Island and Coastal Archaeology* 7:200–218. doi:10.1080/15564894.2011.619245.

Pannell, S. 2006. Welcome to the Hotel Tutuala: Fataluku accounts of going places in an immobile world. *The Asia Pacific Journal of Anthropology* 7(3):203–219. doi.org/10.1080/14442210600965158.

Población, E.A. 2013. Fisheries and food security in Timor-Leste: The effects of ritual meat exchanges and market chains on fishing. *Food Security* 5:807–816. doi.org/10.1007/s12571-013-0308-2.

Reimer, P., E. Bard, A. Bayliss, J.W. Beck, P.G. Blackwell, C.B. Ramsey, P.M. Grootes, T.P. Guilderson, H. Haflidason, I. Hajdas, C. Hatté, T.J. Heaton, D.L. Hoffmann, A.G. Hogg, K.A. Hughen, K.F. Kaiser, B. Kromer, S.W. Manning, M. Niu, R.W. Reimer, D.A. Richards, E. Marian Scott, J.R. Southon, R.A. Staff, C.S.M. Turney and J. van der Plicht 2013. IntCal13 and Marine13 radiocarbon age calibration curves 0–50,000 years cal BP. *Radiocarbon* 55:1869–1887. doi.org/10.2458/azu_js_rc.55.16947. doi.org/10.2458/azu_js_rc.55.16947.

Roque, R. 2010. *Headhunting and colonialism: Anthropology and the circulation of human skulls in the Portuguese Empire 1870–1930*. Palgrave Macmillan, New York.

Sadek-Kooros, H. 1975. Intentional fracturing of bone: Description of criteria. In A.T. Clason (ed.), *Archaeozoological studies*. North Holland Publishing, Amsterdam.

Shepard, A.O. 1974. *Ceramics for the archaeologist*. Carnegie Institution Publications, Washington D.C.

Shipman, P., G. Foster and M. Schoeninger 1984. Burnt bones and teeth: An experimental study of color, morphology, crystal structure and shrinkage. *Journal of Archaeological Science* 11(4):307–325. doi.org/10.1016/0305-4403(84)90013-x.

Stiner, M.C., S.L. Kuhn, S. Weiner and O. Bar-Yosef 1995. Differential burning, recrystallization, and fragmentation of archaeological bone. *Journal of Archaeological Science* 22:223–237. doi.org/10.1006/jasc.1995.0024.

White, J., and W. Henderson 2003. Pottery anatomy: Review and selection of basic nomenclature as a step toward a searchable rim form database for the Sakon Nakhon Basin. *Bulletin of the Indo-Pacific Prehistory Association* 23:35–49.

Appendix

Table 5.A1. Leki Wakik excavated material weights (in grams except as noted).

Test Pit	Spit	Sediment (kg)	Non-artefactual stone (kg)	Artefactual stone	Fully marine mollusc shell	Mangrove-based mollusc shell	Freshwater mollusc shell	Unidentified aquatic mollusc shell	Terrestrial mollusc shell	Coral	Earthenware pottery	Tradeware (glazed) ceramic	Mammal bone	Bird bone	Fish bone	Crustacean and urchin	Seed	Concrete	Metal	Total artefact weight (g)
A	1	83.3	19.9	3	165.3	4.6	62	58.2	-	-	-	11.4	2	-	-	0.1	-	-	-	306.6
A	2	88	42.7	6.3	233.3	2.8	59.6	81.2	-	1.1	115.4	4.4	3.4	-	-	-	-	21.6	-	529.1
A	3	82.9	49.5	0.7	42.5	0.1	2.3	6.1	-	0.7	47.9	-	15.4	-	0.1	0.9	-	-	-	116.7
A	4	78	43.7	0.3	98.9	-	0.5	13.6	-	-	17.9	-	0.1	-	0.1	0.3	-	-	-	131.7
A	5	107.6	41.5	-	14.4	-	-	2.5	-	-	3.4	-	-	-	-	-	-	-	-	20.3
A	6	71.9	69.7	-	50.1	-	1.1	2.7	-	-	-	-	-	-	-	0.2	-	-	-	54.1
A	7	83.2	40.9	-	5.6	-	-	-	-	-	2.2	-	-	-	-	-	-	-	-	7.8
A	8	62.6	47.6	0.4	-	-	-	-	-	-	-	-	-	-	-	-	-	-	-	0.4
A	Total	657.5	355.5	10.7	610.1	7.5	125.5	164.3	0	1.8	186.8	15.8	20.9	-	0.2	1.5	-	21.6	-	1166.7
B	1	71.1	NR	-	14.5	-	0.2	21	10.5	-	2.7	-	0.4	-	-	-	0.3	-	-	49.6
B	2	92.1	-	-	265.2	0.7	3.2	15.1	0.2	-	130	3.9	2.4	-	-	-	-	-	-	420.7
B	3	62.8	42.3	-	163.5	-	2.9	26.6	1.3	-	116.3	0.6	39.9	-	-	-	-	-	-	351.1
B	4	38.8	8.3	0.4	112.9	-	3.3	6.7	-	-	87.8	8.4	0.5	-	-	-	-	-	-	220
B	5	62.7	16.6	-	45	-	6.9	20.3	0.7	-	58.8	1	1.8	-	-	-	-	-	-	133.5
B	6	40.2	10.3	-	26	-	2.2	11	-	-	18.7	-	-	-	-	-	-	-	-	58.9
B	7	44.5	13.8	-	81.1	-	14.1	10.2	0.5	-	65.5	20.6	25.9	-	-	-	-	-	-	217.9
B	8	82.5	32.2	0.3	40.5	-	11.9	30.6	0.3	-	82.4	9	77.9	-	-	-	-	-	-	252.9
B	9	76	29.1	5.1	129.6	-	16.5	28.1	-	-	170.8	1.9	0.3	-	-	-	-	-	-	352.3
B	10	54.9	-	12.8	104.3	-	13.7	11.7	-	-	37.9	2.7	17.9	0.2	-	-	-	-	-	201.2
B	11	63.9	28.2	1	64.6	-	10.3	4.1	-	-	7.5	1.9	-	-	-	0.1	-	-	-	89.5
B	12	89.8	37.6	-	1.6	-	1.5	2.9	-	-	36.5	-	1.2	-	-	-	-	-	-	43.7
B	13	68.7	36.7	-	-	-	0.7	0.4	-	-	1	-	-	-	-	-	-	-	-	0
B	14	NR	-	-	-	-	-	-	-	-	-	-	-	-	-	-	-	-	-	2.1
B	Total	848	255.1	19.6	1048.8	0.7	87.4	188.7	13.5	0	815.9	50	168.2	0.2	0	0.1	0.3	0	0	2393.4

Test Pit	Spit	Sediment (kg)	Non-artefactual stone (kg)	Artefactual stone	Fully marine mollusc shell	Mangrove-based mollusc shell	Freshwater mollusc shell	Unidentified aquatic mollusc shell	Terrestrial mollusc shell	Coral	Earthenware pottery	Tradeware (glazed) ceramic	Mammal bone	Bird bone	Fish bone	Crustacean and urchin	Seed	Concrete	Metal	Total artefact weight (g)
C	1	49.4	48	0.4	139.1	17	0.6	87.2	37.4	14.7	398.1	128.3	0.5	–	–	–	–	–	–	823.3
C	2	64.9	50.1	2.8	306	–	0.6	62	–	55.9	722.2	81	–	–	–	–	–	–	5.7	1236.2
C	3	84.7	59.8	–	150.2	–	4	84.6	7.9	94.8	701.2	9.2	12.8	–	–	–	–	–	–	1064.7
C	4	89.7	102.5	9.4	63.2	7.1	2.7	34.2	4.7	29.3	195	5.9	–	–	–	–	–	–	–	351.5
C	5	82.6	50.8	–	4.7	–	1.1	4.7	–	–	26.3	35.5	–	–	–	–	–	–	–	72.3
C	6	103.6	43.2	1.2	2.2	–	1.3	0.4	0.6	–	2.3	–	–	–	–	–	–	–	–	7.4
C	7	62.3	45.9	–	–	–	0.4	–	–	5.2	–	–	–	–	–	–	–	–	–	6.2
C	Total	537.2	400.3	13.8	665.4	24.1	10.7	273.1	50.6	199.9	2045.1	259.9	13.3	0	0	0	0	0	5.7	3561.6
D	1	94.8	41.7	9.1	116.8	–	41.1	62.5	6.6	23.5	482.5	–	1.3	–	–	0.1	–	–	–	743.5
D	2	57.2	23.7	1.9	138.5	10.3	6.1	14	17.4	3.9	200.8	1.6	21	–	0.1	0.1	–	–	–	415.7
D	3	65.7	25.4	–	81.1	3.7	3.3	10.3	5.3	0.2	147.5	–	1.9	–	–	0.1	–	–	–	253.4
D	4	60.8	33.5	1	22.3	0.5	1.8	5.8	1.2	7.7	27.6	–	3.3	–	0.2	–	–	–	–	71.4
D	5	62.6	32.4	–	7.8	–	–	0.9	3.7	–	19.1	–	3.1	–	–	–	–	–	–	34.6
D	Total	341.1	156.7	12	366.5	14.5	52.3	93.5	34.2	35.3	877.5	1.6	30.6	0	0.3	0.3	0	0	0	1518.6
E	1	0	144.8	–	–	–	–	–	131.9	–	–	–	–	–	–	–	–	–	–	161.3
E	2	24.2	49.9	–	10.5	–	0.4	5.9	78.2	–	8.6	–	1.4	–	–	–	4	–	–	183.9
E	3	16.6	21.1	–	60.7	–	8	2.9	44.7	–	31.3	–	–	–	–	–	1.4	–	–	1132.4
E	4	129.6	175.8	0.6	524	5.9	39.1	57.4	41.8	54.8	317.4	8.4	79.2	–	0.3	0.1	0.5	–	–	1132.4
E	5	86.9	49.6	2.5	233.5	6.4	6.8	0.5	1.4	13	331.8	–	6.8	–	0.1	0.6	–	–	–	643.8
E	6	39.3	19.3	0.3	56.4	–	2.5	7.1	1.1	–	28.3	–	1	–	–	–	–	–	–	97
E	7	42.3	36.1	–	16.5	–	–	2.3	–	–	15.3	–	0.9	–	–	–	–	–	–	36.1
E	Total	338.9	496.6	3.4	901.6	12.3	56.8	76.1	299.1	67.8	732.7	8.4	89.3	0	0.4	0.7	5.9	0	0	2254.5
All		2722.7	1664.2	59.5	3592.4	59.1	332.7	795.7	397.4	304.8	4658	335.7	322.3	0.2	0.9	2.6	6.2	21.6	5.7	10894.8

Source: Authors' summary.

Table 5.A2. Leki Wakik radiocarbon results.

Sample ID	Test Pit	EU	In situ code	Material	Taxon	Lab ID	pMC	RC age (BP)	1σ Error	Cal start (AD)	Cal end (AD)
LW-A7	A	7		charcoal		D-AMS 009704	121.96	Modern			
LW-B3_001	B	3	1	marine shell	Cypraeidae	D-AMS 009698	92.72	607	23	1646	1803
LW-B3	B	3		charcoal		D-AMS 009703	98.55	117	24	1682	1924
LW-B4_002	B	4	2	marine shell	Turbo chrysostomus	D-AMS 009697	92.28	645	24	1574	1705
LW-B4_006	B	4	6	charcoal		D-AMS 009702	97.90	171	25	1667	1892
LW-B6_002	B	6	2	marine shell	Conomurex luhuanus	D-AMS 009696	92.00	670	29	1544	1689
LW_B7_004	B	7	4	charcoal		D-AMS 009701	96.81	260	25	1635	1799
LW-B10_006	B	10	6	charcoal		D-AMS 009700	94.86	424	25	1446	1623
LW-B10_007	B	10	7	marine shell	Turbo chrysostomus	D-AMS 009695	90.96	761	22	1484	1631
LW-B12_002	B	12	2	marine shell	Tridacna crocea	D-AMS 009694	88.22	1007	25	1310	1418
LW-B12	B	12		charcoal		D-AMS 009699	95.65	357	26	1491	1641
LW-B14	B	14		marine shell	Nautilus sp.	D-AMS 009693	87.06	1113	24	1237	1336
LW-C1	C	1		charcoal		D-AMS 009705	Failed				

Calibration performed using OxCal 4.2 (Bronk Ramsey 2009) using the SHCal13 (Hogg et al. 2013) and Marine13 (Reimer et al. 2013) calibration curves for charcoal and marine shell, respectively. Calibrated dates intervals shown are the 95.4 per cent intervals. D-AMS 009705 did not produce valid results. The local ΔR calibration offset is unknown for any species in Timor-Leste, so no ΔR was applied to the shell dates.

Source: Authors' summary.

Social history of forts

6

Social drivers of fortified settlements in Timor-Leste

Andrew McWilliam

Introduction

In a number of publications, archaeologists Peter Lape and C.-Y. Chao have proposed a 'climate change' model to account for the emergence of fortified structures and 'defensively oriented settlement sites' in Timor-Leste. Specifically, they argue that during the late Holocene (post-AD 1000), processes of fortification were driven by severe and rapid climatic events associated with the El Niño Southern Oscillation effect (ENSO) (Chao 2008; Lape 2006; Lape and Chao 2008). The critical ENSO impact was decreasing, leading to variable rainfall and protracted droughts during the period beginning c. AD 1000, and rising to a peak period AD 1300–1400. The effect of variable rainfall, it is argued, resulted in food scarcity and gave rise to the construction of defensive fortifications, particularly in areas with permanent water flows that remained agriculturally viable during drought. According to Lape and Chao, people built forts to protect themselves against others who lived in more distant or adjacent regions and who were suffering food shortages.

Lape and Chao advance a number of related factors that purport to support their predictive model of where fortified settlements might be found. They argue that fortifications appeared in the landscape in regions that contained resources tolerant of climate change, thus creating conditions of relative surplus, and that were also adjacent to regions with resources intolerant of climate change, thus creating conditions of relative deficit. To test their predictive model, archaeological investigations were carried out in selected areas of Timor, especially the northeastern coastal districts of Manatuto and Lautem where a series of 28 defensively located hilltop and stone-fortified former settlements were excavated and/or sampled. They find general support for their hypothesis, arguing that the spatial data supports a conclusion that fortifications were built preferentially in areas containing drought resistant resources (2008:19).

In the following paper, the utility of this climate-based model of settlement fortification is called into question and an alternative analysis is presented that foregrounds a range of prospective social drivers that might better explain the historical shift towards defensive settlements and the structural characteristics of their built forms. While not discounting the importance of environmental dynamics on Timorese livelihoods and residential choice, a factor that continues to play a significant constraining role in relation to Timorese food security, it is argued that the evidence points more to sociohistorical factors as drivers of change than any marked variations in rainfall patterns and agricultural production. Specifically, I argue that the novel and combined impact of Portuguese colonialism and Sulawesi-based Islamic trading interests from the middle of the sixteenth century set in train a transformative shift in Timorese social relations and residential patterns that gave rise to the emergence of fortified hilltop settlements. The paper sets out four central elements of that transformation and, importantly, argues not for a definitive or original date for fortification, for which strong evidence remains elusive, but rather for an historical period of time when the need for a defensive posture became irresistible.[1]

Fortified settlements in Timor: Structure and forms

Timor is littered with the remnants of old fortified settlement sites, many of which were lived in and used by Timorese communities until well into the twentieth century and remain important cultural sites to the present day. There is therefore a considerable body of ethnohistorical information and local narratives about the use and characteristics of these sites, including their structural functions and significance in former times. In the following analysis, I draw on archaeological and ethnographic interpretations that focus on fortified settlement sites in the far eastern district of Lautem. Here there is a considerable density of fortified sites including a number that have been excavated by Lape (see 2006; Lape and Chao 2008). The region therefore provides a direct comparative context for addressing the Lape–Chao hypothesis.

One important category distinction made by resident Fataluku-speaking farming communities in Lautem is that between former sites of habitation, known as *lata paru* (past settlements) or *lata irinu* (old settlements), and the concept of a fortified settlement described by the term *pa'amakolo*. The latter word is a composite construction of *pa'a* (to pile up) and *makolo* (dense or wide walls). Places known as *pa'amakolo* tend to share a number of common structural features (see also Lape 2006). They include:

- Enclosing structures, commonly comprising double rows of dry stacked limestone walls (1–4 m in height and 1–2 m wide at the base), are infilled with a distinctive limestone rubble, known as *horo*, that litters much of the kastic limestone forest floor in Lautem. The walls form massive perimeter barriers and some sites have a series of walled perimeters in varying degrees of integrity.
- Walled settlements are typically located in highly defensive locations, on hilltops or steep cliffs, and enclose areas ranging from 500 m² to 3000 m².
- Many forts feature defensive stone gateways with narrow off-centre entrances that can be guarded from above. Some have slitted apertures suggesting that weapons were used to guard or fire upon the entrances. The gateways typically open onto an internal walled space (*laca*), which is said to be the area where visitors were greeted.
- Many forts have extensive groves of cactus (including prickly pear) near the entrance and lining the surrounding walls, providing an additional defensive barrier.[2]
- *Pa'amakolo* tend not to have internal water sources, but all are generally located in close proximity to substantial springs. According to local informants, in the past water was stored within the fortified sites in earthenware jars.
- Other common internal features of the sites are massive stone graves (*calu luturu*), some of which are reported to form large reusable tombs holding numerous burials (*poko caru*),

---

1   A modified version of this argument was published in 2012 as S. O'Connor, A. McWilliam, J.N. Fenner and S. Brockwell 2012. Examining the origin of fortifications in East Timor: Social and environmental factors. *The Journal of Coastal and Island Archaeology* 7(2):200–218, doi.org/10.1080/15564894.2011.619245. That paper focused specifically on the 'origins' of fortification while I am more concerned here with factors that both initiated and reproduced their form.

2   Prickly pear (*Opuntia elatior*) was an early twentieth-century invasive species in Timor that expanded to plague-like proportions, as it did elsewhere in the region, including Australia. I have argued that it provided a means of encouraging protected settlements out of the mountain forts and into lower-lying terrain (see McWilliam 2000:465).

ceremonial dancing grounds (*sepu*) and typically distinctive sacrificial posts (*ete uru ha'a* or *sikua*), which remain sites of sacrificial veneration for customary owners of the former settlements.

- All the sites are considered the abode of spirits, and thus potentially dangerous to health and wellbeing. They form part of a complex of beliefs and taboos referred to as *tei* (pl: *teinu*), a concept that combines moral authority and protective familiarity with elements of dangerous uncertainty and spiritual retribution.
- A great number of the fortified sites remain actively tended and visited periodically for group-specific sacrificial rituals and commensal gatherings with group origin ancestors.

Archaeological evidence

The present paper is based on a collaborative research project between anthropology and archaeology that is exploring the history and prehistory of the distinctive fortified settlements on the island of Timor in eastern Wallacea, which point to a past period of heightened insecurity and inter-group warfare. Three related questions are guiding the research. First, when was the main period for the initiation of fort construction? Second, what were the prevailing environmental and social conditions of those times? And, third what were the key factors that may have motivated people to develop highly defensive settlement locations?

The project has focused enquiries in the Lautem district and teams have excavated a number of sites, including the prominent fortified coastal sites at Ili Vali (near Com) known as Macapainara–Sirivairara in 2008 (Chapter 2, this volume), and a fortified site above the present-day settlement of Moro-Parlamento, known as Vasino in 2009 (Chapter 4, this volume). The decision to pursue these particular sites was partly for reasons of access and permission from both local and national authorities, but also to develop a wider comparative repertoire of excavated sites in the region. Preliminary results from the excavations indicate that they provided domestic living spaces in conjunction with their role as defensive fortifications.

In addition to these sites, the project team has located and mapped another dozen or so fortified settlements and collected preliminary data on oral histories, contemporary use and significance from local Fataluku communities who maintain strong cultural attachments to the places in question. These sites are located at Moro-Parlamento, Ira Ara, Tutuala and the forested Vero River valley to the south of Tutuala (Figure 1.1, this volume). The location of sites that includes fortified settlements is illustrated by Lape (2006:286, Figure 1). The map illustrates the relative density of defensive fortified sites in this area of Timor and further survey work is likely to yield additional locations.

During 2008, three test pits were excavated within the fortified headland site, Ili Vali (Macapainara), each to a depth of c. 1.5 m (see Chapter 2, this volume). The excavations contained abundant earthenware pottery, animal bones, stone artefacts and charcoal, a wide range of shellfish and small quantities of ceramic tradeware from China and Europe. Wild animals were represented at lower levels and domesticates, especially buffalo, pig and dog, predominate in the higher or more recent levels. The assemblages generally confirm Peter Lape's earlier findings, as do the results of preliminary dating for shell and charcoal excavated from the test pits at Macapainara.

Table 6.1 illustrates a sequence of dates derived from Macapainara. The results are quite clear and consistent. Of interest is the range of overlapping time periods for shell and charcoal, which shows that the earliest recorded date is AD 1500 with a concentration of material falling within the seventeenth to eighteenth centuries.

Table 6.1. Macapainara radiocarbon dates.

Context (spit)	Lab no. (charcoal)	2δ 95.4% cal. age range (AD)	Lab no. (shell)	2δ 95.4% cal. age range (AD)	Overlap (AD)
A2	Wk-24947	1700–1960	Wk-24956	1672–1960	1700–1960
A8	Wk-24948	1690–1950	Wk-24957	1470–1830	1690–1830
A13	Wk-24949	1640–1960	Wk-24958	1430–1720	1640–1720
C2	Wk-24950	1600–1950	Wk-24959	1615–1960	1615–1950
C7	Wk-24951	1690–1960	Wk-24960	1430–1710	1690–1710
C13	Wk-24952	1500–1800	Wk-24961	1420–1720	1500–1720
D2	Wk-24953	1700–1960	Wk-24962	1490–1880	1700–1880
D8	Wk-24954	1650–1960	Wk-24963	1510–1960	1650–1960
D15	Wk-24955	1800–1950	Wk-24964	1290–1550	nil

Source: From O'Connor et al. (Chapter 2, this volume).

Preliminary dating of recovered ceramics shows that most of the sherds are of Chinese origin with some likely Vietnamese tradeware. Markings and other visual identifiers give indicative dates of manufacture between the sixteenth and early nineteenth centuries. Tradeware sherds were not found to the base of the artefact-bearing deposit, indicating that habitation of the site may have been established as early as the fifteenth century, which coincides with a period when tradeware was in short supply (Bulbeck 1992). The ceramic dates appear to be in close agreement with the radiocarbon dates for charcoal. They point to an origin for the fortifications at Ili Vali, suggesting that the fortification pattern was undertaken no earlier than the sixteenth century.

In support of this finding, one of our colleagues, Jack Fenner, has undertaken a Bayesian analysis for the charcoal-based dates from Macapainara (Chapter 2, this volume). His analysis demonstrates that there is a 99.6 per cent probability that the material derives from post-AD 1500, and an 89 per cent probability that it does not appear before 1650. By 1725 the probability factor is down to 68.9 per cent, falling to 28.4 per cent by 1775. Based on this analysis, the early date probabilities for charcoal cluster around the early eighteenth century.

Comparing these findings with those reported by Lape and Chao (2008; Chao 2008) finds several correspondences. Chao (2008), for instance, excavated a series of fortified hilltop sites in the Manatuto district (100 km west of Lautem on the north coast) during 2004–2006. While a range of radiocarbon dates was obtained from eight locations, fully 70 per cent of the identifiable sherds were dated within the period 1550–1650, and a further 22 per cent of the samples in the period 1650–1725. In other words, 92 per cent of the excavated material postdates AD 1550. Just 5 per cent of the sherds were dated prior to 1550. Lape and Chao acknowledge that 'the hilltop sites in Manatuto were mostly occupied from the mid-16th to the early 18th century AD' (2008:18). Data derived from the fortified sites in Tutuala/Lautem (Lape 2006; Lape and Chao 2008), using a combination of radiocarbon, OSL, TL and AMS[3] dating techniques, obtained a wider range of dated material ranging from 2300 BC to AD 1920. However, as Lape and Chao acknowledge, these sites may have been occupied prehistorically, but 'were likely fortified in the 15th–19th centuries AD' (2008:16).

---

3   Optical stimulated luminescence (OSL), thermo-luminescence (TL) and accelerator mass spectrometry (AMS) radiocarbon dating.

Assessing the evidence

How does this new information mesh with the Lape and Chao model of climate change–induced defensive settlements? We think there are a number of logical and evidential problems. First, among the findings of recent analysis and dating of excavated material from the site Macapainara is the confirmation of a concentration of radiocarbon dates around the seventeenth century, while preliminary dating of Chinese and possibly Vietnamese ceramic sherds reveals a range of material from the sixteenth to early nineteenth centuries. These dates are in general accord with those published by Lape and Chao (2008), who found that the majority of the dates for the fortified sites they analysed clustered within the AD 1450–1650 period. More specifically, they note that the hilltop sites in Manatuto were the only places that people chose to live by the sixteenth and seventeenth centuries, while numerous earlier sites 'on terraces and floodplain were abandoned during this period' (Lape and Chao 2008:18). They acknowledge the 'problematic disjunction' between their model and the calibrated dating of the fortified sites sample, that cluster 'around the 1450–1650AD period, which is later than the El Niño frequency peak of 1300–1400AD', and which they have argued was the climatic precursor to fortification (2008:19).[4] Their best response is that these later sites may have arisen:

> as a result of social forces indirectly related to resource shortages and may have been an adaptation to a system that had already begun to be fortified several hundred years earlier. (2008:19)

The fact is, however, that there is little evidence of this earlier systemic process of climate-induced fortification.

The Lape and Chao model relies heavily on the viability of agriculture in close proximity to fortified settlements, particularly the existence of irrigated cropping of cereals in order to make their case: 'Land even just a few hundred metres away from the river may be totally unproductive if it is too difficult to irrigate' (2008:14). The logical difficulty with this argument is that the principal pattern of livelihood in Timor for centuries, as far as we can tell (Glover 1972; Oliveira 2008), has been a mixture of swidden farming and hunter-gathering regimes that are highly attuned to seasonality and optimise the use of multiple food resources. A concentration on irrigated cereal agriculture was the exception and highly restricted in area. The further assumption that group mobility, and therefore access to wider food resources, was constrained by clan boundaries and limited by internecine rivalries is not credible. Mobility and social alliances across boundaries are fundamental features of Timorese traditional upland agricultural systems and have their cultural roots in antiquity. While mutual enmities and feuding were undoubtedly a feature of these clan-based identities, limited population numbers constrained any capacity to guard boundaries from interlopers.

Another logical problem can be described under the general principle that 'poor folks do not generally attack rich folks'. If there were groups of people who suffered acute food shortages due to drought, they would be unlikely to attack fortified groups who had all the advantages of resources and numbers to prevail. It seems much more likely that prosperous fortified settlement communities would direct their aggression towards similarly equipped counterparts who represented more direct threats.[5] The premise of defending attacks from the impoverished starving margins is therefore an unlikely one and unsupported by any material evidence.

---

4 It is somewhat misleading to make the comment that 'In all three areas fortifications appear on the landscape between 1150–1550 AD' (Lape and Chao 2008:18). In fact, the 1150 date from Manatuto was only found in one isolated charcoal date when the great majority of dates lie between the sixteenth and eighteenth centuries (Lape and Chao 2008:18). Problems with the radiocarbon calibration curve are also acknowledged, which can return uncertainties spanning 200 years.

5 Thanks to Jack Fenner for this observation.

Social drivers of fortification

In exploring the possibility of alternate drivers for settlement fortification, I do not discount the influence of dynamic environmental effects on Timorese livelihoods. Reid, for example, has argued that the period AD 1640–1670 was very dry in Southeast Asia, with deleterious socioeconomic consequences (1993:291–298). But this period does not coincide with the critical period presented in the Lape and Chao model, nor is it clear that these effects had any significant influence on the Timorese environment. By contrast, we would argue that, in the case of Timor-Leste, the evidence points much more strongly to social drivers of change in settlement patterns than it does to environmental factors signalled by marked variation in rainfall distribution. This argument is one that aligns much more closely with the available archaeological evidence, particularly the conclusion that the impetus and widespread emergence of fortified settlements occurred in a period postdating the early sixteenth century (1500s) and well into the seventeenth century.

The history of Timor during this period coincided with a series of intense economic and social transformations linked to a unique combination of factors. Specifically, these influences centred on the arrival of European colonialism in the guise of Portuguese and later Dutch trading interests and corresponded with the emergence of powerful Islamic sultanates in eastern Wallacea, all vying for economic and political advantage. The impact of this volatile convergence of interests had demonstrable, dramatic and long-term repercussions for island societies in the archipelago, Timor included. While the specific contours of these repercussions cannot be charted with precision, there are four significant social drivers of change that are likely to have had major impacts on Timorese social relations and livelihoods, and may well have promoted fortified settlement strategies. The four interrelated drivers of changing settlement strategies comprise: (1) a sandalwood trading boom from the late sixteenth century; (2) the introduction of maize as a staple food crop into Timor in the same period; (3) new trade in advanced weaponry, particularly artillery and firearms; and (4) a significant increase in demand for trade in human slaves. I deal below with each of these prospective social drivers separately, but it is evident that there may well be considerable overlap and correspondences between the elements, which could have contributed to intensified pressures on local residential communities, particularly in far eastern Timor-Leste. I suggest that these processes, or some combination of effects, may well have led to inter-group conflict, reprisals and defensive fortifications.

Increased demand for sandalwood (1580s–1700)

The intricate history surrounding the sandalwood trade from Timor has been the subject of numerous detailed studies (e.g. Boxer 1947, 1948; de Roever 2002; Fox 1977; Gunn 1999; Ormeling 1956). All highlight the ancient origins of the trade and its association with early Javanese sea merchants and Chinese traders. The advent of the Portuguese and later Dutch trading interests, specifically in search of sandalwood trading profits, dramatically increased the political complexity of maritime trading relations and led to an unremitting plunder of stocks across the island from the mid-seventeenth century.

Direct Portuguese sandalwood trading in Timor was initiated in the early sixteenth century, when trading relations were established with strategic ports on the north coast such as Manatuto, Adê (Vemasse), Com (Lautem) and Lifau (Oecussi). By the early seventeenth century, the demand and extraction of high-quality white sandalwood (*Santalum album*) had expanded significantly. Profits in sandalwood were substantial, as much as 100 per cent return on investment by the 1590s

(Ptak 1987:103–4), which by then far outweighed the potential profits to be gained from beeswax and slaves, two other sought-after commodities. As Hägerdal notes, these latter commodities, 'were certainly of enduring interest to traders of the archipelago but would probably not have motivated ambitious European schemes of exploitation of Timor in their own right' (2012:12).

Boxer cites the case of:

> [A]n English merchant who called at Batavia (Java) in 1625, reporting that between 10 and 22 Portuguese galliots called at Macassar [Sulawesi] yearly from Macao, Malacca and ports on the Coromandel coast. They arrived in December and left again in May, using Macassar as an entrepôt for the sale of Chinese silks and Indian cotton textiles, which they exchanged for sandalwood in Timor. (1948:177)

Antonio Bocarro, writing in 1635, highlighted the importance of the sandalwood trade and noted that '[I]n fact sandalwood became so popular that it was used as a kind of currency in the Solor-Timor area' (cited in Ptak 1999:105).

An important component of the sandalwood trade was that profits also accrued to local Timorese rulers and their political allies who supplied the fragrant timber from the coastal ports and obtained prized trading goods in exchange. According to the chronicle of Duarte Barbosa (1521:196), ships going to Timor picked up the mainstay products of sandalwood, honey, beeswax and slaves, against the payment of an array of external goods: iron, axes, knives, swords, cloth from Pulicat in India, copper, mercury, vermillion, tin, lead and coral (beads) from Cambay in India). Another seventeenth-century observer, Saris, spoke of the sandalwood sold (along with 'great cakes' of beeswax) in the markets of Bantam for 'great profit', and traded 'against items of high regard in Timor such as; chopping knives, small bugles, porcelain, coloured taffaties and pieces of silver' (cited in Gunn 1999:65). Similarly, early Dutch observer, Crijn van Raemburch (1614), commented:

> [O]n Timor in buying sandalwood one must engage in endless negotiations with the king and noblemen. The felling and transportation to the coast is carried out by the ordinary people. The greater part of the profits go to the rulers. (cited in Ormeling 1956:177)

Timorese political communities best placed to profit from the boom in sandalwood trade were those with exclusive access to and control over productive sandalwood resources, much of which flourished on the raised, red calcareous soils and monsoon forest vegetation in the hinterlands of Timor. If the extent to which rivalries over the control and production of sandalwood contributed to the emergence of fortified settlements in the region remains uncertain, the lucrative bounty and material wealth that could be gained through trade undoubtedly contributed to a degree of competition and possible resource conflicts between rival centres. Control over sandalwood production and trade brought prosperity and enhanced status to well-placed political communities, making them possible targets of avarice among neighbouring groups.

The high point of trading in sandalwood was reached by the mid-eighteenth century, but it remained profitable until well into the nineteenth century and provided an important source of economic benefits for favoured coastal communities. By way of example, the Portuguese historian Figueiredo recorded the comments of former Timor-Leste Governor Viera Godinho (1784), who was complaining about the volume of contraband trade occurring with Dutch, Chinese and Makassarese merchants dealing 'especially in sandalwood and slaves' (2000:710–711).

The introduction of maize

The advent of an aggressive Portuguese colonialism in the Timor region also brought with it a number of associated developments that had a significant impact on Timorese livelihoods and demographics. One of these developments was the introduction and adoption of maize (*Zea mays*) as a staple crop in Timorese food production. While there is no clear evidence for precisely when maize was introduced in Timor, it is reported to have been established in neighbouring Maluku by the 1540s where it could have easily been transported to Timor (Cinatti 1964:180).[6] By 1658 it was already reported as the main crop in western Timor (Reid 1993:19; Hägerdal 2012:30).[7] From 1672 the Dutch VOC (Vereenigde Oostindische Compagnie: the Dutch East India Company) was also active in promoting the production and dissemination of maize as part of an attempt to improve native cultivation (Fox 1977: 76).

William Dampier, who visited the north coast of Timor in 1699, made some relevant observations on patterns of Timorese livelihoods. He noted that:

> Their common subsistence is Indian corn which every man plants for himself. They take little Pains to clear their land; for in the dry Time, they set Fire to the withered Grass and Shrubs, and that burns them out a Plantation for the next wet season. What other grain they have besides Indian corn, I know not. Their plantations are very mean; for they delight most in hunting; and here wild Buffaloes and Hogs enough, though very shy, because of their so frequent hunting. (1703:170)

The introduction of maize represented a major change in Timorese diets and allowed for substantial food surpluses and very likely higher populations.[8] According to Fox, for example, maize probably replaced a multi-crop swidden system based around millet with some rice, legumes and tubers, which would have supported a population of less than 10 to 14 persons per km^2. Maize, by contrast 'provided the Timorese with the potential to support a population several times that density' (Fox 1988:268).

There is in fact very little direct historical documentation of the demographic impact of the widespread adoption of maize across Timor. But one of the consequences, as Fox has suggested, is that maize 'seems to have triggered local group expansion among the Timorese' where 'voracious methods of slash and burn cultivation required new land and produced a mobile society of shifting local cultivators' (1988:269). The long-term effects of this expansion of shifting cultivation included a marked decline in the forest ecology across the island, but a more immediate impact may well have been increased competition over land and food resources among growing populations and therefore a point of tension between rival groups.

Trade in firearms and gunpowder (sixteenth to eighteenth centuries)

Perhaps the most important social driver for inducing defensive strategies among Timorese populations was the development of a bourgeoning trade in firearms and gunpowder. Logically this factor may well have given rise to the characteristic features of fortified defensive settlements

---

6   Timor was for several centuries within the colonial administrative sphere of Ambon (Maluku)-based traders.

7   Cinatti also cites a report of 1624 that identifies maize (*zaburro*) as 'so inexpensive that it has become the main nourishment of the natives' (1964:183). However, Cinatti acknowledges that the term *zaburro* was also indistinctly employed for sorghum and some varieties of millet.

8   Other New World crops that found their way into Timorese cultivation systems and continue to provide important supplementary food production include pumpkin/squash (*Cucurbita* spp.), cassava (*Manihot utilissima* Pohl.), sweet potato (*Ipomoea batatas* Poir.), peanuts (*Arachis hypogaea*), papaya (*Carica papaya* L.) and tomato (*Solanum lycopersicum*), among others.

in far eastern Timor with the use of coralline rubble (*horo*) as a dense filler between two rows of dry stacked stonewalls. Certainly, comments from local Timorese colleagues readily identify the massive stone walls as a defence against penetrating firearm attack.

Although cannon and gunpowder were Chinese inventions and had been known for centuries, it was the arrival of the Portuguese in the Indian Ocean at the end of the fifteenth century, with far superior weaponry, that irrevocably changed the nature of Asian maritime trade and power relations.[9] As Chase has argued:

> [W]hat had brought the Portuguese to Calicut in India in 1498 was spices, but it quickly became apparent that they had nothing anyone wanted, except bullion from the New World, to exchange for those spices. Fortunately for the Portuguese, what they did have were cannon … Operating at such a great distance from their home country, Portuguese ships relied on superior firepower to offset superior numbers … The Portuguese advantage was not commercial but military. (2003:134)

Chase offers the following description of the Portuguese caravels that were positioned off the Malabar (Kerala) coast in 1501.

> Each of the caravels carried thirty men and four heavy guns below, and above, six falconets and ten swivel guns placed on the quarter deck and in the bows, and two of the falconets fired astern; the ships carried six guns below on the deck, and two smaller ones on the poop, and eight falconets above and several swivel guns, and before the mast two smaller pieces which fired forwards. (2003:134)

Bristling with firepower, the Portuguese used their military advantage to considerable effect through what Chase refers to as the 'organised use of violence for economic means' (2003:134). As a diplomatic tool, Portuguese firearms were also given away to curry favour with local rulers. This was despite their own reluctance to arm potential rivals and despite papal bans on selling of weapons to 'infidels' (Chase 2003:138; see also Boxer 1965). For other groups who resisted Portuguese entreaties, the response was typically more belligerent. An early report of Portuguese efforts to engage the sandalwood trade directly on Timor provides a sense of the methods employed. As Gunn notes,

> The expedition of Jorge Fogasa, undertaken in 1516 successfully brought back to Malacca lucrative amounts of sandal. But it was also apparently the case that Fogasa resorted to force in the act of collection, perhaps sowing the seeds of future conflict. As recorded in a letter from Malacca to King Manuel (Portugal) 'they left a land in revolt, since the Portuguese men bludgeoned the merchants of the land'. (1999: 55)

Timor-Leste, in particular, appears to have been a target of Portuguese coercive trading strategies. Hägerdal, for example, has argued that in East Timor (in contrast to the western portion of the island), Portuguese expansion was 'to a much higher degree a question of brute force' and they had a poor reputation for 'brutal and overbearing treatment of local grandees and populations. The domains were smaller and weaker than in the west and easily fell prey to a determined military' (2012:19–20).

> In the low-technological Timorese society, firearms, western methods and maritime skills had a severe impact. Small detachments of musketeers would be decisive for the outcome of armed conflict on the island … The mobility of the sea borne Portuguese [and later Dutch] gave them the possibility to keep large stretches of the coastland in check. (2012:28)

---

9   Chinese sources from the 1500s and 1600s are full of comments on the superior quality of foreign firearms, and foreign observers likewise commented on the inferior quality of Chinese ones. China acquired European muskets sometime in the mid-1500s (Chase 2003:145).

Hägerdal's point is supported by Gunn who argues in relation to the colonising process that:

> Portuguese incorporation was not achieved without extremes of violence, acts of high plunder and massive deracination if not genocide of the victims of such unequal exchanges in naval and military technology. (1999:15)

As has been noted, the Timor trade in sandalwood and, to a lesser extent, in beeswax[10] and slaves (see below) provided the Timorese with access to outside goods; namely, basic commodities such as iron tools and luxury goods such as cloth, alcohol and porcelain plates. But significantly, as Fox has commented, above all the trade provided a means of warfare, a steady supply of muskets (1988:270). Aggressive maritime colonialism and access to weapons, especially firearms, exacerbated conditions for armed warfare, rebellion and punitive raiding between Timorese residential communities. These factors contributed in no small way to establishing a long-term social and political environment of violent conflict conducive to the development of fortified structures and, in the process, the emergence of an elaborate cult of headhunting across Timor (see Forbes 1885; McWilliam 1996). Hägerdal makes a similar point, writing that, 'it is just possible that intra-island warfare was stimulated in the course of the seventeenth century by the intervention of foreign groups' noting that 'there is rarely or never mention of firearms and gunpowder traded for sandalwood in the early historical sources (prior to the 1620s)' (2012:19).[11] This period includes long-term Chinese engagement in sandalwood and associated trading in Timor, which appears to have been negotiated on generally peaceful terms.

The most popular firearms were lightweight and mobile ones: muskets and swivel guns (Chase 2003:139; also Andaya 1992:388). As more manoeuvrable cannon and muskets were introduced by Europeans and later manufactured in Southeast Asia, this tended to give rise to a small number of powerful kings able to monopolise the new technology in their domains (Reid 1988:128). A further key factor in the dissemination of firearms into Timor and the wider region was local production of weapons, probably initiated by the Portuguese distribution of weapons to their native allies.[12] Reid (1988:136) has noted that, under King Tunipalangga (1548–1566), bricks, gunpowder, cannons and various other items were first manufactured in Makassar (Sulawesi). Reportedly, by the turn of the seventeenth century, King Matoaya of Tallo (South Sulawesi) introduced the manufacture of cannons and small muskets, and was himself 'skilled at making gunpowder, fireworks and flares, as well as being an accomplished marksman' (Villiers 1985:44–45). At this time, the Makassarese ruler of Goa (South Sulawesi) could reportedly bring '100,000 men into the field armed with blowpipes, poisoned arrows and four thousand guns, most of them obtained from the Portuguese' (Villiers 1983:42).[13] As Reid notes, '[i]n practical terms, [those] rulers able to deploy handguns effectively were the ones best able to transform the political landscape in their favour' (1988:224).

The fall of the Portuguese-controlled trading entrepôt Malacca to the Dutch in 1541, saw the Makassarese kingdoms rise in importance and trading influence. Converting to Islam in 1605, Makassar had grown into an important state by 1630, exercising suzerainty not only throughout Sulawesi but extending to Seram and Buru and as far as Timor, Solor and Bima (Gunn 1999:77).

---

10 Beeswax has long been exported from Timor. Collected from wild honeybee hives in forest trees, the wax became particularly popular during the nineteenth century to serve the bourgeoning batik industry.

11 Timor also produced the ingredients necessary for the early Catholic Dominican Order's gunpowder manufacture. The earth yielded saltpetre, which the local rulers offered, 'willingly to the religious' and there was wood from which charcoal could be made (Villiers 1985:70).

12 Villiers has observed that 'in exchange for rice and other commodities … the Portuguese provided the Makassarese with European and Japanese firearms and weapons for which they gained a special papal dispensation from the prohibition against selling weapons to unbelievers' (1985:41, see also descriptions by Boxer 1965).

13 By the early seventeenth century, the Portuguese were being pressured by the growing strength of the Dutch VOC and initially found useful allies in the Makassarese.

A key event in the Timor context was the maritime attack in 1640 on Portuguese and Timorese settlements by the Makassarese King of Tallo, Toemamalijang (also known by his Islamic name, Moezhaffar). Although estimates vary, the attack on the Portuguese fortification at Larantuka (eastern Flores), involved up to 150 ships and some 6000 men. They then sailed on to Timor, where the fleet split, half heading to the south coast of Timor, the remainder sailing along the northeast coast where they 'vanquished' the strategic Timorese ports of Manatuto, Adê and Hon,[14] which subsequently came under their control (de Roever 2002:235).[15] The capacity of Makassarese maritime power can be appreciated in the following early seventeenth-century observation of Torres in his voyages into the Arafura Sea;

> At the extremity of this country [Southern Philippines/Maluku] we found some clothed Moors, with artillery for service, such as falconets and swivel guns, arquebuses[16] and white weapons. They go conquering these people who are named Papuas and preach to them the sect of Mahomed'. (Letter of Luis Vaez de Torres, July 1607 in de Morga 1964:415)

There is little documentation of the impact of these attacks on Timorese settlements, but at the very least the events highlight the uncertain and conflict-riddled times of seventeenth-century Timor. This was a period when armed reprisals and threats were always closely entangled with opportunities for maritime-based trade, and where defensive fortifications and a ready supply of firearms and gunpowder were the strategic technologies of the day.[17] As a potential driver for the emergence of fortified settlements in Timor, the coercive threat of attack with high-powered weaponry may well have been a central factor.

It is worth noting that the value of firearms to Timorese communities continued unabated for generations. In his description of Timor in 1829, for example, Müller stressed the importance of muskets to the Timorese:[18]

> The trade in flintlock rifles is the most advantageous … that can be conducted on Timor … The rifle belongs, above all, to the most important piece of inheritance, to the costliest valuable that can pass from father to son; indeed a Timorese would often more easily and more happily do without a house and livestock, even a wife and child, rather than without such a weapon. (1857: Vol. 2 234, cited in Fox 1988:270)

The slave trade

The fourth and final prominent driver for change in premodern Timor was the rise of commercial slavery and the trade in human beings as part of a broader engagement with maritime trading powers. Slavery has a long and ignoble history in eastern Wallacea, where control over labour was always a critical component of local power relationships and a measure of political status. Forms of debt bondage within hierarchical patron–client relationships were therefore common features of the island societies and bonded individuals (slaves) became defined as a strata of social

---

14 Likely to be a version of the Lautem coastal port known as Com.

15 The attack also reached the nearby island of Alor, a Makassarese dependency, although the Dutch, according to VOC Governor General Cornelis Speelman, refused to recognise the claim (de Roever 2002:236).

16 An earlier and rather unwieldy form of the matchlock musket.

17 Makassarese trading dominance on the northeastern ports of Timor continued until the successful Dutch attack on Makassar itself in 1667, after which the region was subject to renewed struggles for economic advantage between the Dutch and Portuguese.

18 During the eighteenth and nineteenth centuries, firearms became widespread on Timor and were apparently conducive to the disappearance of traditional weapons such as blow pipes, bows and shields (Hägerdal 2010:115). They remained an ubiquitous possession of all Timorese households until the late twentieth century. It was only in West Timor during the mid-1980s, for example, that muskets and various homemade firearms stopped being used as an everyday item, following sustained police pressure to confiscate civilian-held weapons.

status. As Reid has noted, 'the system of bonding based on debt was one where loyalties between "owner" and "slave" were strong and intimate, but also became transferable and saleable' (Reid 1988:129).[19]

Slaves as a tradeable commodity are mentioned in the earliest accounts of European records of contact with Timor. Barbosa's account from 1518, identifies 'sanders-wood, honey, wax, slaves and also a certain amount of silver' as traded items from the island (Dames 1921:195–96). Slavery in eastern Wallacea flourished following both the adoption of Islam across the Indonesian archipelago and the rise of European mercantilism and colonialism in Southeast Asia. As Reid has noted, with the Islamisation of Java and the extension of sharia law forbidding enslavement, the major Muslim cities from the late sixteenth century were supplied with slaves from beyond the frontier of Islam. Certain small Islamic sultanates, notably Sulu, Buton (Sulawesi) and Tidore (Maluku) began to make a profitable business of raiding for slaves in eastern Wallacea (Reid 1988:133). A further attraction of sourcing slaves from non-Islamised islands like Timor, as Reid has also observed, was that '[s]ince slave export [is] almost invariably linked with internal disunity, the stateless societies and micro-states of eastern Indonesia, New Guinea, Bali and Nias were consistently among the exporters' (1988:133). Drawing on the records of the Catholic Dominican Order mission archives for the period 1568–1579, Artur de Sá records observations that:

> for some years Muslim traders (Mouros) arriving in Timor via Makassar (in Sulawesi) were trading for sandalwood (sandâlo), beeswax (cera) and slaves (escravagem) from two settlements on Timor, Manatuto and Adê. (cited in McWilliam 2007a:223)

A key impetus for slaving and slave-trading in the eastern archipelago, including Timor, was the Dutch (VOC) violent acquisition of the islands of Banda in neighbouring Maluku from 1621. This action was part of their attempts to monopolise the production and trade in spices, notably nutmeg and mace for which Banda was a key source (see Andaya 1991:83). As Fox has noted:

> After establishing their first fortification, the Dutch set about, in 1621, to enslave, expel or exterminate the entire local population of the islands that they controlled, to divide the productive nutmeg producing land into parcels (*perken*), and then to repopulate the islands with slaves and indentured convicts from all parts of the Indies. (1991:9)

While the documentary evidence of slave-trading from the eastern extremities of Timor at this time is patchy, it is apparent that Timor and particularly the eastern end of the island were closely drawn into the slaving trade networks. Evidence for this development is derived from fragmentary historical documentation and the ethnohistories of resident Fataluku communities. According to Sutherland (1983:267), for example, the Dutch East India Company (Vereenigde Oostindische Compagnie, or VOC), with their endless need for labour, drew upon indigenous slave-trading networks and probably stimulated their expansion and intensification. Kisar, the small island off the northeast coast of Timor, became a transit station for slaves who were sent to work in the nutmeg plantations on Banda (Rodenwaldt 1927:19). At the time, the Dutch were particularly desperate for slaves following the forceful deportation of the native inhabitants from Banda and the view that slaves from areas such as Malabar and the Papuan islands were vulnerable to various types of illness (Andaya 1991:83).

The subsequent decision by the VOC in 1689 forbidding the use of slaves from large tracts of the western archipelago because of their 'record of violence against their masters', increased demand for slaves from the east. So-called '*freeburgers*' and '*Mardykers*' (freed slaves of Christian Asian origin) were licensed to supply the VOC and relied on their extensive knowledge of local trade networks to secure quality slaves (Andaya 1991:83; Ellen 2003). Although local merchants were

---

19   Ellen noted of the premodern Moluccas islands, 'slaves traditionally are distinguished between those exchanged or bought … and those captured in war' (2003:41).

initially excluded by the VOC from dealing in slaves, as with the spices trade, they were soon able to evade the controls and to profitably restore their involvement (Andaya 1991:88). The attraction of sourcing slaves from eastern Wallacea was officially enhanced by a Dutch colonial ordinance of 3 October 1703, which permitted voyages to Timor and Makassar (Sulawesi) specifically to obtain slaves under licence from the Governor General of the VOC (Fox 1983:259).

If the scale of the commercial export of slaves out of Timor during the colonial period is indeterminate and may never have reached the proportions reported for neighbouring islands such as Sumba and Manggarai in western Flores, there was always a ready market for Timorese slaves. This was a fact reported by numerous observers until the late nineteenth century (see, for example, de Freycinet 1827; Gunn 1999; Kolff 1840).[20] Gunn reports, for example, that 'by the end of the seventeenth century (1699) the Timor trade in sandalwood, gold, wax and slaves had become Macau's main source of revenue' (1999:79). More significantly, George Earl, who travelled to Timor in the 1850s, makes the following comments about the Lautem region of far eastern Timor:

> The slaves, who once constituted the chief article of export from the Portuguese settlements on the island, were chiefly obtained, either by force or barter, from these tribes, and were usually brought to the settlements overland … They are described as being extremely cautious in their transactions with strangers, even with those who have held intercourse with them for years; and probably they have good reason to be so, for the great slave mart of the Bughis and Macassar traders, Kapalla Tanah, or the Land's-End, is in their immediate neighbourhood. (1853:181, 182)

> The traders are allowed to land, but not to leave the beach, even to procure water which when their visitors require a supply, is brought down by the natives themselves in bamboo buckets and deposited on the beach. (1853:183)

Two points are worth highlighting here. First, the site that Earl refers to as 'Kapalla Tanah, or the Land's-End' (Headland), is most probably a translation of the old Fataluku name of Valu Beach, Mua Cao Pasaré ('the Headland market'), where local ethnohistorical accounts support Earl's description of trade, and where it is recalled that human slaves (*akanu*), whether war captives or debt bonded dependants, were regularly traded for gunpowder and ammunition.[21]

An insight into those dynamics can be appreciated from the oral histories of residents of the port settlement of Com, to the north and west of Kapalla Tanah. Com port is a sheltered natural anchorage, which has long served as an entrepôt for regional trading opportunities (see McWilliam 2007b). Oral histories of the senior clans of the settlement, Konu Ratu, point to an enthusiastic historical engagement in slaving and sandalwood trading. According to their testimony, there is a strong relationship between endemic warfare, the maintenance of fortified settlements and the enslavement of rival groups as war captives. Konu controlled the port of Com (a Portuguese corruption of the word Kon(u), taken from the resident land owning group) from their fortified settlements (Kon ara and Lor lafae) overlooking the anchorage. Their strategic position enabled them to control the terms of trade. In particular, for the supply of able-bodied human slaves, they secured key exchange goods in the forms of muzzle-loader guns (*fotu*), ammunition (*fotu kafu*) and gunpowder (*aranaku*). Local tradition also points to regular exchanges with Makassarese (Sulawesi) traders, for gunpowder transported in large bamboo containers. In these exchanges one large bamboo container was traded for one human slave (*tau tau ukani = ma'alauhana*

---

20   When Kolff visited Dili in 1825, he commented that, 'Slaves were frequently offered to me on sale, the Commandant among others, wishing me to purchase two children of seven or eight years of age, who were loaded with heavy irons. The usual price of an adult male slave is forty guilders, that of a woman or child being from twenty five to thirty. These unfortunate people are kidnapped in the interior and brought to Dili for sale, the Governor readily providing the vendor with certificates under his name and seal, authorizing him to dispose of the captives as he may think fit' (1840:34–35).

21   Another trade item that local Fataluku recall as a prized trade item was '*koichila*' or custard apples that were widely propagated in the area and were another Portuguese import from the 'New World' (see Cinatti 1964:185).

ukani). The benefits of this trade were significant and during this (undated) period, the Konu Ratu leadership gained the reputation as being *Orang Kai*[22] (from Malay meaning 'wealthy'). According to local knowledge, Konu Ratu formerly owned large numbers of slaves who served the ruling house, preparing gardens, tending animals, cutting timber and tapping palms for the production of liquor (*tua harak*). Additional slaves for trade were also secured from allied *ratu* (clans) in the hinterland; all seeking weaponry to defend their home territories and avoid the threat of enslavement themselves should they be unable to repel their enemies.

A second point raised by the Earl observations on slave-trading is that it was evidently still in operation at the time of his visit, but we gain no insight into the origins of the trade in the region, and therefore how long the 'great slave mart' had been operating. In this regard an important historical feature of the eastern extremity of Timor has been its long-term engagement with Bugis and Makassarese traders from Sulawesi. The maritime attack by the Makassarese King of Tallo, Toemamalijang, in 1640 subordinated the coastal ports on the northeast coast of Timor, which lasted until 1667 when the Dutch conquered the city of Makassar itself. In the interim, Timorese settlements felt the impact of a three-way struggle for control between Portuguese, Makassarese and Dutch authorities. De Roever (2002:235) reports that subsequently some of the 'rajas' of East Timor began offering an annual tribute to Makassar that included 50 slaves as well as stockpiles of sandalwood. It is also reported that the Makassarese came yearly with five, six, or more ships and traded (bees)wax, sandalwood, tortoiseshell and amber in return for cloth (see Coolhaas 1968:Vol. III 930).

Slave-trading and the lucrative opportunities for trading in human cargo were therefore important elements in the political and economic dynamics of premodern Timor, one that inevitably made enemies out of others and fostered a social climate of defensive readiness. The regional slave trade out of Timor continued for centuries and experienced renewed intensity in the late eighteenth and early nineteenth centuries, this time partly in relation to indigenous political centralisation elsewhere in eastern Wallacea, especially the regional sultanates of Ternate, Tidore and Buton (Ellen 2003:102).

Conclusions

In their 2008 paper on environmental drivers for fortification, Lape and Chao draw inferences from the contemporary record of dynamic variations in monsoon rainfall across Timor to compare the sometime grievous impacts of weather patterns on rural livelihoods. Drawing by analogy on the damage that occurred to seasonal maize production in Timor-Leste during the 1997–1998 ENSO, they suggest that 'the unpredictability of precipitation, timing and stability during El Niño events may have had similar catastrophic impacts on other crops with similar scheduling regimes' (Lape and Chao 2008:15).[23]

These patterns are undoubtedly influential factors affecting subsistence food production and rural livelihoods for a majority of Timor-Leste households. They often result in crop losses and, sometimes, outright crop failure, leaving Timorese farmers struggling with food shortages and reduced circumstances. This is a long-term legacy of the uncertain monsoon environment

---

22 A term used widely across the Malay trading world, including the neighbouring islands of Moluccas where the *Orang Kaya* represented an oligarchy of elders from small but wealthy communities who had established a 'mercantile aristocracy' (see Villiers 1981:728–729; also Goodman 1998).

23 The argument here is partly based on the assertion that most rainfall in Timor occurs during November to March with little precipitation at other times, and that the main El Niño effects are typically felt in the period December–February. While this is true for the north coast of Timor-Leste, it is by no means the norm elsewhere. The southern hinterland, for example, experiences double or extended monsoon rainfall seasons, and much of Lautem in the far east receives a substantial period of rainfall during May to July, allowing for increased food production and multiple cropping (see Lape and Chao 2008:15).

in which they live and one that has encouraged the development of highly resilient Timorese communities who focus on diversified food production, foraging strategies and complex exchange relationships that reproduce enduring forms of social capital.

In this paper, I have argued that these features of Timorese social and economic life are certainly important adaptive mechanisms for successful livelihood strategies and that seasonal variation in rainfall patterns may well put additional stress on different communities at different times. But we do not see evidence that these environmental stress factors are causally implicated in the emergence of fortified stone structures in Timor. To the contrary, the weight of evidence points to an enthusiastic process of defensive fortification emerging in eastern Timor well after the high point of the great El Niño warming that had peaked by the beginning of the fifteenth century (AD 1400). The drivers of that later process, I propose, were fundamentally social ones and intimately linked with the transformative changes that accompanied the advent of European colonialism and the development of aggressive Muslim maritime trade in the eastern Indonesian archipelago. Guns, sandalwood, slaves and new forms of sustenance provided a novel and potent mix created by globalised mercantile forces that combined to produce a social climate fostering conflict and favouring defensive residence. I do not discount the possibility that climatic factors may have contributed to these pressures, and future archaeological and ethnohistorical investigations will seek to expand the available evidence in this regard, but to date the weight of argument looks to be in favour of social drivers.

References

Andaya, L.Y. 1991. Local trade networks in Maluku in the sixteenth, seventeenth and eighteenth centuries. *Cakalele: Maluku Research Journal* 2(2):71–96.

Andaya, L.Y. 1992. Interactions with the outside world and adaptation to Southeast Asian Society, 1500–1800. In N. Tarling (ed.), *The Cambridge history of Southeast Asia*. Volume 1. Cambridge University Press, Cambridge. doi.org/10.1017/chol9780521355056.008.

Barbosa, D. 1521. *A description of the coasts of East Africa and Malabar in the beginning of the sixteenth century*. Translated by H.E.J. Stanley. Hakluyt Society, London. www.gutenberg.org/files/38253/38253-h/38253-h.htm. Accessed 21 March 2020.

Boxer, C.R. 1947. *The topasses of Timor*. Indisch Instituut, Amsterdam.

Boxer, C.R. 1948. *Fidalgos in the Far East, 1550–1770: Fact and fancy in the history of Macao*. Nijhoff, The Hague.

Boxer, C.R. 1965. Asian potentates and European artillery in the sixteenth to the eighteenth centuries: A footnote to Gibson-Hall. *Journal of the Malaysian Branch of the Royal Asiatic Society* 38(2):156–172.

Bulbeck, F.D. 1992. A tale of two kingdoms: The historical archaeology of Gowa and Tallok. Unpublished PhD thesis, Australian National University, Canberra.

Chao, C.-Y. 2008. A microregional approach to the social dynamics in the Late Prehistoric Manatuto, East Timor, 11th–18th century. Unpublished PhD thesis. University of Washington, Seattle.

Chase, K. 2003. *Firearms: A global history to 1700*. Cambridge University Press, Cambridge.

Cinatti, R. 1964. Useful plants in Portuguese Timor: An historical survey. *Actas, Colóquio Internacional de Estudos Luso-Brasileiros* 1:177–190.

Coolhaas, W.P. (ed.) 1968. *Generale Missiven van Gouverneurs-Generaal en Raden aan Heren XVII der Vereenigde Oostindische Compagnie, 1665–1674*. Volume 3. Nijhoff, Gravenhage.

Dames, M.L. (ed.) 1921. *The book of Duarte Barbosa*. The Hakluyt Society, London.

Dampier. W. 1703 (1939). *A voyage to New Holland in the year 1699*. Volume 3 Part 2. Argonaut Press, London.

de Freycinet, L.C.D. 1827. *Voyage autour du Monde, execute sur les corvettes S.M. l'Uranie et la Physicienne pendant les années, 1817, 1818, 1819, 1820: Historique du voyage*. Tome, Paris. doi.org/10.5962/bhl.title.63985.

de Morga, A. 1964. *The Philippine Islands, Moluccas, Siam, Cambodia, Japan and China at the close of the sixteenth century*. Translated by H.E.J. Stanley. Hakluyt Society, London.

de Roever, A. 2002. *De Jacht op Sandelhout: De VOC en de Tweedeling van Timor in de Zeventiende Eeuw*. Walburg Pers, Zutphen.

Earl, G.W. 1853. *The native races of the Indian archipelago: Papuans*. H. Bailliere, London. doi.org/10.5962/bhl.title.101733.

Ellen, R. 2003. *On the edge of the Banda zone: Past and present in the social organization of a Moluccan trading network*. University of Hawai'i Press, Honolulu. doi.org/10.1515/9780824844608.

Figueiredo, F. 2000. Timor. In A.H. de Oliviera Marques (ed.), *História dos Portugueses no Extremo Oriente*, Volume 3, pp. 697–793. Fundação Oriente, Lisboa.

Forbes, H.O. 1885. *A naturalist's wanderings in the Eastern archipelago: A narrative of travel and exploration from 1878 to 1883*. Harper and Brothers, New York. doi.org/10.5962/bhl.title.36489.

Fox, J.J. 1977. *The harvest of the palm: Ecological change in Eastern Indonesia*. Harvard University Press, Cambridge, Massachusetts.

Fox, J.J. 1983. 'For good and sufficient reasons': An examination of early Dutch East India Company ordinances on slaves and slavery. In A. Reid (ed.), *Slavery, bondage and dependency in Southeast Asia*, pp. 246–262. University of Queensland Press, St Lucia.

Fox, J.J. 1988. The historical consequences of changing patterns of livelihood on Timor. In D. Wade-Marshall and P. Loveday (eds), *Contemporary issues in development: Northern Territory: Progress and prospects*, Volume 1, pp. 259–279. North Australia Research Unit, The Australian National University, Darwin.

Fox, J.J. 1991. Before Cook: 18th century accounts of life in Eastern Indonesia. Unpublished paper presented at the National Library of Australia, Canberra.

Glover, I. 1972. Excavations in Timor: A study of economic change and cultural continuity in prehistory. Unpublished PhD thesis. The Australian National University, Canberra.

Goodman, T. 1998. The *sosolot* exchange network of Eastern Indonesia. In J. Miedema, C. Ode and R.A.C. Dam (eds), *Perspectives on the bird's head of Irian Jaya: Proceedings of the conference, Leiden, 13–17 October 1997*, pp. 421–454. Editions Rodopi B.V., Amsterdam.

Gunn, G.C. 1999. *Timor Loro Sae: 500 years*. Livros do Oriente, Macau.

Hägerdal, H. 2012. *Lords of the land, lords of the sea: Conflict and adaptation in early colonial Timor, 1600–1800*. KITLV Press, Leiden. doi.org/10.26530/oapen_408241.

Kolff, D.H. 1840. *Voyages of the Dutch brig of war Dourga through the southern and little-known parts of the Moluccan archipelago and along the previously unknown southern coast of New Guinea performed during the years 1825 and 1826*. Translated by G.E. Earl. James Madden and Co., London.

Lape, P.V. 2006. Chronology of fortified settlements in East Timor. *Journal of Island and Coastal Archaeology* 1(2):285–297. doi.org/10.1080/15564890600939409.

Lape, P.V. and C.-Y. Chao 2008. Fortification as a human response to late Holocene climate change in East Timor. *Archaeology in Oceania* 43(1):11–21. doi.org/10.1002/j.1834-4453.2008.tb00026.x.

McWilliam, A. 1996. Severed heads that germinate the state: History, politics, and headhunting in Southwest Timor. In J. Hoskins (ed.), *Headhunting and the social imagination in Southeast Asia*, pp. 127–166. Stanford University Press, Stanford.

McWilliam, A. 2000. A plague on your house? Some impacts of *Chromolaena odorata* on Timorese livelihoods. *Human Ecology* 28(3):451–469. doi.org/10.1023/A:1007061632588.

McWilliam, A. 2007a. Looking for Adê: A contribution to Timorese historiography. *Bijdragen tot de Taal-, Land- en- Volkenkunde* 163(2/3):221–238. doi.org/10.1163/22134379-90003684.

McWilliam, A. 2007b. Harbouring traditions in East Timor: Marginality in a lowland entrepôt. *Modern Asian Studies* 41(6):1113–1143. doi.org/10.1017/s0026749x07002843.

Oliveira, N.V. 2008. Subsistence archaeobotany: Food production and the agricultural transition in East Timor. Unpublished PhD thesis. The Australian National University, Canberra.

Ormeling, F.J. 1956. *The Timor problem: A geographical interpretation of an underdeveloped island*. J.P. Wolters, Groningen.

Ptak, R. 1987. The transportation of sandalwood from Timor to China and Macao, c. 1350–1600. In R. Ptak (ed.) *Portuguese Asia: Aspects in history and economic history (sixteenth and seventeenth centuries)*, pp. 87–109. Franz Steiner Verlag, Stuttgart.

Ptak, R. 1999. *China's seaborne trade with South and Southeast Asia 1200–1750*. Aldershot, Singapore.

Reid, A.J. 1988. *Southeast Asia in the age of commerce 1450–1680*. Volume 1. Yale University Press, New Haven.

Reid, A.J. 1993. *Southeast Asia in the age of commerce 1450–1680*. Volume 2. Yale University Press, New Haven.

Rodenwaldt, E. 1927. Die Mestiezen auf Kisar. Med Dienst Volksgez 2dlm, gr 8 Deel 1(XVII).

Sutherland, H. 1983. Slavery and the slave trade in South Sulawesi 1660s–1800s. In A. Reid (ed.), *Slavery, bondage and dependency in Southeast Asia*, pp. 263–285. University of Queensland Press, St Lucia.

Villiers, J. 1981. Trade and society in the Banda Islands in the sixteenth century. *Modern Asian Studies* 15(4):723–750. doi.org/10.1017/s0026749x0000874x.

Villiers J. 1985. *East of Malacca*. Calouste Gulbenkian Foundation, Bangkok.

7

The indigenous fortifications of South Sulawesi, Indonesia, and their sociopolitical foundations

David Bulbeck and Ian Caldwell

Introduction

This contribution brings together the historical and archaeological evidence for the Indonesian province of South Sulawesi (Figure 7.1) relevant to current debates on the development of fortifications in the Indo-Pacific region during the second millennium AD. The province of South Sulawesi is well placed for this task because of indigenous written historical traditions that cover much of the period of interest (Caldwell 1988: 171), and European accounts from the early sixteenth century onwards (Pelras 1977). In addition to archaeological surveys of historical sites undertaken across much of the province (Table 7.1), a cluster of fortifications near Bone's capital of Watampone have been recorded in sufficient detail for inclusion here (Appendix K).[1]

South Sulawesi's diversity of agro-climatic regimes provides a unique insight into proposals that link fortification development with resource availability and climatic stress. The climate varies from perhumid and equatorial north of the Gulf of Bone, associated with sago production, to monsoonal across the peninsula. Between May and late July, the eastern part of the peninsula experiences a mild rainy season, while the southern and western peninsula enjoys a dry season of increasing aridity from the north to the south. As one approaches the south coast, where several months may pass without rain, the landscape turns from green to brown. Between October and April the eastern side of the peninsula and Selayar Island experience a dry season marked by occasional, local rainfall, while on the west side an ample monsoon starts in December and continues through to late February. Rainfall along the peninsula's coastal cordilleras either drains to the coast or fills the Walennae River and inundates the central lowlands where the Walennae and Cenrana rivers meet (Bulbeck 1992). Bunded rice paddies dominate the rural landscape around the central lowlands and along the coastal plains. In highland or drier regions where the possibility of rice production is limited, arboriculture, maize and root crops are important. Sources of protein include poultry, goats, cattle, and sea and freshwater fish.

---

1 This contribution covers archaeological fieldwork and textual research up to 2012, when the original manuscript was submitted for intended publication. Subsequent related studies are not considered here.

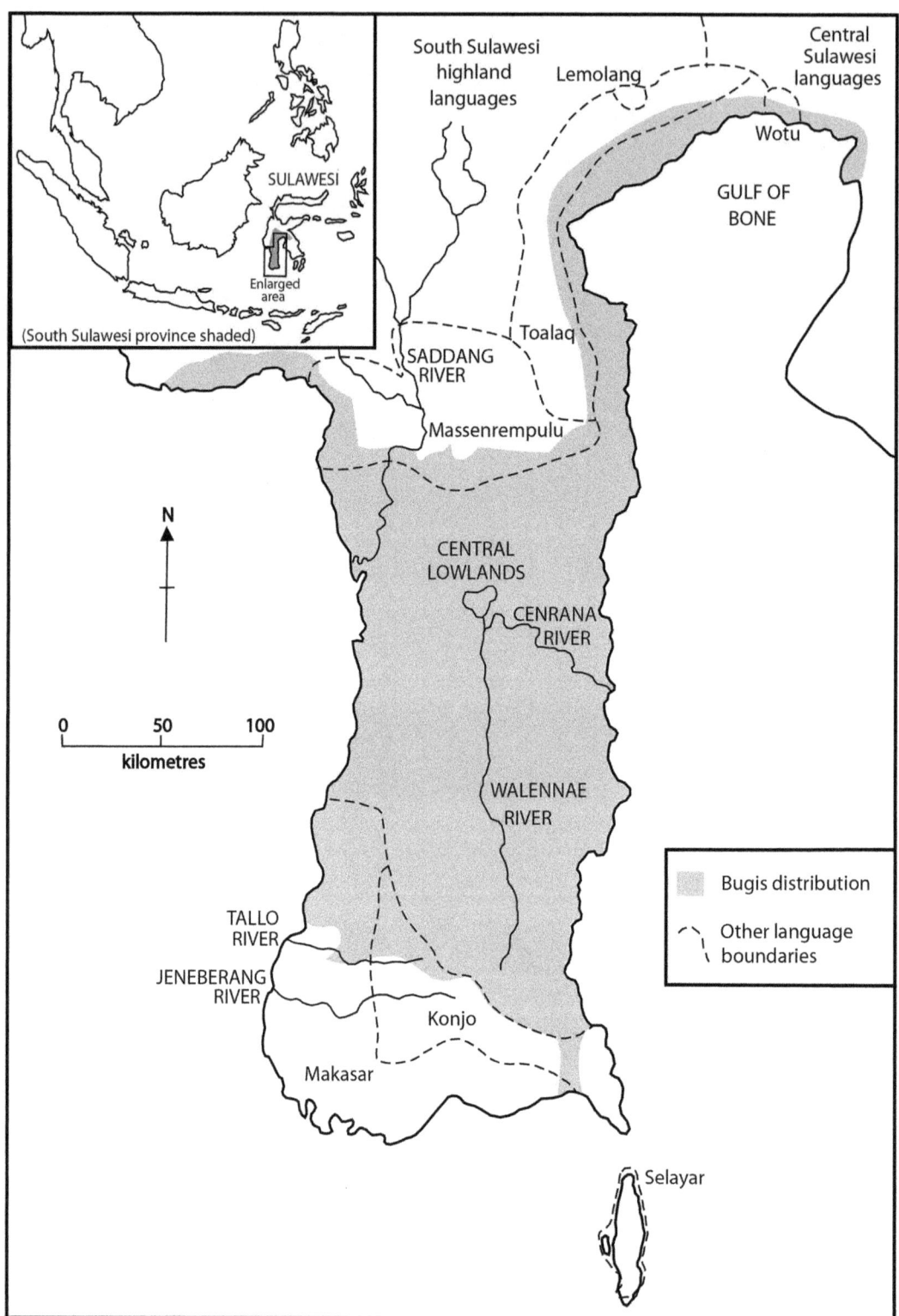

Figure 7.1. South Sulawesi: main topographical features and language boundaries.
Source: David Bulbeck (after Grimes and Grimes 1987: Map 3; Druce 2009: Figure 3.21; OXIS Group 2020).

Table 7.1. Locations (north to south) surveyed in South Sulawesi for historical sites.

Surveyed city/regency/regencies	Target site(s)	Sampling strategy	Approximate chronological coverage (AD)	Reference(s)
North and East Luwu	Iron-industry related sites*	Local reports/surface survey	1st–20th Cs	Bulbeck and Caldwell 2000
Palopo city, Luwu	Tompotikka fort	Surface survey	16th–19th Cs	Mahmud 1993
Enrekang (central Saddang River)	Mortuary sites; fortifications	Local reports/surface survey	17th–20th Cs	Makkulasse 1986; Somba 2009, 2010
Pinrang, Suppa, Sidenreng Rappang	Pre-Islamic sites	Local reports/surface survey	13th–19th Cs	Druce 2009
Pare-Pare city	Bacukiki site complex	Local reports/surface survey	17th–19th Cs	Muhaeminah 2010
Barru	Islamic heritage sites	Local reports/surface survey	17th–20th Cs	Masdoeki 1984
Wajo	Tosora fort; nearby settlements*	Local reports/surface survey	17th–19th Cs	Kallupa 1985; Nur and Hakim 2010
Soppeng	Pre-Islamic sites	Textual toponyms/surface survey	13th–19th Cs	Kallupa et al. 1989
Cenrana Valley	Historical sites*	Textual toponyms/surface survey	13th–18th Cs	Mahmud 2000; Bulbeck and Caldwell 2000
Lamuru	Lamuru Islamic cemetery	Surface survey/restoration	17th–19th Cs	Muttalib 1978
Pangkajene	Sengkae fort*	Textual toponym	15th–17th Cs	Fadillah and Mahmud 2000
Sinjai	Hilltop sites; Balangnipa fort	Local reports/surface survey	14th–19th Cs	Kallupa 1984; Muhaeminah 2009; Hasanuddin in press
Makassar and hinterland	17th-C. and earlier sites	Textual toponyms/local reports/surface survey	13th–19th Cs	Bulbeck 1992
Takalar	Islamic heritage sites	Local reports/surface survey	17th–19th Cs	Masdoeki 1985
Bulukumba	Historical sites	Local reports/surface survey	14th–20th Cs	Muttalib 1983
Bantaeng	La Tenri Ruwa Islamic cemetery; pre-Islamic sites	Local reports/surface survey/restoration	11th–19th Cs	Muttalib 1980; Bougas 1998; Fadillah 1999; Nayati 2000
Jeneponto	Pre-Islamic sites	Local reports/surface survey	13th–16th Cs	Caldwell and Bougas 2004
Selayar	Pre-Islamic sites; Buki kingdom	Local reports/surface survey	12th–18th Cs	Wibisono 1985; Muhaeminah and Mahmud 2009

* Fieldwork investigations included extensive excavation as well as documentation of surface remains.

Sources: See references throughout table.

The people of South Sulawesi are conventionally divided into three major linguistic groups, although in reality the situation is more complex. The Bugis are the most numerous with a population of approximately 4 million, followed by the Makasar with a population of approximately 2.5 million.[2] The highland-dwelling Toraja groups living along the Saddang River and its tributaries have been little investigated in terms of their historical archaeology (apart from the Massenrempulu region) and need not concern us here. The distribution of the Bugis (Figure 7.1) suggests that over time they have infiltrated the homelands of neighbouring ethnic groups, including speakers of Massenrempulu, Toalaq and Central Sulawesi languages (including

---

[2] Broad figures extrapolated from *Indonesia's Population Census* (Sudarti Surbakti et al. 2000) and *CIA World Factbook*. Speakers of languages belonging to the Makasar group include 200,000 Konjo and 90,000 speakers of Selayar (Grimes and Grimes 1987:28–29).

Padoe) to the north, and the Makasar and Konjo languages to the south. In terms of religious affiliation, the Bugis and Makasars have by and large converted to Islam, beginning around AD 1600.

South Sulawesi offers a wealth and variety of fortifications, varying from simple earth mounds (formerly supporting defensive fences of iron or bamboo) set around modest habitation sites to brick fortresses enclosing areas of up to 84 hectares, and earthen fortresses enclosing areas of up to 2 km². The scattered literature on these fortifications (e.g. Perelaer 1872; Andaya 1981; Bulbeck 1998) has generally endeavoured to link them to particular military conflicts, without any attempt to synthesise the wealth of relevant historical and archaeological evidence within a general framework of armed combat and political centralisation in South Sulawesi during the second millennium AD.

In synthesising this evidence, we are in a position to test the model for Indo-Pacific fortifications proposed by Field. According to Field (2008:3–4), the construction of fortifications as the defended occupation of a settled location can be expected at locations with resources that are densely distributed and temporally predictable. Further, during periods of climatic unpredictability, one can expect increased conflict between these settled populations, stimulating the construction of additional fortifications and strengthening of existing fortifications. One such period of climatic unpredictability across much of the Indo-Pacific, according to Field (2008:6), would have been the 'Little Ice Age' after c. AD 1300.

East Timor is the closest place to South Sulawesi where an association between climatic unpredictability and fortification construction has been investigated. During the middle second millennium AD, north coastal East Timor witnessed a remarkable phase of indigenous fort construction involving the building of hundreds of stone-walled structures on hilltops and cliff edges, the remains of which are still visible today. Lape and Chao (2008) relate this phenomenon to a dramatic shift in landscape use and settlement patterns after AD 1000 and propose a causal link between fortification building and a hypothesised period of reduced rainfall associated with ENSO (El Niño Southern Oscillation). They argue that a drying of Timor's climate after c. AD 1000 and the consequent unpredictability of rainfall-dependent resources produced social stresses that stimulated the building of hilltop forts (Lape and Chao 2008:12).[3]

Despite the physical proximity of South Sulawesi and East Timor, their climates are very different. North coastal East Timor is one of the driest regions in Island Southeast Asia, as it falls within the 'permanently dry' zone characterised by 9 to 12 months a year that receive an average rainfall of less than 100 mm. The closest similarity in South Sulawesi is the 'seasonally dry' pockets in the southwest and southeast corners of the peninsula, and the island of Selayar, which on average receive less than 100 mm a month for 5 to 8 months a year (Monk et al. 1997: Figure 2.17). The greater susceptibility to drought of north coastal East Timor means that the ENSO-focused model of Lape and Chao (2008) would not be expected to apply to the parts of South Sulawesi that experience more reliable rainfall. Nonetheless, with reference to Field's (2008:4–6) overarching model, we would still expect to see an increase in fortification construction related to climatic unpredictability after AD 1300 and particularly between the sixteenth to eighteenth centuries.

---

3   Lape and Chao base their climatic reconstruction largely on a proxy record from Ecuador that indicates 'a dramatic increase in El Niño events well above modern levels from 1100–1600 AD, with a peak from 1300–1400' (2008:15). A sediment core from Kau Bay in Halmahera has now been used to reconstruct century-scale climate variability within the Indo-Pacific Warm Pool over the past 3500 years. From this, Langton et al. (2008:795) infer 'diminished ENSO amplitude or frequency, or a departure from El Niño-like conditions during the Medieval Warm Period and distinctive, but steadily decreasing, El Niño activity during and after the little ice age'.

Based on the previous discussion, the methodology for our study is as follows. Chronology of site occupancy, which is central to our investigation, relies on identifications of dateable imported ceramics at the sites, records of the sites in indigenous and European sources, and Carbon-14 dating for a few sites. We start by reviewing the occupation history of hilltop settlements in South Sulawesi sites including both fortified and unfortified sites. Where traces of fortifications are still visible, these invariably involve stone walls, reflecting the ready availability of stone on hilltops, the improvements to habitation space and gardens from the removal of surface rock, and the difficulties in uphill transportation of other construction materials. We then turn to sites in non-hilltop settings and in particular those with evidence for fortifications rather than the hundreds of non-fortified sites (see Table 7.1 references) whose coverage would be unwieldy. The materials used for fortification are of relevance here both as indicators of the sturdiness and durability of the walls and also access to the introduced technology of brick manufacture. Where the settlement history of these non-hilltop sites evidently included periods with and without functioning fortifications, this is particularly valuable information for identifying the times when a strong defensive capacity and its purpose were most crucial. Times of intensified fortification are set in their historical context both at the scale of local conflict and in terms of peninsula-wide political developments. If the climate-focused models of Field (2008) or Lape and Chao (2008) apply to South Sulawesi, then these 'times of war' should correspond to periods of climatic deterioration. If this expectation fails then an explanation based on factors other than climate should be sought.

Background history to South Sulawesi

This section provides a brief summary of South Sulawesi's history during the second millennium AD as background to our coverage of critical sites in the sections that follow.

Political centralisation in South Sulawesi in the form of historical kingdoms (or complex chiefdoms) dates back to the fourteenth century. These kingdoms were based on bilinear descent groups, either a single ruling descent group or a mutually beneficial alliance between two to five descent groups, which traced their origins to a founding apical figure (Bulbeck 1992; Caldwell 1995; Bulbeck and Caldwell 2008; Druce 2009). By the fourteenth century, South Sulawesi had developed trade links with Java, as shown by its four identifiable toponyms recorded in the *Desawarnana*, Javanese court poem written in 1365 (Robson 1995). The four toponyms (Figure 7.1) are: Selayar, which is an island; Luwuq,[4] located on the Gulf of Bone but possessing lands in the western Cenrana valley (Bulbeck and Caldwell 2000); and in the Makasar-speaking part of the peninsula, Makassar[5] and Bantaeng, both of which may refer to a wider area than today's matching toponyms would suggest (Caldwell and Bougas 2004; Reid 1983).

European advances in military technology, introduced to archipelagic Southeast Asia after the Portuguese conquest of Melaka in 1511, increased the scale and intensity of armed conflict in South Sulawesi. Under the joint stewardship of the Goa and Talloq kingdoms, Makassar rose to the status of an emporium by the mid-sixteenth century and over the following decades acquired muskets, brick-making technology, warships and cannons (Reid 1983). Privileged access to firearms enabled the rulers of Goa and Talloq to obtain numerous military victories between the 1540s and 1565, mostly in South Sulawesi but also as far afield as northern Sulawesi and the islands of Sumbawa and Flores. In 1565, as a response to the growing power of Makassar, the Bugis kingdom of Bone forged a defensive alliance with its neighbours, Soppeng

---

4 Please note our use of 'q' to denote a glottal stop in the names of historical kingdoms. This has the advantage of distinguishing them from their modern Indonesian administrative counterparts.

5 Spelled with a double s; the modern name of the city.

and Wajoq, which restricted Goa–Talloq's late sixteenth-century conquests to other regions of South Sulawesi. In the first half of the seventeenth century, Goa–Talloq successfully subjugated Bone and imposed its authority across South Sulawesi and surrounding islands (Andaya 1981; McWilliam et al. 2012).

Goa–Talloq's seventeenth-century primacy over its Bugis and Makasar neighbours depended on its ability to maintain Makassar as an independent emporium where Moluccan spices could be traded in defiance of the monopoly claimed by the Netherlands East India Company (Vereenigde Oostindische Compagnie, or VOC). This situation held until 1667, when the VOC assembled a naval force with unmatched cannon fire and forged a crucial alliance with Arung Palakka, a minor noble from Bone whom the VOC had previously employed as a mercenary. The VOC warships and Arung Palakka's ground troops besieged and occupied the port city of Makassar, and after a brief resistance destroyed the Makassar empire. Following this victory, the VOC claimed most of the southern coastline by right of conquest and added much of the western coastal plain to its possessions by 1669 (Andaya 1981). Working closely with Bone, the VOC administered Makassar until 1800, when the Netherlands government acquired the now bankrupt company as a crown colony. Following a brief period of British administration in the early nineteenth century, the Netherlands colonial government used Makassar as a base to exert increasing control over South Sulawesi. In 1905–1906, the Dutch completed the process of incorporating the traditional kingdoms of South Sulawesi into the colonial administration in a series of short and occasionally bloody confrontations (De Klerck 1975).

Political developments in the South Sulawesi peninsula from the thirteenth to twentieth centuries were underpinned by large sedentary populations that grew significantly as a result of the expansion and intensification of agriculture (especially wet rice cultivation) after c. 1300 (Macknight 1983; Caldwell 1995; Bulbeck and Caldwell 2008). The growing agricultural wealth of South Sulawesi's kingdoms is reflected in the earliest European accounts of the peninsula. In 1544, a Portuguese visitor to the west coast, Antonio de Paiva, noted that:

> The island is rich in all kinds of foodstuffs, of rice and meats … buffalo … pig … chickens … goat … all this in abundance. There are great quantities of fish. (Baker 2005:63)

Paiva's glowing description of the agricultural and general economic prosperity of the peninsula is mirrored in seventeenth-century European reports (Gervaise 1701:14–17; Reid 1988:24–25; Andaya 1981:75–76, 90, 265).

Hilltop sites

If Lape and Chao's (2008) explanatory model for East Timor's fortifications is applicable to South Sulawesi, then the population of South Sulawesi would have retreated to hilltop settlements between AD 1150 and 1700, and settlements in drought-tolerant locations close to drought-susceptible locations would have erected permanent fortifications as additional protection. According to Lape and Chao (2008:18–19), ENSO-stimulated fortification-building in north coastal East Timor peaked between c. AD 1450 to c. 1650. While settlement locations other than hilltops became progressively abandoned, only those settlements in drought-tolerant locations acquired the additional protection of defensive stone walls.[6] These additional defences were required to protect the inhabitants from their counterparts on hilltops in locations more severely affected by drought.

---

6   The naturally defensive location of hilltop settlements is implicit but not clearly stated in Lape and Chao (2008).

7. The indigenous fortifications of South Sulawesi, Indonesia, and their sociopolitical foundations 159

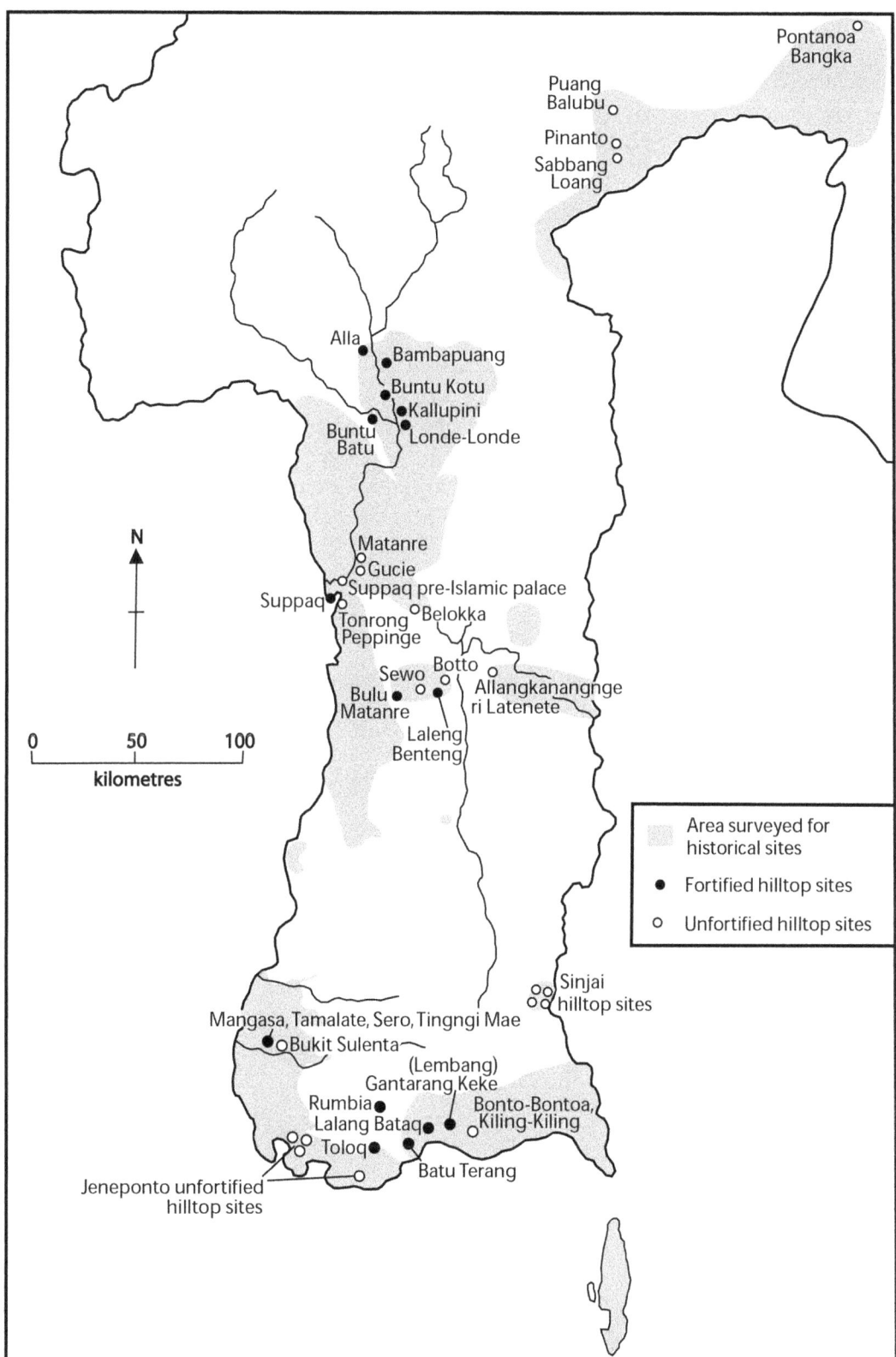

Figure 7.2. South Sulawesi hilltop settlements with and without evidence of fortifications.
Source: David Bulbeck.

Table 7.2 presents the available data on hilltop sites (Figure 7.2) in parts of South Sulawesi with reliable rainfall. The lack of hilltop fortifications in Luwu, Wajo and Sinjai is consistent with the Lape and Chao model as these areas are not prone to drought. However, the presence of both fortified and non-fortified hilltop sites at Goa and Soppeng suggests greater complexity to the construction of fortifications than the Lape and Chao model would allow. For instance, Bulu Matanre in Soppeng protected a mountain pass (Caldwell 1995:397), which may explain why it, and not Sewo, provides evidence for stonewall fortifications. Furthermore, the Suppa and Enrekang hilltop fortifications postdate the period of hypothesised ENSO climatic instability.

Table 7.3 presents the available data on hilltop sites along the more drought-prone southern coast of the South Sulawesi peninsula. The Bantaeng evidence for hilltop fortifications after AD 1300, and their proximity to coeval Jeneponto hilltop (and other) settlements that were generally not fortified, could be regarded as consistent with the Lape and Chao model, inasmuch as Jeneponto is generally more susceptible to drought than is Bantaeng (Caldwell and Bougas 2004). However, there are no accounts, oral or otherwise, of conflict between Bantaeng and its neighbours in the agriculturally marginal land of Jeneponto to the west and Bulukumba to the east. Instead, Bantaeng's fortifications evidently stem from internal conflict during its political integration and/or the need for protection against seaborne attack. In a similar vein, the survival of stone wall defences at Toloq and Rumbia in Jeneponto would appear to stem from their semi-autonomous status and consequent responsibility for their own protection (Appendix E).

Table 7.2. Chronologically dated hilltop sites in parts of South Sulawesi with reliable rainfall.

Site	Approximate dating (AD)	Regency	Fortified?	Reference
Uphill Sabbang Loang	Mid/late 1st millennium, 15th–17th, 19th–20th Cs	Luwu	No	Bulbeck and Caldwell 2000
Pontanoa Bangka	Late 1st millennium, 12th–13th Cs	Luwu	No	Bulbeck 2010
Pinanto hilltop	14th–16th Cs	Luwu	No	Bulbeck and Caldwell 2000
Puang Balubu	14th–16th Cs	Luwu	No	Bulbeck and Caldwell 2000
Allangkanangnge ri Latanete	13th–17th Cs	Wajo	No	Bulbeck and Caldwell 2008
Bulo-Bulo	14th–16th Cs	Sinjai	No	Hasanuddin 2011
Lamatti, Tondong	By 16th Cs	Sinjai	No	Hasanuddin 2011
Batu Pake Gojeng	16th–18th Cs	Sinjai	No	Hasanuddin 2011
Botto	13th–19th Cs (Dutch early/mid-20th C.)	Soppeng	No	Appendix A
Laleng Benteng (= 'within fort')	13th C. onwards	Soppeng	Yes (as of 16th C.)	Appendix A
Sewo Tua	14th–17th Cs	Soppeng	No	Appendix A
Bulu Matanre	14th–17th Cs	Soppeng	Yes	Appendix A
Mangasa, Kale Goa/Tamalate	14th–18th Cs	Goa	Yes (as of 16th C.)	Bulbeck 1992; Appendix B
Bukit Bikuling (Sero)	14th–18th Cs	Goa	Yes (18th C.)	Bulbeck 1992; Appendix B
Bukit Sulenta	17th–18th Cs (graves)	Goa	No	Bulbeck 1992
Tingngi Mae	18th–19th Cs (graveyard)	Goa	Yes (18th C.)	Bulbeck 1992; Appendix B
Suppaq pre-Islamic palace	1300–1700	Suppa	No	Druce 2009
Gucie	1300–1700	Suppa	No	Druce 2009
Tonrong Peppinge	14th–16th Cs	Suppa	No	Druce 2009
Belokka	14th–18th Cs	Sidenreng	No	Druce 2009
Matanre	14th–19th Cs	Sawitto	No	Druce 2009

Site	Approximate dating (AD)	Regency	Fortified?	Reference
Suppaq fort	18th–19th Cs	Suppa	Yes	Appendix C
Buntu Kotu	17th–19th Cs	Enrekang	Yes	Appendix D
Londe-Londe	19th–20th Cs	Enrekang	Yes	Makkulasse 1986
Kallupini	19th–20th Cs	Enrekang	Yes	Makkulasse 1986
Buntu Batu	19th–20th Cs	Enrekang	Yes	Makkulasse 1986
Bambapuang	19th–20th Cs	Enrekang	Yes	Makkulasse 1986
Alla	19th–20th Cs	Enrekang	Yes	Makkulasse 1986

Sources: See references throughout table.

Table 7.3. Chronologically dated hilltop sites in drought-prone parts of South Sulawesi.

Site	Approximate dating (AD)	Regency	Fortified?	Reference
Bonto-Bontoa	1000	Bantaeng	No	Bulbeck 2010
Kiling-Kiling	1000–1200	Bantaeng	No	Bulbeck 2010
Lembarang Gantarang Keke	13th–17th Cs	Bantaeng	Yes	Bougas 1998
Gantarang Keke	13th C. onwards	Bantaeng	Yes	Bougas 1998
Lalang Bataq (= 'within walls')	Ceremonial site by 15th C.	Bantaeng	Yes (implied)	Bougas 1998
Benteng Batu Terang	16th–19th Cs	Bantaeng	Yes	Appendix E
Karaengloe (Sapanang)	14th–17th Cs	Jeneponto	No	Caldwell and Bougas 2004
Bangkala Loe	By 17th C.	Jeneponto	No	Caldwell and Bougas 2004
Tanatoa	14th–16th Cs	Jeneponto	No	Caldwell and Bougas 2004
Banrimanurung hill	By 16th C.	Jeneponto	No	Caldwell and Bougas 2004
Toloq, Rumbia	By 16th C.	Jeneponto	Yes	Caldwell and Bougas 2004

Sources: See references throughout table.

South Sulawesi non-hilltop fortifications

Lape and Chao (2008:18) described a process of increasing abandonment of East Timor settlements other than those on hilltops between the twelfth and seventeenth centuries. Quite the reverse is apparent for South Sulawesi, where the same period witnessed a proliferation of non-hilltop settlements in the Bone coastal plain (Macknight 1983), Makassar and its hinterland (Bulbeck 1992:463), Luwu (Bulbeck and Caldwell 2000:69, 99) and the Ajattappareng lowlands (Druce 2009:Chapter 5). Fortifications were erected as part of this process (Figure 7.3), which may be consistent with Field's (2008:3) general model for Indo-Pacific fortifications provided that we find evidence that these fortifications defended densely distributed and temporally predictable resources. To do so, our supplementary material sifts through a considerable body of historical and archaeological evidence. Our summary of the findings is provided in Tables 7.4 to 7.7.

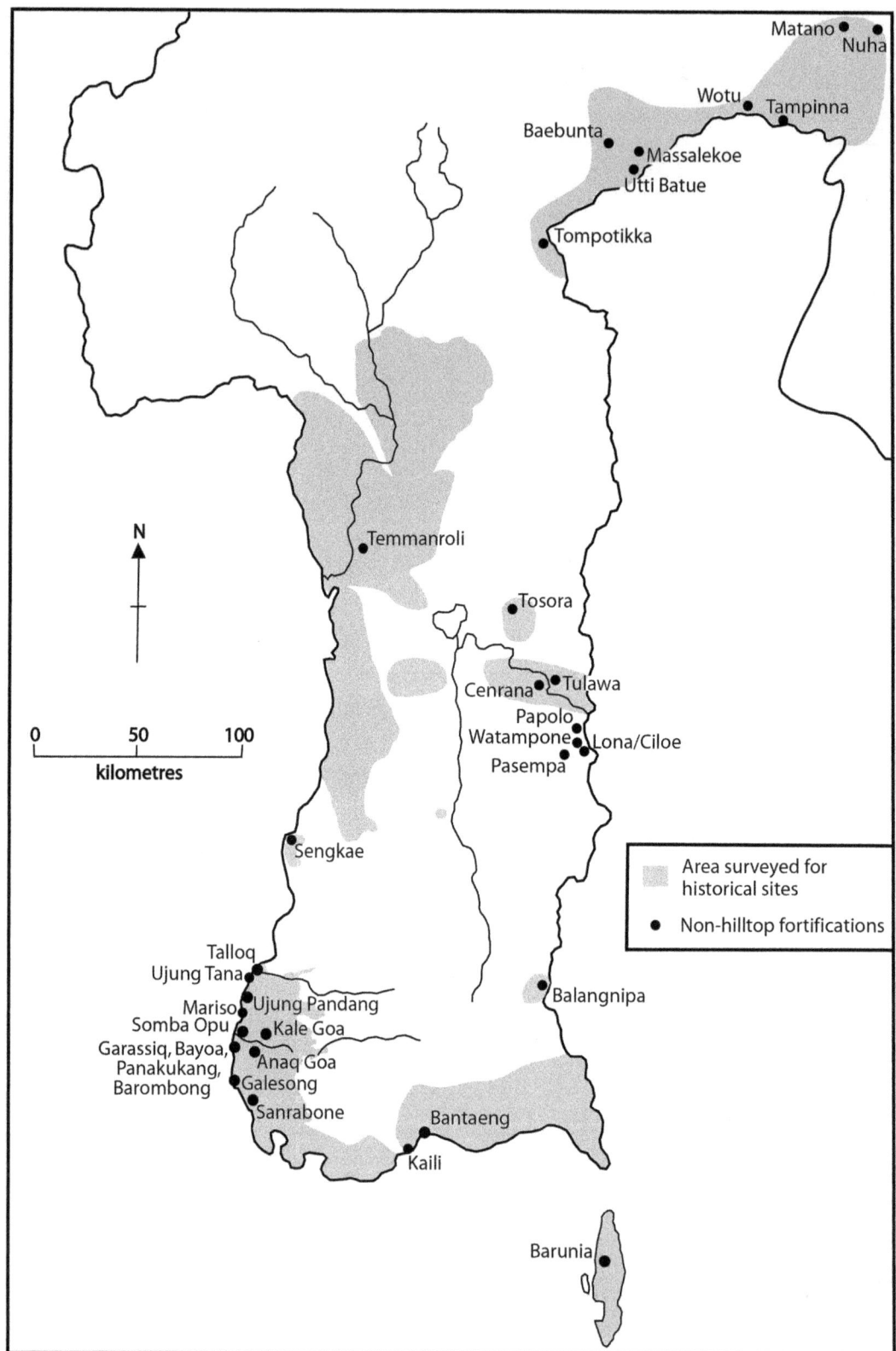

Figure 7.3. South Sulawesi fortifications (excluding fortified hilltop sites).
Source: David Bulbeck.

7. The indigenous fortifications of South Sulawesi, Indonesia, and their sociopolitical foundations

Table 7.4. South Sulawesi non-hilltop fortifications in locations near hilltop fortifications.

Fortification	Form and dimensions	Material	Purpose	Fortification period (AD)	Habitation period at site (AD)
Temmanroli, Sawitto	Semicircular, 14 ha	Earth (?)	Palace centre defence	By 18th C.	14th–18th Cs
Kale Goa	Pentagonal, 84 ha	Earth walls encased with brick	Palace centre defence	c. 1540–1778	14th–18th Cs
'Head Quarters No. 1' (Figure 7.A2), Kale Goa	Unknown	Unknown	Palace perimeter defence	(Late) 18th C.	Unknown
Benteng Malengkeri (Figure 7.A2), Kale Goa	Unknown	Unknown	Palace perimeter defence	18th C.	18th C.
'No. 3' (Figure 7.A2), Kale Goa	Unknown	Unknown	Palace perimeter defence	(Late) 18th C.	Unknown
Benteng Bisei (Figure 7.A2), Kale Goa	Unknown	Unknown	Palace perimeter defence	(Late) 18th C.	Unknown
Benteng Kanonderong (Figure 7.A2), Kale Goa	Unknown	Unknown	Palace perimeter defence	(Late) 18th C.	Unknown
Benteng Bone in Makassar (Figure 7.A2)	Unknown	Unknown (timber?)	Military installation	c. 1739–1900	Unknown
Benteng Kaili, Bantaeng	Unknown	Earth	Unknown	Unknown	Unknown
Bantaeng	Unknown	Unknown	Port defence	By 1666	14th/15th C. onwards

Sources: See Appendices B, C and E.

Table 7.5. Fortifications in Makassar and its hinterland (excluding Kale Goa).

Fortification	Form and dimensions	Material	Purpose	Fortification period (AD)	Habitation period at site (AD)
Somba Opu	Quadrangular with southern extension, 16–20 ha	Mostly walls of solid brick; some dressed masonry	Port and palace centre defence	c. 1540–1701	16th–18th Cs
Talloq	Parallelogram, 40 ha	Stone walls (some dressed masonry), and earth walls encased with brick	Port and palace centre defence	c. 1615–1701	14th C. onwards
Garassiq	Triangular, 2.1 ha	Earth and brick	Port defence	1630s–1701	14th C. onwards
Bayoa	Triangular, 2.6 ha	Earth and brick	Port defence	1630s–1670	15th C. onwards
Panakukang	Quadrangular, 1 ha	Bricks and coral blocks in earth wall	Port defence	1634–1670	15th C. onwards
Barombong	Unknown	Earth and brick	Port defence	1635–1670	17th C. onwards
Somba Opu – Barombong wall	c. 4 km long	Single brick wall	Port defence	1630s–1670	14th C. onwards
Ujung Tana	Unknown	Stone	Port defence	1634–1720s	Unknown
Ujung Pandang	Parallelogram, 1.7 ha	Mainly earth?	Port defence	1634–1667	By 16th C. onwards
Mariso	Unknown	Unknown	Port defence	1634–1670	Unknown
Ujung Tana – Somba Opu wall	c. 10 km long	Single brick wall (?)	Port defence	1634–1670	Unknown
Anaq Goa	Parallelogram, 15 ha	Walls of earth with a brick spine	Military installation	c. 1750–1780 (?)	15th and 18th Cs (main phases)
Sanrabone	Quadrangular, 22 ha	Earth walls encased with brick	Harbour and palace centre defence	1630s (?) –1781	14th C. onwards
Galesong	c. 3.5 km length in total	Seven walls and raised tongues of earth	Harbour defence	1667	1st millennium onwards

Sources: See Appendices B, F and G.

Table 7.6. Other Makasar and Bugis non-hilltop fortifications.

Fortification	Form and dimensions	Material	Purpose	Fortification period (AD)	Habitation period at site (AD)
Sengkae	Quadrangular including river front, 10 ha	Stone foundations	Port defence	c. 1500–1600	15th–17th Cs
Balangnipa	Quadrangular, 0.5 ha	Timber	Port defence	1557–1863	By 16th C.
Barunia (Selayar)	Quadrangular, 2.7 ha	Stone walls	Palace centre defence	Late 18th to 19th C.	Late 18th to 19th C.
Papolo	Unknown	Unknown	Military installation	c. 1565	Unknown
Pasempa	Three interlocking walls, 500 m in length	Mainly earth	Military installation at overland pass	c. 1643–1905	Unknown
Watampone	Quadrangular, 100 ha	Earth walls with timber and bamboo	Palace centre defence	Late 16th C. – 1905	14th C. onwards
Lona/Ciloe redoubts (Bajoe)	Three quadrangular redoubts, 1 ha in area	Unknown	Port/palace centre defence	c. 1859–1905	Unknown
Cenrana ('Istana la Patauq')	Two quadrangular enclosures, 180 ha in area	Gates of stone blocks, earth and uncoursed rubble walls	Military installation/palace centre defence	1671–c. 1760	c. 1500–1760
Benteng Tulawa	Unknown	Unknown	Military installation	c. 1745–1760	Unknown
Tosora	Quadrangular, 100 ha	Earth walls	Palace centre defence	c. 1639–1840	16th C. – late 19th C.
Utti Batue	Single wall, 1.5 km long	Earth	Port/palace centre defence	c. 1450–1600	c. 1400–1600
Massalekoe	Sigmoid wall, 500 m long	Earth	Palace centre defence	c. 1600–1620	c. 1600–1620
Tompotikka (Palopo)	Parallelogram, 200–250 ha	Earth walls	Port/palace centre defence	c. 1620–1840	14th C. onwards

Source: See Appendices H–M.

Table 7.7. Non-Bugis non-hilltop fortifications in Luwu Regency.

Fortification	Form and dimensions	Material	Purpose	Fortification period (AD)	Habitation period at site (AD)
Wotu	Sigmoid wall, c. 550 m long	Earth	Harbour defence	c. 1620–1820	15th C. onwards
Tampinna	Wall up to 250 m long	Probably earth	Maritime traders' defence	c. 1620?–1700	c. 1400–1700
Baebunta	Triangular (southern border formed by river), 6 ha	Earth	Palace centre defence	c. 1800–1850	15th C. onwards
Matano	Eleven curvilinear segments, 550 m long in total	Earth	Population concentration defence	19th C.	12th C. onwards
Nuha	Single wall	Earth	Population concentration defence	Undocumented	12th C. onwards

Source: See Appendix N.

Makassar (Goa–Talloq)

Makassar and its hinterland are the location of the major concentration of indigenous fortifications in South Sulawesi. Tumapaqrisiq Kallona, who ruled the rising agrarian kingdom of Goa from 1511 to 1546, incorporated the port settlement of Makassar in the early sixteenth century and c. 1540 held onto it against a combined assault from Goa's neighbours (Bulbeck 1992:117–119). The Portuguese adventurer Antonio de Paiva visited Makassar in 1544 and 'arrived in the aforesaid port, a large city called Gowa' (Baker 2005:72). In later years, Goa's partner-kingdom of Talloq, which lay immediately north of Makassar, had at least an equal role in administering Makassar and constructing its impenetrable coastal defences (Reid 1983).

In the sixteenth century, Goa fortified its original, hinterland palace centre of Kale Goa and subsequently erected a fortified palace centre at the coastal location of Somba Opu. In the early seventeenth century, Talloq fortified its coastal palace centre and in the 1630s, in the face of rising military threats from the VOC, a line of forts and a connecting wall were erected between Somba Opu and Talloq (Appendices B and F). Most of Makassar's coastal fortifications were razed in 1670 in accord with the conditions of Goa–Talloq's surrender to the VOC (set out in the Treaty of Bungaya in 1667), but this event by no means marked the end of Goa–Talloq's fortifications. For instance, the 1701 reimposition of the Bungaya treaty required Goa–Talloq to raze the several coastal fortifications it had since rebuilt (Patunru 1983:73). In the late eighteenth century, a popular resistance against the VOC led by Goa was accompanied by the erection of brick fortresses in the Makassar hinterland at Anaq Goa and Goa's original heartland of Kale Goa (Appendix B).

Two further fortification developments south of Makassar were intimately connected to the fortunes of Goa–Talloq. One was Benteng Sanrabone, a brick fortress built before the 1670s and probably during the 1630s. The second was the complex of earthen walls at Galesong which were evidently constructed in their full entirety in 1667 to defend Makassar from the advance of enemy troops from the south (Appendix G).

Other southern South Sulawesi fortifications

Three further indigenous forts are located in southern Sulawesi. Located to the north of Makassar, Sengkae was the sixteenth-century palace centre (Appendix H) of the kingdom of Siang, which was an early sixteenth-century competitor of Goa prior to its mid-sixteenth-century conquest by Goa (Bulbeck 1992). On the eastern coast of the peninsula, at Sinjai, Balangnipa is remembered by local historians as a wooden fort dated to between the mid-sixteenth and nineteenth centuries (Appendix I); one of the lesser kingdoms instrumental in the Balangnipa fortifications, Bulo-Bulo, was a seventeenth-century ally of Goa–Talloq (Bulbeck 1992). Finally, despite its mark in South Sulawesi's early history, Selayar has failed to yield evidence for fortifications before the eighteenth century. The island's only fortress, Barunia, was probably erected in response to increasing VOC control over Selayar at the time (Appendix J).

Bone and Wajoq

The Bugis kingdom of Bone originated during the fourteenth century in the vicinity of the present-day regional capital of Watampone (Macknight 1983). Bone played an important part in the political history of South Sulawesi between the sixteenth and early twentieth centuries as reflected in its rich fortification records (Appendix K). Bone provided strong resistance against Goa–Talloq's military campaigns in the sixteenth and seventeenth centuries and established itself as a major powerbroker in Makassar between 1667 and c. 1800. The kingdom maintained its status as the most powerful of the South Sulawesi kingdoms throughout the nineteenth century (Reid 1990:103), notwithstanding its expulsion from Makassar in the early nineteenth century, and military assaults on Watampone by the English in 1814, and by the Dutch in 1824, 1859 and 1905 (De Klerck 1975). The first three campaigns saw little in the way of fighting because the Bone forces fled to Pasempa in the highlands. Bone's army was finally defeated by the Dutch at Watampone in 1905 and the kingdom was incorporated into the Netherlands Colonial State.

Wajoq was one of the oldest Bugis kingdoms, and its heartlands lay along the Cenrana valley, east of South Sulawesi's central lowlands. Tosora (Appendix L) was Wajoq's capital by the sixteenth century, but its walls (remains of which are visible today) were reportedly built between 1636 and 1643 (Duli 2010:148). Wajoq's relations with its southern neighbour Bone oscillated between uneasy truce and open warfare. In the late 1730s, Arung Sengkang became ruler of Wajoq and staged a campaign against Bone, culminating in 1739 with the assault by Arung Sengkang, assisted by Karaeng Bontolangkasa, on the Bone and VOC positions in Makassar (Patunru 1983). The VOC countered by driving Arung Sengkang back to Wajoq; a map of Snout's 1740 campaign against Wajoq (de Roever and Brommer 2008:166) shows Wajoq's troops lined up against the VOC/Bone troops along the Cenrana, the latter assisted by a contingent of Tanete troops attacking Wajoq from the west.

Luwu fortifications

The Bugis kingdom of Luwuq rose to prominence between the fourteenth and sixteenth centuries, based on its control over high-quality iron from the highland regions of Rongkong and Lake Matano. From the fourteenth to seventeenth centuries, Luwuq's capital was located at Malangke on the northwest coast of the Gulf of Bone. In the early seventeenth century, the kingdom appears to have experienced a political and economic crisis and around 1620 moved its palace site to Palopo, today the provincial capital of West Luwu (Bulbeck and Caldwell 2000).[7] Hereafter, Luwuq functioned as a minor maritime trading power, controlling the traffic in dammar and other forest products from the northern reaches of the Gulf of Bone and the south central Sulawesi highlands until the Dutch occupation in 1905 (Caldwell 1988:196). In accord with the historical and archaeological evidence on the history of Luwuq, we date its fortifications at Malangke to the fifteenth to sixteenth centuries and its earthen fortress at Palopo to the seventeenth to eighteenth centuries (Appendix M).

Luwuq was qualitatively different from the other Bugis kingdoms in that its realm included multiple non-Bugis groups, such as the coastally based Wotu and Bajao sea gypsies, and more hinterland-based groups, such as the Lemolang and Padoe. The relocation of Luwuq's capital to Palopo in the seventeenth century evidently opened the way for local ethnic tensions to spill over, as reflected in the seventeenth-century conflict between the Wotu and Bajao (Bulbeck and Caldwell 2000), and the nineteenth-century construction of defensive fortifications by the Lemolang residents at Baebunta and the Padoe residents at Matano. Another Padoe settlement, Nuha, also has earthen walls, which may also be of nineteenth-century construction even though evidence for their chronology was not collected (Appendix N).

Fortification building materials

Tables 7.2 to 7.7 demonstrate the preferential use of local building materials for fortifications. Stone was used for building fortifications, not only on hilltops (as observed in our Introduction) but also at Benteng Barunia, located in the Selayar hinterland, and for a minority of coastal fortifications. Away from hilltops, earth was the predominantly used material, except at Makassar

---

7 Palopo was first occupied at an earlier date, based on the thirteenth- to fourteenth-century ceramic sherds recovered from an area of tumuli within the site (Bulbeck 1996–97:1047).

and its hinterland, which (along with Sanrabone) have the only fortifications where bricks were used. Bricks are hard-baked earth and so reflect the use of local material in fort construction. Goa–Talloq's capacity to fire bricks, along with the unique use of fine masonry at Benteng Talloq and Somba Opu, including stone blocks sourced to a quarry on the middle Jeneberang River (Bulbeck 1998), underlines the technological advantages Goa–Talloq acquired during the time Makassar operated as an independent emporium (Reid 1983; Bulbeck 1992).

Discussion

One strength of the South Sulawesi evidence is that, in most cases, a site's occupation history can be distinguished from the period for which there is archaeological and/or historical evidence of fortifications (Tables 7.2–7.7). The distinction makes clear that the building of enduring defences around settlements was not an integral part of initial occupation, and that when it did occur it was usually for a strategic military purpose. Defences such as a protective fence or hedge may well have been erected at sites during their 'non-fortification' period, but the same caveat would also apply to the 'unfortified' East Timor sites reported by Lape and Chao (2008). Were the South Sulawesi fortifications a response to ENSO-related climatic instability, they should have been built between AD 1100 and 1600, with a peak of construction in the fourteenth century (Lape and Chao 2008:15; Langton et al. 2008: Figure 3A). In reality, many sites remained occupied without evidence of fortifications for much or all of this period, with the earliest evidence for fortification postdating 1600 (e.g. Bukit Bikuling, Bantaeng, Temmanroli, Talloq, Garassiq, Galesong, Sanrabone, Palopo, Baebunta, Wotu, Tampinna and Matano). In addition, more fortifications appear to have been in use throughout the period 1650–1850 than at any point up to 1600 (Figure 7.4).

One possibility to be considered is that there was a relationship between fortification building and climatic desiccation, both in East Timor and South Sulawesi, only partially related to ENSO effects. On the world stage, the eleventh to thirteenth centuries were a warm, wet interval (Lamb 1995), despite the onset of more frequent ENSO events (Langton et al. 2008). The peak in ENSO frequency at c. 1300 may have been associated with the transition to the Little Ice Age, whose effects were most marked between the sixteenth and eighteenth centuries (Field 2008:6).[8] A fourteenth- to eighteenth-century chronology would provide a reasonable match for the South Sulawesi fortifications (Figure 7.4) and also for the East Timor fortifications, with their evidence for a building peak of 1450–1650 and sustained occupation into the early eighteenth century (Lape and Chao 2008:18). In the absence of palaeoenvironmental data from either East Timor (Lape and Chao 2008:15) or South Sulawesi, it may be reasonable to hypothesise an increase in fortifications in both regions at a time of increased rainfall unpredictability associated with the Little Ice Age (cf. Field 2008:4). However, it would be premature to assume that climatic desiccation caused the increase in fortifications without evidence on the scale of conflict in the region (Field 2008:6–7). Furthermore, to understand the constriction history of South Sulawesi fortifications, it is important to recognise the two broad periods involved.

---

8   While there is little consensus on precisely when it began, or when it ended, it is generally agreed that a period of global cooling set in around 1200, leading to the dreadful European summers of 1315–1317. The climate continued to cool until 1500, when evidence from England, Europe, America and New Zealand points to 'generally rather warmer conditions … than in the previous century' (Lamb 1995:211). After 1500, temperatures declined again, reaching a nadir in the 1690s with a series of cold, wet summers and bitter winters. During this decade, temperatures in England and on the continent averaged 1.5–2°C lower than those of today, shortening the growing season by up to two months. Lamb (1995:212) writes that from the mid-sixteenth century onwards, 'the evidence points to the coldest regime … at any time since the last major ice age ended ten thousand years or so ago. *It is the only time for which evidence from all parts of the world indicates a colder regime than now.*' [Authors' italics.]

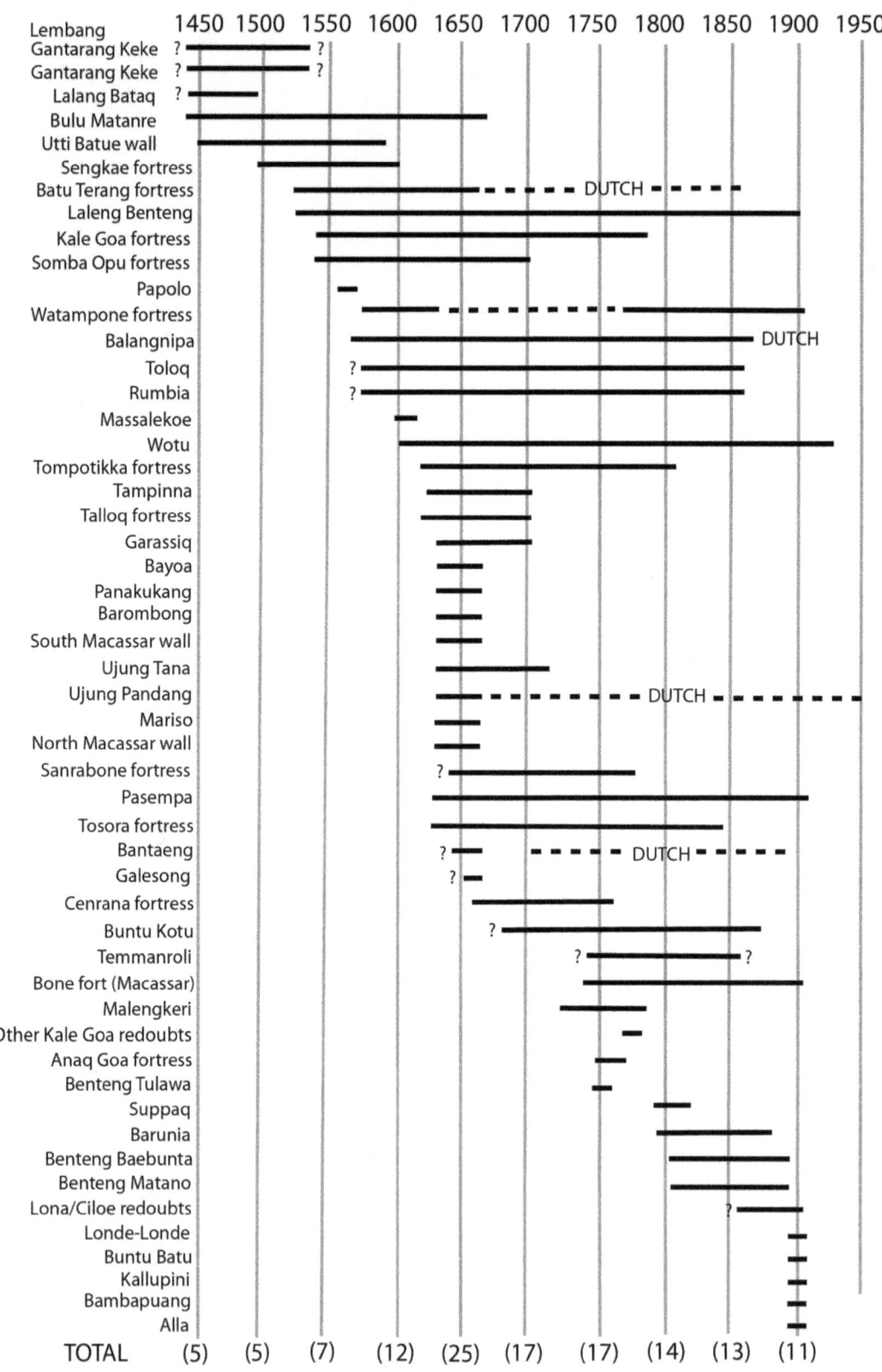

Figure 7.4. Time chart of South Sulawesi's dated fortifications.
Source: David Bulbeck.

The first period, up to the 1530s, involved the building of defended hilltop settlements, as well as two early fortifications at coastal trading centres (Utti Batue and Sengkae). This was a building phenomenon broadly similar to that described by Lape and Chao for East Timor, although in South Sulawesi we can ascribe the hilltop fortifications to the political unification of Bantaeng (Appendix E) or, in the case of Bulu Matanre, the defence of a strategic mountain pass. Political unification in South Sulawesi began c. 1300 or slightly earlier in a number of widely separated locations (Bulbeck 1996–97:1049–1050; Bulbeck and Caldwell 2000; Caldwell and Bougas 2004; Bulbeck and Caldwell 2008). Broadly speaking, the fourteenth through fifteenth centuries was a period of internal state-building and consolidation. Warfare in this period occurred mainly within what were to become the historical kingdoms of South Sulawesi. Only in the sixteenth century did armed conflict spill over into open warfare between the kingdoms as they started to vie for wider supremacy, as foreshadowed by the Utti Batue and Sengkae fortifications.

The second period, starting from the 1540s, predominantly involved fortifications at Makassar, or fortifications (such as Benteng Papolo) erected in resistance against whoever controlled Makassar, or fortifications (such as the Cenrana fortress) that functioned as outposts of a powerful faction in Makassar. Control of the port city of Makassar, and its growing trade relations with other areas of the archipelago, was the key to the political integration of South Sulawesi. This was effectively achieved when Goa–Talloq conquered Bone c. 1640, with the result that the late 1660s occupation of Makassar by the alliance between the VOC and Bone led to a changing of the guard rather than political fragmentation. Despite two serious challenges during the eighteenth century and a brief British interregnum, the Dutch retained control of Makassar and effectively prevented any single native kingdom from dominating the peninsula. The story of mid-sixteenth to mid-seventeenth-century fortifications is centred on Makassar and the task of preventing any serious challenge to control of this important harbour. This policy was continued after 1667 by the Dutch through their construction of Fort Rotterdam and the prohibition of indigenous fortifications along the west coast. Only the fortifications at Luwu inland from the Gulf of Bone appear to have been built according to a rhythm other than control over/defence against Makassar (Appendices M and N). Unlike the agrarian kingdoms to its south, Luwuq's economy was based on its ability to maintain order among the settlements that bartered iron and other hinterland produce at Luwuq's port-capitals of Malangke up to c. 1600 (Bulbeck and Caldwell 2000) and Palopo between the seventeenth and early nineteenth centuries (van Braam Morris 1889).

The three main purposes of sixteenth-century and later fortifications were port defence, palace centre defence and military installations (Tables 7.4–7.7). The purposes of port and palace centre defence were often combined when maritime trade was critical to a kingdom's economy. Control over fertile wet rice land was also an important stimulus for the fortification programs at Makassar (affording control over the Maros and southwest coastal rice lands), Watampone, Wajoq and Temmanroli. The combination of archipelagic trade and control over rice-growing lands has been recognised as central to the historical process of political unification in South Sulawesi (Bulbeck and Caldwell 2008). In a development that does not appear to have transpired in East Timor, fortification programs shifted (as it were) from the natural defensive location of hilltops to prime economic locations for maritime trade and wet rice production (locations with concentrated and temporally predictable resources, in Field's (2008:3) terms). Only when the Dutch advanced on Massenrempulu to complete their colonisation of South Sulawesi do we find a return to a predominance of hilltop fortifications.

The fourteenth to sixteenth centuries appear to have been a period of largely uninterrupted economic and demographic growth in South Sulawesi, and the onset of durable fortifications should be viewed in this context rather than as a response to climatic desiccation. Nonetheless, we leave open the possibility of a relationship between South Sulawesi's mid-seventeenth-century political integration and the effects of the peak of the Little Ice Age. Writing of the widespread economic downturn in Southeast Asia after 1630, Reid (1993:291) makes the statement that 'The most truly global explanation of the "general crisis" is … the gradual decline in temperatures during the seventeenth century'. A part of this 'general crisis' may possibly have been due to specific ENSO effects: Quinn et al. (1978) have demonstrated a correlation between El Niño events in Java, while tree rings from the teak forests of east central Java show the period 1598–1679 to be the worst substantial period for rainfall between 1514 and 1929 (Reid 1993:291). While the effects of the Little Ice Age upon the humid tropics remain unclear, they probably include a greater variability of short-term changes in the weather. Lamb (1995:219–220) points out that it is precisely at such periods of global cooling that climatic conditions are most variable. Combined with increased dryness, such conditions would result in less predictable yields and more frequent harvest failures. By the mid-seventeenth century, populations in South Sulawesi may have been close to carrying capacity despite the widespread felling of forests and their replacement by agricultural lands (especially wet rice fields). The peninsula-wide scale of conflict in South Sulawesi after the early seventeenth century might possibly have been exacerbated by such a crisis, as reduced rainfall and smaller harvests met rising populations and hungry stomachs. This possibility remains to be examined.

Conclusion

The proximate cause for the major period of fortification construction and use in South Sulawesi between the mid-sixteenth and early twentieth centuries was the struggle for political supremacy across the peninsula. European weaponry and other technological advances played a major role in escalating the scale of warfare in the South Sulawesi peninsula. The virtual monopoly that the west coast alliance of Goa and Talloq enjoyed over European firepower between the mid-sixteenth and mid-seventeenth centuries enabled Makassar to rule increasingly large swathes of the peninsula. The partnership between the VOC and the east coast kingdom of Bone was the major political force in the peninsula between the late seventeenth and late eighteenth centuries, despite several challenges to the partnership's supremacy. Between the early nineteenth and early twentieth centuries the European administration in Makassar (starting with the British administration of 1811–1816) exerted increasing colonial control over South Sulawesi. For climatic unpredictability to have been the causal factor for South Sulawesi's increase in fortifications, it must also have been the cause for an increasing role in European military technology in South Sulawesi—a speculative proposition for which no evidence has been found. Perhaps climatic instability associated with the Little Ice Age, associated with reduced—not enhanced—ENSO activity, was a dominant cause for the increase in fortifications in the agriculturally marginal belt of north coastal East Timor. But on present evidence this was not the case in South Sulawesi.

Acknowledgements

We are grateful to Campbell Macknight for access to texts and illustrative documents in his possession, as well as advice and comments on drafts of this paper. Budianto Hakim of Balai Arkeologi Makassar accompanied David Bulbeck during the survey of the Watampone fortifications in December 2010 and Bantaeng fortifications in October 2011. The detailed comments of two anonymous referees are gratefully acknowledged.

References

Andaya, L.Y. 1981. *The heritage of Arung Palakka: A history of South Sulawesi (Celebes) in the seventeenth century*. Verhandelingen van het Koninklijk Instituut voor Taal-, Land- en Volkenkunde 91. Martinus Nijhoff, The Hague. doi.org/10.26530/oapen_613368.

Baker, B. 2005. South Sulawesi in 1544: A Portuguese letter. *Review of Indonesian and Malaysian Affairs* 39:61–85.

Bigalke, T.W. 2005. *Tana Toraja: A social history of an Indonesian people*. Singapore University Press, Singapore.

Bougas, W.A. 1998. Bantayan: An early Makassarese kingdom. *Archipel* 55:83–123. doi.org/10.3406/arch.1998.3444.

Boxer, C.R. 1967. *Francisco Viera de Figueiredo: A Portuguese merchant-adventurer in South East Asia, 1624–1667*. Martinus Nijhoff, The Hague. doi.org/10.26530/oapen_613438.

Budiarta, H. 2007. Taking and returning objects in a colonial context: Tracing the collections acquired during the Bone-Gowa military expeditions. In P. ter Keurs (ed.), *Colonial collections revisited*, pp. 123–143. CNWS Publications, Leiden.

Bulbeck, D. 1996–97. The Bronze–Iron Age of South Sulawesi, Indonesia: Mortuary traditions, metallurgy and trade. In F.D. Bulbeck and N. Barnard (eds), *Ancient Chinese and Southeast Asian Bronze Age cultures*. Volume II, pp. 1007–1076. Southern Materials Center, Taipei.

Bulbeck, D. 1998. The construction history and significance of the Makassar fortifications. In K. Robinson and M. Paeni (eds), *Living through histories: Culture, history and social life in South Sulawesi*, pp. 67–106. The Australian National University, Canberra.

Bulbeck, D. 2010. Uneven development in southwest Sulawesi, Indonesia during the Early Metal Phase. In B. Bellina, E.A. Bacus, T.O. Pryce and J. Wisseman Christie (eds), *50 years of archaeology in Southeast Asia: Essays in honour of Ian Glover*, pp. 152–169. Bangkok: River Books.

Bulbeck, D. and I. Caldwell 2000. *Land of iron: The historical archaeology of Luwu and the Cenrana Valley. Results of the origin of complex society in South Sulawesi Project (OXIS)*. Centre for South-East Asian Studies, University of Hull, Hull.

Bulbeck, D. and I. Caldwell 2008. *Oryza sativa* and the origins of kingdoms in South Sulawesi, Indonesia: Evidence from rice husk phytoliths. *Indonesia and the Malay World* 36:1–20. doi.org/10.1080/13639810802016117.

Bulbeck, D. and B. Prasetyo 1998. Survey of pre-Islamic historical sites in Luwu, South Sulawesi. *Walennae* 1:29–42.

Bulbeck, D. and B. Prasetyo 1999. The origins of complex society in South Sulawesi (OXIS). Unpublished final report to Lembaga Ilmu Pengetahuan Indonesia.

Bulbeck, D., D. Bowdery, J. Field and B. Prasetyo 2007. The palace centre of sago city: Utti Batue site, Luwu, South Sulawesi, Indonesia. In M. Lillie and S. Ellis (eds), *Wetland archaeology and environments: Regional issues, global perspectives*, pp. 119–141. Oxbow Books, Oxford.

Bulbeck, F.D. 1992. A tale of two kingdoms: The historical archaeology of Gowa and Tallok, South Sulawesi, Indonesia. Unpublished PhD thesis. The Australian National University, Canberra.

Caldwell, I. 1988. South Sulawesi A.D. 1300–1600: Ten Bugis texts. Unpublished PhD thesis. The Australian National University, Canberra.

Caldwell, I. 1995. Power, state and society among the pre-Islamic Bugis. *Bijdragen tot de Taal-, Land- en Volkenkunde* 151:396–421. doi.org/10.1163/22134379-90003038.

Caldwell, I. and W.A. Bougas 2004. The early history of Binamu and Bangkala. *Bijdragen tot de Taal-, Land- en Volkenkunde* 160:456–510. doi.org/10.1163/22134379-90003720.

CIA World Factbook. www.cia.gov/library/publications/resources/the-world-factbook/index.html. Accessed 23 March 2020.

Cummings, W.P. (ed. and trans.) 2007. *A chain of kings: The Makassarese chronicles of Gowa and Talloq.* Koninklijk Instituut voor Taal, Land- en Volkenkunde, Leiden. doi.org/10.26530/oapen_376974.

Cummings, W. 2011. *The Makassar annals.* Koninklijk Instituut voor Taal, Land- en Volkenkunde, Leiden.

De Klerck, E.S. 1975. *History of the Netherlands East Indies.* Volume II. B.M. Israël NV, Amsterdam.

de Roever, A. and B. Brommer 2008. *Indische Archipel en Oceanie. Groote Atlas van de Verenigte Oost-Indische Compagnie.* Volume III. Atlas Maior, Voerburg.

Druce, S.C. 2009. *The lands west of the lakes: A history of the Ajattappareng kingdoms of South Sulawesi 1200 to 1600 CE.* Koninklijk Instituut voor Taal, Land- en Volkenkunde, Leiden. doi.org/10.26530/oapen_381395.

Duli, A. 2010. Peranan Tosora sebagai pusat pemerintahan kerajaan Wajo abad XVI – XIX. *Walennae* 12:143–158.

Fadillah, M.A. 1999. Survei dan ekskavasi Bonto-Bontoa, Bantaeng Timur: investigasi awal. *Walennae* 3:13–38.

Fadillah, M.A. 2000. Arkeologi dan Sejarah kuna Wotu: Catatan survei dan eksksavasi. In M.A. Fadillah and I. Sumantri (eds), *Kedatuan Luwu: Perspektif Arkeologi, Sejarah dan Antropologi*, pp. 159–195. Lembaga Penerbitan Universitas Hasanuddin, Makassar.

Fadillah, M.A. and M.I. Mahmud 2000. *Kerajaan Siang Kuna: Sumber Tutur, Teks dan Tapak Arkeologi.* Balai Arkeologi Makassar, Makassar.

Field, J.S. 2008. Explaining fortifications in Indo-Pacific prehistory. *Archaeology in Oceania* 43:1–10. doi.org/10.1002/j.1834-4453.2008.tb00025.x.

Gervaise, N. 1701. *An historical description of the kingdom of Macassar in the East-Indies.* English translation of the original 1688 publication in French. Thomas Leigh and D. Midwinter, London.

Grimes, C.E. and B.D. Grimes 1987. *Languages of South Sulawesi.* Pacific Linguistic Series D–No. 78. The Australian National University, Canberra.

Hadimulyono, dkk. 1985. Studi kelayakan bekas ibu kota Kerajaan Wajo (abad XVII) di Tosora, Kabupaten Wajo Sulawesi Selatan. Unpublished. SPSP Sulselra, Ujung Pandang.

Hasanuddin 2011. Megalithic sites in the district of Sinjai, South Sulawesi, Indonesia. *Bulletin of the Indo-Pacific Prehistory Association* 31:76–84. doi.org/10.7152/bippa.v31i0.10660.

Heersink, C.G. 1994. Selayar and the green gold: The development of the coconut trade on an Indonesian island (1820–1950). *Journal of Southeast Asian Studies* 25:47–69. doi.org/10.1017/s0022463400006676.

Kallupa, B. 1984. *Taman Purbakala Batu Pake Gojeng, Kabupaten Sinjai, Sulawesi Selatan.* Proyek Pemuguran dan Pemeliharaan Peninggalan Sejarah dan Purbakala Sulawesi Selatan, Makassar.

Kallupa, B. 1985. *Study Kelayakan Bekas Ibu Kota Kerajaan Wajo (Abad VXII) di Tosora Kab. Wajo Sulawesi Selatan.* Proyek Pemugaraan dan Pemeliharaan Peninggalan Sejarah dan Purbakala Sulawesi Selatan, Makassar.

Kallupa, B., D. Bulbeck, I. Caldwell, I. Sumantri and K. Demmanari 1989. *Survey Pusat Kerajaan Soppeng 1100-1986.* Privately published, Canberra. ISBN 073-1690-78-8.

Lamb, H.H. 1995. *Climate history and the modern world.* 2nd edition. Routledge, London.

Langton, S.J., B.K. Linsley, R.S. Robinson, Y. Rosenthal, D.W. Oppo, T.I. Eglinton, S.S. Howe, Y.S. Djajadihardja and F. Syamsudin 2008. 3500 yr record of centennial-scale climate variability from the Western Pacific Warm Pool. *Geology* 36(10):795–798. doi.org/10.1130/g24926a.1.

Lape, P.V. and C.-Y. Chao 2008. Fortification as a human response to late Holocene climate change in East Timor. *Archaeology in Oceania* 43(1):11–21. doi.org/10.1002/j.1834-4453.2008.tb00026.x.

Ligtvoet, A. 1880. Transcriptie van het dagboek der vorsten van Gowa en Tello. *Bijdragen tot de Taal-, Land- en Volkenkunde* 28(4):1–259. doi.org/10.1163/22134379-90000513.

Macknight, C.C. 1983. The rise of agriculture in South Sulawesi before 1600. *Review of Indonesian and Malaysian Affairs* 17:92–116.

Macknight, C.C. 1993. *The early history of South Sulawesi: Some recent advances.* Centre of Southeast Asian Studies Working Papers 81. Monash University, Clayton.

Mahmud, M.I. 1993. Struktur Kota Palopo Abad XVII – XIX Masehi: Studi Arkeologi tentang Pemahaman Eksperiensial dan Cita-Pikiran. Sarjana thesis. Hasanuddin University, Makassar.

Mahmud, M.I. 2000. Pemukiman kuna Cenrana, Bone: Beberapa aspek sejarah sosial Bugis. *Walennae* 5:43–64.

Makkulasse 1986. *Laporan Pengumpulan Data 'Peninggalan Sejarah dan Purbakala' Kabupaten Enrekang.* Suaka Peninggalan Sejarah dan Purbakala Sulawesi Selatan, Makassar.

Masdoeki 1984. *Laporan Pengumpulan Data Peninggalan Sejarah dan Purbakala di Kabupaten Barru.* Suaka Peninggalan Sejarah dan Purbakala Sulawesi Selatan, Makassar.

Masdoeki 1985. *Laporan Pengumpulan Data Peninggalan Sejarah dan Purbakala di Kabupaten Takalar.* Suaka Peninggalan Sejarah dan Purbakala Sulawesi Selatan, Makassar.

McWilliam, A., D. Bulbeck, S. Brockwell and S. O'Connor 2012. The cultural legacy of Makassar stone in East Timor. *The Asia Pacific Journal of Anthropology* 13(3):262–279. doi.org/10.1080/14442213.2012.674054.

Monk, K.A., Y. de Fretes and G. Reksodiharjo-Lilley 1997. *The ecology of Nusatenggara and Maluku.* Periplus, Hong Kong.

Muhaeminah 2009. Benteng kolonial Belanda di Balangnipa Kabupaten Sinjai. *Walennae* 11:51–64.

Muhaeminah 2010. Situs Bacukiki di kota Parepare peluang pemanfaatan sebagai obyek wisata budaya. *Walennae* 12:177–188.

Muhaeminah and I. Mahmud 2009. Pusat peradaban abad XV–XVIII kerajaan Buki Selayar Sulawesi Selatan. *Walennae* 11:139–160.

Mundy, R. 1848. *Narrative of events in Borneo and Celebes, down to the cccupation of Labuan: From the journals of James Brooke, Esq., Rajah of Sarawak, and Governor of Labuan. Together with a narrative of the operations of H.M.S. Iris.* Volume 1. John Murray, London.

Muttalib, M.A. 1978. *Petunjuk Singkat tentang Kompleks Makam Kuno Raja-Raja Lamuru.* Kantor Suaka Sejarah dan Purbakala, Wilayah Propinsi Sulawesi Selatan, Makassar.

Muttalib, M.A. 1980. *Naskah Studi Kelayakan. Makam La Tenri Ruwa (Raja Bone ke XI), Bantaeng, Sulawesi Selatan.* Proyek Pemuguran dan Pemeliharaan Peninggalan Sejarah dan Purbakala Sulawesi Selatan, Makassar.

Muttalib, M.A. 1983. *Laporan Pengumpulan Data Peninggalan Sejarah dan Purbakala di Kabupaten Bulukumba.* Proyek Pemuguran dan Pemeliharaan Peninggalan Sejarah dan Purbakala Sulawesi Selatan, Makassar.

Nayati, W. 2000. Laporan Survei Arkeologi Daerah Kabupaten Bantaeng, Sulawesi Selatan. Unpublished report. Makassar.

Nur, M. and B. Hakim 2010. Telaah awal tembikar Wajo. *Walennae* 12:189–194.

OXIS Group 2020. Pre-Islamic South Sulawesi. oxis.org. Accessed 23 March 2020.

Patunru, D.A.R. 1983. *Sejarah Gowa*. Yayasan Kebudayaan Sulawesi Selatan di Makassar (Ujung Pandang), Makassar.

Pelras, C. 1977. Les premières données occidentales concernant Célèbes-sud. *Bijdragen tot de Taal-, Land- en Volkenkunde* 133:227–260.

Perelaer, M.T.H. 1872. *De Bonische Expeditiën Krijggebeurtenissen op Celebes in 1859 et 1860 volgens officiëele Bronnen Bewerkt*. Gualth Kolff, Leiden.

Quinn, W.H., D.O. Zopf, K.S. Short and R.T.W. Kuo Yang 1978. Historical trends and statistics of the Southern Oscillation, El Niño, and Indonesian drought. *Fishery Bulletin* 76:663–678.

Reid, A. 1983. The rise of Makassar. *Review of Indonesian and Malaysian Affairs* 17:117–160.

Reid, A. 1988. *The lands below the winds. Southeast Asia in the age of commerce 1450–1680*. Volume 1. Yale University Press, New Haven.

Reid, A. 1990. Bone and Soppeng: Vanished Bugis kingdoms. In T.A. Volkman and I. Caldwell (eds), *Sulawesi: The Celebes*, pp. 102–105. Periplus, Singapore.

Reid, A. 1993. *Expansion and crisis. Southeast Asia in the age of commerce 1450–1680*. Volume 2. Yale University Press, New Haven.

Robson, S. (trans.) 1995. *Desawarnana (Nagarakrtagama) by Mpu Prapanca*. KITLV Press, Leiden.

Roessingh, M.P.H. 1986. A pretender to Gowa's throne: The war of Batara Gowa I. Sangkilang in south west Celebes, 1776–c. 1790. In R. Russ and G.D. Winius (eds), *All of one company: The VOC in biographical perspective*, pp. 151–177. Hes Uitgevers, Utrecht.

Schilder, G., J. Moerman, F. Ormeling, P. van den Brink and H. Ferwerda 2006. *Atlas Isaak de Graf. Groote Atlas van de Verenigte Oost-Indische Compagnie*. Volume I. Atlas Maior, Voerburg.

Somba, N. 2009. Jejak-jejak arkeologis di kaki Gunung Bambapuang Kabupaten Enrekang, Sulawesi Selatan. *Walennae* 11:107–124.

Somba, N. 2010. Ciri budaya Austronesia di kawasan Enrekang Sulawesi Selatan. *Walennae* 12:1–10.

Stavorinus, J.S. 1798. *Voyages to the East Indies*. Volume 2. Translated into English by S.H. Wilcocke. G.G. Robinson and J. Robinson. Dawsons of Pall Mall, London.

Suaka Peninggalan Sejarah dan Purbakala Sulawesi Selatan 1984. *Laporan Pengumpulan Data Peninggalan Sejarah dan Purbakala di Kabupaten Bantaeng*. Makassar.

Sudarti Surbakti, R. Lukito Praptoprijoko, Satwiko Darmesto 2000. *Indonesia's 2000 population census: A recent national statistics activity*. BPS Statistics Indonesia, Bangkok.

van Braam Moris, D.F. 1889. Het landschap Loewoe. *Tijdschrift van het Bataviaasch Genootschap van Kunsten en Wetenschappen* 32:497–555.

van Rijneveld, J.C. 1840. *Celebes, of Veldtogt der Nederlanders op het Eiland Celebes in de Jaren 1824 en 1825*. Broese, Breda.

Wallis, H. (ed.) 1965. *Carteret's voyage round the world 1766–1769*. Volume II. Hakluyt Society, Cambridge University Press, Cambridge, Massachusetts. doi.org/10.4324/9781315570914.

Wibisono, C.S. 1985. Sebaran situs kubur sebagai studi awal pola pemukiman di Pulau Selayar. *Rapat Evaluasi Hasil Penelitian Arkeologi II*, pp. 370–383. Pusat Penelitian Arkeologi Nasional, Jakarta.

Appendices

Appendix A: Hilltop sites in the kingdom of Soppeng

Table 7.2 identifies as hilltop sites the two prominent peaks of Botto and Laleng Benteng in the current *kabupaten* capital of Watansoppeng, but in fact Watansoppeng itself could be considered a hilltop site. The township sits on a plateau perched above the confluence of the Soppeng and Masewali rivers, leaving only its western flank vulnerable to attack across flat terrain. There is no evidence that enemy troops ever entered Watansoppeng, although Soppeng did concede its vassals along the lower Walennae to Goa in the mid-sixteenth century (cf. Caldwell 1995: Figure 2; Cummings 2007:33). The construction of the stonewall defences recorded at Soppeng's traditional palace, Laleng Benteng, is dated to around the time of Soppeng's unification (Kallupa et al. 1989).

Sewo and Bulu Matanre were two hilltop settlements in the mountains with heavy rainfall immediately to the west of Watansoppeng. Both were first occupied in the fourteenth century and abandoned around 1700 (Kallupa et al. 1989). Sewo sits on a defensible hill, while Bulu Matanre was a fortified mountain settlement dating back to the early fifteenth century (Caldwell 1995:397). Its low stone walls surrounding garden beds recorded during the site survey (Kallupa et al. 1989:49–50) may have been built from the remains of the settlement's stone walls.

Appendix B: Kale Goa and Anaq Goa

By the fourteenth century the emergent kingdom of Goa was based at Kale Goa, a settlement focused on two hillocks overlooking the Jeneberang River, 6 km from its mouth (Bulbeck 1992:219–220). Kale Goa's early fortifications included earth walls erected during Tumapaqrisiq Kallona's reign (1511–1546), brick walls during the reign of his successor Tunipalangnga (1546–1565) and refurbished brick walls during the reign of Sultan Alauddin (1593–1639). Bulbeck (1992:216) attempted to explain the fortress remains at Kale Goa in terms of these three building episodes, but we now suspect that at least some of the fortifications, in particular the 8 m thick walls facing the Jeneberang (Figure 7.A1a), are of later construction (Figure 7.A1b). We note that Goa had been forced by the VOC to demolish Kale Goa's walls in 1676, having rebuilt them using the loose bricks of the demolished fortress (Andaya 1981:174).[9] As documented below, Kale Goa was a functioning fortress in the late 1700s, having presumably been restored earlier in the century.

The c. 1776 Dutch sketch of 'Goa' in de Roever and Brommer (2008:195) can be identified as Kale Goa from toponymic and physiographic matches (Figure 7.A2):

- Data to the immediate north of the fortress
- Bisei at the northeast of the fortress
- Bonsong/Lonjo Boko at the east of the fortress
- Sero at/on a hill to the immediate east of the fortress
- Pandang at the southeast of the fortress
- Tinggi Mae on a hill to the immediate southeast of the fortress
- Mangasa at the south of the fortress
- Taeng across the river to the immediate southwest of the fortress
- 'Grave of the King of Goa', which could correspond to either the early eighteenth-century Arung Palakka cemetery or the seventeenth/eighteenth-century royal Goa graves at the east.

---

9 Andaya calls them 'red stones', a literal translation of *batu merah*, a local synonym for *batu bata* (bricks).

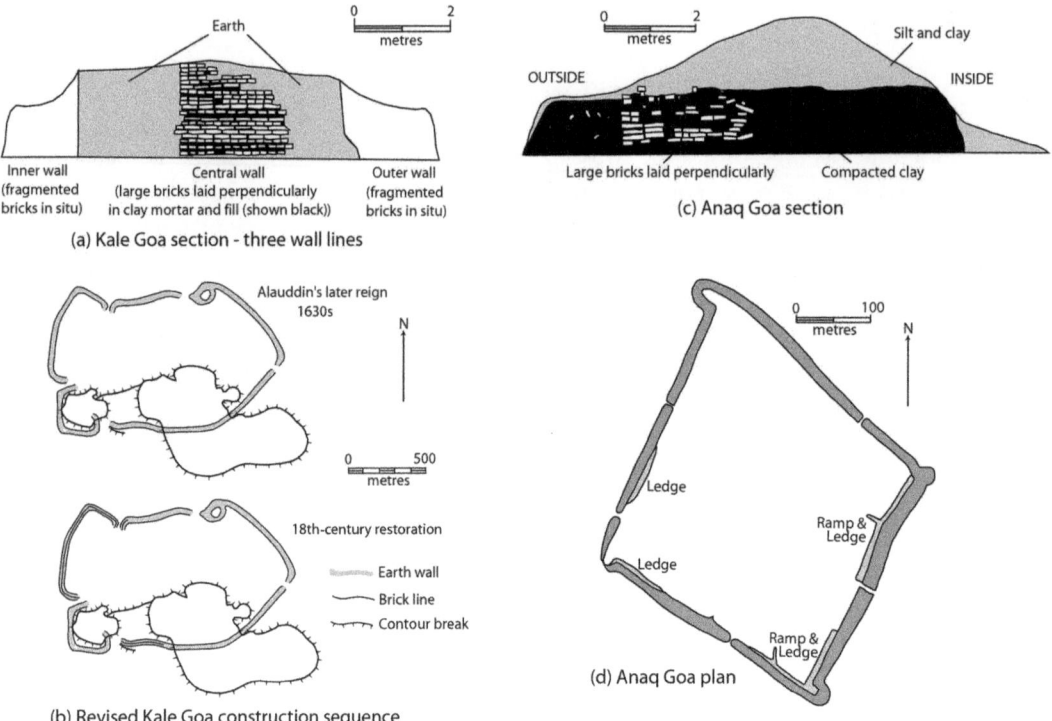

Figure 7.A1. Cross-section and plans for Benteng Kale Goa and Anaq Goa.
Source: David Bulbeck (after Bulbeck 1992).

We cannot make sense of all of the Dutch toponyms but draw attention to important eighteenth-century associations: Goa erected a royal residence at Sero in 1703; Malengkeri was the 1727–1735 residence of the Goa king; Tinggi Mae was the place where the Goa king prayed for rain in 1736; and Mangasa was the place where the Talloq king went fully armed in 1748 (see Cummings 2011:145, 223, 245, 248, 267). In addition, the palace (*benteng*) of Bone is shown as situated close to Kale Goa. This may indicate the approximate location of Bone's military headquarters in Makassar after its earlier headquarters at Bonto Alaq were burnt down during Wajoq's 1739 assault on Makassar (Patunru 1983:79).

The reason for the sudden Dutch interest in Kale Goa was the threat posed by I Sangkilang, a Makasar man of obscure origins, who appeared in 1776 claiming to be the king of Goa whom the Dutch had expelled from South Sulawesi a decade earlier. I Sangkilang led a popular uprising against Dutch positions south of Makassar and, in 1777, occupied Maros, Talloq and, finally, Goa, where he was installed as ruler. The Bugis toponyms at the north of Kale Goa and the Talloq contingent at Kale Goa's eastern flank, c. 1776 Dutch sketch of 'Goa' (Figure 7.A2), evidently represent Goa's allies positioned in an attempt to defend the Goa citadel.[10] In the end, the VOC proved victorious, razing Kale Goa's walls during its assault in 1778 and driving I Sangkilang into the mountains. The VOC reinstated Sultan Zainuddin as Goa's ruler, but in 1781 forbade Goa from rebuilding Kale Goa's walls (Patunru 1983:85–89; Roessingh 1986).

---

10 Datu Baringang was the Bone war commander who attacked I Sangkilang in Maros in 1777 (Patunru 1983:86). The Goa–Talloq royal diary notes the establishment of peaceful relations between Tanete (Agannionjoq), Soppeng and Bone in 1750 (Ligtvoet 1880:220, 229).

7. The indigenous fortifications of South Sulawesi, Indonesia, and their sociopolitical foundations

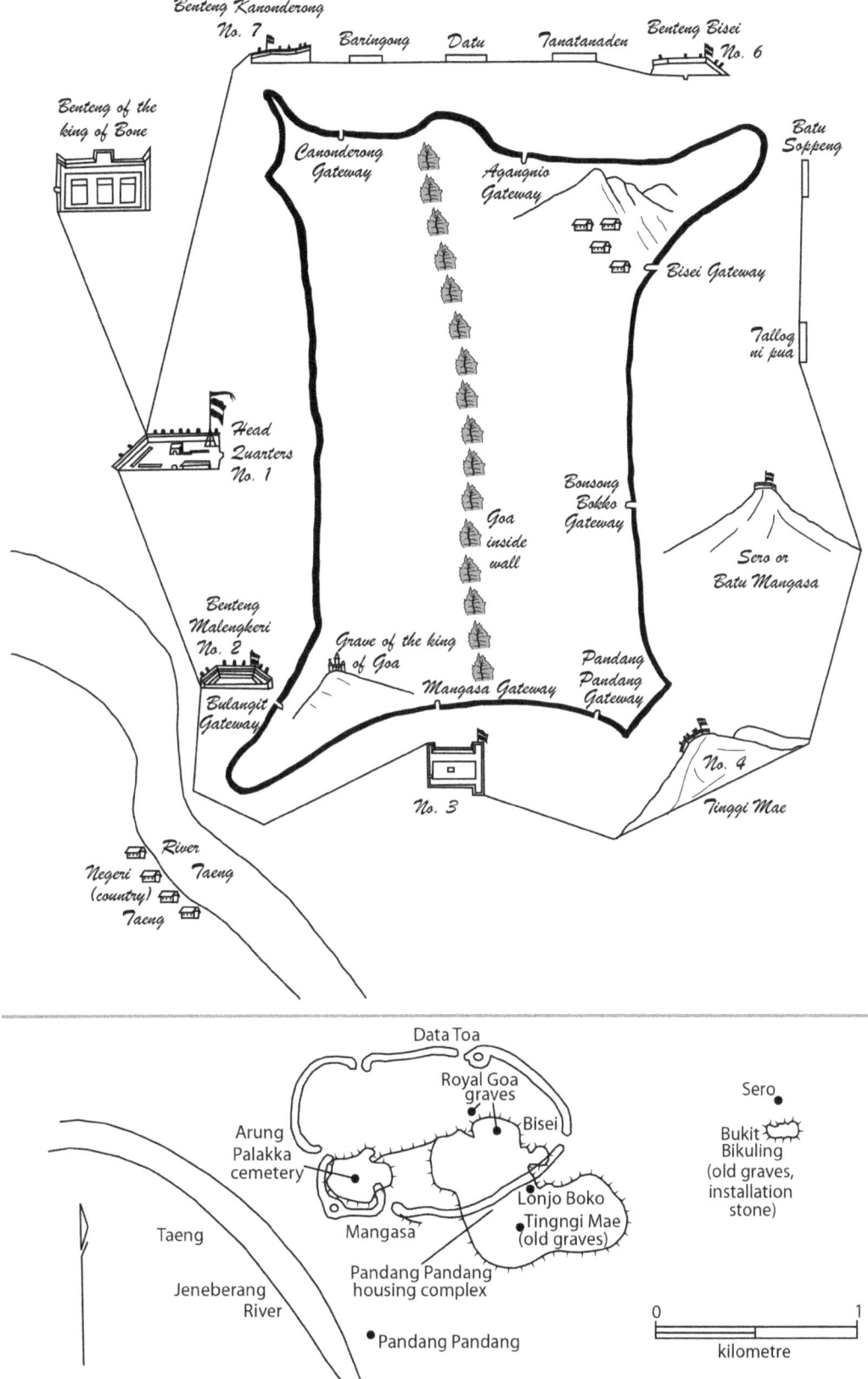

Figure 7.A2. 'Dutch sketch of Goa c. 1776' (above) compared to relevant data from Bulbeck's (1992) survey of Kale Goa (below).
Source: David Bulbeck.

Benteng Anaq Goa was interpreted by Bulbeck (1992:262–264) as a mid-sixteenth-century fortress built by Tunipalangnga for his son, Karaeng Anaq Goa, who died in childhood. One of Bulbeck's reasons was that there is no other pre-1700 reference to Anaq Goa; a second was that the inner spine of large bricks within its 8 m thick walls resembled the inner spine of large bricks along Kale Goa's western wall (Figure 7.A1c). However, the authors have found Anaq Goa depicted on a 1752 map of southern South Sulawesi (de Roever and Brommer 2008:164–165) and now believe that the structural resemblance of the walls could be explained by an eighteenth-century construction date for both fortifications, for reasons explained below.

Ceramic evidence points to more substantial occupation at Anaq Goa between 1650 and 1800 than between 1500 and 1650 (Bulbeck 1992: Figure 8.3). This cautions against dating the fortress's occupation to a time before 1650. In addition, the virtually pristine condition of the fortress suggests a relatively recent chronology, as well as implying that the site has been spared military engagement. The fact that 1751 was the last year for which entries appear in the 'Makassar Annals' (Cummings 2011) might explain its lack of reference to Anaq Goa were it constructed after this year. On balance, acknowledging the ambiguities in the evidence, we prefer a mid-eighteenth-century dating for Anaq Goa's construction (Figure 7.A1d) and surmise that it was never used as a military installation.

Appendix C: Ajattappareng fortifications

Ajattappareng is the name for the confederation of Bugis kingdoms of Sidenreng, Rappang, Sawitto, Alitta and Suppaq, which jointly ruled the fertile wet rice lands between the mouth of the Saddang and South Sulawesi's central lowlands. Druce (2009: Appendix B) surveyed six hilltop settlements, only one of which was fortified. The last is a hilltop of around 1.4 hectares overlooking the eighteenth-century to modern-day port of Suppaq, where Druce (2009:129–131, Figure B.18) recorded nineteenth-century sherdage. This is clearly the fort at Suppaq sketched by van Rijneveld (1840: Plate 2), which forms part of his account of the 1824 Dutch attack on Suppaq, following three unsuccessful assaults on Suppaq by the English in 1814 (De Klerck 1975:146). The construction of the fort was thus evidently a response to European colonial expansion.

Druce (2009:125–126) mapped the outline of a fortress that reportedly extended over 14 hectares at Temmanroli. This fortress served as the palace centre of the early rulers of Sawitto in the fourteenth or fifteenth century. While the date of construction of the fortress is unknown, it includes the grave of a major eighteenth-century ruler, and would appear to have been functional at the time Sawitto relocated its palace centre to Lalle Lama in the nineteenth century.

Appendix D: Enrekang (Massenrempulu) fortifications

The Massenrempulu fortifications reveal a dichotomy between Benteng Buntu Kotu on the one hand, and Benteng Londe-Londe, Kallupini, Buntu Batu, Bambapuang and Alla on the other. Benteng Buntu Kotu has abundant habitation evidence (Somba 2009), but no record of involvement in the early twentieth-century conflict between the Dutch and the Massenrempulu polities. The remaining five fortresses were used in the Massenrempulu resistance against the Dutch but show minimal evidence of habitation (Makkulasse 1986; see also Bigalke 2005). According to Makkulasse (1986), Massenrempulu was traditionally ruled by a confederation of chiefdoms including Enrekang (the main population centre in Islamic times), Maiwa and other constituents including Alla, Malua, Buntu Batu, Kassa, Batulappa and Duri at various times in the past. In 1905, the ruler of Enrekang and his commanders strengthened the fortifications near Enrekang as Dutch troops marched on the region. The Dutch captured the forts at Alla and Buntu Batu in 1907 but, once pacified, Enrekang was left largely in peace and not fully incorporated into the Dutch colonial administration until 1921.

Somba's report on Islamic and pre-twentieth-century non-Islamic burial mortuary locations at Buntu Kotu (2009) provides no period of occupation or date of the construction of the fort's undressed stone walls. From her report, however, we hazard a seventeenth- to nineteenth-century date of construction. This may imply that at least some of the other Massenrempulu fortifications could have origins that predate the nineteenth century. All of these (apart from Alla, which was defended naturally by a steep drop around its entire perimeter) had walls of undressed stone (Makkulasse 1986).

Appendix E: Fortifications in the kingdom of Bantaeng and in Jeneponto

According to Bougas (1998), the township of Bantaeng first emerged as a population centre in the fourteenth or fifteenth century, in concert with the expansion of wet rice agriculture and maritime trade. Bantaeng subsequently incorporated the small kingdoms of Gantarang and Kaili that had developed respectively along the rivers to the immediate east and west, despite a failed revolt by Kaili in the 1500s. In the sixteenth century, several of the Bantaeng polities (and Jeneponto and Bulukumba) suffered military conquest at the hands of Goa–Talloq (McWilliam et al. 2012).

Bougas (1998:93, 94) suggests that the settlement of Gantarang Keke, which lies 10 km upstream from the coast in a ridge of land between the Patte and Biang Keke Rivers, may once have been fortified, and that the remains of a wall behind the primary school may once formed part of the settlement's defences. He states that Gantarang Keke, which lies 2 km downstream, 'seems originally to have been fortified', but offers no evidence (Bougas 1998:95). We would argue that the fortification traces in Bantaeng reflect heightened defence requirements relating to the birth pains of political integration and the threat of distant military attack. We therefore date the reported (Lembang) Gantarang Keke fortifications to the time of Bantaeng's political integration and Goa–Talloq's conquest of 'Gantarang'.

Another apparent fortress, Benteng Kaili, refers to a location near the mouth of the Kaili River, just west of Bantaeng township, where informants reported the existence of earth walls, since washed away by a recent flood (Bulbeck field notes, 8 October 2011). A second coastal fortification can be inferred from Andaya's (1981:82–87) account of the several forts built by Goa–Talloq at Bantaeng in its failed attempt in 1666 to block the VOC advance on Makassar. While there is no information in Andaya (1981) or any other source on fortifications at Bantaeng township prior to 1666, we can assume that a fort of some description had long defended 'the largest and most prosperous city in the south' (Andaya 1981:82). The traces of fortifications that can be seen today at Bantaeng township (5° 33′ 04.2″ S 119° 57′ 09.4″ E) are the remnants of a brick wall and Dutch barracks built by the VOC adjacent to the former residence of the allied ruler of Bantaeng (Bulbeck field notes, 8 October 2011). Local informants maintain that this was also the place where the VOC forces defeated those of Goa–Talloq. This points to this as a likely location for any pre-1666 fortifications at Bantaeng township.

The best archaeologically documented Bantaeng fortification is 'Benteng [fortress] Batu Terang', described by Bougas:

> The principal feature of the site was a large and impressive *benteng* or fort that dominated the top of the hill. The walls of the fort were ± 2 kilometers in length, 3 to 4 meters thick and flat on top. They varied in height, depending on the terrain, from 1 to 8 meters (*Suaka*, 1984:36). These fortifications were only constructed on the northern, eastern, and southern parameters of the town. [11] The main gate seems to have been placed in the eastern wall, facing the rising sun. No wall was built on the western side of the settlement, since the site was protected by the steep descent of the land to the Panaikang River, that bordered the western slope of the hill. The stones, that once formed the wall, have unfortunately been cannibalized by local farmers and very little remains of the *benteng* wall today. (1998:118)

---

11   Three walls of some 2 km in length imply a defended area of around 40–50 ha.

Kaili's revolt in the 1500s may explain the initial construction of hilltop fortress of Batu Terang, but its commanding view over the Bantaeng township, and its abundance of sixteenth- to nineteenth-century habitation debris (Bulbeck field notes, 8 October 2011), imply that it retained its status as a strongly defended area for up to four centuries. After Bantaeng had become a fully integrated political entity, including its period as a VOC stronghold, Benteng Batu Terang may have assisted Bantaeng's defence as an outlook post or withdrawal refuge. There were at least two eighteenth-century uprisings by Makasars against the Dutch presence in Makassar, and Bantaeng was sacked during both of them (Patunru 1983).

As for Jeneponto, Caldwell and Bougas (2004:498) report an extant oral tradition of the unification of Bangkala, one of the two Jeneponto kingdoms, following a ferocious battle between two smaller polities. There may have originally been fortifications of some description in Jeneponto but the only surviving examples are the remains of stone walls at Toloq and Rumbia in upland Jeneponto. The likely explanation here is that Toloq and Rumbia were semi-autonomous and largely responsible for their own protection (Caldwell and Bougas 2004). Both were vulnerable to attack because of their remoteness from Binamu, east Jeneponto's political centre, to which tributary chiefdoms looked in times of insecurity.

Appendix F: Makassar fortifications

Somba Opu

The coastal fortress of Somba Opu, 6 km southeast of Makassar, had earthen walls during the reign of Tumapaqrisiq Kallona and brick walls during the reign of his successor Tunipalangnga, before being fully rebuilt in 1631. Seventeenth-century Dutch sketches of Somba Opu need to be interpreted with care as all fail to depict the fortress's southern extension. However, they provide useful information on internal structures and evidence that the fortress had originally extended northward beyond the extant archaeological remains (Bulbeck 1998).

The 1667 Treaty of Bungaya allowed Somba Opu to remain standing, but continued resistance by the Makassar forces convinced the VOC of the need to destroy this important fortification. The closing chapter of the Makassar War in 1669 saw Bugis troops storm Somba Opu, aided by cannon fire from the VOC warships anchored offshore (Andaya 1981:130–132). In 1694, Sultan Abdul Jalil rebuilt Somba Opu and reoccupied it as Goa's palace centre, but in 1701 the VOC forced him to demolish it (Patunru 1983:72–73). Nonetheless, Somba Opu remained an important population centre, as shown by textual references to Somba Opu in 1724 and 1747 (Cummings 2011:210, 266), until the VOC occupied it in 1778 as part of the expulsion of I Sangkilang. The 'kingdom' of Somba Opu and the area of Sapirea (today a large village) were then placed under VOC control in 1781 (Patunru 1983:89). In accord with the above textual references, Somba Opu appears as a settlement on late seventeenth- to mid-eighteenth-century maps of South Sulawesi, before being depicted as an island without a settlement c. 1810 (de Roever and Brommer 2008:157, 162–165, 174–175).

Benteng Talloq

In the early sixteenth century the mouth of the river Tallo (which had been inhabited since at least the fourteenth century) became the palace centre of Talloq. The earliest evidence for the construction of Talloq's fortress at the mouth of the river dates to c. 1615 (Bulbeck 1992:410, 416). Although the walls were reportedly razed in 1670 (Cummings 2011:77), either the demolition was incomplete or it was soon followed by restoration, given that a 1693 map of Makassar (de Roever and Brommer 2008:162–163) shows a large, quadrangular compound at Talloq. The demise of Benteng Talloq as a functioning fortress presumably dates to the 1701 reimposition of the Bungaya Treaty, which, as noted above, stipulated the demolition of Goa–Talloq's rebuilt coastal fortifications. What remained of the walls in the mid-1980s consisted of coursed, dressed masonry or interior and exterior casings of bricks enclosing earth (Bulbeck 1992: Figure 12.1).

Makassar's coastal wall

A crucial ingredient in Makassar's capacity to resist seaborne assaults by the VOC between the 1630s and 1667 was its chain of coastal forts between Ujung Tana and Barombong, linked by a semi-continuous line of coastal wall (Bulbeck 1998:80–82). The coastal fortifications from Somba Opu to Barombong are well documented in textual sources and archaeological data that confirm or complement each other. The Bayoa, Garassiq, Panakukang and Barombong forts, and the connecting coastal wall, were first built at around 1634 and refurbished after the VOC occupied Panakukang briefly in 1660.[12] The 1693 map of Makassar (de Roever and Brommer 2008:162–163) shows a small fort at Garassiq, presumably one of the rebuilt coastal fortifications that Goa was forced to re-demolish in 1701.

As early as the 1980s, an archaeological survey of the coastal fortifications north of Somba Opu was impossible because of Makassar's urban growth. One of the few sources of useful data is a VOC sketch showing the size of the Ujung Pandang fort (Schilder et al. 2006:302).[13] The construction of Makassar's defences is credited to Talloq's Sultan Awalul Islam. This evidently took place during the 1630s after he had vacated the Talloq throne and moved to Bonto Alaq (located centrally within Makassar) to focus on the city's administration (Bulbeck 1992:429). The Talloq chronicle specifies stone walls at Talloq (confirmed archaeologically) and Ujung Tana, as well as unspecified fortifications at Panakukang and Ujung Pandang (Cummings 2007:88). Based on the archaeological survey of coastal fortifications south of Somba Opu, it is likely that Ujung Pandang was predominantly earthen, while the coastal wall from Ujung Tana to Somba Opu was built of brick (Table 7.5). Ujung Tana may have been the last surviving coastal fortification as it is shown on a 1720s map of Makassar (de Roever and Brommer 2008:157).

Appendix G: Fortifications to the south of Makassar

Sanrabone

An excellently preserved fortress, Sanrabone lacks documentary evidence on its construction history, other than a 1774 observation by Stavorinus (1798:211) that it was built at around the same time as Talloq and Somba Opu. Analysis of brick metrical data supports approximate contemporaneity of construction of all three fortresses (Bulbeck 1998:83, 91). The fact that the VOC/Bugis forces deliberately bypassed Sanrabone during their 1667 assault on Makassar (Andaya 1981:87) also suggests its fortress had been built by that date. The lack of a VOC claim on Sanrabone as a spoil of war may have prompted Goa to install Abdul Jalil as Sanrabone's ruler in 1668, prior to his ascension to the Goa throne in the following year. We can be confident that Benteng Sanrabone had been erected by the mid-1670s based on reports that Goa–Talloq's remnant naval forces were harboured in the Sanrabone River in 1675, and that the Goa regalia were held in safekeeping at Sanrabone in 1678 (Bulbeck 1998:82–83).

---

12 The data in Table 7.5 on the pre- and post-fortification occupation of the sites along the southern coastal fortifications are from Bulbeck (1992). Dutch sketches of the VOC occupation of Panakukang and the 1667 siege of Makassar (Boxer 1967: Plate III; de Roever and Brommer 2008:180) can be useful for understanding the southern coastal fortifications (but also misleading, as in their depiction of Panakukang as a large fort).

13 The VOC was not interested in the Ujung Pandang fortress as such. The purpose of the sketch was to document the initial construction of Fort Rotterdam, the VOC stronghold in Makassar. This involved building stone walls around the Ujung Pandang fort, which had been surrendered in good condition by Goa–Talloq to the VOC in 1667 as required by the Treaty of Bungaya.

The continued importance of Sanrabone is clear from its royal eighteenth-century graves (Bulbeck 1992: Photo E-3), its consistent depiction on VOC maps dating from 1693 onwards (de Roever and Brommer 2008:152, 154–158, 160, 162–165, 168, 174) and its early eighteenth-century role as a southern outpost of Goa (Cummings 2011:169–258). Sanrabone was the original centre of the popular revolt led by I Sangkilang in 1776; its independence ended in 1781 when Goa transferred Sanrabone to the VOC as part of their peace treaty (Patunru 1983:85, 89).

Galesong

Galesong appears to have been an important harbour for some two millennia (Bulbeck 2010:163). At this 'fortified city' (Andaya 1981:88) in 1667, some 30,000 Makassar troops were defeated by 10,000 Bugis ground troops and 250 VOC infantry. This engagement cleared the way for the Bugis troops' northward march on Makassar to besiege the city from its south (Andaya 1981). Bulbeck (1992:712–713, Figure E-4) undertook a comprehensive survey of Galesong that failed to reveal evidence of brick or stone defences, but mapped a total length of 3.5 km of raised earthen features running parallel with or perpendicular to the shoreline. Although Bulbeck interpreted these features as natural cheniers that could well have acted as natural defences, bolstered by timber palisades, it seems more likely that they are remnants of earthen wall defences, consistent with their height of up to a metre or more. Galesong almost certainly would have had defences of some description throughout much or all of its lengthy period of settlement. However, the archaeologically recorded remnants can all be attributed to the 1667 battle, one of the decisive engagements in the Makassar War.

Appendix H: Sengkae (Siang)

Excavations at Sengkae, the fortified palace centre of the Makasar-speaking kingdom of Siang, 25 km north of Maros, revealed a stonewall foundation and fifteenth- to seventeenth/eighteenth-century ceramics. The size of the defended quadrangular area appears to have been approximately 400 m north–south by 250 m east–west, with the northern border formed by a former river channel (Fadillah and Mahmud 2000:45). A Malay presence had apparently been established at Siang by 1494 (Baker 2005:73), and by 1534 the Portuguese were beginning to show an interest in the area (Pelras 1977:228–230). Although Goa conquered Siang by at least 1546 (Bulbeck 1992: 124), it remained a main stopover for Portuguese in South Sulawesi until 1547 (Pelras 1977:233), which suggests that Sengkae's fortifications remained intact after Goa's conquest.[14] However, the kingdom of Siang was based at Sengkae only between the fifteenth century and c. 1600, after which date the river channel north of the fortress became silted up, hindering navigable access to the sea (Fadillah and Mahmud 2000:101). Based on this evidence, we propose a dating of c. 1500–1600 for the Sengkae fortress. Nonetheless, the kingdom of Siang remained sufficiently important in the following centuries to be one of major suppliers of rice to the VOC in 1669 (Andaya 1981:265) and to appear on Aubert's map of 1752 (de Roever and Brommer 2008:164–165).

Appendix I: Balangnipa (Sinjai)

According to local historians in Sinjai, the Dutch fort at Balangnipa on the coastal plain had originally been a Bugis fort. They claim that the Dutch replaced the Bugis timber structures when they built their own fort of concrete blocks in 1863, covering a quadrangular area of 0.5 ha. The Bugis predecessor was first built in 1557 and strengthened after the triple alliance of Bulo-Bulo, Lamatti and Tondong in 1696. The fortress defended the mouth of the Tangka River near Balangnipa, which had been a minor port from at least the sixteenth century (Muhaeminah 2009).

---

14 Antonio de Paiva did not describe any fortifications at Siang in 1544, nor at Suppaq and Makassar, which he also visited (Baker 2005). This lack of evidence can be attributed to Paiva's minimal physical description of any of these places.

Appendix J: Barunia (Selayar Island)

The fort of Barunia on the island of Selayar is one of 20 surveyed sites associated with the kingdom of Buki, which was locally prominent between the fifteenth and eighteenth centuries. Physical traces of Buki's defences are scarce except at Barunia, which is enclosed by a limestone wall and retains six cannons from an original number of perhaps 30. The Buki rulers moved from the coast inland to Barunia in the late eighteenth century in response to increasing VOC control (Muhaeminah and Mahmud 2009). Their relocation should be viewed in the context of the physical proximity of Buki to Benteng, Selayar's administrative capital, which grew in importance as a company outpost during the eighteenth century (Heersink 1994: 49–51). The name Benteng (fortress, fortified settlement) implies that Buki previously had some sort of coastal fortification there, but there are no reports of pre-Dutch fortifications within Benteng.

Appendix K: Bone

The oldest recorded Bone fortification is that of Papolo. Goa staged a failed assault on this fort in 1565, as recorded in both of the Goa and Bone chronicles (Cummings 2007:36; Macknight 1993:22).[15] The Goa chronicle also notes that Bone constructed a stockade at Pasempa (Cummings 2007:49) where Goa, assisted by Wajoq, Soppeng and Luwuq, attacked and defeated Bone in 1643 and 1644 (Andaya 1981:40–41). Described by the English in 1814 as 'very difficult to vanquish' (De Klerck 1975:146), Pasempa was depicted in 1859 as a set of three walls flanking the trail from Palakka (near Watampone) to Wajoq (Perelaer 1872: volume 2, folding chart 3). The walls, with their combined length of 500 m, produced three bottlenecks along the trail and also blocked off movement into the gorge, where a ford had been built across the Pasempa river. As late as 1905, Pasempa served as a retreat for the Bone forces following the fall of Watampone (Budiarta 2007:130).

For nearly a century, Bone maintained a palace centre 30 km northwest of Watampone near the mouth of the Cenrana River. This fortified settlement was built by Bone in 1671 to block off Wajoq's access by river to the sea (Andaya 1981:143). Aubert's 1752 map shows Cenrana (and not Watampone) as a fortified palace centre, flanked by a smaller 'Benteng Tulawa' across the river (Wallis 1965: Figure XIX). A late seventeenth-century VOC map of Cenrana (Andaya 1981: Map 8) and a series of surveys and excavations (Bulbeck and Caldwell 2000:80–82; Mahmud 2000:44–61) make it one of South Sulawesi's best-documented fortifications (Table 7.5). By the 1760s, Bone had returned to Watampone, to judge by the lack of any reference to Cenrana in VOC 1760s correspondence on Bone (Wallis 1965: 368–435).

The Chronicle of Bone makes it clear that the kingdom's palace centre, Watampone, was surrounded by a wall in the late sixteenth century (Macknight 1993:22). According to Drs Asmat (pers. comm., 22 December 2010), the original Watampone fortress was built to a height of 3 m by La Tenrirawe Bongkangnge (r. 1568–1584) before La Maddaremmeng Matinroe ri Bukaka (r. 1625–1640) increased the walls' height to 7 m. This was the fortress that defended Watampone at the time of the Dutch attack in 1905, represented as late as the 1950s by remnant earthen walls up to 5 m high. These claims, which are not found in any written source of which we are aware, may reflect a still-extant oral tradition. In support of Drs Asmat's claim as to the operational status of the Watampone fortress as late as 1905, the fortress is clearly depicted on a topographical map dated to c. 1859 (Perelaer 1872: volume 1, folding chart 1).[16] However, when

---

15 A local historian, Drs Asmat Riady Lamallongeng, accompanied Bulbeck to what he claimed was the site of the fort (S 04° 31' 25.2" E 120° 19' 12.0") but no physical traces were visible.

16 Toponyms in present-day Watampone that match the fortress outline include Saliwengbenteng, Lalebata and Jalan Benteng. A remnant section of earthen wall corresponding to the fortress's southeast corner was recorded by David Bulbeck and Sue O'Connor at 04° 33' 07.5" S 120° 20' 19.5" E on 22 December 2010.

James Brooke visited Watampone in 1840 (Mundy 1848:131), he reported no fortifications, noting that the inhabitants had only recently started returning after the Dutch had burnt the capital to the ground in 1824. On balance, we conclude that the foundations of the Watampone fortress remained intact between the late sixteenth and early twentieth centuries, although we have no evidence for the fortress' use in the defence of Bone between the 1640s and 1750s.[17]

Appendix L: Benteng Tosora (Wajoq)

At the time of his visit to Wajoq in 1840, Brooke described Tosora as:

> a large straggling city, greatly in decay; the ancient boundary of which is marked by a fortification, which embraces a space of several miles in circumference, and occupies to the eastward a slightly elevated ridge, and to the westward sinks to a swamp. Not many years since, the main stream of the Sadang [*sic:* Cenrana] river ran near the southern limit of the town, though it has now receded three miles or more, leaving a deep but narrow channel bounded by swamps. (Mundy 1848:79–80)

From this description, Tosora's original area can be identified with the quadrangular area of Desa Tosora to the north of a chain of ponds linked by a channel (Hadimulyono 1985:103), even though the remnant fortifications have been reduced to two ruined earth walls of 3 km total length (Duli 2010:148). Brooke added that the population of Tosora was about 6000 but must have originally been at least four times that number, and that the Wajoq nobility resided outside of Tosora except when convening there for meetings. This account is consistent with the archaeological evidence for Tosora's final abandonment during the late nineteenth century (Hadimulyono 1985:78; Duli 2010:157).

Appendix M: Luwuq palace centre defences

Earthen walls have also been recorded in association with Luwuq's fifteenth- to sixteenth-century capital at Utti Batue (Bulbeck et al. 2007), and at Benteng Massalekoe, to the immediate north of Malangke Beccu, where Luwuq's capital was briefly located c. 1600 (Bulbeck and Prasetyo 1998). We propose that a levee of the Rongkong River at a site called Dadekoe provided a natural defence for the Utti Batue residents when the settlement was first established. The fifteenth-century use of Dadekoe for burials (Bulbeck and Prasetyo 1999:25) implies the erection of the earthen wall at Utti Batue's doorstep by that date.

The earthen fortress of Benteng Tompotikka at Palopo, mapped by Mahmud (1993) is the largest of the Luwu fortifications. We date the period of the fortress' construction and maintenance to Palopo's first two centuries as Luwuq's capital after c. 1620. Brooke's account of his four days in Palopo in 1840 includes no mention of fortifications, although he did note that Luwuq was in a state of anarchy having recently emerged from a civil war between two contenders for the throne (Mundy 1848:154–155). Disuse of Benteng Tompotikka by the nineteenth century is confirmed by the lack of any reference to fortifications in van Braam Morris's detailed 1889 account of Palopo or the literature on the 1905 Dutch occupation of Palopo.

Appendix N: Non-Bugis fortifications in Luwu

The Wotu people are coastal traders who first settled current-day Wotu town in the fifteenth century (Bulbeck and Caldwell 2000:51). The remnant fortifications at the town of Wotu, mapped by Fadillah (2000:165), are best interpreted as a sigmoid wall of c. 550 m length. Local information and archaeological evidence collected by Fadillah (2000:182, 185) date its construction and maintenance to between c. 1600 and the early twentieth century. Defensive

---

17 Watampone additionally had forward defences at its estuary of Bajoe in 1859 (Perelaer 1872: Plate V) and 1905 (Budiarta 2007:130).

earthen walls are also reported at Tampinna, which was occupied by Bajao sea gypsies between c. 1400 and 1700, before being laid waste by Wotu. Although no archaeological traces have been recovered, the walls were said to have run along the site's southern border as defined by the Tampinna River (Bulbeck and Caldwell 2000:45).

Baebunta was a Lemolang polity closely linked to Luwuq when the latter's capital was based at Malangke. The fort of Benteng Baebunta (Figure 7.A3) reputedly dates to the nineteenth century, although evidence for habitation within the fortified area dates back to the fifteenth century (Bulbeck and Caldwell 2000:55).

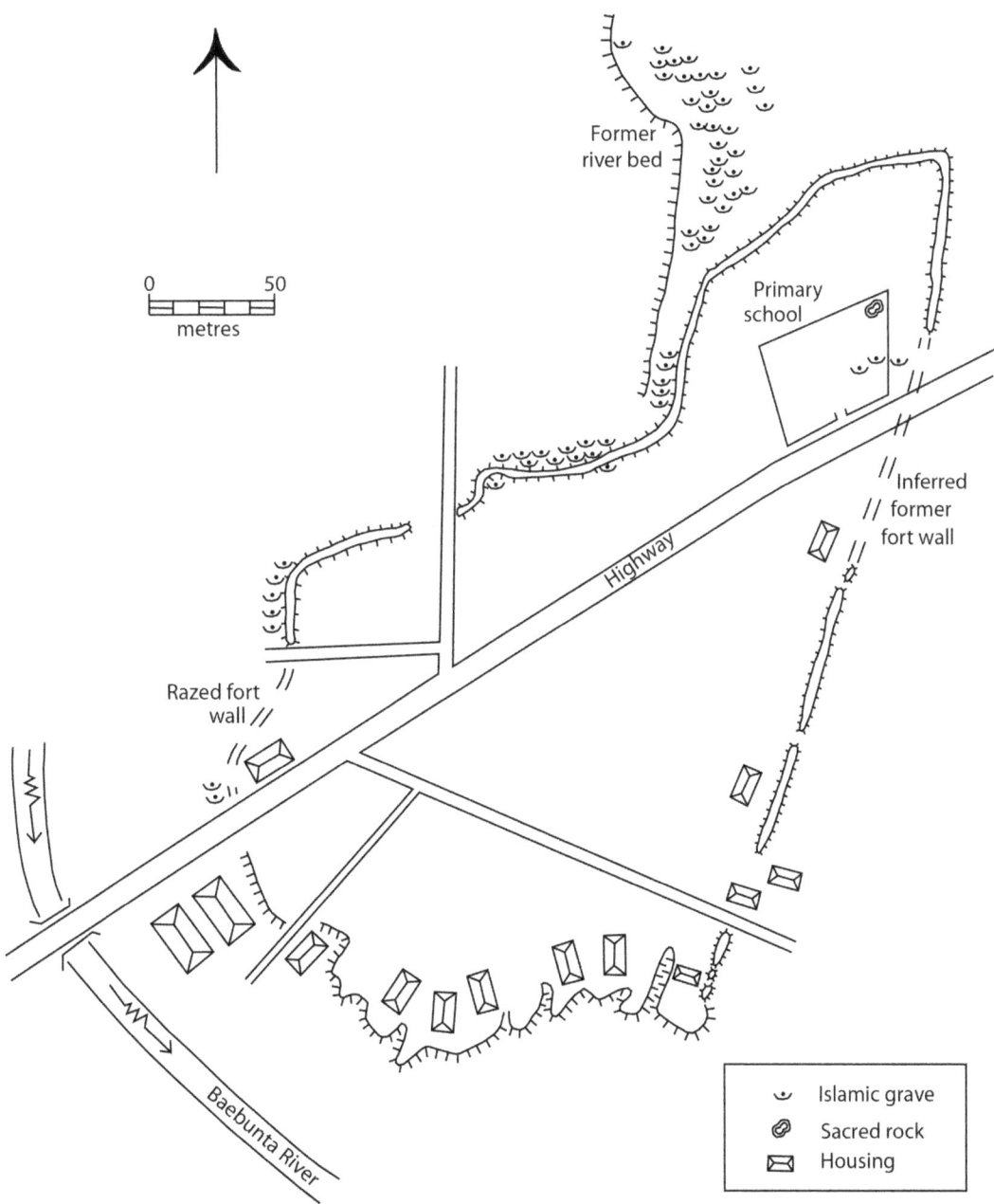

Figure 7.A3. Plan of Benteng Baebunta, Luwu (theodolite and staff survey).
Source: David Bulbeck.

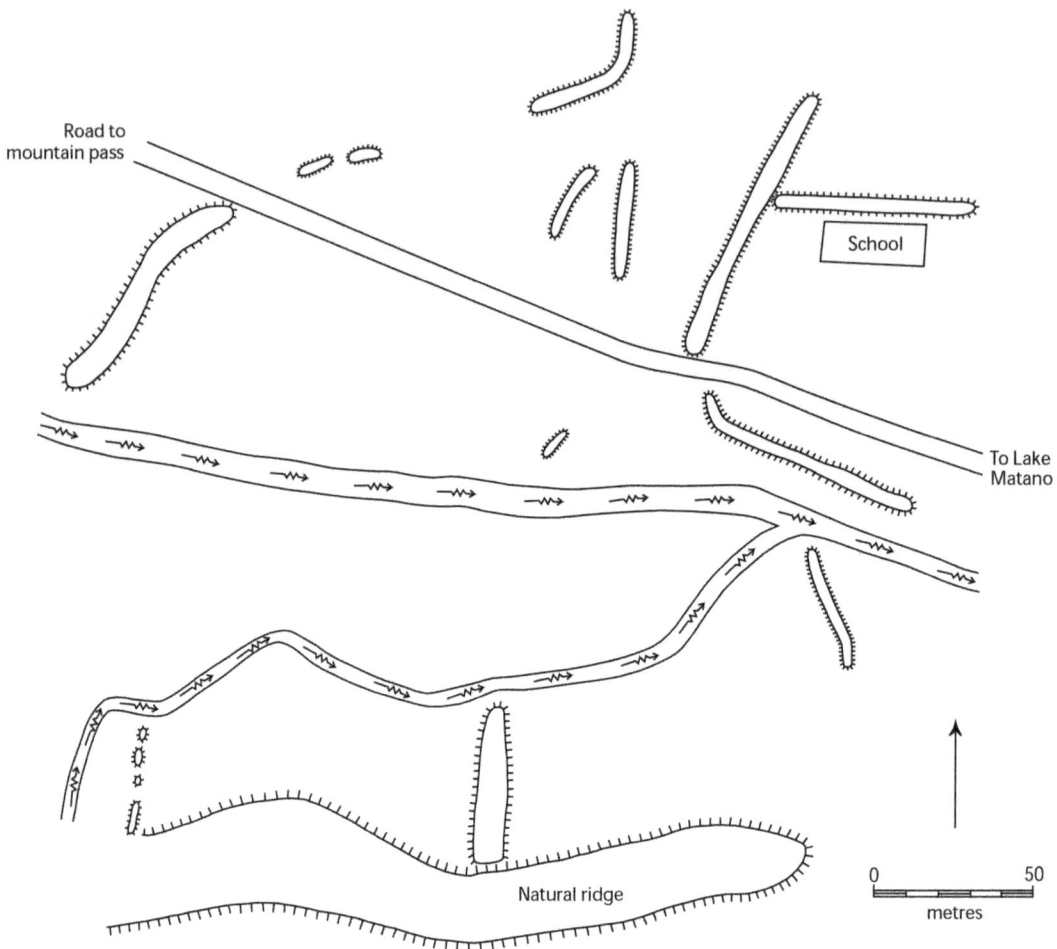

Figure 7.A4. Plan of Benteng Matano, Luwu (theodolite and staff survey).
Source: David Bulbeck.

A complex of defensive walls (probably crowned by bamboo spikes), known as Benteng Matano, was recorded at the western margin of Matano village on the west shore of Lake Matano (Figure 7.A4). According to the local inhabitants, who speak the Padoe language, the walls were built in the nineteenth century to protect them from their neighbours' headhunting raids. The late construction of Matano's defences would appear to reflect the anarchic condition of nineteenth-century Luwuq. Nuha, on the north shore of Lake Matano, also has the remnants of an earth wall up to 60 cm in height and 3.8 m in width at the base. On 27 February 1999, the South Sulawesi archaeologists Gunadi, Tanwir Wolman, Sarjiyanto and Agustiawan collected local information that the wall had once run to the immediate north of Nuha, extending from the Laki River at the west to the Nuha foothills at the east. Permanent habitation at Nuha and Matano dates back to the twelfth century, respectively associated with the production and the export of Lake Matano iron (Bulbeck and Caldwell 2000: 23, 28, 33).

8

Forts on Buton Island: Centres of settlement, government and security in Southeast Sulawesi

Hasanuddin

Introduction

From its establishment in the late sixteenth century, the Buton Sultanate, located at the southeast tip of Sulawesi (Figure 1.1 this volume), lay at the interface of the competing ambitions of the Makassar empire of southwest Sulawesi to the west and the Ternate empire of the northern Moluccas to the east (Andaya 1993). Geographically, the Buton Sultanate controlled a maritime area composed largely of multiple surrounding islands (Sarjiyanto 1999). Of these, Buton, Muna, Kabaena and Wawonii islands make up an archipelago. The Tukang Besi cluster of small islands to the southeast of Buton consists of Wangi-Wangi, Kaledupa, Hoga, Tomia and Binongko islands and their offshore islets. In addition, to the north of Muna lies Tiworo Island, surrounded by several groups of small islands, stretching in a chain from Siompu, Kadatua, Liwuto and Talaga islands to Rumbia and Poleang on the Southeast Sulawesi mainland. The straits between the islands are named the Buton Strait, Muna Strait and the Tiworo Straits respectively. For a map of the places referred to here, and the locations of the subdistricts with the forts referred to in this paper, see Sarjiyanto (1999:104).

The term Butonese covers the inhabitants of all former lands of the Buton Sultanate (Southon 1995) and extended to the southern portions of Southeast Sulawesi mainland. These lands reveal considerable diversity in cultural traditions and languages. Two main groups of languages can be distinguished, both belonging to the Western Malayo-Polynesian branch of Austronesian; those in the north of Buton Island, which belong to the Bungka-Mori group and are closely related to languages on the Southeast Sulawesi mainland; and those spoken elsewhere in the regency, which are classified in the Buton-Muna group (Bisht and Bankoti 2005:187).

Over 100 forts are associated with the Buton Sultanate (Sarjiyanto 1999). The best known of these is the imposing Buton Palace, located in the regency's capital city of Bau-Bau and completed in 1634 by the sixth Sultan of Buton, La Buke (Nur and Awat 2010). According to tradition, there were also a number of other important forts in operation earlier than, or contemporary with, the main fortified palace on Buton, including Fort Wabula, Fort Liwu, Fort Kombeli and Fort Takimpo, described in more detail below.

This paper summarises the results of an archaeological survey of fortified settlements, and structures associated with the Buton Sultanate, in contemporary Southeast Sulawesi province. The research was undertaken by a team from the Makassar Branch of the Indonesian Archaeological Service. Field visits and site documentation were supplemented with interviews and discussions among local resident communities who sustain oral traditions and ceremonial associations with the sites.

Geography and human ecology of Buton Regency

Buton Regency is located within the Wallacean zoographical region and is rich in floral and faunal biodiversity, including coral reefs and tropical ecosystems. The region lies between latitude 4° 25′–5° 45′ E and longitude 120° 30′–123°30′ S and is bounded by the Banda Sea to the east, the Flores Sea to the south, the Bone Gulf to the west and Muna regency to the north. The main crops include maize and tubers. Buton Island is rich in natural resources, including asphalt beds which have been mined and processed, as well as identified reserves of petroleum and gold (Wikipedia 2020).

Annual rainfall in Buton averages around 1904 mm with an average number of 109 wet days per year. The average temperature is approximately 27°C, fluctuating between 21°C and 35°C. From November to April, monsoon winds blow from west to east, carrying moisture and causing heavy rainfall. In the dry season, from May to October, the wind blows from east to west, carrying little moisture (Indonesia Tourism 2017).

The geology of Buton Island presented here is adapted from the 'Local historical manuscript' published by the Bau-Bau City Government Culture and Tourism Office (Anon. n.d.; see also Kandari et al. 2015). Buton Island, which was the centre of Buton Sultanate, consists of sedimentary rocks. Large rivers traverse the northern and central part of the island, although with little water during the dry season. The southern part of the island is rocky and largely barren. In general, the Buton Sultanate lands consisted of rocky plains and hills. Buton Regency is located on the migration path for large pelagic fish (tuna and skipjack) crossing between the Pacific Ocean and the Indian Ocean. As well as the prospects for offshore fishing, the open water surrounding Buton Island has long been used for coastal fisheries.

In addition to its marine wealth, the Buton Sultanate exploited its tropical forests for their abundance of products, such as rattan, resin and various types of high-quality timber, used for making medicines, home furniture and notably the 'Lambo' sailboats. Buton Regency also sits at the crossroads of trade and commerce between the east and west parts of the Indonesian archipelago. The combination of poor prospects for agriculture and strategically located expanses of sea led the people to choose a maritime life.[1] Buton people sailed to all corners of the Indo-Malaysian Archipelago, in boats that ranged in size from small craft accommodating a few people, to large vessels that could carry about 150 tons of goods. The Butonese became renowned as brave seamen and adroit merchants throughout the Indo-Malaysian Archipelago (Southon 1995).

Theoretical orientation

The long history of settlement on Buton has left a vital ancestral legacy of cherished customs and traditions. An example is the *kande-kandea* traditional feast still held in villages to pray for a sustainable and prosperous livelihood (Kumparan 2019). During this harvest festival, traditional dance and martial arts are performed and the elders give customary commandments

---

1   As testified by Coen in the early seventeenth century (Colenbrander 1919): 'Dit is een groot ende oock peupuleert landt, hebbende schoon hout daer- van men na wens ende begeerten vaertuych souden connen maken, als men maer volck brochte'.

to young people based on the experiences of the ancestors. Another example is the traditional festivity formerly known as *wapulaka* performed in various villages (Bahari, Wabula, Bungi, Pasarwajo and Lasiimu). It serves as a discussion forum to address issues on social relations within the community and on access to natural resources protected by the stipulations of customary law (Baubau Post 2018).

The cooperative attitude that representatives of Buton society have to its traditions was witnessed firsthand by the research team from the Makassar Archaeology Office. To collect local information on Benteng Wabula, we initially aimed to interview informants in Wabula. In response to our request the community held a general meeting in the village hall attended by 32 people, including bearers of custom (*pemangku adat*), community leaders and the local authorities (the subdistrict head and Wabula village head). The meeting was designed to authorise a mainstream perception of the fort's historical and cultural background. The Buton cooperative attitude is built on the foundations of respect for the transcendent beings in the supernatural world. When several Wabula villagers escorted the team to Benteng Wabula, they asked permission of the tomb they believed to house the major ancestral figure of Wa Kaa Kaa, and 'reported' to her the aims and goals of the activities conducted by the Archaeology Office team. Similarly, the *kande-kandea* traditional feast involves prayers to transcendent ancestors performed as a voluntary pact to attain the communal goal of social identification and legitimation.

The cultural history of Buton can thus be viewed as its sociocultural symbol, which is the product of the sociocultural identity or 'local knowledge' of its people and remains important as a driving force in every walk of life (see Gosden 1994). However, while Buton's traditions are the receptacle of accumulated wisdom, they are susceptible to erosion by modern values. Buton's cultural history could quickly disappear if conflicting concepts inspired by modernity were allowed to confront it relentlessly. There is an urgent need to document Buton's cultural heritage before its traditions die out and are relegated to the status of myth.

This danger confronts the material culture in Buton, whose ruins and other physical remnants can still be observed, and which have contributed significantly to placing Buton's cultural history in a broader context. Unless Buton's built heritage is managed professionally and effectively, using a sociocultural approach customised to each region and recruiting the archaeological evidence to enrich the identification of Buton's sociocultural identity, its cultural significance will not be realised. The political importance during Buton's history of the four forts described here is the motivation for their study, including their implications for former settlement patterns and general community life (Hasanuddin 2010).

Research methodology

With the foregoing theoretical perspective, the questions to be explored in the research on Fort Wabula, Liwu, Kombeli and Takimpo are:

a. How was the fort architecture designed and constructed?
b. Besides being used as a fort, do the structures reveal evidence of residential compounds?
c. What were the cultural and historical conditions when the forts had a defensive function?

To address these questions, this research aims to:

a. Obtain data from archaeology, history and oral traditions to understand the buildings' structure.
b. Collect historical data from the literature and oral tradition to develop a historical periodisation for the forts and the roles they played.

c. Research any building components contained within the forts.

d. Understand the cultural history of Buton society of relevance to the forts when they were in operation.

Research activities were carried out in two stages: first, by conducting a survey of surface archaeological data to record artefacts and traces of buildings; and second, conducting largely unstructured interviews with traditional community leaders familiar with the heritage of the structures in order to gain insights into the cultural history of the forts. All artefacts collected from the sites were classified and analysed in the context of their functional relation to building foundations, and the sociocultural significance of the archaeological materials according to local respondents.

A short history of Buton

The official language of the Buton Sultanate was a local language, Wolio, but Arabic was also used for preparing documents, and the Malay language (Bahasa Melayu) was also spoken throughout the territory. Etymologically, the name of Buton, according to local tradition, comes from Butu, a type of poisonous banyan (*Barringtonia asiatica*). The locals adopted this nickname as a marker from the archipelagic seafarers who often stopped for shelter in the island. When Islam came to Buton, there was an attempt to link the name with the Arabic language. It was said that the word Buton came from the Arabic word *bathni* or *bathin*, which means a stomach or womb (Rosdin 2014).

Prior to adopting Islam, the Buton Sultanate was the Buton kingdom, known as far away as Java by the time of the Majapahit empire. In his famous Sumpah Palapa oath, prime minister Gadjah Mada mentioned Buton. The existence of Buton as a country was recorded in the *Desawarnana* poem written by Mpu Prapanca in AD 1365 (Robson 1995). It was described as a village where the sages lived in a garden furnished with a giant phallus and water channels. The king was called Yang Mulia Mahaguru (the Honourable Grand Master).

Buton's early prominence is reflected in an oral tradition recorded by the Portuguese explorer Antonio Galvão when he visited the northern Moluccas in the late 1530s. According to this story, a prominent elder of the clove-producing island of Bacan ordered his men to cut some rattan but when they did this, blood gushed out and drew his attention to four serpent eggs hidden in the rocks. The elder guarded the eggs, which later hatched into the children of the king of Bacan, the king of the people of Papua, the king of Buton-Banggai and the woman who married the king of Loloda Island. These four were the ancestors of all the kings of these islands, reflecting a symbolic unity which underlies the continuing appeal of this tradition (Andaya 1993:53).

According to Buton's own oral tradition, Buton was established as a country by four people who came from the Malay Peninsula to Buton in the early thirteenth century AD. The four founding fathers, Sipanjonga, Simalui, Sitamanajo and Sijawangkati, are called the Mia Patamiana. Sipanjonga, Sijawangkati and their followers settled the Gundu-Gundu territory, while Simalui, Sitamanajo and their followers settled Parangkatopa. When Sipanjonga's group arrived at Buton (then called Kalampa), they raised their flag called *longa-longa*, the flag of the Malay kingdom. This became the official flag of the Buton kingdom. Simalui's group moved from place to place until they met the Sipanjonga group. The two groups then intermarried (Rosdin 2014).

Sipanjonga married Simalui's sister, Sibaana, and had a son named Betoambari. Betoambari later married Wasigirina, the daughter of King Kamaru, and had a son named Sangariarana. Betoambari became the ruler of Peropa, and Sangariarana ruled the Baluwu territory. This resulted in four villages tied in kinship, namely Gundu-Gundu, Barangkatopa, Peropa and Baluwu (Hasanuddin 2010).

Later, the four villages formed a union called the Empat Limbo, with each village represented by its leader, who was titled Bonto. The four Bonto also appointed their leader, who was titled Patalimbona (Rosdin 2014). The Empat Limbo acted as the legislative body to appoint and crown a king, and also brought into the union other, smaller kingdoms that had started to emerge in Buton, such as Tobe-Tobe, Kamaru, Wabula, Todanga and Batauga. Thus the Buton kingdom was established with the appointment of Wa Kaa Kaa (a woman married to Si Batara, a descendant of Majapahit royalty) as 'Raja I' in 1332 (Hasanuddin 2010).

Wabula tradition has a slightly different account for the inauguration of the Wolio/Buton kingdom. A man named Rajawangkati founded the kingdom of Koncu. Wa Kaa Kaa, also known as Toweke, was interested in local political developments if she was allowed to be ruler. Rajawangkati willingly crowned Wa Kaa Kaa as the first 'Kolakino' of Koncu. They shared political power according to the following formula. The legislative power, the highest power, fell into the hands of Rajawangkati or his successors who were called *namapusaka*, or the natives. The executive or the legislative mandate fell into the hands of Wa Kaa Kaa and her successors, called the Anano Bangule. If the Anano Bangule could not meet the requirement of providing a ruling 'Kakolaki' (or 'Parabela'), the executive power was taken over by the *namapusaka*.

The Buton kingdom flourished during the reign of six rulers up to 1542. Two rulers, Bulawambona as well as Wa Kaa Kaa, were queens. The reign of these two queens shows that women were equal to men in Buton society at that time. Islam made its initial entry to Buton Island as early as 1412. The *ulemma* Sayid Jamaluddin was invited by Raja Mulae Sangia i-Gola who converted to Islam shortly after. Missionary activity was continued for over a century later, which ushered in Buton's Sultanate phase. According to the main account, the saint responsible was Syeikh Abdul Wahid bin Syarif Sulaiman al-Fathani, reputed to have come from Johore via Ternate. In addition to converting the populace of Callasusung (Kalensusu), a region within the Buton realm, he converted Buton's sixth king, Lakilaponto (also known as Timbang Timbangan or Halu Oleo), in 1542. Lakilaponto thus became the first sultan with the title Sultan Murhum Kaimuddin Khalifatul Khamis. The Sultanate phase ended with the 38th and last sultan, Muhammad Falihi Kaimuddin, whose reign ended in 1960 (Hasanuddin 2010).

The influence of Islam was considerable, especially in the elements of Sufism. The laws of Buton were called the *Murtabat Tujuh* ('Seven Grades'), a popular term in *tasawwuf* (the spiritual dimension of Islam). These laws regulated the duties, functions and positions of the Sultanate ministers. The judicative body was run strictly without discriminating between members of the royal family, the sultan's retainers and the subjects. This was evident in the enforcement of law in Buton. Out of 38 sultans reigning in Buton, 12 of them were punished for violating their oath of office. Among them was the eighth sultan, Mardan Ali, who was sentenced to death by tightening a rope around his neck until it snapped, a form of execution known as *gogoli* (Kompas 2010).

After Lakilaponto converted to Islam, the Buton Sultanate flourished and reached its golden age in the seventeenth century. Buton ruled all of Buton Island and some neighbouring islands but allowed for regional autonomy by recognising 72 *kadie* (small areas). Buton built a strong relationship with Luwu, Konawe and Muna in Sulawesi. In the economic sector, money as a medium of exchange was introduced, called *kampua* (made of cotton spun into thread and woven traditionally to make cloth). Taxation was initially collected from each rural district by an officer named the *tunggu weti*. However, following economic development the *tunggu weti* was elevated to the position of *Bonto Ogena* (high minister), and additional duties were added to his portfolio including finance and heading the Siolimbona—similar to the modern chairman of a legislative body (Purwanto 2016; Rosdin 2014).

Buton was an island region set strategically in the sea-trade route connecting spice-producing islands in the east and the traders from the west of the archipelago. Because of its strategic location, Buton was vulnerable to external threats, both from pirates and from foreign kingdoms that wanted to conquer it. To ward off these threats, a multilayered defence system was established. The first layer consisted of four *Baratas*, namely *Wuna, Tiworo, Kulisusu* and *Kaledupa*, and the second layer consisted of four *Matana Sorumba*, namely *Wabula, Lapandewa, Watumotobe* and *Mawasangka*. The third layer, of spiritual defence, consisted of four people called the *Bhisa Patamiana* (Hasanuddin 2010).

Forts in Buton

To strengthen the multilayered defence system of the Buton Sultanate, forts and defence posts were built from the late sixteenth century. Forts are scattered across Buton's length and breadth, with its diverse language and customs. Examples include Fort Bonelaio on Siompu Island, Fort Lasalimu in Lasalimu village and Fort Ereke in North Buton (author's field notes). Chief among them is the Buton Palace, also known as Fort Wolio (Sarjiyanto 1999), a massive military defensive fortification overlooking Bau-Bau city, which stands magnificently even today (Nur and Awat 2010). It was located in an elevated position 3 km from the beach so that the plains and ocean around the Bau-Bau Gulf could be seen clearly from the fort. The outer brick wall was 2.74 km long, enclosing an area of over 4000 ha. The walls are 1–2 m thick and 2–8 m high, equipped with 16 bastions and 12 gates.

Four smaller forts (*benteng*) were surveyed on Buton Island as part of the author's research. Fort Koncu (or Fort Wabula) and Fort Liwu lie within a kilometre of each other in Desa Wabula (Wabula subdistrict) on the southeast coast of the island. Two other fort sites, Kombeli and Takimpo, lie within the Pasar Wajo subdistrict due east of Bau-Bau city. All of them are built from quarried blocks of naturally occurring coral limestone. Their geographical location and altitude above sea level are presented at Table 8.1.

Table 8.1. Geographical details of the four surveyed Buton forts.

Fort	Latitude	Longitude	Altitude above sea level	Setting
Koncu	05° 37' 07.1" S	122° 49' 30.4" E	325 m	Limestone hilltop
Liwu	05° 37' 04.6" S	122° 49' 32.1" E	301 m	Limestone hilltop
Kombeli	05° 32' 41.9" S	122° 49' 13.1" E	150 m	Limestone hillside
Takimpo	05° 32' 47.3" S	122° 51' 02.5" E	179 m	Limestone hilltop

Source: Author's summary.

Fort Koncu (Fort Wabula)

Fort Koncu features high plastered walls made of coral rocks. It contains an ancient tomb and is the site of the former grand meeting house called *galampa* in the local language. According to local tradition, this was the settlement of the first ruler of Koncu, Wa Kaa Kaa, and her closest kin. The walls were used as the border between Wa Kaa Kaa's living quarters and those of her guards. The fort can be categorised as a simple royal residential compound. There is no evidence of architectural elements of bastions, army barracks or logistics storage often found in the defensive forts of other parts of Indonesia, such as Somba Opu (Reid 1983:144–145) or Cenrana (Andaya 1981:Map 8) in South Sulawesi. Nor are there any traces of a town square abutting the palace, as found in Islamic cities in Indonesia such as Yogyakarta and Banten in Java and Palopo in South Sulawesi.

Figure 8.1. A steep section of the route to Fort Koncu.
Source: Photo courtesy of Hasanuddin.

Fort Koncu is also known as Kampung Bugi Lama or Kampung Wabula II (Figure 8.1) and access to the site involved a 75 km drive from Bau-Bau to Wasuemba (Wabula village), followed by a trek of 3 to 3.5 hours through woods along village footpaths. The footpath became steeper some 6 km from the village (Figure 8.1).

Figure 8.2. The remaining wall structure of Fort Koncu on the eastern side.
Source: Photo courtesy of Hasanuddin.

The walls of coral rock and limestone surrounding the compound (Figure 8.2) taper inwards vertically, from a thickness of about 310 cm at the base to 150–200 cm towards the top. The average height of the walls varies from 300 to 500 cm, according to the contour of the land on which they were built. In the northern and southern parts, the walls curve to adjust to the contour of the land, so this opposing pair of walls is not symmetrical. Also, along part of the eastern perimeter, a steep 60 m cliff abuts the fort, and no rock structure was built here. There is only one entry gate (*lawa* in the local language) to the fort, located between the eastern and northern sides and referred to as Lawa Lakedo.

Apart from the walls, another visible structure at the site is a rectangular building with ceramic flooring and a zinc roof. This is believed to be the place where the first ruler, Wa Kaa Kaa, was buried (Figure 8.3). On its surface an oval block of limestone has been laid, festooned with offerings placed there by visitors to her gravesite on important days in the Islamic calendar (e.g. Bulan Suci Ramadan) to seek blessings at the site. The reconstruction of the gravesite follows the north–south orientation of Islamic graves in Indonesia, although there are no tombstones to mark the location of the head or feet, as is often found with Islamic graves.

The uneven ground surface found around the building is typical only of ancient tombs and so supports the belief that this was a royal burial site. However, it calls into question any claims that a former palace was located at the site. Surveys conducted at the location revealed the presence of sharp-pointed coral rocks, but nothing in the way of artefacts, such as earthenware or ceramic fragments, to indicate human settlement in the past.

Our informants took us to a nearby location, with a relatively flat surface on the west side of Fort Koncu, declaring it as the place where Wa Kaa Kaa's palace once stood. Here there was no sign of foundations or a cornerstone at the indicated location, just a small wooden building erected on one post by the local people as a memorial to the palace. The masted wooden building serves as a site for ritual activity and offerings.

Figure 8.3. Wa Kaa Kaa's grave.
Source: Photo courtesy of Hasanuddin.

Inside Fort Koncu, natural stone features are placed adjacent to each other separated by a small passage through which visitors can enter the fort. According to the local people, this was the location of the royal agreement slab. The stone is engraved with etchings that are generally vertical and have an average length of 10 cm (Figure 8.4). According to our informants, wrongdoers who had violated the customary law were brought before this place for their verdict to be delivered. The most severe punishment was for the convicted offender to be bound and thrown into the sea alive, a punishment still practised during the pre-Islamic era, for instance in Tammejarra, Mandar, West Sulawesi and Jera Pallette, Bone, South Sulawesi.

Figure 8.4. An etched rock said to have been the place of royal agreement.
Source: Photo courtesy of Hasanuddin.

The other main finding during the survey was a circular arrangement of limestone blocks with a rock in the middle bordering a 60 cm deep hole, located on the west side of Wa Kaa Kaa's grave (Figure 8.5). The circular stone structure evokes the *temu gelang* (meeting circle) commonly found at megalithic sites in Indonesia, especially Soppeng in South Sulawesi. In other areas, such as Bantaeng and Bulukumba in South Sulawesi, similar stone arrangements are thought to represent symbolically the centre of the world (Bugis = *pocci tana*, *pocci Butta*). Although our informants were unsure as how exactly to interpret this feature, it is likely to be a microcosmic representation of the human world—in view of its shape, its location within the sacred area at the top of a mountain, the reputation of Koncu as the oldest village in Wabula, and Wa Kaa Kaa's palace site.

Figure 8.5. Limestone arrangement in the shape of a ring thought to symbolise the centre of the world.
Source: Photo courtesy of Hasanuddin.

In addition, there is an upright limestone monolith that has not been used in building the walls. It was a place of ritual ceremonies for residents preparing to go to war, like the one found in the ancient Sengkae fort of the Siang kingdom of South Sulawesi (Fadillah and Mahmud 2000:28).

Fort Liwu

Early in Buton's history, the population evidently abandoned Fort Koncu and relocated to Liwu, an area about 1 km to the north. The likely causes were increasing population growth and the prospects to facilitate access and enhance relationships with outsiders. This is because Liwu's location is very strategic, making it ideal as a location for defensive settlement. From Liwu, activities in the neighbouring mountains and the Flores Sea can be monitored (Hasanuddin 2010).

Pedestrian travel from Fort Koncu to Fort Liwu was relatively easy. The track followed an undulating surface along the edge of the cliff to reach the east–west oriented limestone plateau crowned by the fort (Figure 8.6). To reach Fort Liwu from the Wasuemba coastal village, the track negotiates steep uphill pathways through the woods.

Fort Liwu was built of uncoursed, local coral rocks, like Fort Koncu, but it clearly functioned as a defensive fort. The walls were built in two sections, with the outer section higher than the inner. In addition, the fort has a rectangular shape with a bastion at each of its four corners (Figure 8.7). Each of the four sides has an entrance gate with a different name, namely *lawa magasa* for the north gate, *lawa E'e* for the east gate, *lawa amagasa* for the south gate, and *lawa Wolio* for the west gate. Three of the entrance gates can be accessed by land, but *lawa E'e* (the water gate) can only be accessed from the seaside.

Figure 8.6. The ruins of the wall structure of Fort Liwu.
Source: Photo courtesy of Hasanuddin.

Figure 8.7. One of the corner bastions of Fort Liwu.
Source: Photo courtesy of Hasanuddin.

Figure 8.8. One of the ancient cannons in Fort Liwu now placed on the coast at Wabula.
Source: Photo courtesy of Hasanuddin.

An ancient cannon was once located inside the fort but has been moved to Wabula coastal village and placed near the village meeting house (Figure 8.8). In its shape and size, it resembles other cannons associated with Buton Sultanate forts. The Fort Liwu cannon is 116.5 cm long with the diameter on the front muzzle 7 cm. It was welded together from six components, and has two reinforcing rings with a diameter of 5 cm. The cascabel (subassembly of a muzzle-loading cannon) is 2 cm long, and the breech in the ignition hole at the back of the cannon has a diameter of 3 cm.

The plateau occupied by Fort Liwu is wide enough to accommodate residential areas. The structures inside the fort include ancient tombs (Figure 8.9), the former mosque and the ruins of houses. Although the surrounding land slopes steeply, it can be used to plant coconuts and other crops. Inside Fort Liwu, some fragments of foreign ceramics, particularly from China, were recovered. Plastic litter was found scattered around the settlement remains even though the site was abandoned in 1962, according to our informant, when the inhabitants were relocated to the lowlands to facilitate their administration. At the time of the survey, the fort surroundings were choked with reedy grass up to 1.6 m, largely obscuring the ancient tombs and hindering the recovery of surface archaeological fragments. Nonetheless, the survey revealed enough of the fort structure for its plan to be sketched (Figure 8.10).

Figure 8.9. One of the ancient tombs inside Fort Liwu.
Source: Photo courtesy of Hasanuddin.

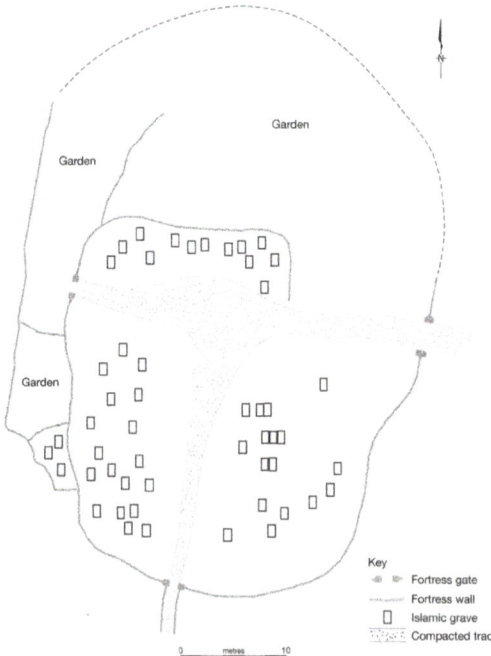

An important structure of the fort is the wall at the centre of the fort, which used to be the *mihrab* of the fort's mosque (Figure 8.11). The other components of the mosque were relocated and rebuilt in Wabula village when Fort Liwu was abandoned. These heritage remains of the fort's small mosque are a visible reminder of Buton's history. They point to leadership of the community by the Buton ruler who had embraced Islam during his reign.

Figure 8.10. Plan of Fort Liwu in Wabula.
Source: Makassar Archaeology Office, redrawn by CartoGIS ANU.

Figure 8.11. The former *mihrab* (a niche in the wall of a mosque) inside Fort Liwu, which also functioned as a tomb.
Source: Photo courtesy of Hasanuddin.

Valuable information is provided by Johannes Elbert's photographs, published in 1911, of Fort Liwu (which he called Fort Wabula).[2] Elbert's photographs confirm the status of Benteng Liwu as a defensive fort and helped breathe life into its archaeological vestiges. One photograph shows one of the entrance gates to Benteng Liwu (Hasanuddin 2010: Foto 4). Above the gate is a guard post made of a thatched-roofed wooden construction with a bamboo ladder. The rooftop of the guard post is shaped like a pineapple. The same sort of guard post above the entrance gate can also be found in the Buton Palace at Bau-Bau. The pineapple symbol is strongly associated with the Buton Sultanate and features as a decorative carved emblem in contemporary designs of Buton architecture.

Fort Kombeli

Fort Kombeli, which is also commonly known as Fort Liwu, lies within the territory of Kombeli village, Pasar Wajo subdistrict. The coral rock walls, built to adjust to the sloping contour of the land, are around 1 m in height, but some parts are difficult to observe because the fort is split by a deep ravine. Three gates were located on the south, west and east sides. It is likely that there had been a gate along the north wall as commonly found in Buton forts, but our survey could not locate it as it was now ruined or buried underground. The south gate is 150 cm tall and 125 cm wide. The west gate (Figure 8.12) is 180 cm wide and 140 cm tall, flanked by walls around 110–140 cm thick.

---

2   Fort Wabula refers to the whole area to the top of the mountain encompassing the Fort Liwu site.

Figure 8.12. One of the gates into Fort Kombeli on the western side.
Source: Photo courtesy of Hasanuddin.

A great variety of tombs and tombstones are scattered across the interior of the fort, including the ancient tombs of the traditional leaders named the *parabela*. However, many of these tombs have been restored by the relatives of the deceased by building a cement wall around them (Figure 8.13). There is a rectangular-shaped tomb made of coral rock, which lacks a tombstone (Figure 8.14). The tombstone of another grave is shaped like a human head. This tombstone must have been made recently because, although made from coral rock, cement was used to help fashion the shape.

Figure 8.13. The restored tomb of one of the *Parabela*.
Source: Photo courtesy of Hasanuddin.

Figure 8.14. Fort Kombeli tomb made of coral rock.
Source: Photo courtesy of Hasanuddin.

Fort Takimpo

Fort Takimpo, located in Takimpo village in Pasar Wajo subdistrict, was restored by the Southeast Sulawesi Provincial Government in 2006. It is ovoid in shape and the coral stone walls adjust to the land contours (Figure 8.15). The walls are 2 m tall and 1.5 m wide (Figure 8.16). The fort has five gates, a main gate located on the east (Figure 8.17), two gates along the west and a single gate to the south and the north. Each gate served as a bastion, with additional stone structures that included a guard post beneath and surveillance post on top. Each gate also has a roofed wooden building originally equipped with a pair of cannons, although none of these can be seen today.

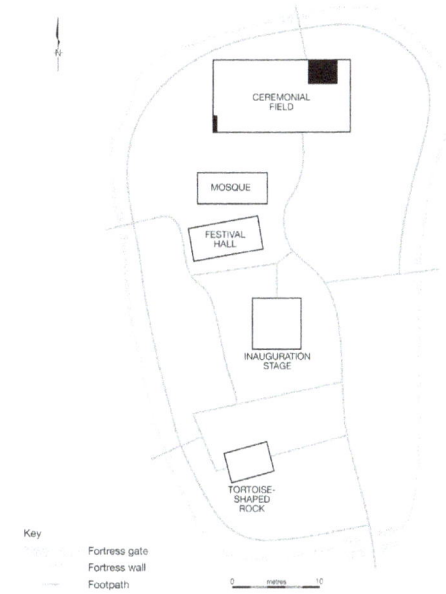

Figure 8.15. Plan of Fort Takimpo.
Source: Makassar Archaeology Office, redrawn by CartoGIS ANU.

Figure 8.16. Fort Takimpo walls.
Source: Photo courtesy of Hasanuddin.

Figure 8.17. Main gateway into Fort Takimpo.
Source: Photo courtesy of Hasanuddin.

The fort allows a view over the surrounding topography, including the shoreline on the northern side, the hills and moderately shallow valleys on the east and southern sides, and a steep drop on the western side (which disappears from view). The surrounding hills were cultivated with seasonal crops.

The mosque, inauguration stone and ancient tombs inside the fort were restored by the Southeast Sulawesi Provincial Government in 2006. The mosque inside the fort is square in shape and has four main pillars (*soko guru*) directly supporting a multi-tiered roof structure. The western side has a niche extended outward from the wall called the *mihrab*, used by the *imam* to lead prayers (Figure 8.18). All these features are typical of ancient mosques in Indonesia.

At the top of the plateau near the mosque, there is a field that was formerly used as a place of ceremony. At that time, the royal flag was always raised there. To the east, there is an inauguration stage with coral rock structures shaped like chairs with back supports (Figure 8.19). According to the local people, the inauguration stage is still used to induct local leaders such as the *parabela*, *moji* and *waci*.

There is little information available on the historical function of the fort. According to local people, the fort was used to defend themselves against pirates and especially Tobelo raiders from Halmahera in neighbouring Maluku province, whom they feared most. The Tobelo reportedly often attacked the village to plunder their wealth and kidnap women and girls.

Figure 8.18. Mosque inside Fort Takimpo.
Source: Photo courtesy of Hasanuddin.

Figure 8.19. The inauguration stage in Fort Takimpo.
Source: Photo courtesy of Hasanuddin.

Discussion

For populations without the technology to build defended settlements, sites difficult to access in the highlands would have offered a degree of security thanks to the natural protection of a deep river valley or steep cliffs. But as agriculture expanded, the lowlands would have offered the greatest opportunity for population increase due to the minimisation of time and energy costs in gathering life-supporting natural resources. Areas richest in natural resources would have become centres of social and cultural activity (Subroto 1983:1178). This would have included the establishment of rulership to coordinate adaptation to the abundant natural resources, expansion of food diversity, and distribution of human settlements to exploit the available resources. It also included defence, because the survival of society required a place of refuge during wartime as well as a centre of government. The Buton forts reflect not only the economic ability of the ruler, but also the presence of territorial forces to defend the people from external attack (Sarjiyanto 1999:99). Thus, we see that the defensive walls at Fort Koncu and Fort Liwu in Wabula enclose visible reminders of the former social order including ancient tombs, remnants of a palace, a place of agreement and a former mosque. In addition, the defensive purposes of the Buton forts were assisted by their position on locally elevated terrain.

In particular, the large number of fortifications in Buton can be understood in the context of the rising tensions between major maritime powers during the sixteenth and seventeenth centuries. During the late sixteenth century, Buton acknowledged Ternate as overlord and protector, but it fell prey to constant attack by Makassar with the turn of the century, followed by conquest in 1626. In 1667, Buton entered a treaty with the Dutch East India Company (Vereenigde Oostindische Compagnie, or VOC) during the prelude to the successful assault by the VOC on Makassar, after which Buton was returned to Ternate, which had also allied itself with the VOC (Andaya 1981, 1993). In addition to these large-scale conflicts, Buton also had to deal with tensions inside its insular domain, such as those presented by Tiworo Island with its strong presence of Samar 'sea gypsies' (Gaynor 2016). The perils of seaborne attack explain why the Liwu and Takimpo forts, as well as the Buton Palace, are notable for their elaborate defensive structures, such as bastions and their commanding view overlooking vital coastal landing sites. Forts like these make it difficult for an enemy to attack and break their lines of defence, which the enemy would have to do to seize land or control of a kingdom. These forts served as military defence posts, and displayed the concentration of power and control over the local economy in order to maintain the existence of the kingdom and its rulers.

The same strategy was followed by foreign powers when they pushed into the Indonesian Archipelago during the same era as the Buton forts proliferated. Initially the Portuguese, then the Dutch, English and Japanese maritime traders established networks of strategic fortified sites across the archipelago. These forts functioned not only as a shelter from belligerent local populations but also as a defence when the foreign powers went to war against each other over their competing economic interests. The forts were established as military and trading posts, their position determined by the imperative to control economic activities along river, land and sea routes. It is not surprising to find Dutch forts or Japanese bunkers established along the waterfront, a river delta or busy road travelled by traders and merchants.

Foreign colonial powers brought with them modern weaponry, and advanced fort construction technologies. A common characteristic of Portuguese and Dutch forts is a rectangular shape with bastions (rectangular or round in shape) at every corner to serve as monitoring posts—a feature emulated on the major Buton fortresses. The imperial powers also styled their forts according to the architecture of their home country, using bricks (such as Fort Banda built by the Portuguese in Maluku) or volcanic tuff stone plastered with cement and limestone (such as Fort Rotterdam in Makassar). Local adoption of introduced technology can be seen with the various brick forts built by Goa–Talloq in its defence of Makassar against the Dutch (see Chapter 7, this volume), and the use of brick in the Buton Palace and some other Buton forts.

Conclusion

The diverse social and cultural traditions of Buton Island indicate a pluralist and open society that welcomed external influences and sought to benefit from them while protecting its own interests. The Butonese, like the Bugis and Mandars, are renowned as seafaring people who traded widely and opened their minds to lifestyles in faraway places. In the process, they gathered a great diversity of trade goods and ideas to benefit social and cultural life in Buton. Evidence of this engagement can be seen in the relics and cultural heritage found to this day across Buton.

Archaeological surveys using an ethnohistorical approach have demonstrated the fortified status of the Koncu, Liwu, Kombeli and Takimpo forts on Buton Island. All four were built on elevated locations, and all of them except Kombeli on hilltops. The unelaborated coralline rock walls of Fort Koncu show that this site was a basic fortified residence, not a military defence post. Architecturally, Fort Liwu resembles Buton Palace in many aspects, including the shape of the entrance door, the two-layered walls, the bastion and the location of the former mosque.

After restoration by the Provincial Government of Southeast Sulawesi, Fort Takimpo and its building components can clearly be seen today. However, they still require ongoing maintenance and protection from the combined impacts of weathering and human agency.

Fort Koncu and Fort Kombeli lie in ruins, with their coral stone walls heavily degraded. If the forts are not restored promptly, the ruins will eventually disappear without a trace, leaving only a legend without physical verification. These forts are important relics of the multilayered defence system of the Buton kingdom that began as early as the fourteenth century AD, and as symbols of the greatness and power of the kingdom of Buton in the context of its cultural history. The Buton Culture and Tourism Office should coordinate with local households to discuss the management prospect of the forts or to develop Koncu and Kombeli into sites for cultural tourism. The forts on the Wakatobi Islands, which formed part of the defensive structure of the Buton Sultanate (Rosmawati 2018), are an example of the potential of these defensive structures for cultural tourism initiatives (Khiri Travel 2017). In the restoration effort, the rules of preservation must be followed, with emphasis on the authenticity of form and compliance with the available data, such as that collected through research by the Makassar Archaeology Office. Building components should not be added without drawing on evidence of pre-existing structural forms because such additions would mask the cultural significance of the forts.

References

Andaya, L.Y. 1981. *The heritage of Arung Palakka: A history of South Sulawesi (Celebes) in the seventeenth century*. Verhandelingen van het Koninklijk Instituut voor Taal-, Land- en Volkenkunde 91. Martinus Nijhoff, The Hague. doi.org/10.26530/oapen_613368.

Andaya, L.Y. 1993. *The world of Maluku: Eastern Indonesia in the early modern period*. University of Hawai'i Press, Honolulu.

Anonymous n.d. Local historical manuscript. Bau-Bau City Government Culture and Tourism Office, Bau-Bau.

Baubau Post 2018. Tradis pindoko wapulaka, aset budaya busel yang hampir punah. *Bau-Bau Post*, baubaupost.com/2018/02/15/tradisi-pindoko-wapulaka-aset-budaya-busel-yang-hampir-punah/. Accessed 4 February 2020.

Bisht, N.S. and T.S. Bankoti 2005. *Encyclopaedia of South-East Asian ethnography*. Angus and Robertson, Sydney.

Colenbrander, H.T. 1919. *Jan Pietersz. Coen: Bescheiden omtrent zijn Bedrijf in Indië*. Part 1. Martinus Nijhoff, The Hague.

Elbert, J. 1911. *Die wissenschaftlichen Ergebnisse der Sunda-Expedition des Frankfurter Vereins für Geographie und Statistik*. Jean Roux, Frankfurt am Main.

Fadillah, M.A. and M.I. Mahmud 2000. *Kerajaan siang kuna: Sumber tutur, teks dan tapak arkeologi*. Balai Arkeologi Makassar, Makassar.

Gaynor, J.L. 2016. *Intertidal history in Island Southeast Asia: Submerged genealogy and the legacy of coastal capture*. Cornell University Press, Ithaca. doi.org/10.7591/9780877272304.

Gosden, C. 1994. *Social being and time*. Blackwell, Oxford.

Hasanuddin 2010. Eksistensi benteng Wabula sebagai bentuk pertahanan berlapis Kerajaan Buton Sulawesi Tenggara. *Walennae* 12(1):21–37.

Indonesia Tourism 2017. Southeast Sulawesi, Wakatobi. www.indonesia-tourism.com/south-east-sulawesi/climate.html. Accessed 4 February 2020.

Kandari, A.M., S. Kasim, M.A. Limi and J. Karam 2015. Land suitability evaluation for plantation forest development based on multi-criteria approach. *Agriculture, Forestry and Fisheries* 4(5):228–238. doi.org/10.11648/j.aff.20150405.15.

Khiri Travel 2017. The magical Wakatobi Islands. khiri.com/discovery/the-magical-wakatobi-islands/. Accessed 4 February 2020.

Kompas Travel 2010. Pulau Makasar dan cerita masa lalu. Kompas.com travel.kompas.com/read/2010/03/13/15410668/Pulau.Makasar.dan.Cerita.Masa.Lalu. Accessed 24 March 2020.

Kumparan 2019. Kande kandea festival budaya buton yang jadi ajang mencari jodoh. kumparan.com/kendarinesia.id/kande-kandea-festival-budaya-buton-yang-jadi-ajang-mencari-jodoh-1rHrPUBsEn9. Accessed 4 February 2020.

Nur, M. and R. Awat 2010. Menemukan kearifan lingkungan dalam pola pemukiman Keraton Buton. *Walennae* 12(1):53–64.

Purwanto, M.R. 2016. Acculturation amongst wisdom, law and Sufism in forming Martabat Tujuh Enactment of Buton Sultanate. *International Journal of Humanities and Management Sciences* 4(3):288–292. www.isaet.org/images/extraimages/EA0416024.pdf. Accessed 24 March 2020.

Reid, A. 1983. The rise of Makassar. *Review of Indonesian and Malaysian Affairs* 17:117–160.

Robson, S. (trans.) 1995. *Desawarnana (Nagarakrtagama) by Mpu Prapanca*. KITLV Press, Leiden.

Rosdin, A. 2014. Buton, Islamization and its manuscripts tradition. *International Journal of Nusantara Islam* 2(2):101–116. journal.uinsgd.ac.id/index.php/ijni/article/view/75. Accessed 24 March 2020. doi.org/10.15575/ijni.v2i2.75.

Rosmawati 2018. The roles of the Liya and Kaledupa forts at Wakatobi as defensive forts of the Buton Kingdom. In M.R. Abdul Wahab, R.M.A. Zakaria, M. Hadrawi and Z. Ramli (eds), *Selected topics on archaeology, history and culture in the Malay world*, pp. 55–72. Springer, Singapore. doi.org/10.1007/978-981-10-5669-7_5.

Sarjiyanto 1999. Eksistensi kerajaan Buton: Kajian: benteng-benteng masa kesultanan. *Walennae* 3(1): 97–106.

Southon, M. 1995. *The navel of the Perahu*. Research School of Pacific and Asian Studies, The Australian National University, Canberra.

Subroto, P. 1983. Studi tentang pola pemukiman arkeologi kemungkinan-kemungkinan penerapannya di Indonesia. *Pertemuan Ilmiah Arkeologi III*, pp. 1176–86. Pusat Penelitian Arkeologi Nasional, Jakarta.

Wikipedia 2020. Buton. en.wikipedia.org/wiki/Buton. Accessed 4 February 2020.

9

Forts of the Wakatobi Islands in Southeast Sulawesi[1]

Nani Somba

Introduction

The Wakatobi Islands are part of a larger archipelago known as the Tukang Besi Islands, located in the Flores Sea to the southeast of Buton Island (Figure 1.1 this volume). Wakatobi is an acronym of the four main islands that make up the group, namely Wa (Wangi-Wangi), Ka (Kaledupa), To (Tomia) and Bi (Binongko) (Wikipedia 2020). This name was first used in 1959, when the Wakatobi region was administratively separated from the Buton Regency.

The islands contain a rich cultural heritage record, but to date there is no management strategy to protect and enhance the cultural resources of Wakatobi. This study aims to provide an inventory of the forts present on the islands to assist in the development of a management strategy. The methods used include a surface survey, observation of the cultural relics and interviewing residents with knowledge of the issues under investigation.

The Wakatobi forts cannot be appreciated in isolation from the kingdom of Buton, which is recognised as one of the key maritime kingdoms instrumental in the acclaimed spice trade from the Maluku Islands during the sixteenth and seventeenth centuries (Andaya 1991). The Wakatobi forts had their origins during this period when they were developed as part of Buton's four buffer zone (*Barata pata mplena*) system of governance. The *Barata pata mplena* included the locations of Kolensusu (based on the Buton mainland), Kaledupa (Wakatobi Islands), Muna and Tiworo (both on Muna Island). This was a multilayered defence system designed to protect the Buton kingdom from foreign, especially European, intervention. Evidence from two of the four Wakatobi forts, Fort Kaledupa and Fort Liya will be presented in this paper. They were developed as part of the defence system of the wider kingdom with its large and imposing central fort (Wolio) overlooking the anchorage at Bau-Bau, the centre of the Buton Sultanate. One of these fortified sites, Fort Liya, has been subsequently developed as a tourist attraction, so its investigation was a priority to provide information and advice on tourism and conservation strategies to the local government.

---

1 Manuscript received 2011; translated from Indonesian by A. McWilliam 2013; edited by D. Bulbeck 2013.

The history and geography of the Wakatobi Islands

There are two origin stories about the names of the Tukang Besi Islands. The more prosaic version is that the phrase derives from the practice of blacksmithing (*tukang besi*) which was a common practice by the people of the islands. During a visit to Binongko Island, a Dutch man named Hoger saw a lot of people busy making tools from iron, and so he called the area *Toekang Besi Eilanden* ('Blacksmith Island', see Hamid 2007:36). However, another story assigns the name to Tulukabesi, the king of Hitu (in Maluku), who took up arms to oppose the Netherlands East India Company (Vereenigde Oostindische Compagnie, or VOC). According to the story, armed resistance was provoked by the actions of the VOC in preventing the islanders from felling clove, nutmeg and mace trees as part of imposing its monopoly on the Moluccan spice trade (Abubakar 1999a). The VOC captured Tulukabesi along with about 300 of his followers and exiled them to the eastern part of Buton Island. This did not quell Tulukabesi's hatred for the Dutch, and he resumed his resistance on the nearby island of Wangi-Wangi. The rebellion reportedly spread to the other islands including Kaledupa, Tomia, and Binongko, and so the region was named the Tukang Besi Islands after Tulukabesi (Abubakar 1999a, 1999b).

Before the Wakatobi Islands were controlled by the kingdom of Buton, and prior to the arrival of the Dutch in the sixteenth century, the area was reportedly named *Liwuto Pataanguna*, which means 'Four Islands' in the Wolio language of Buton. Another popular name was *Liwuto Pasi*, meaning 'Coral Islands'. The tropical islands stretch between 5.00° and 6.25° S north to south, and 123.34° and 124.64° E west to east. Wangi-Wangi Island covers an area of 448 km^2, Kaledupa Island 104 km^2, Tomia Island 115 km^2 and Binongko Island 156 km^2. The total area has a combined land mass of 823 km^2 (Rosmawati 2018).

Structurally the Wakatobi Islands comprise a limestone massif, geologically uplifted from the ocean floor. The extensive lowlands or coastal plain are characterised by rocky, porous alkaline soils. Cultivation of any kind is difficult on these barren and unvegetated chalklands where any surface water seeps deep into the ground. Karstic geologies containing underground stores of freshwater have been discovered in each of the four main islands and have long provided a source of brackish water for the residents. The high salt concentration, however, makes the water unhealthy for consumption, particularly during high tides when the sea level rises above the level of the karstic caves. These days there is a regular trade in bottled water (*galon*) for drinking while shallow wells are still widely used for washing and bathing.

The islands also have talc-white limestone uplands. The highest plateau, Tindoi Hill, located on Wangi-Wangi Island, rises more than 770 m above sea level. Mori Hill on Tomia Island is more than 250 m high, Taipabu Hill in Binongko Island is barely 22 m high, while the highest plateau on Kaledupa Island is just 230 m high (Hamid 2007:41). These rock formations enclose accumulations of soil that are sometimes used for agricultural purposes. This occurs particularly on Kaledupa Island, which is more fertile than the other three and produces annual crops of maize and secondary food crops.

In some coastal areas, mangrove forest adds greenery to the otherwise bleached landscape. However, much of the coastline consists of steep, wave-cut cliffs of limestone. Coral reefs around the islands form a narrow strip of shallow water that is protected from the pounding waves of the surrounding seas. The Wakatobi Islands lie at the confluence of the Banda Sea and the Buru Sea in the northeast, the Flores Sea in the southwest and the Buton Sea in the east. This latter has the least forceful waves and the coastal settlement of Ouw in the west is well known and used as a safe harbour for mooring boats.

The Wakatobi seafloor topography includes 25 coral reefs with a total circumference of some 600 km. The reefs include coral beaches, barrier reefs and atolls. They are scattered across an area which is now included in the Wakatobi Islands National (Marine) Park (TNKW). The island region receives a double monsoon, including heavy rains from the west during November to February, and strong winds from the southeast during the dry period July–September. The region is affected by seasonal currents and ocean swells that track the monsoons (Nontji 1987:68), and at times these conditions make seafaring and boat travel a hazardous activity. Given its position and the abundance of reefs, the area also stands out as habitat for abundant fish of many species. Its fisheries production and potential attract local fishing communities from the Wakatobi Islands, as well as commercial interests from other areas of southern Sulawesi.

Written sources are limited on the origins and dates of arrival of the people who now occupy the Wakatobi Islands. Linguistically, the Tukang Besi language is closely related to the Bonerate language, spoken on the Bonerate Islands to the southeast (Donohue 1999), and these two languages belong to the Muna-Buton cluster of Southeast Sulawesi languages (Joshua Project 2020). However, the Wakatobi Islanders are also fluent in Wolio, the language of Buton, which was the unifying language of the areas formerly under Buton's sway (Hamid 2007:59–63). In addition, many people place the Butonese title *ode* before their name ('*La Ode*' for fathers and '*Wa Ode*' for mothers). These sorts of influences from Buton Island are to be expected, as the Wakatobi Islanders were allies of the Buton Sultanate over hundreds of years and participated in a maritime trade network that extended over much of eastern Indonesia as far as the Papuan coast.

The use of *ode* as a title can be traced in Buton to its fourth sultan, La Elangi Dayanu Ikhsanuddin (1578–1615). He initiated Buton's prevailing system of social stratification by recognising upper and lower classes that cut across Buton's four societal groups. The upper class consisted of the *kaomu*, descendants of the first king (Wa Kaka), and the *walaka* (nobles). *Ode* was one of the titles used by members of the upper class to signify their status.

Most of the upper class initially lived within the fortified walls of the palace centre of Wolio but others, such as the community leaders in the rural settlements (*kadie*), lived outside the palace centre. The *koamu* and *walaka* together ruled the lower class, which included the *papara* and *batua*. Whereas the *papara* lived in rural communities and enjoyed considerable freedom, the role of the *batua* was to serve their designated master, both within the sultanate centres and the *kadie* villages.

As the population developed, there was a gradual increase in the number of high-status households who lived outside the palace centre. One area where they became numerous was in the islands of Wakatobi. Those who lived in the outlying districts had to travel to the palace centre at least once a year, specifically to attend a general meeting that coincided with the inaugural feast of *Murtabat Tujuh* (the 'Seven Grades'). If they failed to attend this event, their social status would be downgraded to an intermediate class, either *analalaki* (if they had been *kaomu*) or *limbo* (if they had been *walaka*). This policy was designed to maintain relationships across the upper class group whether they lived within the centre of government or in the regions.

This method of government evolved into the system of four *barata* established during the first half of the seventeenth century. The *barata* were autonomous regions that had their own governing structure but were required to submit to Buton's overall territorial control. One of these *barata*, Kaledupa, was located in the Wakatobi Islands.

Fort Kaledupa

Fort Kaledupa is located in South Olio village, Kaledupa subdistrict, on the island of Kaledupa. To the east of the fortress, there is a coastal plain with settlements and the foreshore of the Banda Sea, while in the west there are steep hills. The fort's position on a limestone hill circumscribed by steep cliffs, and its vantage point overlooking the sea, were ideal for guarding against a seaborne attack. Around the site, both within and outside the fortress, there are houses and food gardens generally planted with cassava, cashew nuts, coconuts and other tree crops.

Fort Kaledupa is quadrangular stone structure with a north–south orientation some 400 m long and 50 m wide. The walls are curved following the contours of the ground surface and so the sides are not symmetrical. There are two main gates positioned at the north and the south respectively. Above the main gates are two wooden frameworks with gabled roofs that serve as guard posts (Figures 9.1 and 9.2). On the northwest side of the main entrance, there is a stone bastion-like structure. It consists of 2 m thick walls that extend outward 3 m to define a doorway 4 m wide. The walls also include three smaller gateways on both sides, spaced more or less evenly apart. The dimensions of these smaller gates are 1–1.5 m wide, and all were crowned historically with a stone structure.

Figure 9.1. Fort Kaledupa.
A. South Gate; B. East Gate; C. North Gate.
Source: Photo courtesy of Nani Somba.

The enclosing walls of Fort Kaledupa are made of dry stacked and finished limestone blocks that are likely to have been quarried from the surrounding landscape and assembled onsite. The size of the stone elements is not uniform, but they are neatly and securely arranged. The walls range from 1 to 2.5 m thick, and from 1.5 to 3 m high. Some parts of Fort Kaledupa are now experiencing considerable damage from weathering and pilfering of stone materials for subsequent repurposing by local farmers. On the east side of the fort attached to the villagers' houses, for example, most of the stonework has been removed over time to build houses, roads and garden fences. Efforts to conserve and protect the fortification have been made by the local government at key sections of the structure, but the site remains vulnerable due to limited conservation resources. Two cannons from Fort Kaledupa are currently stored at the local police station. According to local beliefs, the cannons were used as defensive weaponry when the fort was in active use: one cannon was placed on top of each gate. This suggests that there may have originally been a larger number of cannons but their whereabouts today remains unknown.

During the early seventeenth century, the ruler of Buton submitted to the imperial ambitions of the Makassarese kingdoms of Goa and Tallo in South Sulawesi and converted to Islam, along with the court and kingdom. Evidence of Islamisation in the Wakatobi Islands comes from an old mosque in Kaledupa, the so-called Kaledupa Palace Mosque, located at the west side of the fort near the main north gate (Figure 9.2). The mosque has been subject to restoration work a number of times, but traces of its antiquity are still visible. These traces include its square shape, 14 x 14 m, and the use of limestone blocks for the foundation and supporting walls. The blocks have been stacked together to produce walls 80–95 cm thick and 1.5–2 m high, on which wooden pillars form the framework for the mosque itself.

The front porch has a flight of five limestone steps in the shape of a gate. Each of the four sides of the mosque has a wooden lattice vent to facilitate airflow. The *mihrab* and wooden pulpit are carved with a leaf design (Figure 9.2), and there is a water vessel at the front gate for the ablutions prior to prayer. At the centre of the mosque, there are four wooden pillars once used to support the mosque's superstructure. The roof is two-tiered in a style consistent with local architectural traditions and includes a platform right at the top where a mosque official could stand and call the parishioners to prayer. The spire is decorated with a carved wooden conical crown, and there is a large wooden buffalo-skin drum that was used historically to call the faithful. Overall, the shape of the Old Kaledupa Mosque resembles that of Buton's royal mosque, located in Wolio (Bau-Bau).

Figure 9.2. Kaledupa Mosque.
A. Pulpit; B. *Mihrab*; C. Ancient grave behind mosque.
Source: Photos courtesy of Nani Somba.

On the south and west sides of the fort, there are some abandoned and badly deteriorated ancient graves. Inside the fort, there are around 20 ancient graves scattered around the old mosque (Figure 9.2), which are believed to be the resting places of past nobles and their families. The gravestones are simple in shape, consisting of sepulchre and club-like headstones carved from limestone. This graveyard and the other parts of the fort are still in use by local people as their cemetery.

Fort Liya

Fort Liya is located on Wangi-Wangi Island in a strategic location on a hilltop surrounded by steep cliffs. It enjoys panoramic views over the plains, and to the coast and seas beyond. This elevated location enabled the early detection of potential enemies whether advancing overland or from the sea. The fort is another quadrangular wall structure some 500 m long by 80 m and oriented east to west. The walls along the east–west alignment are straight, whereas the north and south walls wind and curve following the contours on the ground and creating an asymmetrical walled structure. There are two main gates on the eastern and western sides, which extend out like a bastion. These walls forming the bastions are 6 m thick and spaced 7 m apart. They frame the 2 m wide entrance to the inner space. Like the Kaledupa fort, the east and the west walls both have three gates, 1–1.5 m wide, and were formerly crowned by stone structures. Metal-roofed, wooden guard post structures frame the main entrances and are evidently later additions (Figure 9.3).

Figure 9.3. Fort Liya.
A. South Gate; B. West Gate; C. Bulkheads inside fort.
Source: Photos courtesy of Nani Somba.

The walls of Fort Liya closely resemble the construction of the Kaledupa fortification on the neighbouring island. Extensive use is made of dry-fitted limestone blocks of varying size with average dimensions 1.5–2.5 m thick and 1.5–3 m high. The faced stones of the outer walls mask a central core of limestone rubble in the characteristic style of the wider region and are indicative of a structure built to defend against cannon attack. Most of the structure is badly damaged, the result of opportunistic plundering by local people for other purposes including house construction and garden walls. Much of the south wall has collapsed and is now overgrown with a tangle of trees and shrubs and climbing vines. However, the gate on the west side was restored by the local government in an earlier, short-lived phase of heritage conservation and remains in good condition.

Inside the fort, there is a stone wall about 1 m high (Figure 9.3), which is probably the bulkhead between spatial divisions for different functions. Alternatively, the partition may reflect a boundary between status groups within the ruling group. According to local historians, each gate originally had cannons placed on both sides inside the walls. Large cannons were said to guard the two main gates while smaller or medium-sized cannons were positioned at the other gates. In addition, according to a local informant, in historical memory many other places within the fort were defended with 'small bore' cannons along the perimeter. My Wangi-Wangi informant estimated that when the site was actively maintained as a fortified settlement, it featured as many as 32 cannons, including 16 positioned at the respective gates. However, these days there are just eight cannons remaining in the fort, some of which are damaged and badly rusted (see Figure 9.4).

Inside the fort, there are three monumental buildings, the old mosque (Figure 9.4), the *baruga* or traditional meeting house (Figure 9.4) and a traditional residential house built in the 1920s. The *baruga* is a rectangular structure located on an elevated field at the northern end of the fort. The large structure is 16 m long and 12 m wide, while the walls are 3.5–4 m tall and 0.7–1 m thick. On its north side is a huge banyan tree. According to local informants, the *baruga* field was formerly used as a training ground by soldiers attached to the fort, but given its significance as a ritual house, it is also likely to have been used for ceremonies or as a meeting place for deliberations, as is still customary among local residents. The now badly damaged traditional house is located near the south gate of Fort Liya. It is made of timber with solid square pillars. The front part of the house is an open space, while the back of the house contains separate bedrooms and a kitchen.

Figure 9.4. Fort Liya.
A and B. Cannons; C. Ancient mosque; D. *Baruga* and cemetery.
Source: Photos courtesy of Nani Somba.

Near the *baruga* is a cemetery with ancient graves, believed to commemorate the resting places of former nobles and their families. The gravestones are simple in shape, involving only sepulchre and club-like headstones made of limestone. The cemetery and other parts of the fort are still used by local people for burying family members with links to the site. The imported ceramic sherds recovered from the surface of the fort include Chinese (sixteenth to seventeenth centuries), Vietnamese and European wares. Some of the sherds are the vestiges leftover from treasure hunters who looted the area around the old cemetery looking for antiques. However, other sherds would appear to reflect a tradition, practised until today, of adorning gravestones with porcelain plates and bowls and other high-value porcelain and tradeware.

In addition to foreign ceramics, there are sherds of old pottery from utilitarian wares used in daily life. Another interesting discovery found among the surface scatters is a dense distribution of seashells, evidence that the locals have consumed marine shellfish for centuries.

On the southwest side of Fort Liya, there are several old hand-dug wells, both located inside and beyond the walls of the fort. According to several local informants, the wells have been used by local community members for centuries to provide for their freshwater needs. The well within the confines of the fortification highlights a critical source of potable water during times of warfare or assault on the fort.

Discussion

The Kaledupa and Liya forts are well designed as defence posts. Their hilltop location is advantageous for monitoring and resisting the intentions of enemy troops and fending off armed attacks. Both forts also functioned as residential sites, and likely as centres of government during times of instability and threat, not only for local administration, such as it was, but also as outlying district representatives of the kingdom of Buton. These locations were also important in bringing Islamic governance to Wakatobi. Islamic cities in Indonesia were based on a model of palaces, mosques and other royal buildings clustered around the city square. Here the people, who lived for the most part beyond the city walls, had the opportunity to meet the sultan and courtiers of the palace. Built remains that echo this form of government were recorded on Fort Kaledupa and especially in Fort Liya. The survey of Fort Liya also produced evidence for long-term settlement outside of the walls in a pattern that is common throughout the region. During peaceful times people would live for the most part in their food gardens and tree crop plantations, only retreating into the safety of the forts during times of attack or when raiding parties were in the vicinity.

Today, the Wakatobi Islands are a maritime transit zone between the islands of western Nusa Tenggara and the southwestern and southeastern peninsulas of Sulawesi (Makassar and Buton respectively). The maritime trade routes from Seram Island and Buru Island (Maluku) to Timor and Bali (via Sumbawa) also passed through the waters of Bonerate Island and the Wakatobi Island groups. One particularly important period in the archipelago's maritime history covers the centuries of the spice trade, when cloves, nutmeg and mace were produced in large quantities only at Ternate and Tidore, off the coast of Halmahera, and on Banda Island in the middle of the Banda Sea. Long before the height of this spice trade in the seventeenth to eighteenth centuries, trading ships sailed from the spice islands in the east to the port cities in the western archipelago, and onward to China and the Mediterranean Sea. For instance, when the Chinese geographer Wang Ta-yuan visited Java in the 1340s, the local spice trade network had fallen under the hegemony of the Javanese kingdom of Majapahit The Wakatobi Islands, especially Kaledupa and Wangi-Wangi, were already important nodes in the Java Sea maritime trade zone (Reid 1992:2–4; Hamid 2007:73).

Hand in hand with legitimate maritime trading activity was the constant threat of pirates and slave traders, whose areas of operation covered the seaborne trading networks in and around the archipelago. The strategic trading position of Wakatobi made these islands a prime target for pirate groups and other maritime interests sustained by standover tactics and theft. They were also vulnerable to pirate attack due to their geographical isolation from major commercial empires in the eastern waters, such as Goa (southwest Sulawesi) and Buton. The most notorious pirate groups were based in Papua (seventeenth–eighteenth centuries), Tobelo (eighteenth–nineteenth centuries in Maluku), and Lanun, Balangingi and Mangindanao in the Philippines. The Tobelo pirates were particularly notorious for disturbing the peace on the islands of the eastern archipelago. The Kaledupa and Liya forts not only provided hilltop locations well away from any direct pirate attack, but also enabled the inhabitants to observe the approach and defend themselves from unwelcome interests. In addition, the Wakatobi people are renowned for their skills in martial arts, which they like to show off wherever their boats are at anchor (Hamid 2007:77). These skills may well derive from the Wakatobi Islanders' particular need for self-defence, especially during the heyday of the Wakatobi forts from the seventeenth century, when the Islamic kingdoms of Goa and Buton vied for political and commercial superiority against the rival imperial ambitions of Portuguese and Dutch trading interests (see Baker 2012; Chapter 6, this volume).

Conclusions

The Wakatobi Islands are rich with ancient cultural relics, especially the relatively massive stone fortifications established as centres of settlement and defence in the island chain. In addition to Fort Kaledupa and Fort Liya, described here, there are many other defensive forts on these islands, according to an initial inventory of sites undertaken by the local government. The development of these forts was triggered by the islands' strategic geographical location for maritime trade and their role as a colony (*barata*) of the kingdom of Buton, serving as the eastern frontline defensive post. The cultural heritage contained in Fort Kaledupa and Fort Liya, including Chinese porcelains and Vietnamese tradeware, show that the Wakatobi region was integrated into much wider networks of trade that spanned insular Southeast Asia with connections to global markets. Similarly, the existence of old mosques and ancient Islamic-style graveyards indicate that the forts were part of the sixteenth- and seventeenth-century wave of conversion and proselytisation of Islam across the islands, eastern Indonesia and the Papuan coast. Certainly, the strategic shipping and trading position of Wakatobi has encouraged its people to adapt to their maritime environment, making them bold and brave seafarers with a strong maritime tradition as a key characteristic of their shared cultural identity.

References

Abubakar, L.O. 1999a. Armada penjaga keamanan pantai Kesultanan Buton. *Majalah Budaya Buton (Wolio Molagi)* 1:7–8.

Abubakar, L.O. 1999b. Pemahaman tentang sejarah yang bernama Wolio-Buton. *Majalah Budaya Buton (Wolio Molagi)* 1:37–40.

Andaya, L.Y. 1991. Local trade networks in Maluku in the sixteenth, seventeenth and eighteenth centuries. *Cakalele: Maluku Research Journal* 2(2):71–96.

Baker, B. 2012. Indigenous-driven mission: Reconstructing religious change in sixteenth century Maluku. Unpublished PhD thesis. The Australian National University, Canberra.

Donohue, M. 1999. *A grammar of Tukang Besi*. Mouton, Berlin.

Hamid, A.R. 2007. Pelayaran perahu dan DI/TII di perairan Kabaena-Sulawesi Tenggara, 1953–1965. *Lensa Budaya (Jurnal llmu-ttmu Budaya)* 2(1):85–104.

Joshua Project 2020. Bonerate in Indonesia. joshuaproject.net/people_groups/10933/ID. Accessed 20 February 2020.

Nontji, A. 1987. *Laut Nusantara*. Djambatan, Jakarta.

Reid, A. 1992. *Asia Tenggara dalam kurun niaga 1450–1680*. Volume 1. Yayasan Obor Indonesia, Jakarta.

Rosmawati 2018. The roles of the Liya and Kaledupa forts at Wakatobi as defensive forts of the Buton Kingdom. In M.R. Abdul Wahab, R.M.A. Zakaria, M. Hadrawi and Z. Ramli (eds), *Selected topics on archaeology, history and culture in the Malay world*, pp. 55–72. Springer, Singapore. doi.org/10.1007/978-981-10-5669-7_5.

Wikipedia 2020. Wakatobi Regency. en.wikipedia.org/wiki/Wakatobi_Regency Accessed 25 March 2020.

10

Historical and linguistic perspectives on fortified settlements in Southeastern Wallacea: Far eastern Timor in the context of southern Maluku

Antoinette Schapper

The remains of fortified settlements in far eastern Timor have attracted the attention of archaeologists and led to speculation regarding the underlying drivers of fortification. In this paper, I draw attention to the fact that fortified settlements were not a localised development in far eastern Timor, but in fact are characteristic of a large swathe of southern Maluku. Using evidence from the historical record and from language, I contend that fortified settlement-building cannot be attributed to particular climatic or socioeconomic conditions but is best understood as a cultural feature diffused on a regional level.

Introduction[1]

The landscape of the eastern tip of the island of Timor features numerous stone-walled structures in strategic positions. Investigation has revealed the most significant of these to be the remains of old fortified settlements. In the flurry of academic activity that the eastern part of the island has seen in the last decade, these fortified settlements have become the subject of several studies. Out of this work has arisen an academic debate about the forces driving the construction of these fortified settlements. One side has argued that severe climatic conditions in the period after 1000 BP led to shortages of food, which in turn created a need to defend critical settlements with good access to water for crop irrigation. Those on the other side have countered that the dating of the fortifications does not correlate with the relevant palaeoclimatic events known to have taken place in the region, and argue instead that social changes surrounding the arrival of European colonial powers are likely to have driven the conflict that necessitated the building of village fortifications.

---

1   Support for this research has been gratefully received from a Netherlands Organisation for Scientific Research VENI project 'The evolution of the lexicon: Explorations in lexical stability, semantic shift and borrowing in a Papuan language family', by the Volkswagen Stiftung DoBeS project 'Aru languages documentation', and by the Australian Research Council project (ARC, DP180100893) 'Waves of Words'. Many thanks to Toos van Dijk, Roy Ellen, Aone van Englenhoven, Hans Hägerdal, Juliette Huber, Timothy Usher and Emilie T.B. Wellfelt for their generosity in providing me with much useful information and data from their areas of expertise. All errors are my own.

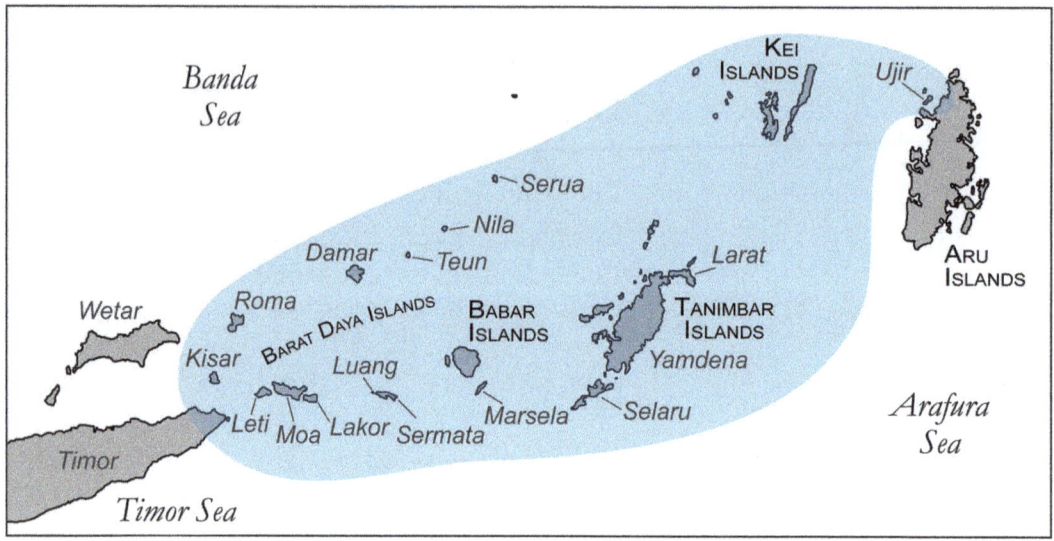

Figure 10.1. Area of southern Maluku and eastern Timor where fortified villages are concentrated (shaded blue).
Source: Antoinette Schapper.

Yet to be considered in this debate is the larger picture of fortified settlement-building in the region beyond the far eastern tip of Timor. Fortified settlements were not a localised development in eastern Timor where specific historical climatic or social conditions held. Fortifications were built widely across the Indonesian archipelago, but stone walls fortifying villages are found with particular concentration in the island region that takes in the southern Moluccan islands from Kisar to Kei (Figure 10.1). That adjacent regions such as the far eastern Tutuala region of Timor and the west coast of Aru also present this settlement pattern historically is highly suggestive of a phenomenon that has diffused from group to group over the region.

In this paper, I contend that fortified settlement-building was a regional phenomenon that spread across southern Maluku, probably during the seventeenth and eighteenth centuries. There are striking similarities across this region in the stone walls fortifying villages, the words used for them and the ways in which they were used and conceptualised. Using descriptions and images from the historical record, I outline the distribution of fortified settlements and paint a picture of their construction and function. Using evidence from language, I show that the term #lutuR, denoting a wall built up from stones, shows signs of borrowing across the region. This indicates that stone wall-building itself, along with the vocabulary with it, diffused across the region. I suggest that as one group built a wall around its village, neighbouring groups were prompted to protect themselves in a similar way. The endemic culture of warfare meant that there was a strong compulsion to adopt village fortifications, thus creating the particular concentration of stone village fortifications attested to in historical accounts and physical remains of which are still visible across the region today.

Fortifications in far eastern Timor-Leste

Archaeological investigation in the eastern half of the island of Timor has seen a flourishing since the declaration of East Timor's independence in 2002. A focal point of activity has been the area at the eastern extreme of the island. While small wall structures are observable across the whole of Timor, this far eastern region is notable for evidencing the archaeological remains of numerous large fortified settlements. This has given rise to a two-sided academic debate about the historical origins and drivers of village fortification.

On the one side, Lape (2006), Lape and Chao (2008) and Chao (2008) have with increasing elaboration put forward the idea that the emergence of village fortification is related to climate change. They argue that El Niño events causing severe climatic conditions, in particular, variable rainfall, would have led to food shortages. This in turn, they argue, occasioned the building of fortifications in areas with valuable water resources for the growing of crops, as groups sought to protect their resources from raiders coming from the surrounding regions. Lape and Chao admit, however, that the dating of the fortified village sites to the period 1450–AD 1650 does not correspond with the known El Niño frequency peak at AD 1300–1400.

Picking up on the lack of dating correlation, an interdisciplinary team out of The Australian National University have disputed Lape and Chao's climate-induced fortification model. O'Connor et al. (2012) bring together a large number of radiocarbon dates from excavations of fortified villages, confirming that settlement activity was only initiated in them from the mid-fourteenth century onwards, too late for that El Niño–driven drought model of Lape and Chao. As an alternative climate-driven model, O'Connor et al. (2012) consider the post-AD 1300 climate transition observed by Nunn (2007) on the basis of examples in the Pacific. In Nunn's (2007) work, it is proposed that the rise of fortification in the Pacific is associated with extended droughts following from changes in monsoon patterns after the transition from the Medieval Warm period to the Little Ice Age from AD 1250–1350. While Nunn (2007) does not discuss East Timor, O'Connor et al. (2012) remark that only the last few decades of the period of widespread climate change in the Nunn model coincide better with the beginning of fortification in East Timor than Lape and Chao's model. However, in the absence of palaeoclimate data for East Timor, the only impact of the Little Ice Age on East Timor that O'Connor et al. (2012) can perceive is a slight lowering of temperatures. This, they conclude, would not have been likely to cause substantial changes in East Timor.

Given the lack of known environmental changes that could have resulted in unpredictability in resource availability, O'Connor et al. (2012) turn to a consideration of social factors that could have given rise to conflict, necessitating the building of fortified settlements. They suggest the following social drivers: population growth arising out of the introduction of maize, slave raiding, competition for valuable trade items such as sandalwood and beeswax, and possibly other unknown internal social developments within the relevant polities in eastern Timor. McWilliam (Chapter 6, this volume) elaborates on O'Connor et al. (2012) and provides more historical argumentation around the proposed social factors that may have initiated and reproduced fortification in eastern Timor. He highlights that this period of fortification aligns with the period of immense economic and social upheaval precipitated by the arrival of Portuguese and then Dutch trading interests, and by the rise of the powerful South Sulawesi trading polities. McWilliam argues that most significant impacts on Timorese social relations and livelihoods were felt from a boom in sandalwood trading from the late sixteenth century, the introduction of maize as a staple food crop in the same period, the new trade in firearms and a significant increase in demand for trade in human slaves. While admitting that the impact on these events on local groups in Timor cannot be tracked with precision, McWilliam suggests that they may well have promoted fortified settlement strategies. However, why the village fortifications are geographically limited to the far eastern part of Timor and not dispersed widely over the whole of the island, where all of these social factors were at play, is not explained.

In sum, for all proposals of drivers of village fortification that we have currently, there remain significant problems in establishing a convincing causal relationship. The climate change–driven models either do not show the right temporal sequencing or cannot be shown to have had an impact that would have effected resource unpredictability, while the suggested social drivers are general factors that were transformative for large swathes of eastern Timor, not simply the areas in which fortifications were found, and whose specific impact on far eastern Timor has not been established.

Historical descriptions of fortified settlements in southern Maluku

While documentary history about the area of far eastern Timor may be lacking for much of the period before the twentieth century (as contended by Lape 2006), the adjacent region of southern Maluku was frequented by Europeans in search of spices and other valuable goods from the sixteenth century and is well-described by numerous visitors from that time. While fortified villages in far eastern Timor are not documented in the historical record during the time of their occupation, they are described in southern Maluku where village fortification was in use until the twentieth century. So even though the archaeology in the region is limited and the construction dates of the fortifications remain to be investigated, the historical record provides a picture of the extent and function of stone fortifications around villages in southern Maluku.

The following sections are comprised of a selection of the written and pictorial sources describing and illustrating the fortified villages in the different island groups of southern Maluku. Most sources available on them come from the late nineteenth and early twentieth centuries. Following this period, village fortifications rapidly became obsolete, as the Dutch colonial powers increasingly exercised control over and imposed stability on the islands.[2]

Kei Islands

Throughout the Kei Islands, villages were once surrounded by sizeable square-shaped stone fortifications topped with hidden gates accessible only via steep ladders:

> The form of these fortifications is everywhere the same. Four strong, thick walls, each 50 to 100 m long, surround a square enclosure. Each wall has in its centre a concealed entrance with stairs, except where a steep adjacent slope makes approach impossible. The ancestors of the Kei people have provided them with prodigious works of this kind, assembling huge blocks of stone into walls a fathom thick and metres in height. (Geurtjens 1921a:270)

In times of war, the walls would be heightened with bamboo and the gates barricaded and *lila* canons put in place (Riedel 1886:225).

Fortified villages appear to have been found widely in the Kei Islands from the middle of the nineteenth century. The resident of Amboina, J.G.F. Riedel in his wide-ranging (1886) work on the people of Maluku and beyond describes villages in Kei located in inaccessible places surrounded by walls made of coral blocks (my bolding):

> With a few exceptions on the islands of Nuhujuut and Nuhutut, the villages of the Kei archipelago are located on the coast in places where water is available. In the past, people say, … they were built on mountaintops and high cliffs, for fear of enemy attack … The villages, the biggest of them containing 60 houses, are surrounded by thick coral stone walls (***lutur***, ***wat lutur***). (Riedel 1886:225)

By the beginning of the twentieth century much of the stone fortification around villages had been removed. In his visit in 1908, the German naturalist Merton found the fortifying walls with steep ladders for entry still in use in a few villages of the mountainous interior (see Figure 10.2).

> Half way up we came to a mountain village surrounded by a stone wall several meters high; at the point of entry stood two wide ladders inside and outside the wall. The interior space was divided by lower walls, 1 to 1.5 m tall, into rectangular courtyards belonging to the individual houses. (Merton 1910:186)

---

2 The following overview of historical records on stone buildings in southeast Maluku was earlier published in Schapper (2019).

Figure 10.2. Layers of stone walls leading up to the gate of a fortified village in the mountains of the Kei Island.
Source: Hugo Merton, 1910.

Little more than a decade later, the Dutch missionary Geurtjens describes the village fortifications as a thing of the past on the Kei Islands:

> In the past, by contrast, the state of war was the norm and the villages were adapted to this situation. Today, peaceful villages can be seen nestling among the greenery in the finest locations along the coast. Formerly they could be found only in the most inaccessible places. It was the steepest of slopes, the most jagged of cliffs, and the grimmest of gorges that made a site suitable for the location of a village. Every village was a fortress, and everybody desired to build a stronghold that would keep the most formidable enemy out. (Geurtjens 1921a:270)

As noted above by Geurtjens, the past state of perpetual warfare between villages was seen to have necessitated the fortifications. Riedel gives an example of the feeble grounds that would lead to war between villages and describes the ritualised way in which the path to war was paved:

> The reason for wars are: appropriation of land, insult, and adultery between inhabitants of different villages, including cases in which when a woman who has married into a strange village is insulted there and sends to her blood relatives a *benaat meak* or token of disgrace, consisting of a little *kabus* (seed fluff of the *Eriodendron anfructuosum*) and some *manuwuun* (chicken feathers), wrapped in a piece of old linen. When a village has decided to wage war, *ravuun*, its chief sends the chief of the other village a piece of *gabagaba* called a *banaat karvevan*, in the form of a sword. If the opposite party does not accept the challenge, the *gabagaba* is returned. But if the other village wants war, an iron machete is sent back in its place. (Riedel 1886:233)

Against this background of readiness to warfare, village walls would have played an important role. Being near indestructible to a native force, they would have meant that very little life would be lost in a conflict. The people of Kei viewed the walls as living entities that, although not demanding, did required tending lest their wrath be awakened:

> In Kei warcraft and history there is no mention of the destruction or capture of such fortifications … It was in fact impossible to take one using Kei weapons. The walls were guardians on whom one could depend for one's safety. No wonder, then, that the thoroughly animistic Kei people viewed their defensive wall as an animated being, a living protector, who furthermore also provided accommodation for the protecting spirits of the tribe. The wall itself was not terribly demanding, and it did not require sacrifices, but if one dared to breach or damage it, then there would be reason to fear its revenge. (Geurtjens 1921a:271–272)

Geurtjens (1921a) recounts that the process of removing walls as part of Dutch pacification precipitated predictions of pestilence now that villages had been 'murdered' and 'unclothed':

> Smallpox, plague and famine would devour the spirits of the wrongdoers, for they had murdered the old walls, destroyed the homes of the spirits: they had stripped their village, torn up its sarong and left it naked and disgraced before the whole world … (Geurtjens 1921a:272)

Aru Islands

Unlike Kei, village fortification was not extensive in Aru. Riedel (1886) notes that, aside from the Dutch-built fort and the attached village of Wokam, there were only two villages with stone fortifications in the Aru Islands in the nineteenth century: Fangabel and Ujir. From as early as the mid-seventeenth century these two villages were in alliance with one another and acted as middlemen for trade between merchants from further west, especially the Makassarese, and the peoples on the eastern side of Aru, with their dense forests populated with birds of paradise and rich seas plentifully supplied with pearls and tortoiseshell (Schapper 2018). Fangabel is no longer inhabited; we have no historical descriptions of the village and there has been no archaeological investigation of the site.[3] By contrast, Ujir stands out in writings on Aru for the vast complex of stone ruins that it is home to.

The first visitor account of the stone structures in Ujir comes from the Dutchman Kolff on his visit in 1825. In particular, he describes the ruins of a stone wall that appeared once to surround the village:

> During our stay here I inspected the environs of the village and saw some former fortifications, the remains of which show that they must once have been very extensive. We also saw traces of a long street, lined by walls, running from the east to the west through the whole village. Here and there we also saw many ruins of stone houses. (Kolff 1828:233)

Almost two decades later, Brumund was equally impressed by Ujir's ruins on his visit in 1843. He also observed the high wall around the village and the stone houses overgrown with plants:

> The village is ringed by a stacked coral stone wall 6 to 8 feet in height, within which still other walls are to be found. There are also some stone houses, all of which are however in ruins, overgrown with bushes and plants. Among these stand the currently occupied houses with their gabagaba roofs, such that the whole scene resembles the ruins of an ancient city that was laid to waste, among which some vagrants have set up camp. These ruins plainly show, as people also confirmed to me, that Ujir was once much richer and more populous. (Brumund 1845:82–83)

---

3   Villagers from nearby Samang said in 2018 that there were no stone structures known at the site of the old village of Fangabel. They observed that it is possible that stones could have been taken from the site for building new structures elsewhere.

Merton also remarked on the extensive stone rubble on his visit to Ujir in 1908. Like Brumund before him, Merton observed not just ruins but also noted that there were many stone walls in use in Ujir village similar to those he saw in Kei:

> The village was itself surrounded by stone walls, and in many cases, the land belonging to a house was also delimited from the neighbouring one by walls, just as we later often saw on the Kei islands. (Merton 1910:166)

The origins of these, at least partially, ruined stone walls observed in the nineteenth and twentieth centuries appear to have been a network of fortifications around Ujir village. These fortifications were encountered by Dutch military forces that attacked Ujir in 1789 as part of reprisals for an assault on the Dutch fort on nearby Wokam. The commander of the expedition against Ujir, Adrianus Anthony's Gravessande, failed in his attempt to take the village, explaining in his report that the heavy walls surrounding the village, along with the Ujirese guns, booby trapping and barricading of entry points, could not be overcome:[4]

> The matter would have been concluded most favourably, if the Alfurs and Backshore people, who appeared in large numbers and joined us, had dared to fight and not been too afraid not only of the enemy (had they been in the forests and fields,[the Alfurs and Backshore people] would have undertaken to haul them out from there!), but also of the guns and strong fortifications (**bentengs**) with which the Ujirese have amazingly strengthened their village, a settlement which nature has helped so extraordinarily [due to its protected position inside a creek] …
>
> Afterwards our people attacked the negeri Ujir for the second time with some fervour, and closed in on the *bentengs* so strongly, that they shot the Ujirese Jaffoera, son of the orangkaya of Fanga-bel Abdul, [and] pulled him from it and took his head; [they] subsequently scaled the second and third of the already mentioned *bentengs*. Some of the enemy fell, among them one person was seen withdrawing to the temple who, judging from his clothing and the circumstances, was considered to be their so-called king Manoeffa who would be Nuku's brother. On this occasion, none of our people fell but several were wounded. Meanwhile, the caltrops with which the ground was littered, the blocking of the roads with felled trees, and the particularly sly damming up of the river created many obstacles for our men. Further circumstances meant that the enemy was in an advantageous position. Other apparent dangers forced us not to go any further, but rather retreat so that the fleet was loaded with suffering wounded people, and not in the condition to go to Goram but had to return. (VOC Archives, VOC 3864, Banda, Secret letters, Report, Banda to Batavia, 4-6-1789, §12)

The Dutch launched two further expeditions against Ujir, eventually taking the village (Tijdschrift voor Nederlandsch Indië 1858). As part of the terms of peace in 1793, the Ujirese were forced to dismantle all but the most essential of their fortifications (Bataviaasch Genootschap van Kunsten en Wetenschappen 1874). One of the most significant *lutur* that remained was that which formed the base of the old mosque (Figure 10.3). The archaeology teams who have visited Ujir suggested that this wall was a repurposing of an original fortified structure (O'Connor et al. 2007).

---

4 Many thanks to Hans Hägerdal for sharing this document and his transcription of it with me.

Figure 10.3. The thick, more than 2 m high *lutur*, or stone wall, that made up the base of mosque of the old Ujir village and which doubled as a fortification, located strategically at the water's edge.
Source: © Emilie T.B. Wellfelt.

Tanimbar Islands

Numerous visitors were struck by the heavily fortified villages of the Tanimbar Islands. Accounts of stone walls in Tanimbar take in the main island of Yamdena as well as the satellite islands of Selaru, Larat and Fordata. Riedel describes the fortifications around Tanimbarese villages as follows (my bolding):

> On the islands of Yamdena and Selaru, fear of enemy attacks means that villages are built by preference on the peaks of raised coral rocks, up to 120 m above sea level. Here access is provided by heavy wooden ladders (*ret*) about 2 m in width. In time of war these ladders are dismantled and stored in the village. These villages, the largest of which contains eighty big wooden houses standing on piles two to three meters high, are surrounded by heavy walls (***lutur***) of stacked coral stones, and further protected by palisades of thorny bamboo, while on the seaward side they are usually shielded by *Pisonia alba* trees. (Riedel 1886:285).

Extensive village fortifications were necessitated by the perpetual state of inter-village warfare that existed in Tanimbar. A picture of the extent can be developed by the accounts of successive travellers to the island of Larat in northern Tanimbar. The English naturalist Forbes stayed in the village of Ritabel in 1882 and encountered many signs of endemic violence:

> The next sight was less exhilarating– on a tree-clad elevation the half-burned and recently deserted village of Ridol; and from the branch of a high tree before us a human arm, hacked out by the shoulder-blade dangled in the breeze, and at no great distance further were recently gibbeted human heads and limbs.

> A state of war, we found, existed between, on the one hand, the villagers of Ridol burnt out by the Kaleobar people, leagued with Waitidal on the north-western corner, which had taken them in, and with Ritabel, our village; and on the other hand, those of Kaleobar, one of the largest villages on the island situated on the north-eastern corner, which was leagued with Kelaan and with Lamdesar, two other villages on the south-eastern coast … Frequent raids had been made recently by these villages on Ritabel, the wife of whose chief had recently been picked off from the outside of the palisade by a lurking Kaleobar marksman, while many of the villagers showed us their recent wounds received in an attack made a few weeks before our arrival. (Forbes 1885:304)

A decade later the warfare between the villages on Larat seemed not to have lessened. Jacobsen (1896:209) did not see himself but reported from one Captain Langen that the village of Ridol had once again been laid to waste.

The resident of Ambon, De Vries, describes the villages of the Tanimbar as having 'a fortress-like appearance' still at the beginning of the twentieth century. He presents a detailed description of the fortifications around the village of Lermatangkort:

> It is built on a high rock plateau, with sharp drops on all sides. From the sea side in particular it is unscaleable, so a tall wooden staircase or ladder consisting of several sections is installed. In wartime these sections are hauled up, completely severing the link with the outside world. The ladder leads to a gate which provides access to the village. The gate is set in a wall of stacked stones, surmounted by a fence of thick, upright bamboo carved at the top into sharp spikes. Cross-beams reinforce the whole structure. The gate itself is so narrow that only one person can pass through at a time. Opposite it on the landward side is a second gate, also with a ladder. These two gates are the only ways into the village. (De Vries 1900:494)

Shortly after this, the traditional pattern of village fortification declined. The Catholic priest Drabbe (1940) describes the walls and the wars that necessitated them as a thing of the past:

> The gate gives access to the village which is enclosed within a wall about 2m high. The wall consists of stacked reef stones. Its remains can still be seen in many places. There are no more complete walls, because, when the Government abolished warfare, the order was given to demolish them … In the past they served to keep enemies outside, and pigs inside. (Drabbe 1940:48)

We see this dramatic decline in fortification comparing images of the village of Omtufu. Drabbe took a photograph of the village when he was stationed in Tanimbar from 1915 (Figure 10.4). We see the old stone wall is reduced to low rubble and without gates. The same village photographed in 1903 shows bamboo palisaded gates with guards standing off to the left (Figure 10.5). In the time of high alert that Forbes observed due to the ongoing war, the gates of Ritabel were similarly palisaded and surrounded by bamboo caltrops:

> All round the village we found a high strong palisade, with a portion removable, however, on the shore side in the daytime. In attempting to pass out by the landward gateway we were at once restrained by several of the villagers following us, who pointed to the ground in an excited manner, demonstrating to us its surface everywhere set with sharpened bamboo spikes, except along a narrow footpath. Their gestures instantly opened our eyes, with an unpleasant shock, to the truth that we were environed by enemies, and the village was standing on its defence. (Forbes 1885:303)

Still Drabbe (1940) was able to record beliefs and rituals to do with the protective stone walls before their falling into disuse. As in Kei, the stone walls of the village were regarded by the Tanimbarese as living entities that needed to be provisioned:

> After the construction of such a village wall a sacrificial feast was also held, involving a communal meal for the whole kampong together with offerings of food first to the wall, then to the village itself, and finally to God. Before everyone began to eat (a large meal of rice with pork), the head of the village founder's lineage group took a portion of rice with a strip of pork fat, *babi dolas*, on top, and placed it on the wall on the seaward side of the village, speaking the words: 'Wall, we have finished stacking you up, do not let your weight press upon us'. Then a portion was placed on the ground in the village, on the seaward side of the dancing and gathering place, and the village sacrificer said to God: 'Friend (the term by which sacrificers and village criers address the Supreme Being), we have fed the wall and the village, keep the weight of the stone from us'. Thereupon the whole community repeated the prayer of the sacrificer. (Drabbe 1940:49)

Figure 10.4. Remains of the stone wall around Omtufu village, Yamdena, Tanimbar Islands c. 1920.
Source: Petrus Drabbe © KITLV 404606.

Figure 10.5. One of the entry gates to Omtufu village, Yamdena, Tanimbar Islands c. 1903, shown in use with palisading of sharpened stakes and two guards standing off to the gate's left.
Source: © KITLV 82675.

Babar Islands

Like their larger and better described neighbours, the Babar islands are known to have been home to villages fortified with stone walls. As always, Riedel provides a clear statement on the extent and type of fortification around villages (my bolding):

> Most villages [on Babar itself] (*let* or *lehol*) are set on high ground above the sea, surrounded by a stone wall (***lutur***) two to three meters high, up to two meters wide. (Riedel 1886:342)

The most detailed description of the fortifications on the Babar islands that we have comes from after the time that they were in use (see van Dijk and de Jonge 1987; Kealy et al. 2018). The anthropologist van Dijk describes the protective *lutur* that traditionally surrounded villages on Marsela, the southernmost island of the Babar group, on the basis of oral traditions:

> In elevated places, we still see the remains of early Marselan villages which were inhabited by various *em* until the beginning of the twentieth century. A village (*lek* or *run*) was really a kind of fort designed to fend off an enemy. The people lived under constant threat of war. Remains of the ring-wall which surrounded the village are still present, often with shooting holes still visible. According to informants, this wall, [whose personal name was] *Wawyèlya*, was at least four meters high and one to one and a half meters thick. Bamboo stakes were fixed on top of the wall to make it even more difficult for an enemy to enter the village … A gate, *worrey*, was equipped with large wooden doors that gave access to the village. (van Dijk 2000:159)

Van Dijk (2000:171) also describes the significance of the village walls. As in the Kei Islands, the walls were conceived as a cloth wrapped protectively around the villagers. If denuded, life would flow away from the village.

A contemporaneous account of the stone walls around villages in Babar comes from a Dutch military expedition to subdue unruly villages on Babar in 1907, which found villages heavily armed against attack. The anonymous author of a report published in the popular contemporary magazine *Eigen Haard* writes of the great surprise they experienced encountering walls that were 'built of stone 2m high and topped with a 2 m high bamboo fence with stakes in between' (1907:795). The force was also warned by the local Dutch official that booby traps of caltrops and pitfalls lay all around stone walls (*Eigen Haard* 1907:794). In the villages of Babar they encountered a large number of guns, with each village yielding up dozens of rifles. The authorities saw these as unnecessary, given the absence of large dangerous animals in the islands, and confiscated them. Pacification was further imposed by giving troublesome villages a few weeks to move out of their inaccessible walled villages and move to the coast, where they would not be tempted to resist the rule of the 'company', as the locals still called at the time. The 1907 expedition also captured the difficult access to villages due to the steep ascents which led up to the walled villages (Figure 10.6).

Figure 10.6. The landward gate of Wakpapapi, Babar, Babar Islands, with a steep ladder leading up to the palisaded stone wall.
Source: *Eigen Haard* 1907:797.

Figure 10.7. Gate over the stone wall of Lawawang village, Marsela, Babar Islands.
Source: Wilhelm Müller-Wismar 1913 © Museum für Völkerkunde Hamburg.

Figure 10.8. Stone wall palisaded with bamboo around Latalola village, Marsela, Babar Islands.
Source: Wilhelm Müller-Wismar 1913 © Museum für Völkerkunde Hamburg.

The German linguist and ethnographer, Wilhelm Müller-Wismar, visited the islands in 1913 and took multiple photos, taking in the fortifications around villages, particularly on the island of Marsela, that show striking similarities with those described for other parts of southern Maluku. Figure 10.7 shows a man-height wall built up with stones; the wall is topped with a gate with wooden doors led up to by steep steps; stakes are embedded in the top of the walls, presumably used for attaching palisading in times of war. Figure 10.8 shows another village surrounded by a stone wall topped with an extensive bamboo palisade and reinforced with piles of logs stacked on the wall. These images show that, although pacification had begun at least in 1907 on Babar Island itself, the traditional fortified village pattern persisted beyond that for some time still.

Leti and Luang island groups

Located in the southeastern corner of southern Maluku, directly adjacent to Tutuala on the eastern tip of Timor, the islands of Leti, Moa, Lakor, Luang and Sermata are also recorded as having their traditional villages fortified. Riedel describes the walls as imposing structures of considerable height and thickness with similar palisades and gates as found in other island groups:

> Most villages are located on isolated knolls or outcrops of coral stone, 20 to 50 m above sea level, and surrounded by a stone wall, *lutru*, three meters tall and one meter thick with two to four entrances or gates, which are closed in times of danger. (Riedel 1886:379)

> Around each village on [on Luang and Sermata] there is a stone wall, *lutru*, 2.25 m in height and 2 m thick. Entry is via two gates, one at the front and one at the rear. The majority of villages are located close to the sea but at some elevation, and where possible in the vicinity of a water source. In the past, bamboo fortifications and caltrops, *hoora*, were placed around them in time of war. (Riedel 1886:317–318)

Figure 10.9. A Letinese walled village in the top right-hand corner of the frontispiece of Barchewitz (1751).
Source: Barchewitz 1751.

It is for islands in this group that we have the earliest account of village fortification. Ernst Christoph Barchewitz was a German in the service of the Dutch East India Company (Vereenigde Oostindische Compagnie, or VOC) stationed on the island of Leti between 1714 and 1720. His travelogue of 1751 provides the first depiction of a stone wall surrounding a village in southern Maluku (Figure 10.9). In his 1730 work he describes the walls as ubiquitous due to the perpetual state of war between villages:

> Directly to the east … surrounded by a strong wall, was the village of Leyduttun. All the villages of Leti had such walls for their protection, because the local rulers were always at war with one another. These walls were made of large flat stones, and provided with holes for shooting. Neither chalk nor lime was used in their construction, the dry stones simply being placed on top of one another. (Barchewitz 1730:212–213)

Fortification continued to be a prominent feature of Leti and Moa in the nineteenth century, with Bosscher (1854:436) remarking that the villages 'could almost be called small forts, untakable for an indigenous enemy'. Still in the early twentieth century De Vries (1900) remarked on the strange walled villages of Leti, similar to those on Tanimbar:

> Toetoekai and Lehoelele are the strangest villages one can imagine. Here are the same fortresses that I had already seen on Tanimbar, but now with the difference that having entered through the gate, one sees nothing but walls! The only access to the village, which is perched up on a rock plateau, is by a staircase leading to the gate. This gate is so narrow that the sedan chair in which I was sitting, an ordinary armchair, could pass through only with difficulty. There are two such gates in the stone wall that surrounds the whole stronghold.
>
> Having squeezed through this entrance, one sees a street ahead, lined on both sides by high walls over which, upon my arrival, the heads of curious inhabitants fleetingly appeared, only to duck away again fearfully.
>
> Behind those walls are the parts of the village which are separated again by stone barriers; and in order to be extra safe, everyone is also protected in the same way. (De Vries 1900:600)

Despite the fact that it appears to have had enormous regional influence (Pannell 2007), there is very little ethnographic or historical documentation of the Luang island group. No descriptions of traditional walled villages on the islands beyond that in Riedel (1886) have been located. Pannell (2007:91) notes the remains of traditional villages are still evident today as a series of multi-terraced, stone-walled compounds on hilltops. Müller-Wismar photographed one of these villages (Figure 10.10), but it is not known whether it was still inhabited at the time.

Kisar and the northern arc of Barat Daya Islands

Kisar and the northern arc of Barat Daya Islands (Roma, Damar, Teun, Nila and Serua) form a loose island chain southwest of the area under discussion. Perhaps with the exception of Kisar, they were out-of-the-way places that have altogether less relevant historical documentation than the other places discussed thus far. Nonetheless, here too we find clear, albeit limited, descriptions of fortified villages.

Figure 10.10. Hilltop fortified village on Luang Island.
Source: Wilhelm Müller-Wismar 1913 © Museum für Völkerkunde Hamburg.

As always, Riedel (1886) is helpful, explicitly stating, even for the remote Roma, Teun, Nila and Serua islands, that villages were fortified with stone walls. For the islands of Kisar and Damar, he provides more information including the local names of the walls (my bolding):

> The villages (*lete*) on Damar are built on the tops of hills, ringed with stone walls, **lutur,** and governed by *orlete* or chiefs and headmen. These chiefs have little influence, however; the heads of the individual houses or families do not permit meddling in their private disputes, which can lead to war. (Riedel 1886:463)

> The old villages [on Kisar], in so far as they have not been destroyed, are ringed by stone walls 5 m in height and 2m thick. These villages have thirty or more houses and are called *heruke lalaape* 'big villages', as distinct from the *heruke tataane* or temporary forts located on flat lands. (Riedel 1886:422)

While Riedel suggests that fortified villages were in decline on nineteenth-century Kisar, they nonetheless remained prominent in the landscape. Jacobsen (1896:118) notes that some hilltop villages still had walls at the end of the nineteenth century. In 1891, when Bassett-Smith visited Damar, the traditional pattern of village fortification was still practised, with each village being 'enclosed by dry-stone wall, having a wooden ladder for means of entrance and exit' (Bassett-Smith 1894:136). The Siboga zoological and hydrological expedition of 1899–1901 through eastern Indonesia photographed these stone walls around some villages on Damar (Figure 10.11). Pannell (1991) observed the remains of stone walls (*lutruni*) surrounding old villages on Damar but makes no mention of any particular cultural significance they may have had.

Figure 10.11. Wulur village on Damar island enclosed by a stone wall visible behind villagers.
Source: Siboga Expedition 1900 © University of Amsterdam Library.

The southern Maluku village fortification pattern

In the descriptions and depictions in the previous sections, a common pattern of traditional fortified settlement across southern Maluku has emerged: villages on hilltop and/or cliff-edge locations encircled by high stone walls with narrow gated entrances, often hidden and only accessible by steep ladders or stairwells that could be dismantled, barricaded and/or booby trapped in times of danger. Across the region, these protective stone walls were made of rough blocks of coral stacked to several metres, often extended in height by bamboo palisades and spotted with holes through which approaching enemies could be shot at. Within villages, numerous smaller walls were frequently present to prevent an invading enemy from storming the village too easily. The villages fortified by these stone walls existed within the context of a highly fragmented political landscape in which the many small polities were in a state of near perpetual warfare with one another. The protecting stone walls occupied an important place in society, offering substantial protection against indigenous forces. They were widely treated by villagers as living entities, provisioned with food and clothing.

The sources we have looked at make clear that fortified villages existed already in the early eighteenth century in some parts of southern Maluku and persisted until Dutch pacification in the early twentieth century. This begin date aligns well with the available radiocarbon dates in eastern Timor, that suggest the widespread emergence of fortified settlements there occurred after the sixteenth century and into the seventeenth century (O'Connor et al. 2012:208–211). The coinciding timing suggests that village fortification in southern Maluku and eastern Timor were part of single historical movement, a point that is reinforced by the linguistic data in the following section.

A linguistic view on stone wall–building

The common pattern of village fortification found across southern Maluku is also reflected in language. In many of the descriptions presented in the previous section the reader will have observed the term *lutur* or similar, used for this protective stone wall. In this section, I apply historical linguistic methodology to throw light on the history of the term #lutuR and, in turn, on the history of the stone building.[5] I show that the evidence from language points to stone wall–building as having diffused across southern Maluku, including far eastern Timor.

One of the central tasks of historical linguistics is to determine the relatedness of languages and group them into families and subgroups of more closely related languages within those families. This is achieved through the application of the blandly named 'comparative method', a set of procedures in which a feature-by-feature comparison of two or more languages with common descent from a shared ancestor is made in order to extrapolate back and hence infer the properties of that ancestor. The principal (but not only) feature comparison that is made across languages to establish relationships is between phonemes, the minimally distinctive sounds of a language. Over time, words change in how they are pronounced. These changes do not typically occur to individual words in isolation; rather, the same sound (often under definable phonetic conditions) tends to change in a regular way across the entire vocabulary of a language. This is known as the principle of regularity of sound change. Languages that show a high degree of regular sound correspondences across numerous form-meaning pairings (words or morphemes with similar meanings) can be deemed related to one another.

Establishing the sound correspondences between related languages makes it possible to uncover further aspects of linguistic history in two ways that are relevant to us here. First, related languages that share sets of sound changes that are not present in other members of the family can be said to form a subgroup, a set of languages that share a common (low-level) ancestor. Knowing the subgroups of a language family and plotting them against geography helps us track the paths of migration and dispersal which populations of speakers have followed in the past. Second, the regularity of sound change also allows us to distinguish words with a common heritage from those that are borrowed. Where two related languages have words of similar meaning that can be related to each other by regular sound changes, that word is regarded as inherited from the common ancestor. Where two related languages have words of similar meaning with only irregular sound correspondences, it indicates that borrowing is likely involved.

The known instances of the term #lutuR are plotted in Figure 10.12.[6] These can be clearly divided into regional blocks on the basis of differences in semantics. In the western half of Timor and the islands to its north, members of the #lutuR set are verbs meaning to pile or stack up stones. In central Timor, members of the #lutuR set are nouns typically glossed as 'fence', but the items appear to denote any kind of man-made barrier demarcating portions of land. In the east of Seram, one language, Seram-Laut, has *lutur* for 'stone or coral fish trap' (Ellen 2003:163). Finally, across a dozen languages in southern Maluku we find members of the #lutuR set denoting walls made of piled-up stones, in some cases, specifically or especially, those around villages.

---

5   In this section, the symbol # marks a word that is not a reconstruction, but rather a generalisation across forms in an etyma set. The symbol * is reserved for words that are truly reconstructable to a protolanguage on the basis of the comparative method.

6   In compiling this data, I looked through sources and dictionaries from the region. This included many languages from the Nusa Tenggara Timur area that ultimately did not evidence a #lutuR word, e.g. Pampus (1999) on Lamaholot in the Solor archipelago, Onvlee et al. (1984) on Kambera on Sumba.

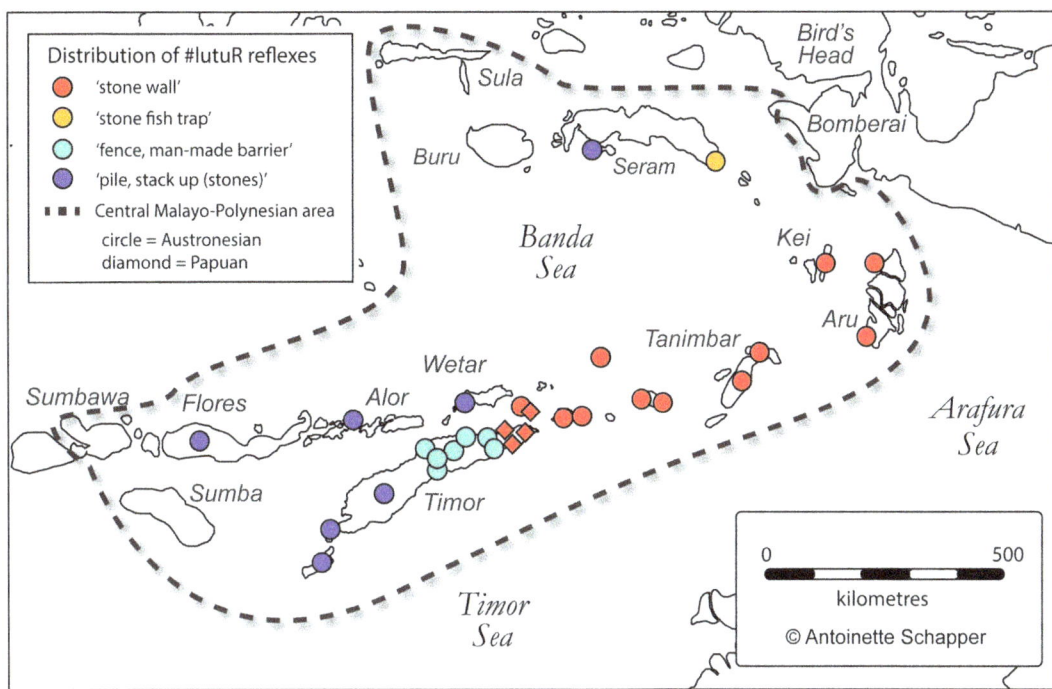

Figure 10.12. Distribution of #lutuR in Southeastern Wallacea.
Source: Antoinette Schapper.

With this last meaning, #lutuR is found is two unrelated families: Austronesian languages, a large family extending from Taiwan in the north to Madagascar in the west and Hawai'i and Easter Island in the east (Blust 2009), and the eastern members of Papuan languages belonging to the Timor-Alor-Pantar family, which is limited to southeast Wallacea (Schapper et al. 2014). Given that these families have no relationship with one another other than areal, this points to #lutuR having been borrowed from members of one family by the other. The direction of borrowing here is almost without doubt from the Austronesian languages into the Papuan languages. Instances of #lutuR are not found in the related Papuan languages of central Timor or Alor-Pantar, but rather are limited to those of eastern Timor and Kisar, adjacent to Austronesian languages evidencing #lutuR with the same sense (a point returned to below). To demonstrate that the term goes back to the common ancestor of the Papuan languages, we would need to find an instance of #lutuR in one of these other languages which form distinct primary subgroups of the family (Schapper 2017). The eastern Timor Papuan groups are, moreover, known to have adopted many cultural categories and associated vocabulary items from Austronesian society (McWilliam 2007).

Table 10.1. Proto-Malayo-Polynesian reconstructions around walls and their building.

*pager	'enclosure; palisade around a village; fence around a planted tree or cultivated field'
*qalad	'fence, wall'
*qatuR	'pave with stones; pile or stack up, arrange, order, put in sequence'
*susun	'stack up, pile in layers'

Source: Blust ACD.

Table 10.2. Austronesian languages with #lutuR 'stack, pile up stones'.

Language	Form	Meaning
Asilulu	lutu	'to arrange (stones) one on top of the other' (Collins 2003:61)
Ili'uun	lutu(r)	'pile up' (Josselin de Jong 1947:125)
UabMeto	lutumbatu	'steenen opstapelen' (Middelkoop n.d.)
Termanu	lutubatu	'steenen opstapelen, vooral onder een boom om er eene rustplaats van te maken; de opgestapelde hoop steenen' (Jonker 1908:335)
Helong	lutaŋ	'opstapelen' (Jonker 1908:335)
Kedang	lutur	'heap, pile, stack up, pile stones on [something]' (Samely and Barnes 2013:383)
Manggarai	katur	'menjusun batu2; susunan batu' < k-lutar 'pagar batu, susunan batu' Verheijen (1967:196, 254)

Source: See references throughout table.

Table 10.3. Austronesian languages with #lutuR 'fence, man-made barrier'.

Language	Form	Meaning
Tetun	lutu	'hedge, fence, enclosure, circular mud wall' (Morris 1984:135)
Tokodede	luto	'fence' Capell (1944:332–333)
Kemak	lutu	'fence' Capell (1944:332–333)
Mambae	luto	'fence' Capell (1944:332–333)
Dadu'a	lutu	'sebe, cerca viva, pagar' (Penn 2006:98)
Waima'a	lʔutu	'fence' (Belo et al. n.d.)
Naueti	ʔlutu	'fence' (Veloso 2016:135)

Source: See references throughout table.

Table 10.4. Austronesian languages with #lutuR 'stone wall'.

Language	Form	Meaning
Kei	lutur	'muur, e.g. *entutlutur* een muur stapelen' (Geurtjens 1921b:103)
Ujir	lutur	'susunan batu, benteng tradisional' (Handoko 2016:170)
	luti	to pile up stones, stone wall (Emilie T.B. Wellfelt pers. comm.)
West Tarangan	lutur	(*archaic*) stone fence, wall, to cover with stones (Rick Nivens pers. comm.)
Fordata	lutur	'gestapelde muur' (Drabbe 1932a:69)
Yamdena	lutur	'muur van opgestapelde steenen' (Drabbe 1932b:65)
Babar	lutur	'steenen muur … van twee tot drie meter hoog, tot twee meter breed' (Riedel 1886)
Central Marsela	lutur	stone wall around a village (Toos van Dijk pers. comm.)
	lukra	stone wall around the garden (Toos van Dijk pers. comm.)
Damar	lutur	'steenen ringmuur' (Riedel 1886)
	lutruni	'village wall' (Pannell 1991:80)
Wetan	lutri	'wall, especially the stone or coral wall round the village' (Josselin de Jong 1987:229)
Luang	lutru	'steenen muur … van 2.25 m hoogte en 2 m dikte' (Riedel 1886)
Leti	lutur ~ lutru	stonewall (Aone van Engelenhoven pers. comm.); 'muur van de negorij, benteng' (Jonker 1932:144)
Kisar	lukur	stone wall, including protective village walls and field garden boundaries (John Christiansen pers. comm.)

Source: See references throughout table.

Table 10.5. Papuan languages with #lutuR 'stone wall'.

Language	Form	Meaning
Fataluku	lutur(u)	any kind of construction involving the stacking of stones, including village and garden walls, dance places and graves (Aone van Englenhoven pers. comm.)
Oirata	lutur(e)	'village wall' (Josselin de Jong 1937:253)
Makalero	lutur	stone wall, including village walls and garden walls (Juliette Huber pers. comm.)
Makasae	lutur	stone wall (Juliette Huber pers. comm.)

Source: See references throughout table.

Yet, because #lutuR is not found outside of southeast Wallacea, we cannot account for it simply as a run-of-the-mill borrowing of an Austronesian etymon into Papuan languages. All the Austronesian languages outside of Taiwan share a common ancestor known as Proto-Malayo-Polynesian (PMP). There is a significant body of work on the history of Malayo-Polynesian languages, and an extensive vocabulary has been reconstructed for PMP. In the domain of wall-building, Table 10.1 gives the relevant reconstructions of PMP lexical items. Noticeably absent from this list is #lutuR, whose reflexes are set out in Tables 10.2, 10.3 and 10.4 according to semantics. There are two possibilities to account for the regional distribution of #lutuR in Austronesian languages: inheritance or diffusion.[7]

Inheritance would mean that this lexeme was innovated in a common ancestor to all the languages. Austronesian languages in this area have been claimed to all belong to the Central-Malayo-Polynesian (CMP) subgroup (Blust 1982/3, 1993) and the term could be traced back to Proto-Central-Malayo-Polynesian (PCMP). The CMP subgroup putatively takes in all Austronesian languages in the Minor Sundic Island Chain east of Bima spoken on the eastern half of Sumbawa, together with all of the islands of central and southern Maluku. Members of the #lutuR set are, however, not in evidence across the whole proposed CMP area. Rather they are limited to the southern arc of islands. And within this arc, languages reflecting #lutuR belong to a range of different primary subgroups of CMP that are not thought to be related to one another below PCMP.

The clustering of the different senses of #lutuR into geographic areas rather than according to subgroups further suggests areal diffusion is a significant factor for understanding the distribution of #lutuR. For example, the central Timor languages (i.e. Tokodede, Kemak and Mambae), which according to Hull (1998) form the 'Ramelaic' subgroup distinct from the other Austronesian languages of Timor, nevertheless use #lutuR in the same way as their nearest 'extra-Ramelaic' neighbours in the eastern half of Timor (e.g. Galoli, Waima'a, Naueti), that is, in the sense of 'fence, man-made barrier'. The areality rather than genealogy of these different semantic clusterings is also seen across familial boundaries. In Table 10.5 we see that the semantics of #lutuR terms in the eastern Timor Papuan languages conform with those of the neighbouring Austronesian languages in the southern Maluku region where village fortification was prevalent. This likely reflects adoption of the term for stone wall–building from that area.

An examination of sound correspondences likewise indicates that #lutuR has been borrowed across the Austronesian languages in the region often with the specific sense of a stone wall fortifying a village. Particularly telling in this respect is the appearance of doublets, two reflexes of the ultimately same ancestral word acquired through different historical routes.[8] In Ujir,

---

7   There is a third logical possibility: chance similarity. However, this is not considered here as the combined lexical and semantic similarities of the forms in Tables 10.1, 10.2 and 10.3 are clearly beyond chance.

8   English is well known for its doublets acquired through contact with other Indo-European languages. For example, *skirt* and *shirt* are both ultimately from Proto-Germanic *skurtjōn-, the former reflecting borrowing from Old Norse *skyrta* and the latter inheritance from Old English *scyrte*.

we find the doublet *lutur* meaning a stone wall fortification (Handoko 2016) and *luti*, which can be a noun meaning 'stone wall' or a verb 'to stack up stones' (Emilie T.B. Wellfelt pers. comm.). Word-final PMP *R is regularly reflected as /i/, as in Ujir *rengai* 'hear' <PMP *deŋeR; the presence of a final /r/ therefore marks Ujir *lutur* as irregular and marks it out as borrowed. By contrast, *luti* looks to be regular, with the loss of unstressed /u/ before /i/ expected. Central Marsela has a similar doublet: *lutur*, denoting a protective stone wall around a village, is irregular, with PMP *t having /k/ as its regular reflex in the language (e.g. *(wo)kel* 'three' <PMP *telu), and indicates that the idea of fortifying villages with a stone wall diffused from elsewhere; *lukra*, denoting a stone wall around the garden, by contrast, shows the expected sound change of PMP *t > /k/ and may be inherited or (seeing as the final /a/ is unexplained) at least borrowed at an earlier stage than *lutur*, before the *t > /k/ sound change took place. Thus, in both Ujir and Central Marsela, the word *lutur* shows clear signs of borrowing in the specific sense of stone wall used for fortification.

Not all languages with an instance of #lutuR show irregular sound correspondences. However, regularity does not rule out an item from being a borrowing. Borrowings can show regular correspondences where the sounds they contain are stable, as the consonants *l, *t and, to a lesser extent, *R tend to be in Austronesian languages in the area under consideration. A pertinent example is Dempwolff's (1938) reconstruction Proto-Austronesian *kuTa 'fortress'; reflexes of this item in Austronesian languages conformed to the established sound correspondences, even though it was known to be a borrowing from Sanskrit that diffused across Island Southeast Asia as part of the Indianisation that took place from around AD 300. That some of the Austronesian reflexes of #lutuR, particularly in the semantic set 'stone wall', show irregularities and that this form–meaning pairing is clearly borrowed into the neighbouring Papuan languages in eastern Timor indicates that the practice of building stone walls, including to fortify villages, diffused across southern Maluku.

Discussion

This paper has sought to add context, both geographical and historical, to the debate about the origins of fortified settlements in far eastern Timor. These village fortifications were part of a common pattern of traditional fortified settlement found across southern Maluku that already existed in the early eighteenth century in some parts of southern Maluku and persisted until Dutch pacification in the early twentieth century. The southern Maluku pattern of settlement fortification consisted of villages on hilltops and cliffs enclosed by stone walls with gated entrances, only accessible by steep stairs. The stone walls were made of rough blocks of coral piled up to several metres in height, often extended with bamboo palisading and surrounded by booby traps. The protecting stone walls of villages offered substantial protection against attack and were often viewed by indigenous peoples as living entities needing food and clothing.

Fortifying a village with walls of piled-up stone is not a radical technological innovation. Walled villages were found scattered about the Malay archipelago in the early modern period. What stands out in southern Maluku and far eastern Timor region is the united vocabulary which is used: #lutuR in the sense of 'stone wall' is used across the whole of the region. Elsewhere in Maluku we find borrowings from western Indonesia are used for stone walls (e.g. Malay *benteng*, ultimately from Min *hông sêng*; Malay *kota*, ultimately from Sanskrit *koṭa*). These terminologies are also found in West Timor and other parts of Nusa Tenggara Timor (e.g. Uab Meto *kot* 'fort' McWilliam 1996:142; Wersing *kot* 'defensive wall' Schapper field notes) as well as in the languages of the trading states of South Sulawesi (e.g. Makasarese *benteng*, *kota*, *lodji*, Cense 1979:932). Even if inspired by fortifications such as these to the west, the linguistics makes clear that the practice of building stone walls used in the fortification of villages spread across southern Maluku including into eastern Timor. The term #lutuR in the sense of 'stone wall' has diffused across the boundaries of the Austronesian and Papuan language families in the region and shows, through recurrent irregularity in sound correspondences, a pattern of borrowing between the Austronesian languages.

We have no accounts of the eastern Timor fortified villages at the time of their occupation. Looking at the southern Maluku villages gives us insights into the likely functioning and significance of village fortification within eastern Timor. Realisation that the eastern Timor fortifications are part of a wider regional pattern also places a question mark on the areally restricted social factors identified by O'Connor et al. (2012) and McWilliam (Chapter 6, this volume) as possible drivers of fortification in eastern Timor. Maize was not a significant crop in most of southern Maluku and so cannot have precipitated a population boom which saw an intensification in territorial warfare there. Similarly, southern Maluku was not a source for sandalwood. The impact of the remaining two factors, a new trade in firearms and a significant increase in demand for trade in human slaves, is difficult to determine. McKinnon questions whether warfare in Tanimbar was really exacerbated by the increased weaponry of the colonial powers:

> from early accounts and from accounts of contemporary Tanimbarese, one perceives that intervillage warfare was a persistent fact of life in the islands. Wars or, perhaps more properly, headhunting raids could be instigated by disputes concerning rights over land and reefs, or by disputes relating to intervillage thefts, adultery, murder or insults. (1991:7)

The historical accounts that we have seen from elsewhere in southern Maluku indicate that low-level warfare and raiding was a cultural practice, not caused specifically by resource scarcity but the normal way of life, with the smallest misdemeanours or offences occasioning violence. Schapper (2019) argues that in the seventeenth century Dutch naval aggression, in particular the massacre of the Bandanese in 1621, caused widespread fear amongst indigenous populations. This is put forth as a potential trigger for the spread in village fortification in southern Maluku, while endemic cultures of warfare meant the trend was continued once established.

This study, finally, highlights how the examination of linguistic data is an important analytical tool with which to deepen our understanding of processes of cultural diffusion. Comparing linguistic vocabularies for fortification in eastern Indonesia has shed significant light on a debate in the archaeological literature, identifying a region in which village fortification diffused widely between communities.

References

Barchewitz, E.C. 1730. *Allerneueste und wahrhaffte ost-indianische Reise-Beschreibung: … benebst e. ausführl. Land-Charte d. Sudwester- u. Bandanesischen Insulen, welche in anderen Land-Charten nicht gefunden, noch in denen Geographien beschrieben werden*. J. Christoph and J.D. Stößeln, Chemnitz.

Barchewitz, E.C. 1751. *Der Edlen Ost-Indianischen Compagnie der vereinigten Niederlande gewesenen commandirenden Officiers auf der Insul Lethy, Neu-vermehrte Ost-Indianische Reise-Beschreibung: Darinnen I. Seine durch Teutsch- und Holland nach Jndiengethane Reise; II. Sein eilff-jähriger Aufenthalt auf Java, Banda und den Südwester-Insuln, Glücks- und Unglücks-Fälle, seltsame Begebenheiten, auch remarquirte rare Gewächse, Bäume, Früchte, Thiere, Fische, Insecten, Berge, Vestungen, Nationen, Gewohnheiten, Aberglauben der Wilden, und viele andere Denckwürdigkeiten mehr; III. Seine Rück-Reise, der dabey erlittene grausame Sturm, und endlich glücklich erfolgte Ankunft in sein Vaterland, umständliche erzählet wird; Nebst einem vollständigen Register*. Johann David Jungnicol, Erfurt.

Bassett-Smith, P.W. 1894. Damma Island and its natives. *Journal of the Anthropological Institute of Great Britain and Ireland* 23:134–141. doi.org/10.2307/2842448.

Bataviaasch Genootschap van Kunsten en Wetenschappen 1874. Tractaat van vreedetusschen de Edele Oost-Indische Compagnie de negorijen van Oedjier en Gabel. *Notulen van de Algemeene en Bestuurs-Vergaderingen van het Bataviaasch Genootschap van Kunsten en Wetenschappen* 11:149–151.

Belo, M. da C.A., J. Bowden, J. Hajek, N.P. Himmelmann and A.V. Tilman n.d. *Glosáriu Waima'a Caisido*. Department of Linguistics, Ruhr-University, Bochum.

Blust, R. 1982/3. More on the position of the languages of Eastern Indonesia. *Oceanic Linguistics* 22/23(1/2):1–28.

Blust, R. 1993. Central and central-eastern Malayo-Polynesian. *Oceanic Linguistics* 32(2):241–293. doi.org/10.2307/3623195.

Blust, R. 2009. *The Austronesian languages*. Pacific Linguistics. The Australian National University, Canberra.

Bosscher, C. 1854. Statistieke schets der Zuidwester-eilanden. *Tijdschrift van het Bataviaasch Genootschap* 2:419–458.

Brumund, J.F.G. 1845. Aanteekeningen gehouden op eene reis in het oostelijke gedeelte van den indischen archipel. *Tijdschrift voor Nederlandsch-Indië* 15:39–89, 251–299.

Capell, A. 1944. Peoples and languages of Timor. *Oceania* 14(4):311–337. doi.org/10.1002/j.1834-4461.1944.tb00406.x.

Cense, A.A. 1979. *Makasaars–Nederlands woordenboek* [Makassarese–Dutch dictionary]. Nijhoff, The Hague.

Chao, C.-Y. 2008. A microregional approach to the social dynamics in the Late Prehistoric Manatuto, East Timor, 11th–18th century. Unpublished PhD thesis. University of Washington, Seattle.

Collins, James T. 2003. *Asilulu-English Dictionary*. Jakarta: Badan Penyelenggaraan Seri Nusa, Universitas Katolik Indonesia Atma Jaya.

Dempwolff, O. 1938. *Vergleichende Lautlehre des austronesischen Wortschatzes, Band 3: Austronesisches Wörterverzeichnis*. Dietrich Reimer, Berlin.

De Vries, J.H. 1900. Reis door eenige eilanden-groepen der Residentie Amboina. *Tijdschrift van het Nederlandsch Aardrijkskundig Genootschap* (2)XVII:467–502, 593–620.

Drabbe, P. 1932a. *Woordenboek der Fordaatsche taal*. A.C. Nix, Bandoeng.

Drabbe, P. 1932b. *Woordenboek der Jamdeensche taal*. A.C. Nix, Bandoeng.

Drabbe, P. 1940. *Het leven van den Tanémbarees: Ethnographische studie over het Tanémbareesche volk*. E.J. Brill, Leiden.

Eigen Haard 1907. Van een kleine expeditie. Beschrijving van de 'excursie' naar Babber (Tenimber-eilanden). *Eigen Haard* 50:794–800.

Ellen, R. 2003. *On the edge of the Banda zone: Past and present in the social organization of a Moluccan trading network*. University of Hawai'i Press, Honolulu. doi.org/10.1515/9780824844608.

Forbes, H.O. 1885. *A naturalist's wanderings in the Eastern Archipelago: A narrative of travel and exploration from 1878 to 1883*. Sampson, Low, Marston, Searle and Rivington, London. doi.org/10.5962/bhl.title.36489.

Geurtjens, H. 1921a. *Uit een Vreemde Wereld of het Leven en Streven der Inlanders op de Kei-eilanden*. Teulings 's Hertogenbosch.

Geurtjens, H. 1921b. *Spraakleer der Keieesche Taal*. Albrecht and Martinus Nijhoff, Weltevreden and 's Gravenhage.

Handoko, W. 2016. Situs pulau ujir di kepulauan Aru: Kampung kuno, islamisasi dan perdagangan. *Kapata Arkeologi* 12(2):163–174. doi.org/10.24832/kapata.v12i2.309.

Hull, G. 1998. The basic lexical affinities of Timor's Austronesian languages: A preliminary investigation. *Studies in Languages and Cultures of East Timor* 1:97–202.

Jacobsen, J.A. 1896. *Reise in die Inselwelt des Banda-Meeres*. Verlag von Mitscher and Röstell, Berlin.

Jonker, J.C.G. 1908. *Rottineesch–Hollandsch Woordenboek*. E.J. Brill, Leiden.

Jonker, J.C.G. 1932. *Lettineesche Taalstudiën*. A.C. Nix, Bandoeng.

Josselin de Jong, J.P.B. 1937. *Studies in Indonesian culture I: Oirata, a Timorese Settlement on Kisar*. Noord Hollandsche Uitgevers Maatschappij, Amsterdam.

Josselin de Jong, J.P.B. 1947. *Studies in Indonesian culture II: The community of Erai (Wetar) (texts and notes)*. Noord-Hollandsche Uitgevers-Maatschappij, Amsterdam.

Josselin de Jong, J.P.B. 1987. *Wetan fieldnotes: Some eastern Indonesian texts with linguistic notes and a vocabulary*. Foris Publications, Dordrecht.

Kealy, S., L. Wattimena and S. O'Connor 2018. A geological and spatial approach to prehistoric archaeological surveys on small islands: Case studies from Maluku Barat Daya, Indonesia. *Kapata Arkeologi* 14(1):1–14. doi.org/10.24832/kapata.v13i2.458.

Kolff, D.H. 1828. *Reize door den weinig bekenden zuidelijken Molukschen archipel en langs de geheel onbekende zuidwest kust van Nieuw-Guinea, gedaan in de jaren 1825 en 1826*. Bij G.I.A. Beijerinck, Amsterdam.

Lape, P.V. 2006. Chronology of fortified settlements in East Timor. *Journal of Island and Coastal Archaeology* 1(2):285–297. doi.org/10.1080/15564890600939409.

Lape, P.V. and C.-Y. Chao 2008. Fortification as a human response to late Holocene climate change in East Timor. *Archaeology in Oceania* 43(1):11–21. doi.org/10.1002/j.1834-4453.2008.tb00026.x.

McKinnon, S. 1991. *From a shattered sun: Hierarchy, gender, and alliance in the Tanimbar Islands*. University of Wisconsin Press, Madison.

McWilliam, A. 1996. Severed heads that germinate the state: History, politics, and headhunting in Southwest Timor. In J. Hoskins (ed.), *Headhunting and the social imagination in Southeast Asia*, pp. 127–166. Stanford University Press, Stanford.

McWilliam, A. 2007. Austronesians in linguistic disguise: Fataluku cultural fusion in East Timor. *Journal of Southeast Asian Studies* 38(2):355–375. doi.org/10.1017/s0022463407000082.

Merton, H. 1910. *Ergebnisse einer Zoologischen Forschungsreise in den Südöstlichen Molukken (Aru- und Kei-Inseln) im Auftrag der Senckenbergischen Naturforschenden Gesellschaft*. Senckenbergische Naturforschende Gesellschaft, Frankfurt am Main.

Middelkoop, P. n.d. Nederlands–Timorees Woordenboek. Unpublished manuscript. KITLV, Leiden.

Morris, C. 1984. *Tetun–English dictionary*. Canberra: Pacific Linguistics.

Nunn, P. 2007. *Climate, environment and society in the Pacific during the last millennium*. University of the South Pacific, Suva, Fiji.

O'Connor, S., M. Spriggs and P. Veth 2007. *The archaeology of the Aru Islands, Eastern Indonesia*. Terra Australis 22. ANU E Press, Canberra. doi.org/10.22459/ta22.2007.

O'Connor, S., A. McWilliam, J.N. Fenner and S. Brockwell 2012. Examining the origin of fortifications in East Timor: Social and environmental factors. *The Journal of Island and Coastal Archaeology* 7(2):200–218. doi.org/10.1080/15564894.2011.619245.

Onvlee, L., U.H. Kapita and P.J. Luijendijk 1984. *Kamberaas (Oost-Soembaas)-Nederlands woordenboek: met Nederlands-Kamberaas register*. Foris, Dordrecht.

Pampus, K.-H. 1999. *Koda Kiwa: Dreisprachiges Wörterbuch des Lamaholot (Dialekt von Lewolema)*. Franz Steiner, Stuttgart.

Pannell, S. 1991. Narrative boundaries, national horizons: The politics of identity in Amaya, Maluku Tenggara, Indonesia. PhD thesis. University of Adelaide, Adelaide.

Pannell, S. 2007. Of gods and monsters: Indigenous sea cosmologies, promiscuous geographies and the depths of local sovereignty. In P. Boomgaard (ed.), *A world of water: Rain, rivers and seas in Southeast Asian histories*, pp. 103–124. KITLV Press, Leiden. doi.org/10.1163/9789004254015_004.

Penn, D. 2006. Introducing Dadu'a: Uma línguade Timor-Leste. Honours Thesis. University of New England, Armidale.

Riedel, J.G.F. 1886. *De sluik- en kroesharige rassen tusschenSelebes en Papua*. Nijhoff., 's Gravenhage.

Samely, U. and R.H. Barnes 2013. *A dictionary of the Kedang language: Kedang-Indonesian-English*. Brill, Leiden.

Schapper, A. 2017. Introduction to the Papuan languages of Timor, Alor and Pantar. In A. Schapper (ed.), *Papuan languages of Timor, Alor and Pantar. Sketch grammars*. Volume 2, pp. 1–54. De Gruyter Mouton, Berlin. doi.org/10.1515/9781614519027-001.

Schapper, A. 2018. *Life and times in Ujir: A community sourcebook*. Yayasan Pustaka Obor, Jakarta.

Schapper, A. 2019. Build the wall! Village fortification, its timing and triggers in southern Maluku. *Indonesia and the Malay World* 47(138):220–251. doi.org/10.1080/13639811.2019.1554778.

Schapper, A., J. Huber and A. van Engelenhoven 2014. The relatedness of Timor-Kisar and Alor-Pantar languages: A preliminary demonstration. In M. Klamer (ed.), *Alor-Pantar languages: History and typology*, pp. 99–154. Language Science Press, Berlin. doi.org/10.26530/oapen_533875.

Tijdschrift voor Nederlandsch Indië 1858. Aroe-eilanden, in vroeger tijd en tegenwoordig. *Tijdschrift voor Nederlandsch Indië* 20:257–275.

van Dijk, T. 2000. Gouden eiland in de Bandazee: Socio-kosmische ideeën op Marsela, Maluku Tenggara, Indonesië. Unpublished PhD thesis. Leiden University, Leiden.

van Dijk, T. and N. de Jonge 1987. The house on the hill: Moieties and double descent in Babar. *Bijdragen tot de Taal-, Land- en Volkenkunde* 143(1):54–104. doi.org/10.1163/22134379-90003341.

Veloso, A. 2016. A grammar sketch of Naueti, a language of East Timor. MA thesis. Leiden University, Leiden.

Verheijen, J.A.J. 1967. *Kamus Manggarai: Manggarai-Indonesia and Indonesia-Manggarai*. Volume 1. Nijhoff, 's Gravenhage.

VOC Archives. VOC 3864, Banda, Secret letters, Report, Banda to Batavia, 4-6-1789, §12.

Conclusion and future directions

11

Surveys of fortified sites in Southern Wallacea

Sue O'Connor, Shimona Kealy, Andrew McWilliam, Sally Brockwell, Lucas Wattimena, Marlon Ririmasse, Mahirta, Alifah, Sandra Pannell, Stuart Hawkins, Mohammad Husni and Daud Tanudirjo

The chapters in this volume offer some insight into how widespread the phenomenon of fortification was throughout the Wallacean archipelago. Chapter 10, in particular, presents historical information and photographic records for a number of fortified settlements in Maluku, providing details on the number of houses they contained and the way in which they operated as defensive structures. This chapter presents additional commentary, locational information and photographic records of fortified settlements recorded during the course of general archaeological surveys on Sumba, Timor-Leste, Kisar, Babar and Wetang Islands (Figure 11.1), the nature of which will be explained in more detail below.

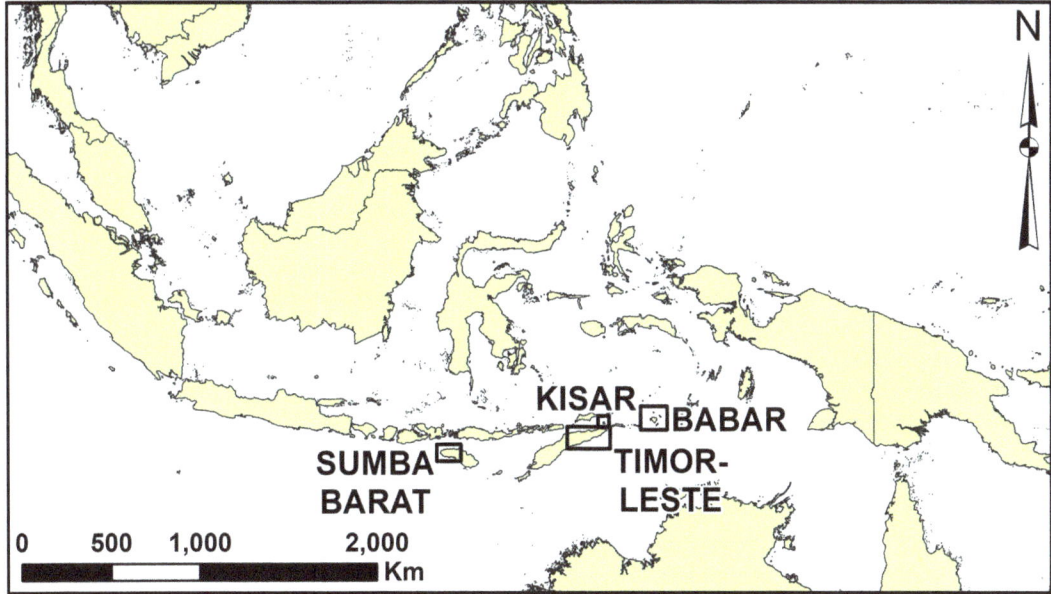

Figure 11.1. Map showing survey locations.
Source: Shimona Kealy, based on coastline data from: 'Global self-consistent, hierarchical, high-resolution geography database'. Version 2.3.7. Released June 2017 (Wessel and Smith 1996).

Fortified built structures discussed in this chapter have been documented in varying degrees of detail. For some, oral history of settlement use was collected, while for others a GPS location and photographic record was all the information obtained. On some islands, such as small Kisar, pedestrian survey of the uplifted limestone terraces rising from the coast within 1 km of the coastline was relatively comprehensive, with approximately 70 per cent of the periphery of the island covered. Our survey of the interior of the island, however, was much more *ad hoc* and areas surveyed were selected on the basis of information provided by local guides. Other areas of Kisar were surveyed using satellite imagery, which was made possible by the low density of vegetation cover. On Babar and Wetang Islands, and on the island of Sumba, the fortified structures described below were found incidentally during the course of fieldwork aimed at locating caves suitable for excavation. Survey of the landscape using satellite imagery failed to reveal fortified sites on these islands due to the dense tree cover and thus lack of ground visibility. On the larger island of Timor, intensive anthropological surveys were undertaken in limited areas, aimed primarily at recording oral histories about land ownership, genealogies, past land use and subsequent resettlement to coastal areas. Collectively these records highlight the remarkable diversity, but also the many shared locational and structural features, of fortified sites in Wallacea.

Fortified settlements in West Sumba

The western portion of Sumba Island was surveyed in the dry season of 2009 by a joint team from The Australian National University (ANU) and the Universitas Gadjah Mada (Sally Brockwell, Sue O'Connor and Daud Tanudirjo). We were based in the main town of Waikabubuk and took day trips by car to sites accessible by road and on foot. Our survey was not systematic or comprehensive due to the pressure of time. We were told about, or taken to, sites by knowledgeable locals and Dr David Mitchell, an Australian medical doctor who had lived and worked as a volunteer in West Sumba from 1968 to 1975, and who has visited often since then. As well as fortified settlements, we also recorded caves with occupation evidence, old villages, graves and coastal artefact scatters and middens. GPS locations and brief descriptions were recorded but no detailed measurements were taken (Figure 11.2; Table 11.1).

Table 11.1. Summary data on fortified sites in West Sumba.

No.	Kecamatan (subdistrict)	Site name	Location	Description	Findings
1	Wanukaka	Paletirua	Lat. -09.770° Long. 119.405° [1]Alt. 147 m	Large fortified village	Stone walls, megalithic tombs, *laca*, pottery
2	Wanukaka	Parimareha	Lat. -09.789° Long. 119.389° Alt. 121 m	Fortified village	3 houses, high stone walls
3	Wanukaka	Kulke	Lat. -09.792° Long. 119.388° Alt. 124 m	Fortified village on top of hill	4 houses, stone walls
4	Loli	Praigege	Lat. -09.554° Long. 119.453° Alt. 539 m	Old walled village on hilltop, large: ~200 m across	Many internal walls, broken graves, pottery
5	Loli	Kodarawa Watuoleate	Lat. -09.543° Long. 119.489° Alt. 514 m	Old site on hilltop above village, small	Very rocky. 2 graves
6	Laratama	Wei Malado	Lat. -09.461° Long. 119.414° Alt. 504 m	Fortified village	Very overgrown, walls, spirit house, graves

Note: [1] Approximate altitude.
Source: Authors' summary.

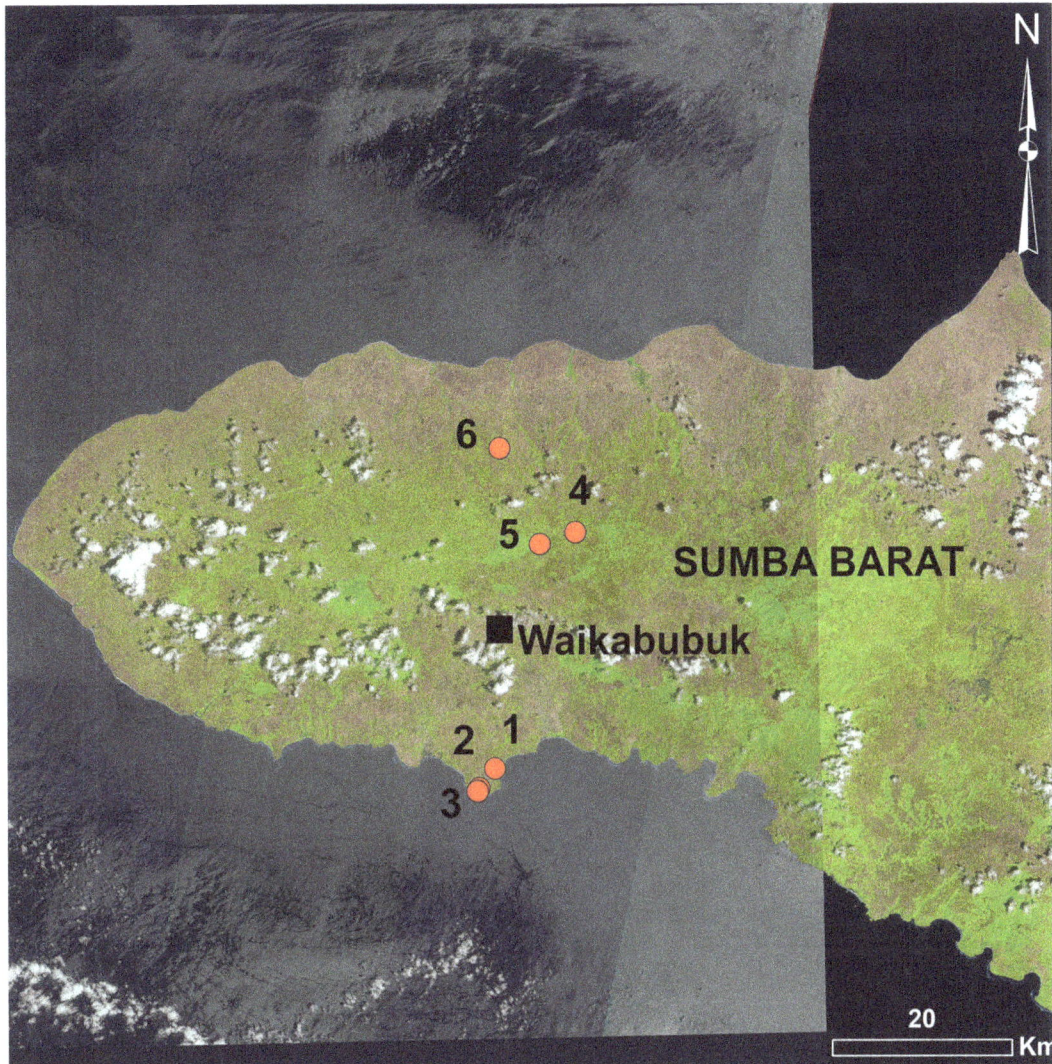

Figure 11.2. Map showing the location of identified fort sites in Sumba Barat (West Sumba).
Sites are numbered based on Table 11.1.
Source: Satellite image from the Sentinel-2A satellite (2019-12-13) obtained from the Sentinel Data Hub (European Space Agency 2019).

The fortified sites described below are all located in defensive positions on hilltops or high cliffs above the sea (Table 11.1; Figure 11.3).

1. Rua is an area with coastal clifftop villages. We visited three villages here, Paletirua, Parimareha and Kulke. Paletirua is a large village with many houses surrounded by stone walls. There is *Pandanus* growing out of them, which is perhaps a defensive feature. The village is located on a steep cliff, 147 m above sea level. It contains many megalithic tombstones and a *laca*—a small open space, which serves as an antechamber prior to accessing the main internal compounds (Figure 11.3). There was pottery by the entrance, including some red slipware.

2. Parimareha is a small village with three houses surrounded by high stone walls. The locals say that it is old.

3. Kulke is a small village with four houses. It is located on top of a hill surrounded by stone walls. At the end of the road next to it, there are steep cliffs rising out of the sea.

4. Praigege is a village on top of a hill at an elevation of 539 m, overlooking the valley in a southerly direction back towards Waikabubuk. It is surrounded by extensive stone walls that are now damaged. It contains internal stone walls as well. There are many degraded graves, also broken, with a *laca* in front of the graves. There is much pottery on the surface. The site was very overgrown so visibility was poor, but it appears that it is extensive, about 200 m across. Our guide told us the village had been abandoned for 100 years.

5. Kodarawa Watuoleate is an old settlement located at an elevation of 514 m on a rocky hilltop above the present-day village. There used to be walls but the stone has been removed to fence the gardens below. The two graves it contains have been looted; however, they are still regarded as being sacred and are mentioned in *adat* (customary law and practice) songs.

6. Wei Malado is an abandoned site in the forest at an elevation of c. 500 m. The whole site was overgrown and ground visibility is poor. It contains a spirit house, monumental tomb stones and the remains of a wall with stone slabs. There are as many as 10 clan tombs here.

Figure 11.3. Paletirua fortified village.

A. Paletirua high walls; B. Praigege walls; C. Paletirua view to sea; D. Paletirua entrance; E. Praigege tombs; F. Paletirua megalithic tombs.

Source: Photos courtesy of Sally Brockwell.

David Mitchell recounted an incident that occurred in West Sumba in 1998 (Dibley 1999), which may recall inter-clan conflicts in past times when forts were actively used as defensive positions against raiding parties. The Loli and Wewewa clans are related through marriage, and share in common churches, schools and businesses, despite some disagreements over land boundaries. Although usually peaceful, on 5 November, 2000 Wewewa men, dressed in traditional cloths and headbands and armed with spears, machetes and rocks, marched on Waikabubuk in the Loli Valley. The Wewewa were acting in reprisal against a Loli mob who had attacked them and looted their houses the previous week as the result of an out-of-control demonstration against local government corruption. The raiding Wewewa stormed into Waikabubuk but were met with an opposing Loli force defending Kampung Tarung, the traditional mother village of the Loli district, standing on the hilltop above the modern town, guarding the rice fields below. The Wewewa were routed, 26 people died from machete wounds and many houses were burnt. Police were sent in and peace was restored quickly by the provincial authorities. However, the incident demonstrates the intensity and sensitivity of inter-clan rivalry even into modern times, and emphasises the necessity for defensive strongholds in the past when there was no higher power to impose order.

Fortified settlements in Timor-Leste

This Timor-Leste compilation brings together the research of a number of contributing authors, completed over a series of exploratory visits to different areas of the territory between 2009 and 2013, and always accompanied by knowledgeable local guides. The listing includes fortified sites identified by local people but not visited by researchers. Table 11.2 presents this data in summary and includes general location information and brief commentary on significance and site features.

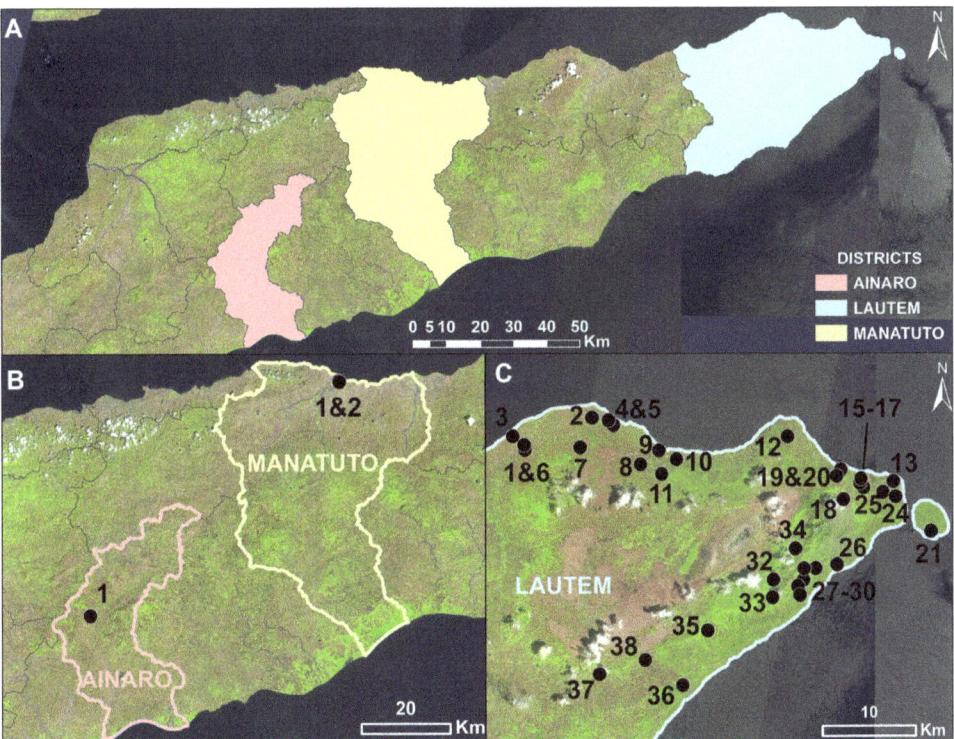

Figure 11.4. Map of fortified sites located in Timor-Leste.

A. Location of the three districts discussed here; B. Sites identified in Ainaro and Manatuto Districts—numbers corresponding to Table 11.2; C. Sites identified in Lautem District—numbers corresponding to Table 11.2.

Source: Satellite image from the Sentinel-2A satellite (2019-12-07) obtained from the Sentinel Data Hub (European Space Agency 2019).

Ainaro District

The Subago fortified settlement in Ainaro was recorded in May 2010 by Sue O'Connor, Sally Brockwell, and Sandra Pannell. Our local guide, Mateus Anaral, said that there used to be houses built inside the walls and that his grandparents were born there. The remnants of large thick walls are still visible on the southern side of Subago (Figure 11.5A) where there was a single narrow entrance. Several stone 'altars' were observed (Figure 11.5B), including one used during the corn harvest to ensure that the crop is abundant.

Figure 11.5. Ainaro survey at Subago.
A. Remnant wall; B. Altar.
Source: Photos courtesy of Sue O'Connor.

Manatuto District

In 2010, two poorly preserved fortified settlements were recorded within the boundaries of the modern township of Manatuto (Figure 11.4C). The survey was carried out by Sally Brockwell, Sandra Pannell, Sue O'Connor, Estefan Guterres and Guterres Karlilo. Other fortified sites were located on the road between the townships of Manatuto and Laclo but these were not explored in any detail as they had been previously recorded by Chou (2013).

Sau Huhun (Galoli) or Sau Tutun (Tetun) (Chou 2013 provides the name Saututo for this fort) is located on the highest point of the ridgeline overlooking the Manatuto Pousada (rest house) (Figure 11.6). The walls of Sau Huhun could scarcely be made out in places, and we were told that the stone had been removed to build the *pousada*. Remnant walls occurred around the east, north and west perimeters. The east and west walls could be traced by a low line of rocks. The walls on the west side were a mixture of built-up soil and rock. Inside the walls in the area where we presume the houses would have been constructed, we located Chinese tradeware, earthenware pottery and marine shells (Figure 11.7).

Figure 11.6. Views towards Manatuto from the remains of the Sau Huhun fortification, showing its defensive position.

Source: Photos courtesy of Sue O'Connor.

Figure 11.7. Sau Huhun fortification.
A. Sally Brockwell pointing to remnant of wall at northern end of the fort; B. Estefan Guterres walking along earth and rock wall remnant; C. Earthenware sherds, broken Chinese Blue and White tradeware and marine shellfish on the surface at Sau Huhun.
Source: Photos courtesy of Sue O'Connor.

On the hilltop opposite the Banda Maria shrine is another fortified settlement with remnant walls. The hill is called Iliheu Tatua (Galoli, *ili* = village, *heu* = new, and *tatua* = old). According to our guide Guterres Karlilo, the hilltop was the former site of a village that was later moved to the edge of the river Meta Laclo during the time of the Indonesian occupation from 1975 to 1999. Remnants of the base of a thick wall on the south side indicate that it was built using two roughly parallel rows of stone infilled with earth. At the base of this hill is a place where there was previously an altar with skulls (Figure 11.8; see Chapter 1, this volume) and in the past fragments of human cranium could still be seen near a large flat stone at this location (Guterres Karillo pers. comm.). They have now disappeared, either taken by people or decayed.

Figure 11.8. Iliheu Tatua hill.
A. Photograph taken in 1913 showing altar with skulls; B. The same view in 2010. The skulls and altar are no longer present.
Source: Photo A by António Nascimento Leitão, courtesy of Natural History and Science Museum of University of Porto, register number MHNC-UP-FCUP-IA-AF-775; Photo B courtesy of Sue O'Connor.

Lautem District

The data in Table 11.2 only reveals a partial view and for the most part focuses on five administrative villages in Lautem municipality (Figure 11.4D). They include Moro-Parlamento, Com, Mehara, Tutuala and Muapitine. A full survey of Lautem itself would likely produce several times this number. Analysis of the named forts, Macapainara (Ili Vali) and Vasino (Moro-Parlamento) are given fuller treatment in Chapters 2 and 4 of this volume and are not addressed here in detail.

During June 2009 surveys were undertaken of the Tutuala area including the Vero River valley and associated forested lands on the seaward side of the Paichao mountain range.[1] The purpose was to locate and undertake visits to a sample of the fortified settlement sites in the region and begin a process of documenting the range and variation found amongst them.

A large number of fortified sites are located in Tutuala subdistrict (see Lape 2006). One of these is the massive fortification Mapulu, located on a forested hilltop in the upper reaches of the Vero River valley, to the south of the current settlements of Cailoro and Vero (Tutuala subdistrict) (Figure 11.4D). The northeastern side of the fort is strategically located on a limestone cliff with a massive dry stone wall providing a secure inner perimeter. A series of low outlying ring walls extend outward on the lower slopes, with large standing stones providing defensive posts. Access to the fort is via a sloping path lined by 4 m high stone walls, including apertures that allow defenders to observe and fire upon intruders, probably with Portuguese-style matchlock muskets or local copies that were in general use from the sixteenth century (Lieberman 2009:422). They were equipped with a trigger mechanism to ignite a gunpowder charge that fired a projectile. The muzzle-loading muskets were unwieldy but lethal when on target, and keenly sought along with gunpowder as a trade item of choice in the eastern islands. The gateway to the fort features a *laca*. Within the fort, the internal space is divided into two general living areas that contain a series of old stone graves (*calu luturu*) and separate open ritual spaces (*sepu*) (Figure 11.9).

According to local knowledge, the full name of the fort is Mapulu Ro Malae. The phrase references a number of groups who resided there and continue to maintain relations of sacrificial veneration to the ancestral presence in the site. This occurs at least annually on the Catholic holy day of All Souls' Day (2 November), known as *vaci i huma'ara*, when relatives visit to clean the graves and ritual spaces and present offerings of candles, betel nut and food to the ancestors. Renu Ratu is the customary land owner (*mua ocawa*, landlord) and responsible for overall site protection. Another group of customary owners of the site is the clan Kukulori, of which the former Falintil guerrilla resistance leader, Konis Santana, was an integral member who found refuge in the site during the armed struggle for independence. Local custodians of the site recall one historical occasion when they fought off the attack of a Portuguese figure, Kiri Kiri (Gregorio) Maulaka, who had marched from Lorehe and attacked the fort with a large contingent of soldiers. They held large boulders above the access path and when the enemy approached the fort they cut the ropes and crushed many of the soldiers. The internal space of Mapulu contains a ritual altar stone (*tei*), that represents the spirit guardian of the land to which offerings and invocations are directed when assistance is sought by the living group of members.

---

1   The Vero valley survey was undertaken Sue O'Connor, Andrew McWilliam, local guides Mario Dos Santos Loiola, Joao Dos Santos and Martinho Dos Santos, and state forestry officers.

Figure 11.9. Mapulu Ro Malae.
A. Perimeter wall; B. Standing stone; C. Entrance to fort; D. Ancestral graves and sitting area.
Source: Photos courtesy of Andrew McWilliam.

A second example of fortifications in the Tutuala area is the hilltop fort Hi Maka Loli, which is located to the northeast of Mapulu fort and immediately south of the main administrative centre of Tutuala. The fortified site has remnant stone walls and a damaged stone gateway that leads to a double internal space. There are numerous large stone graves with pre-Christian headstones (*na otu*) to which sacrificial offerings are made. The ground has extensive scatters of porcelain and tradeware and includes a ritual dancing area with elevated sitting stones (graves) around the space.

According to local knowledge, the fort (*pa'amakolo*) is the historical site for the Vacumura paternal origin group, who moved here following the arrival of their ancestors in Timor-Leste. They maintained trade relations with external visitors and recall using João beach on the north coast of Tutuala as a site where trading and exchange occurred. Over time, as the Vacumura group flourished and expanded, the area became too crowded (*matete*, narrow, crowded). The group largely dispersed to the west, towards the 'wide lands' (*mua maluere*) of Los Palos.

Figure 11.10. Maiana tomb.
Source: Photo courtesy of Andrew McWilliam.

Access to the Vero River valley area is possible via a well-trodden footpath that leads from the settlement of Vero (Tutuala) past the forested hilltop fort of Mapulu, through a series of swidden gardens. It then follows the slope of the Vero River course towards the coast. On the lower reaches of the river, our group visited a range of ancestral locations, including a series of former fortified residential sites that are located at prominent elevated locations on the forested slopes between the Pai Chao mountains and the southeast coast (for extended discussion see Fitzpatrick et al. 2012:160–164).

Fortified sites visited in the Vero valley include Haka Paku Leki, Ili Haraku, Maiana and Pailopo (see Table 11.2 below), all of which were occupied until the early twentieth century but remain important places for ancestral veneration. Each of these sites reflects structural accommodation to the physical properties of the sites, which were often built on existing rocky outcrops and atop cliff faces. Ili Haraki, near the base of the Pua Loki mountain, for example, is fashioned out of a massive rockpile with tactically placed dry stone walls to effect a secure perimeter.

Maiana is one of the smaller fortified sites we recorded. It is situated on a forested hilltop and surrounded by a broadly circular stone wall of substantial proportions. The defensive perimeter also includes areas of spiky cactus (prickly pear) that served as another form of barrier against attack in the past. Maiana is located in the western part of the Vero region close to the historical boundary (the river, *Verkass ver*) that separated the lands of Fataluku clan groups Renu Ratu and Latuloho Ratu based in the adjacent village of Muapitine. The fort site itself is associated with the clan group Aca Cao, which took over from a former group, Pai'ir Ratu, which died out. The site features a large (3 x 1.5 x 1 m) rectangular grave decorated with dressed stone in the style known as '*Makassar mataru*'—Makassar stone (Figure 11.10; also see McWilliam et al. 2012). It sits adjacent to a *sepu* ritual ground in the usual style of the region. There is no local record of previous fighting at the site.

Figure 11.11. Ili Kere Kere, a small overhang on a sheer cliff face in the Tutuala area with stone wall and dancers.

Source: Photo courtesy of Andrew McWilliam. See also Table 11.2 #13.

Table 11.2. Summary data on fortified sites in Timor-Leste, numbered by district and corresponding to Figure 11.4.

No.	Subdistrict	Site name	Location	Description	Notes & significance
AINARO DISTRICT					
1	Ainaro	Subago	Lat. -08.97743° Long. 125.50146° Alt. 1059 m On hilltop next to Ainaro town	Fortified village with large wall on the south side and a single exit and entrance.	Has several stone altars which include one used during corn harvest.
MANATUTO DISTRICT					
1	Manatuto	Sau Huhun	Lat. -08.30936° Long. 126.00586° Alt. 72 m On top of hill, opposite and looking to Manatuto Pousada.	Old Settlement; Has walls on E, W and N sides but only low line of rocks remaining.	Chinese tradeware, pottery, marine shellfish on surface.
2	Manatuto	Iliheu Tatua (name of hill)	Lat. -08.51457° Long. 126.01263° Hilltop opposite Bunda Maria shrine.	Old settlement with altar, remnants of wall on S side.	At the base of the hill skulls are placed above a stone altar; marine shellfish and pottery seen on surface.
LAUTÉM DISTRICT					
1	Moro-Parlamento	Vasino or Wasino	Lat. -08. 36475° Long. 126.93531° Alt. 245 m On the southern edge of Moro settlement in the hill above the north coast (see Chapter 4, this volume).	Site has a large stone grave that is reported to be a group burial tomb (*Poku caru*, to open the basket). Used in living memory but no longer due to Church disapproval.	Former major centre for Pai'ir (Moro) Ratu (also known as *Kota lulunu*). Fort built as result of outbreak of warfare following arrival of Portuguese. Authority granted to related rival group in Lautem. (Uruha'a Ratu—Dom Paulo). José le Sumalai was last 'king' of Vasino before people moved.

11. Surveys of fortified sites in Southern Wallacea

No.	Subdistrict	Site name	Location	Description	Notes & significance
2	Moro-Parlamento	Vasaku	Lat. -08.33500° Long. 126.99935° Alt. 115 m	*Parma kolo*. Has intact walls up to 1.5 m. Only one wall remains. Has double grave.	
3	Moro-Parlamento	Laulau Lokotu	Lat. -08.3520° Long. 126.9237° Alt. 40 m On the eastern side of the road to Moro from coast.	A semi-fortified site overlooking rice fields on the coast.	Said to be dwelling place before relocation to Vasino. Original name of Moro is *Pai Sapolo*. Most stone repurposed to make road to Moro during Portuguese times.
4	Moro-Parlamento	Masui	Lat. -08.33731° Long. 127.01489° Alt. 85 m Beside road west of the settlement of Ira Ara (west of Com).	Fort has been partly dismantled with remnant walls and entrance stones standing (see O'Connor et al. 2012).	Kati Ratu owner of area but fort long abandoned. Site has prominent wooden structure—said to be burial (see Figure 1.4). Graves with 2 uprights. Fort said to have been built by magical means (*masino*).
5	Moro-Parlamento	Ira Ara	Lat. -08.341797° Long. 127.019384° Alt. 100 m Near Ira Ara village, adjacent to large spring and main road to Com.	See Lape et al. (Chapter 3, this volume).	Old site formerly built by Cailoro Ratu who married daughter of Kati Ratu in a classic example of a stranger king mythology (Sahlins 1985:87).
6	Moro-Parlamento	Ira Cao	Lat. -08.36022° Long. 126.93450° Alt. 167 m Directly above church in modern village of Moro, SE of and above the freshwater spring.	Low walls less than 1 m high, as stone has been reused for buildings in modern village. Stone walls and graves overgrown.	Old fortified settlement. Chronological period unknown but used before and into Portuguese times.
7	Moro–Nari area	Ili Fanu, Apa Fanu	On high slopes to the south of Soekili village, Nari.	Fortified site. Not visited.	Little information—Kati Ratu likely (see Viegas and Feijó 2019).
8	Com area	Lor Lafae	Overlooking the port of Com to the east of Etepiti settlement, 1 km inland.	Strategic fortified site. Extensive area of limestone cliffs and walled areas. A number of significant graves.	Fortified settlement of Konu Ratu—main group of Com, which historically controlled trading at the port/anchorage (McWilliam 2007a).
9	Com area	O'o Lo Kon	Lat. -08.3652° Long. 127.0633° Alt. 65 m Immediately above the beach and overlooking the harbour of Com.	Walled site with numerous stone graves.	Early fortified site for Konu Ratu who historically controlled trade in the port (see McWilliam 2007a).
10	Com area	Ili Vali	Lat. -08.37344° Long. 127.08045° Alt. 200 m On bluff overlooking coast 3 km east of Com.	Walled site with extensive internal areas of graves, dancing ground and other features. Developed on two levels (see Chapter 2, this volume).	Main fortified settlement of Fara kati Ratu (*Macapainara-Serevairara*). Appointed Koronel by Portuguese (18th C.). Moved to near coast became Mua Pusu village. In 1976 forcibly relocated to Com by Indonesian military.
11	Com area	Loho Matu Lata	About 2 km above the coast and Mua Pusu settlement area. East of Com.	Strategic fortified location overlooking forested slopes to the coast below.	Large number of old graves, *tei* altars and crumbling stone walls. Actively managed by Loho Matu community in Com.

No.	Subdistrict	Site name	Location	Description	Notes & significance
12	Luikere area	N/A	North of Mehara settlement (east of Com).	Fortified settlement. Not visited.	Former stronghold of Kapitan Ratu.
13	Tutuala–Mehara; northern area	Ili Kere Kere	Lat. -08.393911° Long. 127.289482° Alt. 250 m Clifftop fortified cave site.	Series of overhangs with sheer cliffs on eastern side, partitioned by stone walls (see Figure 11.11) with rock art and sacrificial altar.	Mythic settlement site of Tutuala Ratu. Origin settlement that had mythic large wax candle that attracted seafaring settlers to Timor. Massive stone walls used for defence partition space into three sections (see O'Connor et al. 2011:49–52 for additional detail).
14	Tutuala–Mehara; northern area	Lorilata Namilata	South of Ili Kere Kere.	Walled site with cliffs on eastern side. Has graves, *sepu* ritual ground and sacrificial post (*sikua*).	Tutuala Ratu defensive site. Former fortified residence of Tutuala Ratu. See Pannell (2006) for discussion.
15	Tutuala–Mehara; northern area	Hi Maka Loli	Lat. -08.39967° Long. 127.26070° Alt. 410 m Prominent peaked hill and sheer cliff south of Tutuala kota.	Fortified site with internal graves and porcelain scatters. Front gateway damaged. Fine example of *sepu*.	Owned by Vacumura Ratu. Origin settlement before moving west. All Vacumura Ratu once lived here.
16	Tutuala–Mehara; northern area	Cailoro Lata	Lat. -08.39556° Long. 127.25703° Alt. 350 m Site is proximate to local school in Tutuala near the main church.	Now largely dismantled, rock of the fort was used to build the Tutuala Pousada guest house and police station following Portuguese pacification campaign in 1902.	Formerly a major fortified site. War skulls and *tei* altar in small cave below western cliff of site. Cailoro traded with Makassar at João on the northern coast.
17	Tutuala–Mehara; northern area	Haro	Lat. -08.23.484° Long. 127.15.493° Alt. 376 m Close to current Tutuala Pousada.	Fortified site with damaged walls. See Lape (2006) for sequence and Pannell (2006) for history of use.	Site of former residence of Tutuala Ratu who were moved here in the 1920s when the Portuguese built the *pousada*.
18	Tutuala–Mehara; northern areas	Mapulu Ro Malae	Lat. -08.41049° Long. 127.24127° Alt. 405 m (GPS for entrance to inner walled compound). On forested hill at the top of the Vero River catchment.	Fort has a series of low outer ring walls with standing stones as defensive posts. Massive inner walls and extensive internal spaces.	Formerly three groups lived there: Mapulo Ratu (Renu), Kiki Moru (Koavaca Ratu) and a subsidiary group, Ro Malae. Internal layout reflects these divisions.
19	Tutuala	Jasa Lata	Lat. -08.383117° Long. 127.238650° Alt. 274 m	Fortified settlement with very large walls. Visited with Pedro Morais.	–
20	Tutuala–Mehara; northern areas	Lo Chami	Lat. -08.388783° Long. 127.234683° Alt. 300 m On elevated ridge and hilltop, south of Aldeia Iyoro.	Fort not visited—not permitted—they only attend on All Souls' day/night (*i vaci huma'ara*). Walled site with cliff on one side (see Lape 2006).	Ancestral site for Koavaca Ratu and Paiuru Ratu and former residential site during times of warfare.

11. Surveys of fortified sites in Southern Wallacea

No.	Subdistrict	Site name	Location	Description	Notes & significance
21	Tutuala–Jaco Island	Lai Vai	Lat. -08.4398° Long. 127.3254° Alt. 50 m On southern area of Jaco Island and c. 700 m inland from coast.	Fortified site. *Adat* platform and *tei* stone. Site visited with Orlando Sanchez.	1st walled settlement on Jaco Island. Zenlai Ratu accredited with ownership of former fort before moving to the mainland (*mua lafae*, Timor).
22	Tutuala–Jaco Island	Pitilete	On Jaco Island.	Fortified site. 2nd walled settlement on Jaco Island after Lai Vai.	Zenlai Ratu accredited with ownership of former fort before moving to the mainland (*mua lafae*, Timor).
23	Tutuala–Jaco Island	Honolati	On Jaco Island.	4th walled settlement on Jaco Island after Lai Vai.	Zenlai Ratu accredited with ownership.
24	Tutuala-Valu-Jaco	Lopo Malai	Lat. -08.407850° Long. 127.291567° Alt. 175 m Near Lene Hara Cave, above Valu Beach.	Crumbling remnant fort. Small walled compound. Much of the stone has been repurposed.	Ma'a leki Ratu claims ownership of area—(*mua hocavaru*) Ma'a Leki and Zenlai Ratu controlled trading ports at Mua Cao *pasaré* and Lopo *malar(u)*, (Valu Beach) respectively and received *hiaré* (landing fees). See Lape (2006).
25	Tutuala-Valu-Jaco	Muacao	Lat. -08.40372° Long. 127.27949° Alt. 320 m Near Lene Hara.	Crumbling circular stone settlement. Walls not intact as stone has been repurposed to make garden walls.	Zenlai Ratu moved to this place when they left Lene Hara.
26	Tutuala-Vero River valley, southeast of Paichao Range	Pati-patinu	Lat. -08.4707° Long. 127.2351° Alt. 100 m On elevated bluff overlooking Jaco Island.	Not visited.	Keveresi Ratu—now nearly died out. Mythic place where the land was divided among 14 groups (Pannell pers. comm.) who had settled from outside.
27	Tutuala-Vero River valley, southeast of Paichao Range	Haka Paku Leki	Lat. -08.47427° Long. 127.21465° Alt. 248 m Limestone rocky outcrop to the southeast of the Paichao Range.	Strategic semi-fortified site; has extensive elevated defensive walls lower down and rises to a narrow shelf overlooking the southeast coast. Scatters of pottery on highest points.	The mythical strategic fortress of Renu Ratu, which dominated this area of Ponta Leste.
28	Tutuala-Vero River valley, southeast of Paichao Range	Ili Haraku	Lat. -08.48510° Long. 127.20291° (GPS for inner wall near the gateway.) Alt. 257 m On the upper slopes to the immediate southeast of Paichao Range.	Large fortified site with extensive dry walls. Large cliff face to the east. Inner and outer walls with gateways. Site inhabited in living memory—probably until World War II.	Historically linked to Renu Ratu and their warrior allies Aca Cao Ratu. Recalls wars against Marapaki and Zenlai Ratu who attacked the fort. Renu leader killed, but Aca Cao resisted and forces eventually withdrew. Boundary on the coast between Sere Moko and Sere Lafai.
29	Tutuala-Vero River valley, southeast of Paichao Range	Serelau	Located in hill between coast and Paichao Range, nearby and to the north of Ili Haraku.	Fortified site with stone walls but not sighted. Not visited.	Current owners live in Aldeia Vero (Tutuala). Serelau Ratu (see Fitzpatrick et al. 2012).
30	Tutuala-Vero River valley, southeast of Paichao Range	Maiana	Lat. -08.49096° Long. 127.19747° Alt. 300 m Located east of Ili Haraku as a free-standing hill.	Smaller fortified site with circular walls surrounding a large stone (non-Christian) grave. Massive walls surrounded by prickly pear cactus.	Formerly Aca Cao Ratu granted to Pai'ir Ratu. Large grave with fine Makassar stone-dressed finish (*Makassar mataru*) (see McWilliam et al. 2012). Grave of a Paiuru Ratu close to boundary between Renu Ratu and Latuloho Ratu (Muapitine) at the creek, Verkass Ver.

No.	Subdistrict	Site name	Location	Description	Notes & significance
31	Tutuala-Vero River valley, southeast of Paichao Range	Pai Lopo	Located to the south of Maiana towards Ili Mimiraka and boundary with Pai Chao Ratu land.	Not sighted.	Aca Cao Ratu place.
32	Muapitine–Malahara and southern forests	Pari Loho	Lat. -08.485102° Long. 127.174104° Alt. 500 m Southwest of Malahara settlement 5-6 km in dense secondary forest.	Extensive stone walled fortified site overgrown with large *Ficus* trees.	Part of the lands of Pai Chao Ratu. Former inhabitants (*Kua Mai* Ratu) left the area many years ago. Used as jungle camp by both Falintil and Indonesian TNI[1] soldiers during occupation.
33	Muapitine–Malahara and southern forests	Veter(u)	Located on 'little Pai Chao'. Eastern side of Paichao Range.	Massive limestone outcrop with steep cliffs around much of the structure and stone walled sections. Large double grave site for sacrificial veneration.	Mythological landing site of Pai Chao Ratu, seagoing *perahu* now fossilised and embedded in the land. To the south another walled structure—known as Lamira—former settlement of subsidiary (Paca-Kanaluri) group.
34	Muapitine - Malahara and southern forests	Nofitu	Lat. -08.456269° Long. 127.195125° Approx. GPS Alt. 680 m On prominent hill between Lake Ira La Laru and Pualoki (Paichao mountains).	Fortified sites. Not visited.	Mythic settlement associated with Cailoro Ratu and referring to the morning star (venus, *noi_ipi*). Another related site not located: *No Kafa*.
35	Muapitine - Malahara and southern forests	Mua Pitine Irinu	On upper reaches of Aramoko creek. Located in hills due south of current Mua Pitine settlement.	Reported to be large fortified site. Not visited.	Latu Loho Ratu is the land owner (*mua ho cavaru*). When threatened by 1902 Portuguese campaign, surrendered without losses. Remained inhabited for many years.
36	Muapitine–Malahara and southern forests	Pehe	In elevated position south coast, western side of Aramoko creek.	Not visited. The fort is an ancestral settlement of current members of Lupuloho hamlet in Suco Muapitine.	1908 residents relocated to a road connecting to Lorehe and then moved *en masse* to Los Palos in 1976 by Indonesian army. Key owners are Pui Rili, Aca Cao, Paraluki and Naja Ratu. People still attend rituals and annual *meci* (sea worm) harvest there—footpath to Muapitine (see McWilliam 2007b).
37	Muapitine-Los Palos and southern forests	Belta Tres	In hills 4 km south of Los Palos.	Fortified site. Not visited, Fataluku owners now resident in urban Aldeia of Los Palos, known as Ira Ara. Relocated during occupation.	Members of Ira Ara were staunch supporters of independence and active in armed resistance. Fortified site remains an important place for refuge and sacrificial veneration.
38	Muapitine-Los Palos and southern forests	Lereloho	In the forested hills 3-4 km south of Los Palos.	Fortified site. Not visited. Fataluku owners now resident in urban Aldeia of Lereloho. Relocated during occupation.	Members of Lereloho active in independence struggle and clandestine resistance. Fortified site and general area still regularly frequented.

Note: [1] TNI = Tentara Nasional Indonesia, the Indonesian National Military.

Sources: Authors' summary, see also references throughout table.

Fortified sites on the island of Kisar, Maluku Barat Daya, Indonesia

Kisar was surveyed over two field seasons in 2014 and 2015 by a joint team from ANU, Universitas Gadjah Mada and Balar Arkeologi Maluku. A number of abandoned fortifications were located in open elevated positions, as well as in caves/shelters, during archaeological reconnaissance of the island (Figure 11.12; Table 11.3).

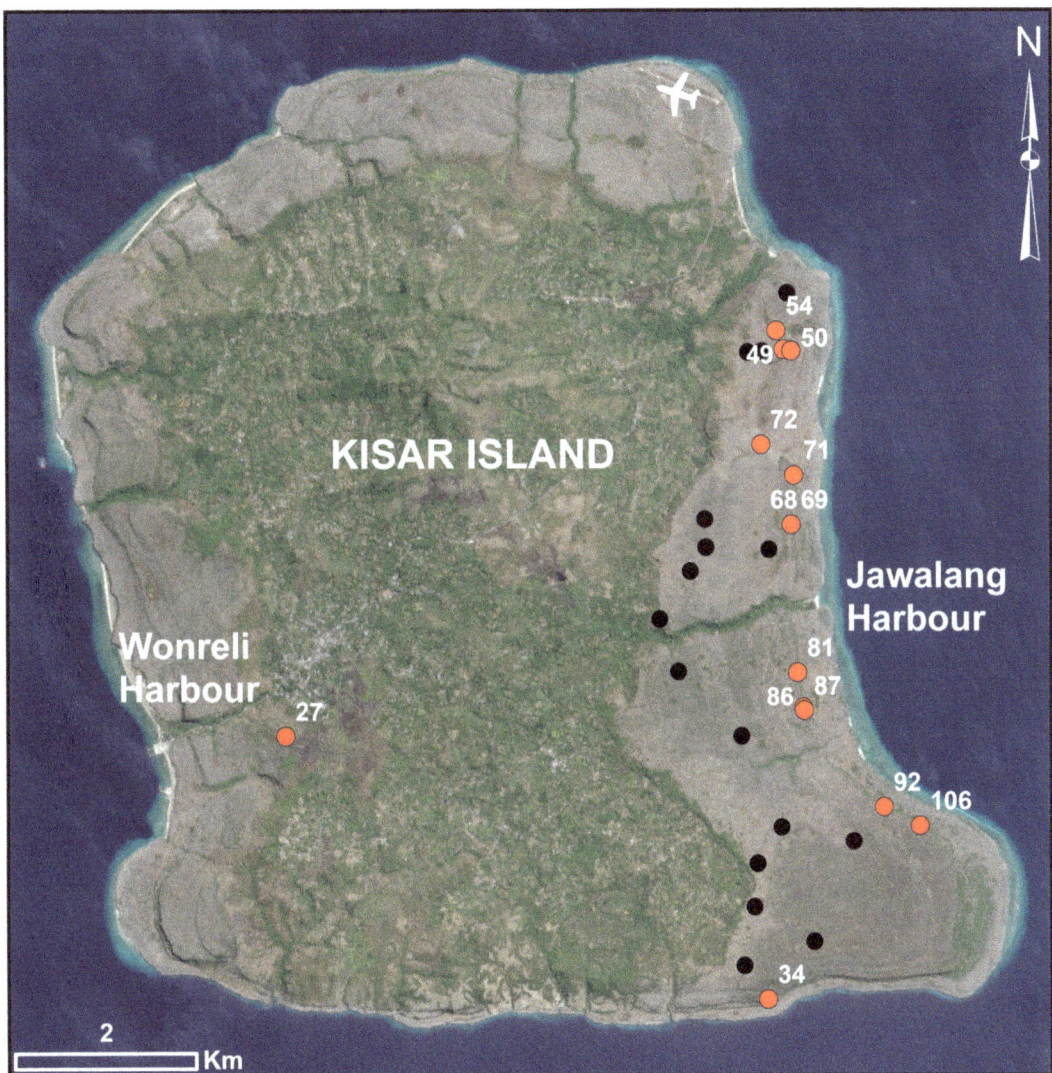

Figure 11.12. Map showing the location of identified fort sites on Kisar island.

Sites identified during pedestrian survey of the island are shown in red and numbered based on their KSR codes (see Table 11.3). Likely additional fort sites identified during remote-sensing surveys (but not yet ground truthed) are shown in black.

Source: Satellite image from the Sentinel-2A satellite (2019-07-10) obtained from the Sentinel Data Hub (European Space Agency 2019).

In 2014, five fortified sites were recorded in Kisar: KSR 27, 34, 49, 50 and 54. KSR 27 is located on the highest point of the hill overlooking the modern town of Wonreli to the north and Wonreli Harbour to the west. Although it would once have had impressive walls, only remnants of these remain today. The walls appear to follow the highest points of the contour of the hill. Local informants stated that the stone from the walls had been reused for other structures after the settlement was abandoned. Features which are probable graves and remnant stone house bases were observed within the walls; however, much of the surface of the hilltop was obscured by dense vegetation.

KSR 34 is a cave that contains a stone altar. Oral history indicates that it was used as a defensive location by local people until World War II, although there is no evidence of stone walling to support this.

KSR 49 is a very large fortification (c. 0.02 km^2/>15,000 m^2) in an open hilltop location (Figure 11.13) with massive fortified stone walls (Figure 11.14). Based on local reports and our satellite survey of the island, KSR 49 is likely to be the largest fortification of its type preserved on the island. Known as the Pur Pura Negeri Lama, it is said to be the original location of the Pur Pura (or Pura Pura) village, now located about 2 km inland to the west. The Pur Pura Negeri Lama is situated atop a bastion of the third limestone terrace (Figure 11.13A). Approximately half to three-quarters of the walls are built along the edge of the terrace cliffs, which rise c. 10 m above the plain and thus are naturally protected by the steep drop-off in elevation (Figure 11.13B). The walls extending up from the cliff edge are similar in construction to those of the Negeri Lama visible to the south (KSR 72), but reach heights of c. 2 m. As well as KSR 72, another fortification slightly to the southwest was clearly visible, however, due to time constraints we were unable to visit it. Later satellite surveys strongly suggest a similarity in design between this Negeri Lama and KSR 49 and 72 (see Figure 11.12 remotely sensed sites).

Figure 11.13. The view from Loi Puru Ula looking north (left) towards the Pur Pura Negeri Lama (KSR 49—indicated), and the view from the Pur Pura Negeri Lama south towards Loi Puru Ula (KSR 68 and 69).
Source: Photos courtesy of Shimona Kealy.

Along the portion of the Pur Pura plateau not edged by steep cliffs, dramatically larger walls have been built (Figure 11.14). Not only do these stone walls reach heights of up to c. 4 m, but they are between 1 and 5 m thick and contain chamber-like areas within the walls (see Figure 11.14C). Narrow passageways allow entrance to the central part of the settlement (Figure 11.14A and D), which contains numerous stone features. For example, KSR 50 is a megalithic complex of shaped and dressed stones positioned in the centre of the KSR 49 fortification, but was recorded as an individual site, as it was enclosed by a separate walled enclosure. The complex includes collapsed menhir-like standing stones (Figure 11.15), and large circular stones of a fine-grained sedimentary rock, which are shaped and dressed and remarkably similar in shape and size to those found in fortified settlements in neighbouring Timor-Leste (McWilliam et al. 2012).

11. Surveys of fortified sites in Southern Wallacea   267

Figure 11.14. The Pur Pura Negeri Lama (KSR 49) showing the significant heights of the walls (A, D); extensive stonework (B) and chambers within the main wall dividing the headland (C).
Source: Photos A and D courtesy of Marlon Ririmasse; photos B and C courtesy of Shimona Kealy.

Figure 11.15. Fallen megalithic standing stones from the old Pur Pura village complex (KSR 50), located within the Pur Pura Negri Lama fortifications (KSR 49).
Source: Photos courtesy of Marlon Ririmasse.

KSR 54 is a very large cave extending into the same limestone terrace upon which KSR 49 is constructed (Figure 11.16). It contains the remnants of carved wooden posts (Figure 11.16B) which were said by our local guides to be part of an old fortified village, however it was unclear if these structures were built within the cave itself or came from the open fortified village KSR 49. KSR 54 did not have evidence of thick walling suggestive of a fortification.

Figure 11.16. Cave (KSR 54) (A) below the Pur Pura Negri Lama containing carved timber post (B).
Source: Photos courtesy of Marlon Ririmasse.

Located just over 600 m north of the Jawalang rock art locality (O'Connor et al. 2018) and 860 m north-northwest of Jawalang Harbour are several fortifications in the Loi Puru Ula locality (KSR 68, 69 and 71). This area consists of a series of largely interconnecting limestone shelters that are located approximately 4 m up the cliff face of the limestone terrace. The floors of these shelters, a number of walls and connecting gateways, and a remarkable staircase to access them all, are positioned at the entrance of KSR 68 (Figure 11.17). The walling and staircase have been constructed from significant quantities of stonework. The staircase, in particular, rises approximately 4 m to reach the shelter floor, is about 1 m wide, and extends an estimated 3 m along the face of the cliff.

Figure 11.17. Loi Puru Ula 1 (KSR 68) fortified rock-shelter with altar (A: viewer's left) and rock wall from base of cliff to the lip of the shelter floor, forming a staircase for access to the site (A: viewer's right). The rock-shelter has a commanding view of the plain below (B).

Source: Photos courtesy of Shimona Kealy.

For the purpose of discussion, we have split the Loi Puru Ula site into its three main shelters, the southern (KSR 68), central (KSR 69) and northern shelters (KSR 71), which are each identifiable by their size and the presence of a stone altar. These three are, however, connected or semi-connected by narrow ledges and smaller shelters. The staircase rises to the floor of the southern shelter and then extends as a raised platform that broadens the shelter floors to the north. Within the southern shelter is a stone altar, built as a semicircular stone wall in the north corner, with a small pillar in the centre of an earth platform (Figure 11.17A). This altar still appears to be of significance today as our guides spent a moment in consultation when we first entered the site, before proceeding to show us around.

Travel to the central shelter (KSR 69) is made significantly easier through the extension of the top of the staircase to the north (Figure 11.18A). This remarkable construction is made from a large accumulation of stone in a wall up the almost vertical cliff of the terrace to the lip of the shelter floor, thereby extending the internal living space. At the floor level, large naturally flat slabs of stone have been placed so as to enlarge the pathway and interconnected concavities of the shelters by about 1 m of flat paved floor. There is a stone wall approximately 0.5 m high separating the central and northern shelters with a small, stepped gateway built-in to provide access between the two (Figure 11.18B). The northern shelter is most notable for the large altar present, constructed of a single large stone slab approximately 1 m² positioned atop smaller stone supports. The surface of the altar has a few small pits, likely formed as a result of grinding (e.g. nuts). The northern most extent of the Loi Puru Ula shelters ends in a squared stone wall about 0.5 m high.

Heading north from the Loi Puru Ula locality, there are a number of hills rising out of an open plain between Loi Puru Ula and the Pur Pura Negeri Lama (Figure 11.13). Approximately 750 m north-northwest of Loi Puru Ula (as the crow flies), situated on the top of one of the central hills, is the remains of an old fortification known as Nomaha Negeri Lama (KSR 72; Figure 11.19). Oral tradition states that this is the old village of Nomaha, now located about 1.5 km inland to the west. A stone wall around 1 m in height follows the topography, and completely encircles the hilltop (Figure 11.19B). Although small in size (c. 650 m²), this centrally located hill has a commanding view of the plain, while its steep sides, topped by the final obstacle of a stone wall, makes access difficult and would have presumably provided its inhabitants with a significant defensive advantage in the event of an attack (Figure 11.19A). From the Nomaha Negeri Lama, there is a view north (c. 1 km) to Pur Pura Negeri Lama (KSR 49).

Figure 11.18. Loi Puru Ula 2 (KSR 69) showing the paved extended shelter floor (A) and stone wall with gate separating the different shelters along the terrace (B).

Source: Photos courtesy of Shimona Kealy.

Figure 11.19. Nomaha Negeri Lama (KSR 72) view from plain looking north-northwest to the hilltop where the fortification is located (A), and the view of the stone wall looking north (B).

Source: Photos courtesy of Shimona Kealy.

South of Jawalang Harbour following the terrace, a series of caves and fortifications were identified during surveys undertaken in 2015. The most northerly of these, Kota Lama 1 (KSR 81), consisted of a cave with fortifications enclosing the northern and southern ridgeline of a ~30 x 10 m extended area of the terrace platform in front of the cave (Figure 11.20). Like many of these fortifications, the site overlooks a large area of the plain below (Figure 11.20B).

Approximately 400 m south of KSR 81, one of the cave sites, Worletiwuru (KSR 86), is partially fortified through the construction of a stone wall. On the south side of the cave a built stone wall forms the northern side of another fortified platform similar to KSR 81, which the locals identified by the name 'Sokon' (KSR 87). The southern walls of Sokon were particularly interesting for the zig-zag pattern by which the walls were constructed to maximise alignment to the terrace ridge (Figure 11.21).

Figure 11.20. Jawalang Selatan Kota Lama 1 (KSR 81) showing stone wall with entrance (A) and the commanding view of the plain to the south-southeast (B).

Source: Photos courtesy of Stuart Hawkins.

Figure 11.21. Sokon (KSR 87) fortification showing stone walls following the ridge (A) with 'z'-shaped constructions (B, in detail).
Source: Photos courtesy of Stuart Hawkins.

Figure 11.22. Jawalang Selatan Kota Lama 2 (KSR 106).
Source: Photo courtesy of Stuart Hawkins.

Further south from KSR 86 and 87, the terrace cliff curves slightly from an easterly facing aspect to a more northerly one. It is along here that Ilese Weraa (KSR 92) and Jawalang Selatan (south) Kota Lama 2 (KSR 106) were located, approximately 450 m apart. Ilese Weraa is an elevated cave with stone arrangements, while KSR 106 is a small, circular fortification on the terrace edge, built of uniformly dark stone (Figure 11.22) and located less than 1 km from the southeastern tip of the island.

Kisar is particularly promising for future fort survey and archaeological study as remote survey of the island using satellite imagery in Google Earth Pro V 7.3.2.5491 (2018a) identified at least 16 additional sites that match the unique features of the open Negeri Lamas identified during the brief ground surveys (see Figure 11.12 remotely sensed sites).

Table 11.3. Summary data on fortified sites in Kisar.

[1]KSR No.	Region	Site name	Location	Description	Findings
27	Wonreli Hill	Negeri Lama Katrow Wakrow	Lat. -08.07879° Long. 127.1603° [2]Alt. 121 m	Old fortified settlements	Grave structure, fragments of pottery.
34	Oirata	Oirata Cave	Lat. -08.10466° Long. 127.2087° Alt. 44 m	Cave with altar	Oral history says this was occupied until World War II.
49	Pur Pura Village	Pur Pura Negeri Lama	Lat. -08.04156° Long. 127.2112° Alt. 54 m	Fortified village	Gate with stone walls.
50	Pur Pura Old Village	Megaliths	Lat. -08.04152° Long. 127.2115° Alt. 54 m	Erected stone and dolmen complex	–

¹KSR No.	Region	Site name	Location	Description	Findings
54	Below Pur Pura Negeri Lama	Pur Pura Negeri Lama Cave 2	Lat. -08.03954° Long. 127.21° Alt. 49 m	Large cave below Pur Pura Negeri Lama	Wood statue said to be part of the old fortified village.
68	Loi Puru	Loi Puru Ula 1	Lat. -08.05843° Long. 127.2114° Alt. 39 m	Fortified shelter	Stone walls, staircase and altar with stone upright. Said to be used for defence against raiding clans.
69	Loi Puru	Loi Puru Ula 2	Lat. -08.05843° Long. 127.2114° Alt. 39 m	Fortified shelter	Stone floor, stone altar, stone gate with step.
71	Loi Puru	Loi Puru Ula 4	Lat. -08.05362° Long. 127.2117° Alt. 40 m	Fortified shelter/cave	Evidence of habitation, such as marine shell and stone wall built inside cave.
72	Loi Puru	Nomaha Negeri Lama	Lat. -08.05062° Long. 127.2083° Alt. 54 m	Negeri Lama	The old fortified settlement of Nomaha.
81	Jawalang Harbour South	Kota Lama 1	Lat. -08.07283° Long. 127.2119° Alt. 43 m	Negeri Lama	Fortified ridge.
86	Jawalang Harbour South	Worleti-wuru	Lat. -08.07628° Long. 127.2125° Alt. 41 m	Fortified cave	Stone wall.
87	Jawalang Harbour South	Sokon	Lat. -08.07656° Long. 127.2126° Alt. 40 m	Negeri Lama	Fortified ridge.
92	Jawalang Harbour South	Ilese Weraa	Lat. -08.08599° Long. 127.2207° Alt. 40 m	Elevated cave	Stone arrangements.
106	Jawalang Harbour South	Kota Lama 2	Lat. -08.08782° Long. 127.2244° Alt. 41 m	Small fort	Small, circular fortification near terrace edge.

Notes: [1] The KSR numbers refer to the complete archaeological survey of the island, thus some numbers are missing from this sequence. [2] Approximate altitude.
Source: Authors' summary.

The Babar Island group

Fortified settlements in the Babar Island group were located by a joint ANU and Balar Arkeologi Maluku team composed of Sue O'Connor, Shimona Kealy and Lucas Wattimena during fieldwork in October 2017 (Table 11.4). The survey was not specifically aimed at locating fortified settlements but was a general reconnaissance for archaeological sites (Kealy et al. 2018). Old fortified settlements in this group were referred to by local guides and landowners as Negeri Lama. One potential Negeri Lama locality was identified atop the north plateau on Wetang island, based on the presence of stone structures and because of its location (#6). A number of larger, significantly better preserved, Negeri Lama sites were identified on Babar Besar Island, all on the east coast with a single exception near the village of Manuwuy in the north (Figure 11.23). The forts have thick stone walls, sometimes up to 1.5 m wide and reaching 2 m high with entrance and exit 'gateways'. The walls of the forts are of varying height; those close to modern settlements and garden areas have often had stone from the walls removed to make modern garden walls or for other construction. The site near Manuwuy (#27) is the clearest example of this and thus the most poorly preserved of the Negeri Lamas visited in the course of the Babar group survey.

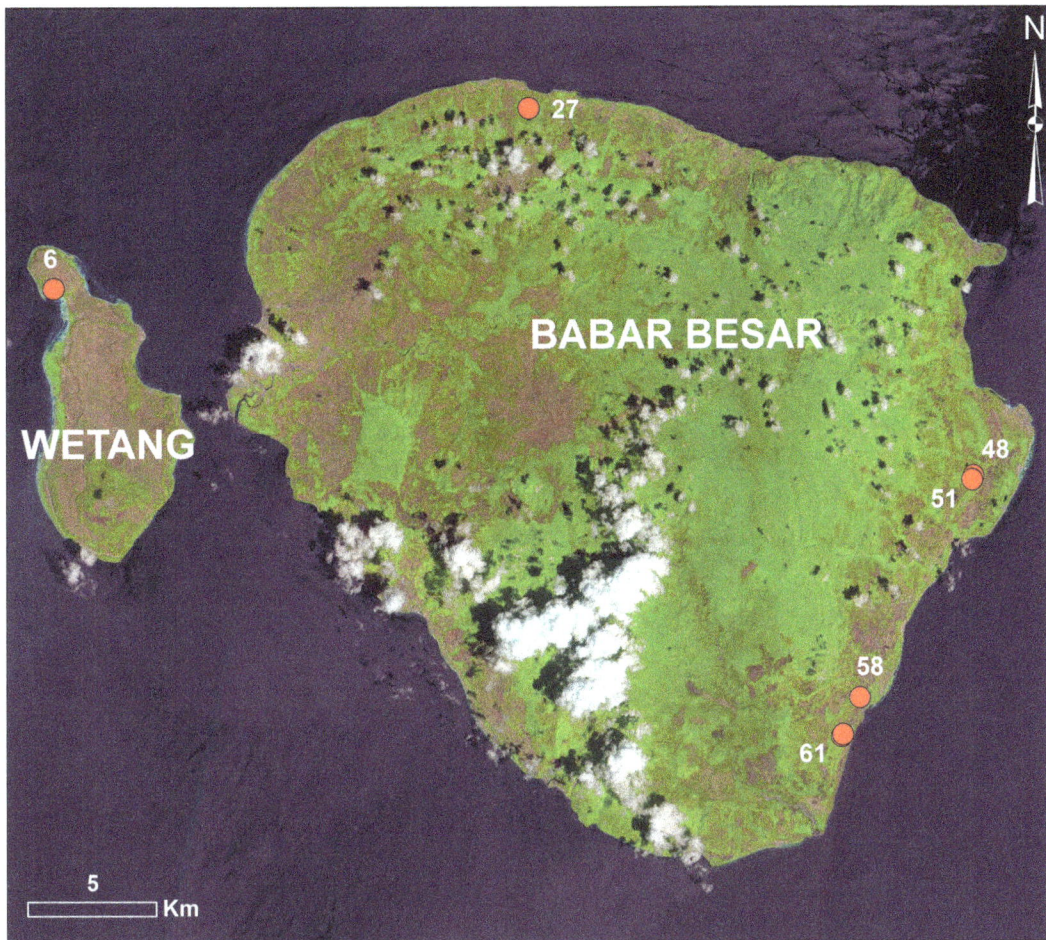

Figure 11.23. Map showing the location of identified fort sites on the islands of Wetang and Babar Besar. Sites are numbered based on Kealy et al. (2018) (see also Table 11.4).

Source: Satellite image from the Sentinel-2A satellite (2019-12-04) obtained from the Sentinel Data Hub (European Space Agency 2019).

The formation of the fort walls is roughly semicircular, with a steep escarpment or drop-off on the unwalled section of the construction providing natural defence. Oral history from local villagers records unanimously that these village settlements were occupied by individual clan groups. They were fortified with high walls for protection against raiding by other clan groups living in similar fortified settlements. In this part of the island, pacification and movement to the current coastal village is said to have occurred with the arrival of missionaries from the German Protestant Bremman Mission in 1917. A centennial celebration in honour of this occasion had taken place a few weeks before we began our survey. Oral history for multiple villages/clans in east Babar Besar begins with the occupation of a few ancestral villages high in the mountains. War and population expansion over time was said to have resulted in the movement of these villages, and sometimes the division of a village into two separate clans that then constructed individual 'new' fortifications on the adjacent lower terrace (closer to the coast). Repetition of this process over time resulted in a series of abandoned fortified villages stepping up into the hills. The modern distribution of present-day coastal villages is a result of pacification, with some clan groups recombining in the larger, coastal settlements.

Figure 11.24. Kukeweble Negeri Lama (#61) showing the high (A), thick (B) surrounding wall constructed of a mix of medium to very large stones (C). In the centre of the Negeri Lama was a circular stone altar under the shade of a Banyan tree (D).

Source: Photos A, B and D courtesy of Shimona Kealy; photo C courtesy of Lucas Wattimena.

The largest, most complete Negeri Lama observed on Babar Besar was the Kukeweble Negeri Lama (#61), covering an area of over 1 ha near the village of Tutuwawan. Located close to the coast on the lowest terrace, Kukeweble represents the final traditional stone-walled settlement of the Tutuwawan ancestors in their move from the mountains to the coast (Figure 11.24).

The three other Negeri Lama visited in east Babar Besar were all further inland and at higher altitude than Kukeweble. Wulua Negeri Lama (#48) is particularly significant for its position directly on the edge of the first major terrace above the coast. The narrow stone-lined gateway to this ancestral village, located atop a c. 50 m steep cliff with surrounding stone walls on all other sides, would have made this Negeri Lama particularly secure against enemy forces (Figure 11.25). Wulyeni Negeri Lama (#56) is also located on the first terrace above the coast. While the smallest of the Negeri Lamas in the area, it has an abundance of earthenware pottery and stone artefacts on the surface, suggesting good potential for in situ archaeological deposit (Figure 11.26).

Figure 11.25. Wulua Negeri Lama (#48) showing narrow stone staircase leading to the gateway on the cliff edge (A), and stone arrangements surrounding the gateway with its commanding view over the plain below (B).
Source: Photos courtesy of Shimona Kealy.

Figure 11.26. Wulyeni Negeri Lama (#56) showing stone stair for entrance (A), circular stone wall (B and D), and stone tools located inside (C).
Source: Photos courtesy of Shimona Kealy.

The most inland fortified Negeri Lama visited was Ilkeoi (#51), and is the second most inland fort of the series, according to the local Kokwari villagers. The oldest, more inland Negeri Lama were not visited on this survey due to their remote forested locations, time constraints and the focus of the survey being more concerned with cave and rock-shelter deposits preserving human occupation records prior to the Negeri Lama period (pre-AD 1300).

Remote survey using satellite imagery (Google Earth Pro V 7.3.2.5491 2018b) was attempted for Babar Besar and Wetang to identify additional fortifications, as conducted on Kisar. However, these islands are more thickly forested than Kisar and the dense vegetation cover makes identification of fortifications from space virtually impossible.

Table 11.4. Summary data on fortified sites in the Babar Island group. Numbers follow full list of survey localities from Kealy et al. (2018: Table 1).

[1]No.	Subdistrict	Site name	Location	Description	Findings
6	Wetang, Nusiata Village	Negeri Lama-Nusiata	Lat. -07.853° Long. 129.525° [2]Alt. 111 m	Possible Negeri Lama on hilltop	Possible remains of stone structure from Negeri Lama.
27	Babar Barat, Manuwuy Village	Hutmiey Negeri Lama	Lat. -07.791° Long. 129.693° Alt. 11 m	Negeri Lama on headland	Stone wall remains indicating Negeri Lama location.
48	Babar Timur, Kokwari Village	Wulua Negeri Lama	Lat. -07.916° Long. 129.851° Alt. 47 m	Negeri Lama on cliff edge	Stone wall and gateway remains of Negeri Lama.
51	Babar Timur, Kokwari Village	Ilkeoi Negeri Lama	Lat. -07.918° Long. 129.850° Alt. 67 m	Negeri Lama in upper terrace	Stone wall and gateway, largely overgrown.
58	Babar Timur, Manuwui Village	Wulyeni Negeri Lama	Lat. -07.992° Long. 129.810° Alt. 46 m	Circular Negeri Lama with well-preserved walls	Stone wall remains of Negeri Lama. Significant surface deposit of pottery and grindstones.
61	Babar Timur, Tutuwawan Village	Kukeweble Negeri Lama	Lat. -8.005° Long. 129.806° Alt. 27 m	Large Negeri Lama on headland	Large, extensive walls, stone altar.

Notes: [1] The numbers refer to the complete archaeological survey of the island, thus some numbers are missing from this sequence. [2] Approximate altitude.
Source: Kealy et al. (2018: Table 1).

It is interesting to note that on Kisar, the villagers stated that they had moved their settlements either inland or to the harbour locations, while on Babar the oldest fortifications were the furthest inland, moving progressively closer to the coast with the modern villages built along the coast. This difference could, however, be a reflection of the differences in topography and infrastructure between the two islands. Kisar is much less mountainous than Babar and has also had its interior cleared and farmed far more extensively than Babar. Additionally, while Babar is currently experiencing a boom in infrastructure construction with an airport and connecting highway to the central harbour, Kisar has had this infrastructure (and more) in place for some time. Thus, access to Kisar's centre is possible by motorised vehicles on well-built roads while the interior of Babar is only accessible on pony back via small trails.

Discussion and conclusion

The survey work undertaken to date indicates that fortification was a widespread phenomenon and was probably a feature of all occupied islands across the eastern Wallacean archipelago during the period c. AD 1400–1880. While no excavation has been undertaken in most of the fortified settlements recorded in this chapter, both the oral history and the cultural material seen on the surface inside the settlements are all consistent with their occupation within this timeframe. In some instances, oral history indicates that these settlements continued to be occupied into the early 1900s or later. For instance, in the Lautem area of Timor-Leste, oral accounts tell of ancestors fleeing their fortified settlements only when they were set on fire under instructions from Portuguese administrators who wanted to relocate the occupants to the coast. Fragments of tradeware, embedded in the soil inside walls and near old graves, includes Portuguese and other European ceramics dating to the mid-twentieth century. On Babar, the oral histories we collected recalled pacification and movement to the coast only in 1917.

The results of the archaeological reconnaissance reported herein indicate that the phenomenon of fort building was more geographically widespread, extending at least as far west as Sumba Island in the East Nusa Tenggara group (Figure 11.1). Schapper (Chapter 10, this volume) provides historical descriptions and photographs of fortified settlements in southern Maluku, encompassing the islands from Kisar in the west to the Kei group in the east. Looking at the historic sources for the area east of Maluku it is clear that similar defensive settlements were built as far east as Papua. Merton (1910) reported that fortifications at Ujir in the Aru Islands were already abandoned when he visited the islands in 1908 (Schapper this volume; Veth et al. 2005). Van der Crab (1864:52) reported fortified settlements built of limestone on the southern shore of the Berau Gulf, which contained deserted houses. Röder (1939–40:7) also reported fortified settlements throughout the MacCluer Gulf area of Papua. He believed that people fortified their villages due to the incursion or influence of Seramese migrants from the west and they were used as defence against firing weapons (Röder 1939–40:10). In writing of one fort in the Fu-um area of Arguni, he stated that the locals,

> have for many centuries been in close contact with the population of the Isle of Ceram in the Moluccas, who sold them guns and gunpowder and probably taught them the art of building fortifications. (Röder 1939–40:10)

One of his illustrations shows an enormous roughly oval-shaped fortification with high, thick walls on the most elevated point of the mountain, which he described as already overgrown and abandoned at the time of his visit (Röder 1939–40:7). Writing in 1939, he stated that the people 'left their former fortified village and settled near the coast in Arguni some thirty years ago'. So, as with many of islands of Nusa Tenggara and Maluku discussed above, settlement along the coast apparently did not occur until the early twentieth century.

The phenomenon of fortification across eastern Wallacea has been under-documented, but remains a heritage narrative of significant historical and cultural importance worthy of further archaeological research. The data in this chapter serve as a guide and starting point for a comprehensive program of research and heritage assessment of fortified settlements, as and when appropriate funding is secured.

References

Chou, C.-Y. 2013. The evolution of natural and social landscapes in late prehistoric East Timor: A historical ecology perspective. In S. Chiu and C.-H. Tsang (eds), *Archaeology and sustainability*, pp. 215–235. Center for Archaeological Studies, Research Center of Humanities and Social Sciences, Academica Sinica, Taipei.

Dibley, T. 1999. Tragedy in Sumba: Why neighbours hacked each other to death in a remote part of Indonesia. *Inside Indonesia* 58(April–June):1–6. www.insideindonesia.org/tragedy-in-sumba. Accessed 15 February 2020.

European Space Agency 2019. Sentinels Scientific Data Hub. scihub.copernicus.eu. Accessed on 19 August 2019 and 2 March 2020.

Fitzpatrick, D., A. McWilliam and S. Barnes 2012. *Property and social resilience in times of conflict: Land, custom and law in East Timor*. Ashgate Press, Farnham.

Google Earth Pro V 7.3.2.5491. 2018a. Kisar Island. 8°4′S 127°11′E. ©2018 AfriGIS (Pty) Ltd. Data SIO, NOAA, U.S. Navy, NGA, GEBCO. Image ©2018 DigitalGlobe.

Google Earth Pro V 7.3.2.5491. 2018b. Babar and Wetang Islands. 7°54′S 129°43′E. Image ©2018 TerraMetrics. ©2018 AfriGIS (Pty) Ltd. Data SIO, NOAA, U.S. Navy, NGA, GEBCO. Image ©2018 DigitalGlobe.

Kealy, S., L. Wattimena and S. O'Connor 2018. A geological and spatial approach to prehistoric archaeological surveys on small islands: Case studies from Maluku Barat Daya, Indonesia. *Kapata Arkeologi* 14(1):1–14. doi.org/10.24832/kapata.v13i2.458.

Lape, P.V. 2006. Chronology of fortified settlements in East Timor. *Journal of Island and Coastal Archaeology* 1(2):285–297. doi.org/10.1080/15564890600939409.

Lieberman V. 2009. *Strange parallels: Southeast Asia in context 830–1830*. Volume 2. Cambridge University Press, Cambridge.

McWilliam, A., D. Bulbeck, S. Brockwell and S. O'Connor 2012. The cultural legacy of Makassar stone in East Timor. *The Asia Pacific Journal of Anthropology* 13(3):262–279. doi.org/10.1080/14442213.2012.674054.

McWilliam, A. 2007a. Harbouring traditions in East Timor: Marginality in a lowland entrepôt. *Modern Asian Studies* 41(6):1113–1143. doi.org/10.1017/s0026749x07002843.

McWilliam, A. 2007b. Customary claims and the public interest: On Fataluku resource entitlements in Lautem. In D. Kingsbury and M. Leach (eds), *East Timor: Beyond independence*, pp. 168–175. Monash Asia Institute Press, Melbourne.

Merton, H. 1910. *Ergebnisse einer Zoologischen Forschungsreise in den Südöstlichen Molukken (Aru- und Kei-Inseln) im Auftrag der Senckenbergischen Naturforschenden Gesellschaft*. Senckenbergische Naturforschende Gesellschaft, Frankfurt am Main.

O'Connor, S., S. Pannell and S. Brockwell 2011. Whose culture and heritage for whom? The limits of national public good protected area models in East Timor. In J.N. Miksic, G.Y. Goh and S. O'Connor (eds), *Rethinking cultural resource management in Southeast Asia: Preservation, development, and neglect*, pp. 39–66. Anthem Press, London. doi.org/10.7135/upo9781843313588.004.

O'Connor, S., A. McWilliam, J.N. Fenner and S. Brockwell 2012. Examining the origin of fortifications in East Timor: Social and environmental factors. *The Journal of Island and Coastal Archaeology* 7(2):200–218. doi.org/10.1080/15564894.2011.619245.

O'Connor, S., Mahirta, D. Tanudirjo, M. Ririmasse, M. Husni, S. Kealy, S. Hawkins and Alifah 2018. Ideology, ritual performance and its manifestations in the rock art of Timor-Leste and Kisar Island, Island South East Asia. *Cambridge Archaeological Journal* 28(2):225–241. doi.org/10.1017/s0959774317000816.

Pannell, S. 2006. Welcome to the Hotel Tutuala: Fataluku accounts of going places in an immobile world. *The Asia Pacific Journal of Anthropology* 7(3):203–219. doi.org/10.1080/14442210600965158.

Röder, J. 1939–40. Kota's in West Nieuw-Guinea (Mac Cluer-Golf). In W.A. Hovenkamp (ed.), *Tijdschrift Nieuw Guinea*. Volume 4, Issue 1–6. The Nieuw-Guinea Comite en Den Nieuw-Guinea Studiekring.

Sahlins, M. 1985. *Islands of history*. University of Chicago Press, Chicago.

van der Crab, P. 1864. Reis naar de Zuidwestkust van Nieuw-Guinea de Goram-en Ceram-Laut Eilanden en Oostelijk Ceram. In B. van Kunsten and A. Wetenschappen (eds), *Tijdschrift voor Indische Taal-, Land-, en Volkenkunde*. Volume 13, pp. 531–556.

Veth, P., S. O'Connor, M. Spriggs, W. Nayati, A. Jatmiko and H. Mohammad 2005. The Ujir site: An early historic maritime settlement in northwestern Aru. In S. O'Connor, M. Spriggs and P. Veth (eds), *The archaeology of the Aru Islands, Eastern Indonesia*, pp. 85–93. Terra Australis 22. ANU Press, Canberra. doi.org/10.22459/ta22.2007.05.

Viegas, S. and R. Feijó 2019. Funerary posts and Christian crosses: Fataluku cohabitations with Christian missionaries after World War II. In R. Roque and E.G. Traube (eds), *Crossing histories and ethnographies: Anthropology and the colonial archive in East Timor*, pp. 107–202. Berghahn Press, New York and London.

Wessel, P. and W.H.F. Smith 1996. A global self-consistent, hierarchical, high-resolution shoreline database. *Journal of Geophysical Research* 101:8741–8743. doi.org/10.1029/96jb00104.

12

Conclusion

Andrew McWilliam, Sue O'Connor and Sally Brockwell

The archipelagic bioregion of Wallacea is named in honour of the pioneering work of nineteenth century naturalist, Alfred Russell Wallace, who recognised its unique endemic ecology and faunal species diversity. Taking this region as a frame of geographic reference, the present edited collection of research papers highlights another form of diversity in the proliferation of indigenous fortified settlements and defensive structures that signify a historical reality of long periods of armed conflict and endemic warfare. With their strategic locations on prominent hilltops, and protective dry stone walls in varying states of preservation, the fortifications stand as mute relics of a turbulent and conflict-ridden past. At the same time, many of these same structures are still viewed as spiritually charged mythic sites connecting contemporary populations to an abiding ancestral presence.

The chapters in this volume present detailed archaeological and ethnohistorical studies of specific fortified settlements, focusing on the regions of Lautem in far eastern Timor-Leste (see Chapters 2, 3, 4, 5 and 6), Sulawesi (see Chapters 7, 8 and 9) and the islands of Maluku Barat Daya (Chapter 10). The examples, discussed in varying degrees of detail, illustrate just how widespread the phenomenon of fortification was throughout the archipelago. Their proliferation also highlights the scope for further research into their provenance and origins. In this concluding chapter, we offer closing commentary and analysis on the historical role of the indigenous fortified structures. In reviewing the comparative evidence, we consider the chronology of fort-building in relation to the factors that prompted the expansion of fortified settlements throughout the region, along with the use of construction materials and common design features.

Fortifications on most of the islands of Wallacea remain undated. Many fortified settlement sites have exotic tradeware occurring as surface occurrences, or on graves, which can be used to provide a relative age for site use. However, this tradeware is likely to date the final period of occupation, rather than the inception of fortification, at any given locale. Only in Timor-Leste is there a large enough sample of excavated and well-dated fortified sites to provide a platform for examining the chronology of fort-building. Even here, a reliable assessment of the timing of initial fort construction is hampered by uncertainties in the radiocarbon calibration curve for this time period, which produces large error ranges on the dates, and by problems relating to the reliability of the provenance of the charcoal and shell dated (O'Connor et al. 2012:206). As Lape and Chao (2008:18) point out, anomalously old ages obtained from the lower levels of excavations within fortifications may relate to earlier use of the hilltop for farming, hunting, collecting and/ or processing wild resources well before the walls and other fortified structures were built. Lape and Chao (2008) report examples of this where radiocarbon ages obtained on charcoal were significantly older than the age of the tradeware in the same stratigraphic unit. Conversely, exotic tradeware may not always provide reliable ages for occupation as, being high-prestige value goods, items may have been heirloomed for a long time prior to breakage. Thus, they may be significantly older than the occupation level from which they were recovered (Fenner and Bulbeck 2013). In summary, a Bayesian analysis of the currently available radiocarbon data set for the Timor-Leste fortifications indicates that fort-building may have been initiated as early as AD 1300, but continued and developed for centuries, becoming widespread between AD 1550 and 1750 (O'Connor et al. 2012:211). Oral history and historic glass bottles corroborate the use of some of these settlements through into the first half of the twentieth century. Whether this chronology can be reliably extended to fortifications on other islands of Wallacea will have to await future excavations. However, it does seem to be provisionally supported by the historic and oral accounts relating to fort use.

In terms of the origins of fortified settlements, research presented in the volume has considered three general drivers that arguably created the need to initiate defensive structures. One argument that has attracted wide scholarly attention is to view sudden climate change as the primary driver of conflict over diminishing food supplies and water resources, in the process generating a defensive posture and readiness among resource rich groups. Peter Lape (2006, Chapter 3, this volume), drawing on his archaeological research in Timor-Leste, as well as comparative work on palaeoclimates in the Pacific (Field and Lape 2010), is a proponent of this view. He offers a convincing model for the widespread emergence of fortification across much of Asia and the Pacific at much the same time. The general argument is for a correlation, or at least a strong association, between extended droughts or some kind of dramatic environmental stress and emergence of fortification (see also Nunn 2007). One suggested period is the cooler climate of the so-called Little Ice Age from AD 1300 to 1400 (Nunn 2007; see also Pearce and Pearce 2010). In the case of Timor-Leste, Lape and Chao (2008) argue for a broadly similar dynamic, proposing that tests for an El Niño Southern Oscillation drought relationship to fortification-building have shown a 'probable' direct causal relationship.

Although the highly suggestive correlation between environmental stress, food shortages and fortification has attracted scholarly support, direct compelling evidence remains limited and provisional. As Lape has acknowledged:

> to adequately test [the] model, a complete survey of fortified settlements in the Ira Ara region would need to be completed, with each site's initial fortification building episode securely dated. The earliest sites should date to times of increasing drought frequency and be located at the boundary of resource-rich and resource-poor areas. (Chapter 3, this volume)

This is a considerable challenge in itself, made more complicated by the difficulty of dating the beginning of fortification due to occupation of the Ira Ara site in the mid-Holocene prior to fort construction (see Chapter 3, this volume; see also Pearce and Pearce 2010:119 for comparable limitations elsewhere, and Chapter 7, this volume). Proponents of the causal climate change link to fortification tend to limit their claims to the immediate defensive impulse to fortify settlements, accepting that subsequent use and further construction may have been prompted by other proximate reasons.

An alternative argument for the drivers of fortification, also addressed in a number of chapters of this volume, has looked to direct external and economic conditions as fundamental to the emergence of defensive settlements. O'Connor et al. (2012) argue that most of the reliably dated structures in Island Southeast Asia are shown to be constructed from the fifteenth century AD, with a peak of fort building occurring between the fifteenth and seventeenth centuries. This is rather later than the climate change models generally allow. However, it is very much coincident with the emergence and expansion of various imperialist political and economic trading interests that were to dominate the region for the next 500 years. The intrusive presence of expansionary trading interests from early Chinese to European, especially Portuguese and Dutch powers, and Muslim maritime kingdoms (e.g. Ternate, Tidore, Bugis, Makassar and Buton) may have generated conditions of endemic rivalry for economic and political ascendancy across the region. This intense competition for supremacy played out in violent struggles over control of trading alliances, especially with diverse coastal settlements. It resulted in shifting patterns of persecution, as well as lucrative opportunities for beneficial alliances (see Hägerdal 2012; Chapters 6 and 7, this volume).

At the onset of these turbulent times, residential settlements had little option but to flee inland in the face of armed onshore raiding parties. The emergence of fortified hilltop settlements in these uncertain coastal contexts was a rational and effective strategy to resist unwelcome incursions, while providing a secure basis for managing and controlling external trade relations. The construction of massive double dry stone walls with coralline rubble infill looks excessive as a defence against gunfire and spear attack, but is an effective shield against high-powered projectiles fired from cannons. Under this alternate scenario, the drivers of fortification are arguably still based around fighting over resources. However, unlike a climate-driven scenario of struggles to secure fertile land and food supplies, it is access to weapons and the associated lucrative trading arrangements that generate the rise of defensive structures. In larger islands, like Timor, Sulawesi and Sumba, inland populations were also ensnared within the intensified struggle for control over trade goods (e.g. sandalwood, slaves, beeswax, food crops), forging alliances with coastal entrepôt and constructing defensive fortifications themselves against depredations and attack by rival groups.

Antoinette Schapper (2019, Chapter 10, this volume) rejects both these analyses and offers a third and alternative theory for the rise of fortification, based upon a persuasive cultural design that diffused across a wide region. Her use of linguistic and historical evidence highlights the widespread, and broadly simultaneous, qualities of fort construction across the islands of southern Maluku and Timor, which she locates largely in the seventeenth and eighteenth centuries. The striking similarities across the region in the nature of the stone walls fortifying villages, the common words used to name them, especially (#lutuR: stone walls) and the ways in which they were used and conceptualised are suggestive of a kind of wholesale replication of a shared vision or model of protective enclosure. Schapper considers this pattern to be linked to endemic levels of pre-existing internecine indigenous warfare that may well have predated European intervention. Evidence from various European observers also highlights the strong spiritual qualities accorded the massive enclosing stone walls, which were thought to provide a protective 'living' agency that went beyond the pure materiality of the stone itself. Evidence from Timor-Leste shares many features of the fortified landscapes of southern Maluku with their ritual spaces (*sepu*), stone altars (*tei*) and ancestral graves (*calu luturu*), along with great variations in the size of the fortified enclosures themselves. The features indicate that these structures were used both as defensive deterrents from armed attack and as sites of ritual commemoration and sacrificial invocation to a protective ancestral presence and power.

In considering the relative merits of these different theories of fortification, it is evident that that the process of building defensive enclosures over time and across the region may well have had multiple drivers and knock-on effects. Climate variability and seasonal drought have long been highly influential elements in the relative success of rain-fed agriculture across Wallacea, and we cannot discount its role in competitive struggles over food supplies. Similarly, the idea of fortification as a kind of cultural model or assemblage of ritually potent features that diffused rapidly across the region in the manner of a cult cannot be wholly discounted. However, its emergence still required a trigger. Schapper (2019, Chapter 10, this volume) suggests that the Dutch East India Company (better known as VOC, after Vereenigde Oostindische Compagnie) massacre of the Bandarese population in 1621—brutally enacted to enforce monopoly control over the nutmeg and mace spice trade—caused widespread fear among indigenous populations, and may have been that trigger. Subsequently, the endemic cultures of inter-village warfare and ritual headhunting meant that the trend was continued once established. However, this explanation brings the argument back once again to economic issues and the highly disruptive influence of the numerous external and imperialist ambitions of maritime trading powers competing for political and economic supremacy. In this context, fear and uncertainty from unseen seaborne attack may well have been a more compelling reason to initiate major defensive fortifications.

It is also difficult to reconcile the fortified settlements described in this volume with much of the theoretical literature relating to the rise of socially and economically stratified societies (although, see Furholt et al. 2019). While monumental architecture can be seen to define vertical relations within society, it is difficult to see the operation of this principle in Wallacea. Some of the settlements were said to have contained 60 or so houses within the walls (Schapper 2019, Chapter 10, this volume), while others, such as Sauo in Timor-Leste as described by Forbes (1989) in 1885, encompassed less than a dozen precariously perched stilt dwellings. In some cases, multiple fortified settlements may have been aligned under the control of a central elite ruler, chief or *raja*, but in others, fortification may have arisen as a local multi-family household response to incursions by raiding parties from neighbouring clans. Some of the forts discussed herein seem to have been occupied for hundreds of years, while others were short-lived. Reasons given for abandonment and relocation of fortified settlements are also multifarious.

In view of these differences, it is not surprising that there are marked disparities in the remains of household items from different fortifications. As well as local earthenware, coastally proximal fortified settlements such as Macapainara (Chapter 2, this volume) and Leki Wakik (see Chapter 5, this volume), contained imported tradeware from China, mainland Southeast Asia and Europe. Vasino (Chapter 4, this volume), in a more inland location, contained only locally manufactured earthenware.

Oral history indicates that, even if there was ostensible elite control over a fortification, the building and maintenance was likely undertaken by members of the clan group, or their dependants who lived within its walls, as opposed to specialist craftspeople or mobile labourers contracted to an elite leader. However, there is no doubt that, as in other parts of the world, 'ritual burials materialized elite control of landscape and ceremony' (DeMarrais et al. 1996:19) and extended the influence of some individuals and families well beyond death. Austronesian society is inherently hierarchical and 'ownership and elite privilege were sanctioned over generations, ascribed to individuals who could claim consanguinity with those interred' (DeMarrais et al. 1996:19; see also Reuter 2007). Large ancestral graves are a common feature of all fortified sites discussed in this volume, regardless of the size of the settlement.

As a final reflection on this study into indigenous forts and fortification of Wallacea, the chapters in the present volume, in addition to their direct archaeological significance, attest to the productive possibilities for collaborative research across a range of disciplines around questions of late Holocene archaeology. In this context, the time depth is such that analysis of excavated archaeological material can be placed directly into comparative perspective with the written historical records, as well as the diverse oral traditions and mythic histories of local residents. The triangulation of these sources of information makes possible a more nuanced and richer interpretation of the significance of these sites than might otherwise be the case where the archaeological evidence lies beyond living memory. Recent work paying closer attention to the value of Portuguese and Dutch archival sources on Timor and the region in order to facilitate ethnographic understanding support this possibility (see Roque and Traube 2019). It is within this expanded field of interactive meaning construction that the present collection offers a set of insightful perspectives on patterns of indigenous fortification across Wallacea. In the process we signpost future directions for productive research and greater clarity on the origins and dynamics of indigenous fortification in Wallacea and beyond.

References

DeMarrais, E., L.J. Castillo and T. Earle 1996. Ideology, materialization, and power strategies. *Current Anthropology* 37(1):15–31. doi.org/10.1086/204472.

Fenner, J.N. and D. Bulbeck 2013. Two clocks: A comparison of ceramic and radiocarbon dates at Macapainara, East Timor. *Asian Perspectives* 52(1):143–156. doi.org/10.1353/asi.2013.0005.

Field, J.S. and P.V. Lape 2010. Paleoclimates and the emergence of fortifications in the tropical Pacific Islands. *Journal of Anthropological Archaeology* 29(1):113–124. doi.org/10.1016/j.jaa.2009.11.001.

Forbes, H.O. 1989 (1885). *A naturalist's wanderings in the Eastern archipelago*. Oxford University Press, Singapore.

Furholt, M., C. Grier, M. Spriggs and T. Earle 2019. Political economy in the archaeology of emergent complexity: A synthesis of bottom-up and top-down approaches. *Journal of Archaeological Method and Theory*. doi.org/10.1007/s10816-019-09422-0.

Hägerdal, H. 2012. *Lords of the land, lords of the sea: Conflict and adaptation in early colonial Timor, 1600–1800*. KITLV Press, Leiden. doi.org/10.26530/oapen_408241.

Lape, P.V. 2006. Chronology of fortified settlements in East Timor. *Journal of Island and Coastal Archaeology* 1(2):285–297. doi.org/10.1080/15564890600939409.

Lape, P.V. and C.-Y. Chao 2008. Fortification as a human response to late Holocene climate change in East Timor. *Archaeology in Oceania* 43(1):11–21. doi.org/10.1002/j.1834-4453.2008.tb00026.x.

Nunn, P. 2007. *Climate, environment and society in the Pacific during the last millennium*. University of the South Pacific, Suva, Fiji.

O'Connor, S., A. McWilliam, J.N. Fenner and S. Brockwell 2012. Examining the origin of fortifications in East Timor: Social and environmental factors. *The Journal of Island and Coastal Archaeology* 7(2):200–218. doi.org/10.1080/15564894.2011.619245.

Pearce, C. and F. Pearce 2010. *Oceanic: Path, sequence, timing and range of Prehistoric migration in the Pacific and Indian Oceans*. Springer, London and New York.

Reuter, T. (ed.) 2007. *Sharing the Earth, dividing the land: Land and territory in the Austronesian world*. ANU E Press, Canberra. doi.org/10.22459/SEDL.10.2006.

Roque, R. and E.G. Traube (eds) 2019. *Crossing histories and ethnographies: Following colonial historicities in Timor-Leste*. Berghahn, New York.

Schapper, A. 2019. Build the wall! Village fortification, its timing and triggers in southern Maluku. *Indonesia and the Malay World* 47(138):220–251. doi.org/10.1080/13639811.2019.1554778.

Contributors

Alifah – Balai Arkeologi, Yogyakarta, Indonesia

Noel Amano Jr – Max Planck Institute for the Science of Human History, Jena, Germany

Anthony Barham – The Australian National University, Canberra, Australia

Sally Brockwell – The Australian National University, Canberra, Australia; University of Canberra, Canberra, Australia

David Bulbeck – The Australian National University, Canberra, Australia

Ian Caldwell – University of the Philippines Diliman, Republic of the Philippines

Judith Cameron – The Australian National University, Canberra, Australia

William R. Dickinson – formerly University of Arizona, Tucson, Arizona, USA (deceased)

Jack N. Fenner – The Australian National University, Canberra, Australia

Jana Futch – Brockington and Associates, Atlanta, Georgia, USA

Prue Gaffey – The Australian National University, Canberra, Australia

Bernard Gratuze – IRAMAT, Institut de Recherche sur les Archéomatériaux, Centre Ernest Babelon, Orléans, France

Hasanuddin – Peneliti pada Balai Arkeologi Makassar, Sulawesi Selatan, Indonesia

Stuart Hawkins – Australian Research Council Centre of Excellence for Biodiversity and Heritage (CABAH), The Australian National University, Canberra, Australia

Mohammad Husni – Balai Arkeologi Maluku, Ambon, Indonesia; Balai Pelestarian Cagar Budaya Maluku Utara, Ternate, Indonesia

Amy Jordan – University of Washington, Seattle, Washington, USA

Shimona Kealy – Australian Research Council Centre of Excellence for Biodiversity and Heritage (CABAH), The Australian National University, Canberra, Australia

John Krigbaum – University of Florida, Gainesville, Florida, USA

Michelle C. Langley – Griffith University, Nathan, Australia

James Lankton – University College London, London, UK

Peter V. Lape – University of Washington, Seattle, Washington, USA

Mirani Litster – The Australian National University, Canberra, Australia; University of Canberra, Canberra, Australia

Andrew McWilliam – Western Sydney University, Liverpool, Australia; The Australian National University, Canberra, Australia

Mahirta – Universitas Gadjah Mada, Yogyakarta, Indonesia

Tim Maloney – Griffith University, Gold Coast, Australia

Sue O'Connor – Australian Research Council Centre of Excellence for Biodiversity and Heritage (CABAH), The Australian National University, Canberra, Australia

Jack O'Connor-Veth – The Australian National University, Canberra, Australia

Sandra Pannell – University of Western Australia, Crawley, Australia; James Cook University, Cairns, Australia

Emily Peterson – University of Washington, Seattle, Washington, USA

Philip J. Piper – The Australian National University, Canberra, Australia

Marlon Ririmasse – Balai Arkeologi Maluku, Ambon, Indonesia; Pusat Penelitian Arkeologi Nasional, Jakarta, Indonesia

Antoinette Schapper – KITLV/Royal Netherlands Institute of Southeast Asian and Caribbean Studies, Leiden, The Netherlands

Nani Somba – Peneliti pada Balai Arkeologi Makassar, Sulawesi Selatan, Indonesia

Daud Tanudirjo – Departemen Arkeologi, Fakultas Ilmu Budaya, Universitas Gadjah Mada, Yogyakarta 55281, Indonesia

Tse Siang Lim – The Australian National University, Canberra, Australia

Lucas Wattimena – Balai Arkeologi Maluku, Namalatu-Latuhalat, Indonesia

Rose Whitau – The Australian National University, Canberra, Australia

Richard C. Willan – Museum and Art Gallery of the Northern Territory, Darwin, Australia